Policy and Marketing Strategies for Digital Media

"The essays in this book provide valuable insights for both professionals and academics on the impact of changes in digital media on public policy and the marketplace."
—*David Ackerman*, *California State University, Northridge, USA*

"This is a collection of important insights from around the world on some of the most important communication issues of our time. It is must-reading for anyone who wants to see the whole picture."
—*Pat Longstaff*, *Syracuse University, USA*

With digital media becoming ever more prevalent, it is essential to study policy and marketing strategies tailored to this new development. In this volume, contributors examine government policy for a range of media, including digital television, Internet Protocol TV (IPTV), mobile TV, and Over-the-Top (OTT) TV. They also address marketing strategies that can harness the unique nature of digital media's innovation, production design, and accessibility. They draw on case studies in Asia, North America, and Europe to offer best practices for both policy and marketing strategies.

Yu-li Liu is professor of the Department of Radio and TV at National Chengchi University in Taiwan. She has published numerous books, including *Multi-Channel TV and Audience*, *Cable TV Management and Programming Strategy*, *Cable TV Programming and Policy in China*, *Radio and TV*, and *Telecommunications*.

Robert G. Picard is director of research at the Reuters Institute, Department of Politics and International Relations, University of Oxford. He is the author and editor of 27 books and an academic expert on media economics and management and government communications policies.

Routledge Studies in New Media and Cyberculture

For a full list of titles in this series, please visit www.routledge.com

Policy and Marketing Strategies for Digital Media

Edited by Yu-li Liu and
Robert G. Picard

Routledge
Taylor & Francis Group

NEW YORK AND LONDON

First published 2014
by Routledge
711 Third Avenue, New York, NY 10017

and by Routledge
2 Park Square, Milton Park, Abingdon, Oxon OX14 4RN

*Routledge is an imprint of the Taylor & Francis Group,
an informa business*

Library of Congress Cataloging-in-Publication Data
    Policy and marketing strategies for digital media / edited by Yu-li Liu and
Robert G. Picard.
        pages cm. — (Routledge studies in new media and cyberculture ; 19)
    Includes bibliographical references and index.
    1. Telecommunication policy.   2. Telecommunication—Marketing.
3. Mass media—Technological innovations.   4. Digital media.   I. Liu,
Yu-li, 1957–   II. Picard, Robert G.
    HE7645.P63   2014
    384.068'4—dc23
    2013047894

ISBN: 978-0-415-74771-4 (hbk)
ISBN: 978-1-315-79430-3 (ebk)

Typeset in Sabon
by Apex CoVantage, LLC

Printed and bound in the United States of America by Publishers Graphics,
LLC on sustainably sourced paper.

Contents

Part III: Marketing Strategies

Figures

Tables

Acknowledgements

This book originated in a conference entitled "The Digital Media and New Media Platforms: Policy and Marketing Strategies," sponsored by the Ministry of Education in Taiwan. We are indebted to many scholars who presented their papers at this conference held in March 2012 at National Chengchi University in Taipei, Taiwan. We would also like to thank the authors who could not attend this conference but were still willing to contribute their works to this book. As editors of this book, we had opportunities to interact with these well-known and knowledgeable authors who made great efforts in writing their chapters. We would also like to thank the anonymous reviewers for recommending our book proposal to the publisher Routledge. Through their comments and criticisms, we have been able to carefully revise our chapters. We would like to acknowledge the assistance of Tiffany Lin in compiling the collection and checking all the tables, figures, and references. Last, but not least, Felisa Salvago-Keyes and Katie Laurentiev of Routledge also deserve special recognition for their support in publishing this book.

Introduction

Yu-li Liu and Robert G. Picard

In recent years, more and more countries have switched off or committed to switching off their analog television broadcast signals, steps that harmonize the fundamental distribution technologies of broadcasting, telecommunications, and other media and make possible a range of new communication services. In this digitized world, the use of digital and new media has become an increasingly important issue. The policies and marketing strategies of the converging media deserve much attention from the public since they may have a significant impact on daily life. In some European countries, the digital TV platform also provides pay-TV services that compete with other TV platforms, such as cable TV, direct broadcast satellite (DBS), and Internet Protocol Television (IPTV). Over-the-Top (OTT) media have also emerged in the market. Some of them have even started to bring threats to the traditional media in terms of watching hours and revenues. In many countries, OTT video services do not require viewers to apply for licenses, nor are such services regulated by communications laws. This again raises the problem of a level playing field and what policy makers are trying to accomplish with public policy.

When facing the convergence of telecommunications, media and the Internet, many countries endeavor to revise their legal framework or communications laws in order to cope with the problems caused by the blurring boundary of the media. Some countries try to revise their communications laws separately; some try to establish new laws to deal with new media; some try to merge their telecommunications laws and electronic media laws; some adopt the vertical model of regulation; and some adopt the horizontal model of regulation. Since 1998, many scholars have started to discuss or propose the layer model, which is believed to provide a better conceptual framework to accommodate convergence.

The EU's Framework Directive classified electronic communications into "electronic communications networks" (ECN) and "electronic communications services" (ECS). Its Audiovisual Media Service Directive (AVMSD) divides the media into linear (television broadcasts) and nonlinear (on-demand) services that are often utilized in response to content regulations under convergence. However, the directive may not be sufficient.

For some newly emerging media, the AVMSD is not applicable. Therefore, in April 2013, the EU released the "Green Paper on Preparing for a Fully Converged Audiovisual World: Growth, Creation and Values" to seek public consultation.

While the EU's horizontal model of regulation is one of the major paradigms for communications laws, the United States' paradigm, also known as the "silo model," is another popular regulatory regime. In addition to that, countries like China, Japan, Korea, and Taiwan also have their own distinctive regulatory approaches. For instance, the issues related to the retransmission of content, network neutrality, and the Internet regulatory regime are some of the major concerns of the regulators and stakeholders in some particular countries. Various countries also go through institutional changes or reforms to different extents in response to convergence. Nonetheless, the most important task is for policy makers to find a regulatory approach that best suits their countries' condition, policy traditions, and culture.

While particular policy issues have become crucial due to the rapid changes in the development of communications technology, the ongoing convergence also calls for innovative marketing strategies from both traditional and newly emerging media. As a matter of fact, convergence has brought forth creative destruction, which is removing value from some media industries and forcing their reconfigurations. The penetration of newly developed technology has transformed the media industry. One example of this disruption can be found in online video distribution. Convergence has allowed the same content to be distributed via both traditional and new media. The truth is that the competition between traditional and new media has become pronounced.

Consequently, both traditional and new media are required to reposition themselves or enhance their competitive edge at both strategic and operational levels. From the perspective of new media, facilitating the process of diffusion has become crucial. While new media platforms may be deemed to be innovative and "new" to consumers, oftentimes their penetration is hindered due to regulations, usability issues, and customers' feelings of indifference to the new services. With an increase in the channels for content delivery, coordination becomes crucial in retaining or gaining customers. These media platforms also require innovative revenue models, through advertisements and paid premium services as well as attractive content and quality, to stay in the market. Due to the disruption to the market brought by convergence, the costs and pricing structures of these services also require further consideration especially because much of the same content is now available on competing platforms.

Convergence has led to a customer-focused marketing approach where the old way of implementing marketing strategies may no longer be as effective as before. In the past, marketers had full control over feeding into consumers' needs with services and products, but today, consumers are open to various sources of information through different channels such as the World

Wide Web, and the markets do not have full control over this relationship anymore. With the prevalence of digital media or even newly emerging media, the understanding of branding techniques in digital media can be useful. Creating, negotiating, and marketing customer relationships are also becoming important.

This book is a collection of 18 academic articles written by well-known scholars from Europe, America, and Asia. Since policies and marketing strategies should go hand in hand for better understanding, the chapters are composed of two major topic areas—namely, policy issues and marketing strategies and the respective country case studies. Each topic area is arranged with overviews to go over the framework and rationale, regional issues analysis, and country studies with a specific national focus. In view of the diverse backgrounds of these authors, this book presents a diversity of perspectives in examining issues related to digital media and new media and reveals the breadth of the issues and debates surrounding the new digital environment.

In brief, part 1 of the book addresses policy issues in regard to digital media. The first chapter is entitled "Digital Television and Switchover Policies in Europe." Petros Iosifidis, as the editor of the *International Journal of Digital Television*, focuses his chapter on the development of digital television in Europe. He also pays particular attention to the public interest obligations and the importance of public policy. Iosifidis assesses the benefits of digital TV and argues that the public interest outcomes arising from the introduction of digital TV will depend on two particular items: universality and accessibility to the public. According to the author, the most efficient model to ensure these values is the introduction of free-to-air digital TV in which public service media play a key role.

In chapter 2, Peggy Valcke and Jef Ausloos address the challenges faced by the current definition and scope of audiovisual media services. In their chapter entitled "Digital Media Policy: 'Television on the Internet: Challenges for Audiovisual Media Policy in a Converging Media Environment,'" they discuss how filtering and personalized mechanisms may help citizens navigate the Internet and obtain tailor-made information in the age of information overload, but these mechanisms also have a tendency to remove the media's power as an editor in terms of what the audience can access. As the authors mention, the current definition and scope of the audiovisual media service directive may not be sufficient. They therefore emphasize the importance of carefully investigating how different actors play their roles under convergence.

Chapter 3 is entitled "Making TV Accessible in the 21st Century." As the current chairman of the International Telecommunication Union Telecommunication Standardization Sector (ITU-T) focus group working on digital media accessibility, Peter Looms reviews the current status of television accessibility and what has been done in this regard. From the author's perspective, the case for access service provision is poorly understood.

However, progress will depend on building awareness among TV stakeholders regarding the nature of the accessibility challenge. In addition to that, stakeholders must know the solutions available and the cost of making television accessible. In the chapter, Looms pays particular attention to the case histories on digital television accessibility and initiatives needed to make TV inclusive in the 21st century.

Chapter 4 by Rob Frieden is entitled "Next-Generation Television and the Migration From Channels to Platforms." In this chapter, Frieden notes that consumers nowadays have access to a large inventory of video content choices via broadband television. Due to factors such as technological innovations, broadband availability, new business plans, and inexpensive high-capacity storage, the Internet is also able to serve as a single medium to deliver services. These factors have contributed to the fact that video content can now be accessed through multiple channels. Therefore, this chapter considers how incumbents and market entrants will respond to changed circumstances in order to preserve or acquire market share, as well as the impact on consumers.

In chapter 5, Amit Schejter and Noam Tirosh discuss the topic of "New Media Policy: The Redistribution of Voice." In each of their developmental stages, media technologies were designed to serve a limited form of democracy, more often than not one that served the rulers no less than the ruled. But contemporary media has the ability to provide an opportunity of voice to many more. Technological capabilities combining four "new media" characteristics—interactivity, mobility, abundance, and convergence—allow making a conceptual leap: from discussing speech in terms of freedom to discussing speech in terms of equality, the conversation about media policy can make a transition from a conversation about liberty to a conversation about social justice.

Part 2 of this book focuses on country case studies related to policy issues. In chapter 6, entitled "Policy Implications from the Changing Market Environment Including Convergence between Telecommunication Services and Broadcasting Services," Yasu Taniwaki, a government official from the Ministry of Internal Affairs and Communications (MIC) in Japan, indicates that changes in the market structure for telecommunications and broadcasting can be conceived in two areas—namely, the horizontally integrated network and the vertically integrated business models. These two approaches may have different effects on regulations. Moreover, the author stresses that the competitive market, the openness of different platforms, and the global coordination of policies should be considered by the regulators under convergence for better adaptation.

Chapter 7 is entitled "Reconsidering the Telecommunication and Media Regulatory Framework in Taiwan: Using the Newly Emerging Media as Examples" by Yu-li Liu. Liu begins by reviewing the major paradigms in the communications laws. By examining the American silo model and the European horizontal model, criticisms of these two regulatory approaches are also presented to see how they may fit the current development of convergence. Aside from these two major paradigms, regulatory approaches from other countries are also addressed to see how regulators deal with newly emerging media such as IPTV and OTT video services. By providing a case study of Taiwan's regulatory framework, the author offers suggestions for future regulatory reforms for these new media platforms.

In chapter 8, Yoko Nishioka and Minoru Sugaya discuss "Japan's Legislative Framework for Telecommunications: Evolution Toward Convergence of Communications and Broadcasting." Under the impact of convergence, Japan was one of the few countries in the world to have successfully reorganized a number of existing acts (in Japan's case, four out of eight) into one converged Broadcasting Act. By detailing the historical development of broadcasting and the characteristics of the Japanese telecommunications legislative framework in general, the authors provide an elaborate review in regard to the institutional changes in Japan.

Chapter 9, entitled "The Impact of Digital Convergence on the Regulation of New Media in Korea: Major Issues in New Media Policy," by Euisun Yoo and Hyangsun Lee examines key issues under convergence in Korea. The chapter discusses major changes in the media regulatory systems, such as the background of the recent adoption of a dual regulatory system with the Ministry of Future Creation and Science (MFCS) and the Korea Communications Commission (KCC) for media businesses. The chapter puts much of its focus on the major pending policy issues in media business regulation and content regulation, such as the retransmission of terrestrial TV broadcasts by pay-TV operators, network neutrality and reasonable network management, and changes in content regulation.

Chapter 10, entitled "Fine-Tuning the Competition: The Case of Singapore's Cross-Carriage Rule in Ending Content Exclusivity," covers a case study in Singapore by Mabel Tan and Peng Hwa Ang. Since Singapore had the highest content exclusivity rate in the world, the government has decided to compel exclusive content rights holders to allow its competitors' subscribers access to the same content, on the same terms, on rival networks. In this chapter, the authors argue about the effectiveness of the policy to end the high cost of content exclusivity and stress that the policy must be expanded beyond cross-carriage and include a more proactive regulatory overview in addressing the monopoly sellers and its oligopolistic buyers in pay TV to ensure that new entrants may access the premium content and thereby foster competition.

The last chapter under part 2, chapter 11 by Miklos Sukosd, is entitled "Inverse Intranet: The Exceptionalism of Online Media Policies in China." After reviewing the cases in democratic countries, the author offers a different perspective in response to convergence in China. According to the author, the formation of China's "inverse intranet" system did not take place by chance. It followed a centralized Internet regulatory regime dominated by two broad strategies: maintain control and stimulate growth. As a result, the state has full control over the content online, and domestic Internet companies are also booming since access to foreign websites is often blocked. In essence, this model contradicts the U.S.-based Internet since it was envisioned as being borderless with a global network commons based on free speech.

Part 3 of the book focuses on the marketing strategies related to digital media and new media. Chapter 12 by Robert G. Picard is entitled "Digital Media and the Roots of Marketing Strategy." The author points out that many media companies are approaching digital platforms as if they were just another place in which to make their offline product available. To achieve success in digital media legacy, media companies need to create new strategies that do more than extend the existing strategies of their offline products. The four *P*'s of marketing (product, price, place, and promotion) are thus important in considering strategies for digital platforms.

Chapter 13 by Richard Gershon is entitled "Digital Media, Electronic Commerce, and Business Model Innovation." The author discusses two important questions in regard to the long-term success of media and telecommunication companies. First, the author looks into what it means to be an innovative media business enterprise, and second, Gershon explores how digital media and business model innovation have been used to transform the field of electronic commerce. The author also chooses three media companies, namely Apple, Netflix, and Amazon.com, to examine their unique business models.

Chapter 14 is entitled "Cross-Media Marketing Strategies" by Bernd W. Wirtz, Philipp Nitzsche, and Linda Mory. The authors argue that the concept of cross-media is referred to as the lateral expansion of media distribution to various media channels or media submarkets. By focusing on the fundamentals, manifestations, causes, and process of cross-media management, this chapter presents various forms of cross-media marketing strategies and success factors in the media sector.

In chapter 15, entitled "Marketing Communications with Networked Consumers and Negotiated Relationships," Edward C. Malthouse and Don Schultz discuss the evolvement of customer relationship management. Under convergence, marketers no longer enjoy absolute control over what goods or services are marketed to consumers. Instead, consumers have more power nowadays due to their easy access to information. In brief, the authors describe how marketing and marketing communication have developed over the past 50 years and the importance of absorbing changes in the emerging markets.

In chapter 16, Robert Pennington discusses the implications of marketing in digital media in "Marketing Self-Branding Strategies for Social Presence in Digital Media." Pennington stresses that societies provide the means to create identity through inventories of signs, and the strategy for consumers is to select brands appropriate to individual identity. Therefore, this chapter discusses the strategy for marketers to meet consumers' identity needs in digital media while maintaining authoritative control over brands for real-world returns.

Part 4 of this book focuses on country case studies. In chapter 17, entitled "Technology and Competition in U.S. Television: Online Versus Offline," Ryland Sherman and David Waterman review the development of online television as well as the disruption it brings to the market. By examining the revenue models and programming of major online television service providers, the importance of content aggregation is also emphasized. A discussion on the factors that are most likely to have an impact on online television in the future is also presented.

In the last chapter of the book, entitled "Multiscreen Services: User-Centric Marketing Strategies," Donghee Shin analyzes the current situation and strategy of device makers and telecommunication carriers, as well as Internet service providers, regarding multidevice services, also known as N-Screen in Korea. The author recognizes the setbacks that hinder the diffusion of multiscreen devices. By using a context-specific extension of the technology acceptance model, multiscreen acceptance is empirically investigated based on usability and quality factors. In essence, this chapter offers insights to facilitate the diffusion of multiscreen devices in the future.

In summary, this book aims to offer valuable insights to readers by examining different aspects of digital media and new media in terms of both communication policies and marketing strategies.

Part I
Policy Issues

1 Digital Television and Switchover Policies in Europe

Petros Iosifidis

INTRODUCTION

This chapter focuses on the developments of digital television in Europe and the public interest obligations (Feintuck & Varney, 2006; Garnham, 1986) that are raised, such as freedom, access, universality, political pluralism and content diversity. The first part of the chapter considers digital TV penetration data from across Europe, as well as the status of national digital switchover plans, stressing that Northern Europe is much more advanced in this regard than Southern and Eastern-Central Europe. National policies are largely determined by markets, political contexts and supranational influences, notably European Union audiovisual policy, which puts pressure on member states to speed up digital switchover. This creates a tension between the push of the EU to harmonize the switchover process and set target dates and the struggle of some of the member states to comply with this policy. The work then assesses the benefits of digital TV (extra channels, converged communications, enhanced interactivity and mobility) and argues that the public interest outcomes from the introduction of digital TV (DTV) will depend on its universality and accessibility to the public. In terms of the strategies that could be employed to accelerate digital uptake, the chapter points to adopting free-to-air DTV. The wide reach of the free-to-view model, in which public broadcasters have a leading role, ensures that the transition to DTV is citizen friendly, that it meets sociocultural issues and that the universality principle is maintained in the digital age.

Digital Switchover and the Development of DTV

In the multichannel digital era with an unprecedented proliferation of sources of communication, most people still rely mainly on television broadcasting in order to be entertained and informed. The development of television has gone through many phases, with the most recent being the introduction of digital television in Europe in the late 1990s. This major phase was subsequently followed by announcements of individual national analogue switch-off plans. These were shortly followed by a European Commission (EC) initiative to harmonize analogue switch-off dates with the year 2012 as a target.

But it is not only Europe, for across the world countries are switching to digital television at dramatic speed. The technology was only introduced a couple of decades ago, and already, in 2012, half of the world's 1.2 billion television households have been converted into digital. The main driver of digital switchover was apparently the increasing spectrum efficiency. Another driver, especially from the late 1990s onwards, were the favourable government policies both in the U.S. and Europe that gave a push for the development of the technology. Market considerations also played a key role, with the electronics industries being keen to develop a new generation of hardware (set-top boxes and satellite dishes). Content-wise, the main driving force in the initial stage of digital TV came from the pay-TV sector, especially digital satellite and secondarily digital cable, though more recently digital terrestrial TV gained momentum and in some countries took the lead from digital satellite and/or cable TV.

The digital switchover has had a great impact on viewers, the broadcasting sector, related industries, the government and society as a whole. Broadcasters benefit because they can adopt a multichannel strategy driven by reduced costs resulting from digitalization. The digital switchover has positive effects on related industries such as technology providers, manufacturers, TV retailers and installers. Spin-off effects for governments are triggered by the freeing up of frequencies that are typically sold at premium rates to mobile TV or mobile telephony companies. Societies as a whole are benefited with the increase in bandwidth for digital media, the digital upgrade of households and the possibility of participating in a pan-European, communal digital television culture.

Some outcomes of switchover are clearly cast as positive to the viewer, with consumer choices increasing with regard to distribution mode, technology and content as a result of digitalization. Viewers are able to watch more television channels with enhanced quality with technologies such as high definition (HD), wherever they are (at home or on the move) and whenever they want (thanks to DVRs and video on demand). Digital television involves much more than just extra channels, and the HD channels is the result of convergence—the blurring of the boundaries of broadcasting, telecommunications and computer technologies, based on digitized electronics.

Diverse Levels of DTV Development

But there are diverse experiences as the development and penetration of digital television has been uneven across the globe. Differences between countries—in size, development, culture and politics—play a great role and rule out any "one-size-fits-all toolkit." The United States completed analogue switch-off (after various postponements) in June 2009. Australia launched its digital terrestrial HDTV in 2001 but then had to postpone the start of switch-off from 2008 to 2013. Digital switchover, understandably, is not a high priority in developing countries, with African countries, for example, expected to convert after 2015. China, the world's biggest manufacturer of TV sets, developed its own set of technical standards and has concentrated first on digitizing its cable TV systems. The process of digital switchover is very slow in China, as it is in most Asian countries. As will be shown in detail in the following, the development of the technology varies widely in Europe; Finland and Sweden were early completers of switchover in 2007, but other countries have yet to complete the process, despite the EU's 2012 deadline. In countries like Germany, Austria and Luxembourg, where cable networks predominated, the process of switchover was much more straightforward.

Returning to the benefits of digital TV for viewers, it is obvious that not all of the new services are available to everyone. Whilst not all consumers have equal purchasing power, citizens' interests are poorly served in terms of access to a universal service. Notions of universal service and access are typically related to sectors such as health care, education and essential services including water, electricity and the telephone service. Universal telephone service, for example, was adopted as a policy objective in both the United States and Europe to encourage economic and social interaction within the individual countries as a way of promoting national unity (Melody, 1990). Most European countries have imposed similar public service obligations on their broadcast media. In contrast to the U.S. broadcasting model, the Western European model developed outside the market. The European broadcasting model—the so-called public service broadcasting model—in its ideal form consisted of a nationwide public monopoly which would universally distribute information, facilitate public debate and contribute towards a common identity in return for a basic, initial payment, usually in the form of an annual license fee. In the course of time, institutions entrusted with these tasks have expanded their activities by venturing onto online media platform. These expansions help the public channels maintain the universality principle in the digital age, but as will be shown in this chapter, these activities have caused controversy and encountered increasing scrutiny from competitors. Meanwhile public channels' development of their web activities is testing the applicability of traditional regulation. As Moe (2008a, p. 220) asks, "How do regulatory frameworks relate to the wider remits?"—"Is it public service media online?"

Today the universal access paradigm can be applied to a wide array of communications and information services, traditional activities or new ventures, offline or online, with the definition of basic access varying from country to country. In countries such as France and Italy, for instance, there is a push for "universal broadband" while in the UK there is a push for a "digital Britain" (Departments of Culture, Media and Society and Department for Business Enterprise and Regulatory Reform [DCMS/DBERR], 2009). The issue of universality is part of the wider debate over what is in the "public interest" in today's competitive and liberalized digital world of media and communications. Media marketization, privatization and concentration bring forward important questions on positive freedoms, such as the right of citizens to have equal access to the technologies and to receive a wide range of opinions and information at affordable prices. Potential conflicts between private profit motivations and social goals like universality, affordability, diversity of views and political pluralism now, more than ever, need to be considered and resolved. The problem remains one of designing media regulation in the public interest, in particular of shaping the technological form and accessibility of digital television.

Governments play an active role in regulating the transition to digital, for they consider it a public policy concern. Adda and Ottaviani (2005) argue that the transition to digital terrestrial television (DTT) is a public policy problem and that governments take an active role in the transition because of the interplay of two motives, one economic and the other noneconomic. First, DTT technology uses a publicly owned, rather than a privately provided, network. Here the government acts as the "private" owner of the network and is interested in solving the coordination problem associated with switching standard. Second, most governments perceive the transition to DTV as having important noneconomic consequences, due to the social role of the media. An increased and more competitive supply of television channels should improve the overall flow of information in the society, with positive economic, social and political effects. Operationally, universal access to the traditional TV channels is seen as a minimal condition to avoid social inequalities. The universality principle implies that switch-off of analogue TV will not be feasible and socially acceptable until almost all viewers have migrated to DTV.

The Nordic European region, and countries like the UK, Germany and Spain, stand as forerunners when it comes to the adoption of DTV services, but, as will be shown in the following, other European countries are lagging behind in terms of both penetration of digital services and awareness of the process of digital switchover. Despite the uneven national developments of DTV, digital switchover is promoted vigorously by the European Commission. According to the e-Europe Action Plan, all member states were required to disclose their national strategies for the switchover from analogue to DTV by the end of 2003.[1] In June 2005 the European Commission published a communication "on accelerating the transition from analogue to digital broadcasting" which urged EU member states to bring forward the likely date of analogue switch-off and called for a coordinated approach to making freed-up spectrum available across the EU. The European Commission (2005) suggested the year 2012 as a possible target for the completion of switchover. Following this, many member states have published plans to terminate analogue terrestrial broadcasting, and some have already done so, but there is uneven pace of digital TV transition across Europe.

The dates for the analogue switch-off that have been set by national governments vary greatly depending, among other factors, upon penetration of digital services, the size of the market, the state of technological infrastructure and public awareness of the process to switchover (Iosifidis, 2005, p. 59). Luxemburg and the Netherlands completed analogue switch-off in September and December 2006 respectively, whilst analogue terrestrial in Finland was switched off on 31 August 2007. Belgium (Flanders), Denmark and Germany are among the list of member states which have already ceased analogue terrestrial transmission. The large British market has started regional switch-off of analogue signals, for the switchover started from the Border region in 2008 and was effectively completed with the Meridian, London, Tyne Tees and Ulster regions in 2012.

According to the European Audiovisual Observatory's latest survey (2012), 22 of the then EU's 27 member states (now 28) have completed digital switchover, as have the non-EU states of Croatia, Switzerland, Norway and Iceland. Pay DTT services are now available in 17 EU countries and 21 European countries overall. Eighty-six new DTT channels were launched in 2012, and HD channels are available in DTT networks in 22 European countries. A total of 33 pay DTT services were available in 21 countries at the end of 2012 following new launches in Belgium and Greece. However, the number of pay DTT subscribers dropped by 13%, with almost 1 million subscribers dropping out of Italy's pay DTT service. According to the European Audiovisual Observatory, 369 new channels launched in the EU across all platforms—DTT, cable, satellite and IPTV—in 2012, with over 40% of these being HD channels. The number of channels closing down fell from 143 in 2011 to 62 in 2012. Poland, Hungary, Bulgaria, the former Yugoslav Republic (FYR) of Macedonia and Greece are scheduled to complete switchover at the end of 2013, with Serbia and Bosnia and Herzegovina to follow in 2014 and the remaining countries—Albania, Montenegro, Romania, Russia and Turkey—in 2015. However, recent developments in Greece, in particular the abrupt government decision to close down public broadcaster ERT in July 2013, may postpone the digital switchover target date.

It can be seen that national governments that are lagging behind in terms of analogue switch-off include some of the Southern European countries as well as the new EU members, who joined in 2004 and 2007. Eastern Europe has its own character in terms of digital TV developments. With roughly half of TV households in Eastern Europe relying on terrestrial television, the region represents a large market for free-to-view multichannel television. However, analogue switch-off in this part of Europe has been hampered by political issues, governments' lack of a political priority and a lack of political consensus that makes it difficult to reach an agreement. There is a lack of sufficient understanding of the issues involved in the digital switchover by regulators and broadcasters, especially with regards to the programming and market issues involved (Iosifidis, 2011a). Public broadcasters in many transition countries still have not consolidated in terms of the transition from state into public service television. Efficient communication practices on the process of digitalization and switch-off are largely unknown to the general population. The digital switchover process has even been dubbed as "premature" by some analysts who claim that the countries are not ready yet for this transformation (Jakubowicz, 2007, p. 21). It seems that digital switchover is a top-down operation, imposed by government policy (where there is one), responding to decisions being taken by the European Union (Jakubowicz, 2007, pp. 35–36). This situation provides a striking example of the way in which the EU's push for the digital economy may result in ill-timed operations in relation to the rollout of DTT, for digital switchover is not likely to be an easy or smooth and trouble-free operation.

Most of the countries with advanced levels of DTV penetration have also set early dates for analogue switch-off. Finland and Sweden, for example, which were committed to making the switchover to digital in 2007, had in 2007–2008 a DTV penetration of above 50%. Norway, with a 2009 switch-off date, also ended 2008 with more than half of its households accessing DTV. Exceptions to this are Britain, arguably the most advanced European country with a DTV adoption well above the European average despite a switch-off date of 2012, and Ireland, which in 2008 had a digital household adoption of 60% but has fixed a late date for switchover.

It is clear that the European market in 2012 remains fragmented with regard to the adoption of technologies, and there is little sign that Europe is developing a homogeneous DTV industry. These variations in the national structure of the television industry create a dilemma for EC regulators in terms of the feasibility of introducing common digital switch-off dates. There is clearly a tension between the macro and the micro levels. At the macro level there seems to be pressure from the EC for member states to hurry towards digitalization in order to create a workable internal market. In effect since 2003, the European legal framework for electronic communications has covered different technological platforms and provided for integrated regulation (European Commission, 2002). The Television without Frontiers Directive (renamed Audiovisual Media Services Directive– AVMSD),[2] which is the cornerstone of the EU's audiovisual policy, has broadened its scope in response to digitalization and convergence and endorsed the view that a common approach to digital switchover and digital dividend[3] will reinforce the overall competitiveness of Europe in the global marketplace, strengthening the position of its media, telecommunications and IT sectors. The AVMSD created the legal framework and the legal certainty which new business models and technological services need in order to achieve full consumer acceptance and to successfully deploy new services, including digital TV, in the internal market. Without doubt, switchover will bring about benefits to viewers and broadcasters, stimulate innovation and growth of the consumer electronics sector and therefore contribute to the renewed Lisbon agenda, which was conceived in March 2000 and aimed to make the EU "the most dynamic and competitive knowledge-based economy in the world" (Lisbon European Council (2000). Hence the earlier the switchover process is started and the shorter the transition period, the sooner these benefits are realized (Iosifidis, 2011a).

However, EC policy towards DTV and switchover stands in tension with the micro level—that is, strategies adopted by individual member states. The EC's proposal for the 2012 deadline for completing terrestrial analogue switch-off may lead some member states to an ill-timed, insufficiently planned and unduly rapid introduction of DTT services to catch up with other more advanced territories (Iosifidis, 2006, p. 264). Each country's policy orientation and market dynamics lead to different development paths to a DTV market. Local TV infrastructure, strength of incumbent service providers, aggressiveness of emerging operators, differing markets and political contexts and both citizens' and consumers' attitudes towards new services either expedite or slow down the uptake of digital services in these countries. Strong DTT uptake in countries where commercial deployments or trials are taking place has a positive impact on their ability to expand subscriber base, but launching the process prematurely for reasons relating to the EU's internal market in countries that are not ready for it may result in the adoption of hazy and inappropriate decisions with regards to programming, financial support mechanisms or the use of frequency spectrum. A main problem is that public broadcasters in most of the countries of the region can hardly play a special role in accelerating the switchover process or raising citizen awareness.

With further exploration along these lines, we may question the extent to which European policy has been effective in driving DTV, particularly geared around universality and a common standard, as central principles. For it is not only the speed of switchover that matters for an effective EC switchover policy, but also the inclusiveness and the principle of universality for achieving a "European digital citizenship," which can be realized by supporting communities in sharing experiences through digital media and by designing inclusive technologies that have the potential to support public communication in a networked European society. One possible way to ensure universal digital services in the new era is to empower public broadcasters to introduce online services and extend their portfolio of platforms and channels. Both national and EU politics are not unfavourable to this, provided that the new services fit with the public remit, add potential value in a public service context and do not distort competition (Bardoel & d'Haenes, 2008, p. 342). Public broadcasters who have traditionally been important conveyors of freely accessible and reliable information should fully use the opportunities offered by digital media. As Nissen (2006) noted, in a report to the Council of Europe's public service broadcasting advisory body, to achieve this they need to operate three types and levels of services: traditional linear programme services for the general public; linear services targeted at special audiences; and personal interactive services. Online services are not acknowledged as an autonomous part of the public service broadcasting (PSB) remit (Moe, 2008b, pp. 320–321), but some public broadcasters' websites, such as the BBC's, offer a fine example of the extension of the "public service" model into the new media. As Christophers (2008, p. 253) argues in relation to programme access and product scarcity, we can read initiatives such as the BBC's Creative Archive project—whereby clips of BBC factual programmes were made available online for free download for noncommercial use—and its interactive iPlayer (offering "catch-up TV" online) as an acceptance that conventional methods of arbitrating access are approaching their sell-by date.

A Council of Europe report (2008) called PSB "a vital element of democracy in Europe" and argued that it should be free to use the new interactive technologies and the Internet in order to level social divisions and combat political and social disengagement. Broadly speaking, there are four areas in which public broadcasters can make a social and cultural difference in the digital world and contribute to the public interest and enhanced civic participation in a democratic society: information (as trusted media brands these institutions can create an online environment and launch web sites where reliable and accredited information proliferates); decentralization and interaction with the citizens (which contribute to creating a civic society at the local, regional, national and international levels—a fine example is the BBC Trust's collaboration with the *Audience Councils* in England, Northern Ireland, Scotland and Wales, which help it understand the audiences' needs, interests and concerns); mobilization (this category focuses on services that assist citizens to be activists with regard to social movements and involvement—a good example is the BBC's Action Network service offering advice and tools to those who wish to run campaigns on mainly local matters); and accessibility (here, DTT is paramount in facilitating the delivery of public service content across various channels and platforms, allowing broadcasters to tailor content to meet specific needs and preferences).

Freeview, Universality and DTT

The previous discussion illustrated that EU attempts to create a coherent and cohesive European digital market stand in tension with member states' own policies, ability to conform, readiness for digital and desire to be part of that market. This section will focus on the specific strategy of DTT adapted to speed up digital uptake which can be considered both as socially acceptable since it ensures universality and a "killer application" since it rockets the pace of digital uptake.

Britain in 1998, Sweden in 1999 and Spain in 2000 were the first to launch DTT with platforms heavily reliant on pay television, but all experienced start-up problems, particularly the British and Spanish platforms which failed financially. In Britain, the digital switchover policy was conceived at the end of the 1990s, in the middle of the dot-com euphoria. The take-up of DTV services was then relatively high, but following the collapse of DTT pay television platform ITV Digital in 2002, the initial high rate was not maintained. This financial crisis was the result of a poor management policy, overbidding for football rights, technical problems (picture freezing and poor geographical transmission coverage) and the decision to give away free set-top boxes to emulate the strategy of pay satellite broadcaster BSkyB (Iosifidis, Steemers, & Wheeler, 2005, pp. 112–114). The simultaneous closure of the Spanish DTT platform, Quiero TV, due to huge debts put the viability of the technology in serious doubt (Iosifidis et al., pp. 115–116). Given the low subscriber base of the Swedish pay DTT platform Boxer, a new strategy across European countries was urgently needed to target more viewers. Until 2002 the economic model for DTV had been largely based on pay television services, which lured customers with exclusive sports and film content. However, saturation of the pay television market refocused attention for DTT platforms to the free-to-view market, and with the launch of the BBC-led Freeview service in September 2002, DTT in Britain has turned into a free-to-air only platform.

Freeview is aimed at an audience confused by DTV and hostile to subscription services. The redirection of DTT towards a primarily free-to-air system has proved compelling to many households, with the platform's share of the DTV market increasing from 10.6% in 2003 to more than 70% in 2012. The subscription-free platform helped both rebuild public confidence in DTV and combat the common misconception that DTV is necessarily pay TV. Since the launch of Freeview, DTV has become considerably more affordable as competition between manufacturers and retailers of Freeview receivers resulted in significant price reductions in the cost of hardware. Perhaps more importantly, Freeview appeals to those who reject satellite and cable pay TV services. In fact, the popularity of free digital service Freeview has contributed to DTV take-up from previously sceptical groups. Early analysis of the demographics of Freeview subscribers reinforces the notion that free-to-air digital customers are largely additional to pay-TV subscribers. In March 2003 a Quest Survey gave demographic data on the types of households that were using each platform and concluded that Freeview had a different profile to other platforms. In particular, the findings suggest that many of Freeview's customers are affluent, older people who have no interest in purchasing satellite or cable pay-TV services.

DTT beyond the UK

Following the British example, other European countries considered launching subscription-free DTT services. The service has been available in Spain since November 2005, when Quiero TV was relaunched with approximately 30 free-to-air national and autonomous regional television and radio services. The popularity of the DTT platform is very significant given that approximately 82% of the 9.3 million Spanish TV households rely on the terrestrial platform for their primary television reception. France, another European country with a large number of analogue-reliant homes (12 million), launched free DTT services in March 2005. Despite the rather late introduction of DTT (attributed to the debate over the choice of standards), the technology is already being adopted widely, thanks to a long tradition of terrestrial TV reception. In contrast Germany met much easier its ambitious target of early analogue switch-off and universality in coverage because barely 5% of German homes rely on analogue terrestrial only, as low-cost cable TV and free-to-air satellite dominate the market. Germany, like most of the Benelux and Nordic countries, has a strong cable infrastructure.

However, the development of DTT has not been a success story uniformly across Europe, particularly in the smaller European countries of Greece, Portugal and Ireland. In January 2006, the Greek public broadcaster ERT launched free-to-air services with three "pilot" channels, but it was only in 2012 that these services attracted relatively good numbers of viewers. ERT does not seem capable of adapting to its new role as leader of digital TV services and private channels only recently involved in DTT services. Market size and the social and political context embedded in Greece—for example, where television took its first steps under a dictatorship regime and was openly used for propaganda purposes—play a defining role in the decision to enter new, unfamiliar and commercially risky activities. Portugal launched its DTT service in the end of 2009 with the public broadcaster PTP providing free-to-view services in partnership with commercial broadcasters, but it is still too early to judge its success. DTT in Ireland was only recently launched, for under legislation in May 2007, public broadcaster RTÉ and the separate broadcasting (BAI) and spectrum regulators (ComReg) were mandated to invite applications during 2008 under the Broadcasting (Amendment) Act 2007. Italy, which has the largest number of homes in Europe relying on the terrestrial platform at nearly 14 million, launched subscription-free DTT services in 2003 operated by Berlusconi-owned commercial channel Mediaset and in 2004 by public broadcaster RAI. However, the country had to make strenuous efforts to convert the 14 million analogue-reliant homes in order to meet its target switch-off date of 2012, given that in the end of 2009 slightly more than 60% were digital homes. The abundance of free terrestrial channels in Italy creates a culture of antipathy towards digital TV as pay TV–led the offerings, which is typical in all Southern European countries.

Alternative means of accessing digital television have not gained similar momentum to that of DTT. In the UK, Sky, alongside other market payers like Virgin Media, is now offering a triple-play package to its customers, featuring free entry-level broadband access, digital TV and telephony. The drivers which have created these favourable conditions—industry convergence and on-demand services—are expected to continue. However, it is notable that triple-play services suffer from drawbacks for both citizens and consumers: for consumers, companies incur considerable costs in offering such services, particularly in the initial stage of their development until economies of scale are realized, and hence jeopardize the universality principle in accessing digital television; for citizens, therefore, DTT offers a viable universal alternative at the national level but does restrict their membership to a networked "European digital citizenship" (Iosifidis, 2011b).

CONCLUSION

As the dominant audiovisual medium, television plays a major role in forming our cultural identity by determining not only what we see of the world, but also how we see it. Universally available terrestrial channels have hitherto ensured access to quality output, often incorporating innovative programming and new forms of creativity. The makeup of the platform environment has now shifted, but DTT offers a unique chance for the public service providers to continue this trend and grant consumer-citizens access to media services of their own choice *and* on fair terms. From this point of view, the establishment of DTT is important, for it makes DTV accessible to a large part of the population, minimizing the number of households which cannot access TV services when switchover takes place. Public broadcasters generally have an important presence on the DTT free platform as a result of "must-carry" rules adopted by governments, but with the exception of the BBC—which has considerably extended its portfolio of platforms and channels—the rest of the public channels are still trying to adapt to their new role as leaders of digital television services and primary contributors to switchover. The BBC may be the "Noah's Ark in the digital world" (to quote its former director general Mark Thompson); the German public broadcasters ARD and ZDF may be encouraged to take an active part in the emergent digital world; and in Norway there might be a broad political consensus to approve an expansive strategy for public institution NRK facing new media platforms (Moe, 2008a), but in the Mediterranean region and Eastern Europe, public broadcasters are in a much weaker financial condition than their Northern and Western European counterparts, and this factor, coupled with political indecision, causes delays in launching DTT services.

Whilst policy intervention to boost DTV uptake may be justified at an EU level to guarantee a coordinated approach to the switchover process and to the use of the available spectrum, the pressure put on at the macro level for new member states to be part of the "digital economy" may not result in positive change, for it could lead to ill-informed policies that are short-sighted. This danger is particularly apparent in countries where DTT penetration rates are low and awareness of the digital switchover process is lagging behind. While countries adopting a DTT policy, such as Britain, Germany and the Nordic countries, seem to conform most closely to EC ideals, in terms of speed of switchover, the smaller and Mediterranean European territories as well as Eastern/Central European countries do not seem capable of catching up with the EC's target date of switch-off. In the UK the BBC's aggressive digital strategy clearly reflects the government's mandate to the BBC to promote digital television to all citizens as part of a policy for a "digital Britain." Meanwhile, some models may be understood to be at odds with universalism. The market—through, for instance, the latest triple-play offerings—can boost DTV adoption, but public policy could also be seen as a necessary precondition to set the switchover process in motion and to implement it from a socially acceptable perspective. Internal market measures must also take "public interest" aspects into account, and DTT policy should aim to conform to universal accessibility.

The free-to-air model of television, in which public broadcasters have a leading role, has therefore played a significant part in Europe's digital TV strategies for it enhanced consumer interest in DTV services. Perhaps more importantly, the launch of DTT services has made digital services more affordable, addressing citizens' interests by maintaining the universality objective in accessing television services in the digital era. For public service broadcasters to remain prominent content providers, in turn enhancing accessibility and promoting digital citizenship, they should expand their activities to more platforms and introduce online services that have truly public value and are available for the whole national population (Iosifidis, 2011b). This way the EU's drive towards switchover as promoting a "European digital citizenship" may relate to the paradigm of universality.

NOTES

1. The e-Europe 2005 Action Plan was launched in the Seville European Council in June 2002 and endorsed by the Council of Ministers in the e-Europe Resolution of January 2003. It aimed to develop modern public services and a dynamic environment for e-business through widespread availability of broadband access at competitive prices and a secure information infrastructure.
2. The TWF Directive was first adapted in 1989 (Directive 89/552/EEC) and amended in 1997 (Directive 97/36/EC). The new Audiovisual Media Services Directive 2007/65/EC was published in the Official Journal L 332, 18 December 2007, and came into force on 19 December 2007.
3. The digital dividend can be described as a spectrum over and above the frequencies required to support existing broadcasting services in a fully digital environment.

REFERENCES

Adda, J., & Ottaviani, M. (2005). The transition to digital television. *Economic Policy, 20*, 160–209.

Bardoel, J., & d'Haenes, L. (2008). Reinventing public service broadcasting in Europe: Prospects, promises and problems. *Media, Culture & Society, 30*(1), 337–355.

Christophers, B. (2008). Television's power relations in the transition to digital. *Television & New Media, 9*(3), 239–257.

Council of Europe. (2008, November). *Strategies of public service media as regards promoting a wider democratic participation of individuals—compilation of good practices.* Report prepared by the group of specialists on public service media in the information society (MC-S-PSM). Retrieved from www.coe.int/t/dghl/standardsetting/media/Doc/H-Inf(2009)6_en.pdf

Departments of Culture, Media and Society and Department for Business Enterprise and Regulatory Reform (DCMS/DBERR). (2009, June 16). *The digital Britain White Paper.* London: Crown Copyright.

European Audiovisual Observatory. (2012). *Survey "Europe moves closer to digital switchover."* Retrieved from www.digitaltveurope.net/37402/europe-moves-closer-to-digital-switchover

European Commission (EC). (2002). *Directive 2002/21/EC of the European Parliament and of the Council of 7 March 2002 on a common regulatory framework for electronic communications networks and services (Framework Directive).* Retrieved from http://eur-lex.europa.eu/LexUriServ/LexUriServ.do?uri=OJ:L:2002:108:0033:0033:EN:PDF

European Commission (EC). (2005, May 24). *Communication on accelerating the transition from analogue to digital broadcasting.* COM(2005) 204 final. Brussels: Commission of the European Communities.

Feintuck, M., & Varney, M. (2006). *Media regulation, public interest and the law.* Edinburgh: Edinburgh University Press.

Garnham, N. (1986). The media and the public sphere. *Intermedia, 14,* 28–33.

Iosifidis, P. (2005). Digital switchover and the role of BBC services in digital TV take-up. *Convergence—The International Journal of Research into New Media Technologies, 11*(3), 57–74.

Iosifidis, P. (2006). Digital switchover in Europe. *Gazette—The International Journal for Communication Studies, 68*(3), 249–267.

Iosifidis, P. (2011a). Growing pains? The transition to digital television in Europe. *European Journal of Communication, 26*(1), 3–17.

Iosifidis, P. (2011b). *Global media and communication policy.* London: Palgrave Macmillan.

Iosifidis, P., Steemers, J., & Wheeler, M. (2005). *European television industries.* London: British Film Institute.

Jakubowicz, K. (2007). Digital switchover in Central and Eastern Europe: Premature or badly needed? *Javnost/The Public, 14*(1), 21–38.

Lisbon European Council, (2000), Presidency Conclusions. Retrieved from www.europarl.europa.eu/summits/lis1_en.htm

Melody, W. (1990). Communication policy in the global information economy: Whither the public interest? In Marjorie Ferguson (Ed.), *Public communication: The new imperatives* (pp. 16–39). London: Sage.

Moe, H. (2008a). Public service media online? Regulating public broadcasters' Internet services—A comparative analysis. *Television & New Media, 9*(3), 220–238.

Moe, H. (2008b). Dissemination and dialogue in the public sphere: A case for public service media online. *Media, Culture & Society, 30*(3), 319–336.

Nissen, C.S. (2006, February). *Public service media in the information society.* Report prepared for the Council of Europe's group of specialists on public service broadcasting in the information society (MC-S-PSB) (Media Division, Directorate General of Human Rights, Council of Europe). Retrieved from www.coe.int/t/dghl/standardsetting/media/doc/H-Inf(2006)003_en.pdf

Quest Survey. (2003). *Multichannel quarterly, Q2 2003.* London: Independent Television Commission.

2 Television on the Internet

Challenges for Audiovisual Media Policy in a Converging Media Environment

Peggy Valcke and Jef Ausloos[1]

The audiovisual media landscape is characterised by a growing convergence of both media services and the way they are consumed and delivered. This convergence—understood here as the progressive merger between traditional broadcast and Internet services[2]—is challenging media policies and regulation across the world. In 2011, for instance, the Australian communications regulator (ACMA) published a report stating that the majority of legislative concepts that form the building blocks of current communications and media regulatory arrangements are either "broken" or under significant strain from the effects of convergence.

The European Commission, too, (re)opened the discussion on the implications of the ongoing transformation of the audiovisual media landscape through the publication of a Green Paper in April 2013 (European Commission, 2013). This Green Paper comes only 5 years (and 4 months) after the adoption of the Audiovisual Media Services Directive (AVMSD) in December 2007 (coordinated in 2010 by Directive 2010/13/EU), which was—at that time—supposed to offer an answer to the merging of previously distinct TV content distribution channels. The AVMSD introduced new definitions and revised existing rules in order to create a level playing field between traditional and new services. Its main objective was to enhance legal certainty and to make the legal framework for the audiovisual sector more future proof and fit for the Internet era (Valcke & Lievens, 2009; Valcke & Lefever, 2012).

The European legislator, however, could hardly foresee the rocketing popularity of online video portals like YouTube and DailyMotion or social media like Facebook and Twitter. Nor did it consider appropriate regulatory responses to current trends such as the integration of Web 2.0 features into modern television sets and the widespread adoption of tablets, games consoles and Blu-ray players—often referred to as "smart TV," "hybrid TV," or "connected TV."[3] In its first report on the application of the AVMSD, the European Commission noted that the emergence of connected or hybrid TV integrating Internet and Web 2.0 features into modern television receivers "marks a new stage in the convergence of Internet and TV," urging the European legislator to test the regulatory framework set by the directive against evolving viewing and delivery patterns (European Commission, 2012).

The aim of this chapter is to contribute to the academic and policy discourse revolving around the future of broadcasting regulation. Is this regulation a legacy from the analogue past, which was characterised by scarcity? Or are there still reasons to impose specific standards (for instance in relation to the prohibition of hate speech, the protection of minors, cultural diversity, or the identification of commercial communications) on certain categories of media types or media content? If so, where—in a digital and converging media environment—should we draw the line between "regulatable" and "unregulatable" content, and whom should be considered as the responsible provider with editorial control?

In the following pages, this chapter will examine the concept of "audiovisual media service" as the fundamental building block in Europe to regulate TV content in an increasingly digital and connected media environment. The various constitutive elements of the legal definition will be dissected so as to identify major fallacies in the emerging connected media landscape. Additionally, it will also explore how different member states have interpreted the scope of the directive and what difficulties national regulators encounter with regard to the applicability—in terms of material scope—to hybrid services, such as news video websites.[4]

UNRAVELLING THE NOTION OF AUDIOVISUAL MEDIA SERVICE

Definition

Seven Cumulative Criteria

With the adoption of the AVMSD in 2007,[5] the European legislator broadened the scope of EU-wide harmonised broadcasting rules to include every "audiovisual media service" (AVMS): "a service as defined by Articles 56 and 57 [ex 49 and 50] of the Treaty of the Functioning of the European Union which is under the editorial responsibility of a media service provider and the principal purpose of which is the provision of programmes in order to inform, entertain or educate, to the general public by electronic communications networks."[6] The idea was to put forward a technology-neutral definition that would cover all comparable video services, irrespective of the platform or technology used to deliver them to the end user. The definition is usually broken down into seven cumulative criteria: an (a) economic service; (b) under editorial responsibility; (c) of which the principal purpose is; (d) the provision of programmes; (e) in order to inform/educate/entertain; (f) to the general public; (g) by electronic communications networks.

How these criteria are further clarified by the AVMSD and interpreted by national media regulators will be studied in the subsequent sections. From this discussion, it will become clear that recent developments in the media landscape—and particularly online—have put some of these criteria to the test. Media regulators across Europe are struggling to apply the criteria to hybrid services such as online news sites or online video platforms that offer both professional and amateur content.

Linear Versus Nonlinear

The notion of AVMS includes both *linear* and *nonlinear* services.[7] The former (also called "television broadcasts" by the directive) are video services provided by a media service provider for *simultaneous viewing* of programmes on the basis of a *programme schedule*. In other words, the media service provider decides on the moment in time when these services are transmitted (push services) and the order in which the programmes are shown. By contrast, nonlinear services are delivered by a media service provider *at a moment chosen by the user* and at his/her individual request on the basis of a catalogue of programmes selected by the media service provider (on-demand or pull services).

The correct qualification as linear or nonlinear service is not without its legal consequences. Based on this distinction, the AVMSD installed a so-called *graduated* (or *two-tiered*) regulatory regime, which implies that linear services are subject to strict rules whereas nonlinear services are only subject to "light touch" regulation.[8] In some member states, these services are monitored by separate regulatory bodies (e.g., the Authority for Television on Demand [ATVOD] versus Ofcom in the UK).

Whereas this distinction was still rather straightforward in 2007, online video playlists and automated selection tools are increasingly blurring the line between the two categories.

Take NMAtv, for example. This popular Taiwanese animated news provider has—amongst others—its own YouTube channel.[9] At first glance, this service bears a lot of resemblance to traditional television services. The videos automatically follow one another in a continuous playback, sometimes interrupted by a commercial break. Moreover, there seems to be at least some level of editorial responsibility over the audiovisual material presented. The individual videos themselves also show a lot of similarities with conventional news reporting, albeit with a playful undertone. If NMAtv were to be qualified as an AVMS (and assuming it would fall under EU jurisdiction), it would be subject to a whole set of rules regarding, for instance, advertising and the protection of minors (particularly relevant taking into account the often racy nature of the videos it offers). If it were to be qualified as a linear service, these rules would be even more stringent (implying, for instance, adding daily limits to the amount of advertising that could be included in the service).

The NMAtv example clearly illustrates the difficulties facing media regulators in Europe. In its Green Paper on Media Convergence (European Commission, 2013), the European Commission questioned whether the distinction between traditional twentieth-century consumption patterns and new/changing on-demand services should still be upheld.

ECONOMIC SERVICE

EU level: The scope of AVMSD is limited to services as defined by Articles 56 and 57 of the Treaty on the Functioning of the European Union (TFEU). These articles cover every type of service with an economic character (i.e., services that are "normally provided for remuneration"). Conversely, the AVMSD excludes "primarily non-economic activities" that are not in competition with TV broadcasting (e.g., private websites, correspondence or privately created content).[10] This last provision specifically aims to exclude audiovisual user-generated content (UGC) that is "shared and exchanged within communities of interest." The most straightforward indicator to identify an "economic service" is when it is provided in return for remuneration. Remuneration, though, does not necessarily have to come from the actual users of the service (but can also come from sponsorship, advertisement or other sources), nor is it required in each individual case. Not-for-profit services, in other words, are not excluded per se. Conversely, the presence of an advertisement on a website does not automatically imply the service is "economic" (Viola & Cappello, 2011).

National implementation: This seemingly clear criterion has led to diverging interpretations by the different media regulators across Europe. Confronted with a growing diversity of business models, some have tried to clarify the scope of services against remuneration. In this regard, the Belgian Conseil Supérieur de l'Audiovisuel (CSA) has specified that compensation does not have to be pecuniary, nor does it have to go to the actual provider. The decisive element is the economic aim or the competition with other services (which can evolve over time).[11] The Austrian Regulatory Authority for Broadcasting and Telecommunications (RTR) has been struggling to assess the economic nature of "video content provided by NGO's which rely on donations," as well as political video blogs (Machet, 2011).

Other national authorities have tried to use this criterion to exclude certain categories. In Slovakia, for example, the Council for Broadcasting and Retransmission (CBR) has stated that government websites, blogs, civil society activist websites and so forth typically do not (or only to a negligible extent) create an economic profit and are therefore unlikely to constitute an "economic service" (Council for Broadcasting and Retransmission [CBR], 2009). In the Netherlands too, services offered by private persons or public enterprises will not be considered unless they are offered for remuneration or are of a clearly commercial nature (Betzel, 2011; Machet, 2011).

Some media regulators have tried to push aside ambiguity and legal uncertainty by introducing a specific financial threshold. In Italy, for example, to be labelled economic service, revenues have to exceed €100,000, measured at least one year after the start-up (Machet, 2011; Gianni et al, 2011).[12] Unsurprisingly, this threshold has given rise to much criticism. Large enterprises could be discriminated against compared to small(er) enterprises in the same situation. Moreover, the practicability of isolating the actual revenues stemming from the AVMS alone might prove to be hard (Betzel, 2011). But, despite its drawbacks, this extra indicator is nonetheless argued to be pragmatic and practical, proportionate and objective (Hermanns & Matzneller, 2011).

Editorial Responsibility

One of the key (and intensely debated) criteria in the AVMSD pertains to the editorial responsibility of a media service provider (not to be confused with the provider's legal liability or social accountability). Article 1(1)(c) of the AVMSD defines editorial responsibility as "the exercise of *effective control* both over the *selection* of the programmes and over their *organisation* either in a chronological schedule, in the case of television broadcasts, or in a catalogue, in the case of on-demand audiovisual media services."

Effective Control
EU level: In line with the intermediary liability exemptions in the e-Commerce Directive 2000/31/EC (2000), service providers that have no actual control over the content itself fall outside the AVMSD's scope of application. Aggregator sites, for example, are often exempted because their control is usually limited to presentational elements only (Betzel, 2011). However, when the role of these assembling/cataloguing services amounts to more than the simple organisation of different channels, editorial responsibility might still arise (Hermanns & Matzneller, 2011). Furthermore, the "effective control" criterion has also been defined as the "power to shape the communicative characteristics of a service" (Schulz & Heilmann, 2008). Finally, Chavannes and Castendyk (2008) have suggested looking at which entity owns the broadcasting rights in order to assess who has "effective control."

National implementation: Member states adopts different interpretations of "effective control." This is demonstrated, for instance, by the diverging qualification of catch-up TV services. Whereas most regulators treat them as a traditional video-on-demand (VOD) service within the scope of the AVMSD (e.g., Flemish Community of Belgium, Slovakia, Netherlands, Ireland and the United Kingdom; see Machet, 2011), the Italian communications regulator *Autorità per le garanzie nelle comunicazioni* (AGCOM) does not consider Internet providers offering "non-linear services with catalogues consisting exclusively of programmes previously broadcast in linear mode (e.g., catch-up TV or archive services)" as AVMS providers (Gianni et al, 2011). AGCOM considers editorial responsibility only to be effective "when selection and organisation are exercised together with the *economic exploitation*" (Machet, 2012). Furthermore, some regulators do not require "effective control" to be practiced permanently. The concrete *possibility* of control suffices according to the Belgian CSA, and if several persons exercise this control successively, the last person is considered to be editorially responsible (Janssen, 2012).

Selection

Effective control over the selection of programmes is generally considered to require a positive action. In other words, editorial responsibility should involve deliberately picking out specific programmes to insert in its service but is not required to determine the actual content itself. This criterion has proven particularly controversial with regard to UGC-platform providers that—arguably—do not make an ex ante selection of content (e.g., YouTube, DailyMotion or Vimeo). Increasingly, however, these services are profiling their audience and using algorithms to provide them with customised video selections. Verweij (2011) even argues that the directive does not require an a priori selection, but that editorial responsibility can also follow from a posteriori removal and the stimulation of users to upload content (the so-called "guided self-selection" model).

Most regulators have not followed this interpretation, though, exactly because these platforms generally only remove content a posteriori (through notice and takedown; see Valcke et al., 2010). According to the Italian AGCOM (2010), "websites that only provide an indexing activity of the content uploaded by users, do not fall under the scope of the regulations." In the UK, ATVOD clearly rejected the "guided self-selection model" in the BNP TV case (Authority for Television on Demand [ATVOD], 2010a), in which it ruled that a specific section on the website of the British National Party (BNP) constituted an AVMS, *despite* the fact that it allowed users to upload their own content. Not only was "the majority of content . . . clearly produced specifically for/by the BNP," users were also unable to upload videos directly, but rather had to send them to an administrative e-mail address instead.

Some media regulators have claimed that the selection must be based on criteria related to the profile of the service as well as the actual content itself (Machet, 2011; Conseil Supérieur de l'Audiovisuel [CSA], 2012). ATVOD, by contrast, has decided that the reasons behind the selection are irrelevant (ATVOD, 2012). In some situations, and particularly if an online platform contains both third-party content *and* editorially selected/organised content, the assessment might be more complicated. In these situations, the Dutch media regulator *Commissariaat voor de Media* (CvdM) argues, a distinction should be made. The platform provider should only be held responsible for its own content, whereas the third-party "channels" on its platform should be regarded as editorially responsible each with regard to their respective content (if the other six conditions are met; see CvdM, 2011; CSA, 2011; Machet, 2011). In other words, professional channels on platforms such as YouTube or DailyMotion (e.g., NMAtv, supra) will likely be regarded as AVMS providers in at least a number of member states, such as the Netherlands, Austria, Belgium, Finland, Italy and Slovenia (Machet, 2012).

Organisation

Effective control over the *organisation*, in the online context, usually refers to the cataloguing and presentation of programmes. In order to qualify, this "organisation" has to bring added value to the service. Electronic programme guides (EPGs) are considered as AVMS in several jurisdictions already (Machet, 2012). Such interpretation depends to a great extent on how EPGs are defined. There is a clear difference, for example, between traditional EPGs and backwards-facing EPGs. The latter are also called enhanced EPGs, offering the ability to go backwards and forwards (allowing viewers to navigate to added value services and other extra features such as remote booking, recording, etc.). There is no clear consensus yet on how to assess either one of these (Machet, 2012). Most regulators *do* seem to agree, though, that merely organising content in alphabetical or chronological order is not sufficient to qualify as an AVMS provider. The same goes for merely making content accessible through a simple search engine (Machet, 2011; CSA, 2012; ATVOD, 2011e).

According to Dutch case law, an organisational element exists when content is put in lists such as "Top Ten," "Promotions," "Most Viewed" and "Recently Added."[13] The Dutch CvdM clearly stated that this organisation might as well result from adding metadata in order to influence the presentation of the content (to categorise or to improve searchability; see CvdM, 2011). The Czech media regulator requires the categories to be structured based on content criteria (e.g., genre; see Machet, 2011), but does not specify whether this can be automated or not. The automated organisation of programmes based on metadata has given rise to many issues, especially when it is unclear who added the metadata in the first place. Who is responsible, for example, when a third party added the metadata? The one who included the metadata, or the one who used it to structure the content? In 2012, ATVOD held BSkyB—as the provider of the Sky Anytime platform—editorially responsible for Viacom channels (Nickelodeon, MTV and Comedy Central) even though it neither added any metadata concerning these channels nor had the ability to change it. ATVOD ruled that the provision of metadata cannot be determinative. Although ATVOD acknowledged that both parties—BSkyB and Viacom—had a role in organising the programmes and held some degree of control, it was Sky that, on the matter of selection, "on balance" held general control by virtue of it having "final say" over the selection of programmes (ATVOD, 2012).

However, BSkyB successfully appealed this decision; Ofcom quashed the determination—amongst other reasons because ATVOD did not sufficiently address whether any contractual provisions settled any ambiguity as to the allocation of editorial responsibility—and referred the matter back to ATVOD for reconsideration.[14]

Identification

The previous sections illustrate the difficulty of identifying the actual editorially responsible entity. Today's rapidly evolving media landscape, with a multitude of different (types of) actors—all influencing the potential AVMS in one way or another or wearing different hats at the same time—has rendered this exercise even harder. According to the European Audiovisual Observatory and Direction du Développement des Médias (DDM) (2009), the one who is editorially responsible is the one whose brand appears in the service. Digital television providers will generally not be seen as editorially responsible for the individual channels included in their packages even though they aggregate the packages and control customers' access to them. At the same time, they *will* be editorially responsible with regard to their own channels and VOD services.

Ofcom recently ruled that a contractual clause designating the party editorially responsible in principle prevails (Ofcom, 2012b).[15] In the absence of such a clause, ATVOD considers the following factors to facilitate identification: provision of relevant viewing information, metadata, branding, sponsorship arrangements and so forth (ATVOD, 2011e). The CvdM looks at who has the last say over the cataloguing and who adds the metadata (e.g., title, category, description, etc.). In other words, even though a platform holder might offer a programme catalogue, it will not have editorial responsibility if the cataloguing is entirely based on metadata over which it has no control. The CvdM also states that, if there are multiple players and if it is impossible to identify one person with effective control over both selection *and* organisation, most weight should be given to the one making the actual *selection* (Betzel, 2011; CvdM, 2011). Surprisingly, the Belgian CSA (2012) states the exact opposite. The organiser (and *not* the selector) would be best placed to implement and apply the parental control, age verification and time limit requirements.

Interpretation problems have also occurred in situations where advertisement is selected and inserted by a (independent) third party (Machet, 2012).

Principal Purpose

Quantitative and Qualitative Factors

Another contentious criterion to delineate AVMS is the notion of the "principal purpose" of a service, which implies that the relevant service should be *primarily* focused on providing programmes. Hence, services in which audiovisual material is merely incidental are excluded. This criterion has been invoked to exclude newspaper websites from the AVMSD. Even though these websites often include videos, these are usually only ancillary to the main purpose (providing written articles). To an increasing extent, however, the accessorial nature of these services is being questioned, and some jurisdictions (e.g., Austria, Belgium, Czech Republic, Norway, Sweden, Luxemburg, etc.) have started to consider newspaper websites (or at least their video sections) as AVMS (Machet, 2012).

In an attempt to create more legal clarity, the European Platform of Regulatory Authorities (EPRA) has identified three different approaches to assess the principal purpose criterion: a quantitative, qualitative and hybrid approach (Machet, 2011). The first rather mechanically evaluates the proportion of audiovisual media in order to assess the principal purpose of the service in general. The *qualitative* approach, on the other hand, evaluates both the intention of the service provider as well as "how the service is perceived by a general audience" (infra). The *hybrid* approach, finally, constitutes a more pragmatic mix of the two other methods. Given the growing convergence between different media, authorities will generally take a hybrid approach to assess the principal purpose. After all, it becomes increasingly difficult to categorise a service provider as *only* providing one specific service (AVMS or not). Both traditional AVMS providers (e.g., broadcasters) and normally excluded services (e.g., newspapers) are expanding their offerings, moving further away from—or closer to—the conventional meaning of an AVMS. This is not to mention the emergence of entirely "new" services (e.g., UGC platforms), which are redefining the very meaning of what constitutes an AVMS. Put briefly, although the proportion of audiovisual material on a website definitely has some influence, it is (usually) insufficient to accurately determine the service's principal purpose. In other words, it is increasingly clear that—from a practical standpoint—one cannot rely on the quantitative approach (only) when assessing media services in such a dynamic environment.

The quantitative approach has—at least partially—been applied in several member states. In Italy, for example, when a service broadcasts for less than 24 hours per week, it is not considered to be an AVMS (Gianni et al, 2011). In the UK, ATVOD (2010b) granted determinative weight to the fact that the audiovisual part of a website contained over 400 videos and constituted a major part of the service as a whole. The CvdM, on the other hand, has clearly criticised this approach as it tries to compare apples with oranges (Machet, 2011).

Most media regulators across the EU have adopted a more hybrid approach. Confronted with ambiguous and multifaceted new services, regulators often examine whether the audiovisual section of a contested service can be considered as a stand-alone service (e.g., ATVOD, 2010f). In other words, when the service as a whole cannot be categorised as an AVMS within the directive's scope, authorities usually investigate whether the service consists of several subservices, each of which might constitute an AVMS on their own. A determining factor in the assessment is whether the audiovisual content forms a coherent consumer offering that can exist autonomously. In order to assess this, multiple factors are relevant. Besides taking into account the amount of audiovisual material (quantitative factor), the CvdM (2011), for instance, suggested looking also at the presentation and/or the use of a separate URL, its recognisability and the relationship with other parts on the website (qualitative factor).

The service provider's marketing strategy is often used as a useful indicator. The use of logos or brands that are generally associated with television (e.g., *Top Gear*, BBC, TV) can be considered too (ATVOD, 2011g; Ofcom, 2012a). The CvdM declared it does not take into account the actual person or company that is offering the service (e.g., traditional broadcaster or not), but does look at the service's functionality, presentation and how it is used and perceived by the public (Hermanns & Matzneller, 2011). In early 2012, for example, the Dutch CvdM ruled that the town of Zeist's website—or any of its subsections—did not constitute an AVMS. Even though the website offers a linear, live video stream, it does not contain a video catalogue, and the provision of videos is clearly not its principal purpose.[16] A similar decision was made regarding a website offering users help and support concerning first aid. Taking into account the presentation of the videos and their relation vis-à-vis the textual part of the website, the CvdM concluded that the service did not have the provision of videos as its principal purpose.[17]

ATVOD considered different factors in different cases: as examples, the provider described its own service as a "digital film and television service" in a communication to its customers (ATVOD, 2010g); the website's homepage featured a trailer and several links to films and TV series that could be downloaded on the site (ATVOD, 2010c); the Terms and Conditions state that the service gives the public access to thousands of film titles (ATVOD, 2010e).

Online News Services

The interpretation of "principal purpose" has led to intense discussions—and diverging solutions—in the context of news video websites offered by newspapers. A landmark case in this regard is the Sun Video case in the UK (ATVOD, 2011f; Ofcom, 2011b; Metzdorf, 2012). Whereas ATVOD had determined that the video section on the tabloid's website constituted an on-demand AVMS, Ofcom overruled its decision. ATVOD's arguments included that (a) a website can contain more than one service; (b) the video is aggregated on a discrete section of the website; (c) it is moreover presented as a consumer destination in its own right (Sun TV); (d) viewers are not invited to consider the content as subsidiary (to the written material); and (e) videos make sense without the textual articles. Ofcom did not agree and found that ATVOD had put too much emphasis on the video section alone, without proper consideration of the overall content and its relation with the video section. It considered the presentation and marketing of Sun TV insufficient to prove principal purpose and found that for most videos, there was a "Read Full Article" link with a text providing more context, meaning, comments and implications. The website's video section was therefore still too intertwined with textual content and could not be considered an AVMS in its own right. Ofcom *did* recognise, though, that services such as the one concerned might in the future develop to a point where the principal purpose changes.[18] According to several media regulators in Europe, this point has already been effectively reached. In four decisions of October 2012, the Swedish Broadcasting Commission considered the video sections of Swedish newspapers' websites (*Helsingborgs Dagblad, Aftonbladet, Dagens Nyheter* and *Norran*) as AVMS. These video sections constituted a significant part of the websites and—more importantly—were considered to be separate services in relation to other content on the websites (organised in catalogues such as "Sports" and "News"; see Swedish Broadcasting Commission, 2012). Also the Danish Radio and Television Board and the Slovak Council for Broadcasting have come to the conclusion that video sections of newspaper websites constitute AVMS (Machet 2012; EMR 2012).

Programmes

In order to qualify as an AVMS, the service has to provide access to "programmes." Article1 (1)(b) of the directive defines a programme as "a set of moving images with or without sound constituting an individual item within a schedule or a catalogue established by a media service provider and whose form and content is comparable to the form and content of television broadcasting." Animations, as in the case of NMAtv, seem to be covered by the notion of "moving images."

The "programme" requirement is—arguably—the most flawed concept with regard to the directive's intention of being "technologically neutral." The directive was meant to apply to certain content in a certain context, regardless of the technology used. Although the reference to traditional TV broadcasting is understandable in the short run (wanting to create a level playing field), it necessarily leads to difficulties in the long(er) run. The rapid transformation of the media landscape challenges the very meaning of what constitutes "an item . . . comparable to . . . television broadcasting" (TV like). Meanwhile, new (types of) services might not constitute "programmes" *stricto sensu*, but regulation might seem sensible nonetheless. This debate leads to a wider discussion on the very rationale behind the AVMSD itself.

Recital 24 explains that the service should "compete for the same audience as television broadcasts, and the nature and the means of access to the service would lead the user reasonably to expect regulatory protection." The recital continues by saying that "the concept of 'programme' should be interpreted in a dynamic way taking into account developments in television broadcasting," for instance, to take into account the trend towards offering videos of shorter duration, produced especially for mobile services ("mobisodes"). It remains unclear, though, how national regulators should apply this criterion to typical online content (e.g., short video clips) that would not constitute a "programme" on traditional television broadcasting. The European Audiovisual Observatory and DDM (2009) expressed concerns on how to interpret trailers, advertisements and videos such as "highlights," since specialised websites only consist of these kinds of videos. Also service providers that traditionally fall within the scope of AVMS regulation do not always offer a concrete TV format anymore. The Czech authority has struggled to qualify TV broadcasters' "services connected to the presentation of certain services or products of companies (e.g., a video guide)" (Machet, 2012).

A wide variety of factors is being used by media regulators to assess the TV likeness of a certain service and to judge whether form and content of the service concerned are comparable to TV programme conventions. The CvdM will not consider raw audiovisual material, lacking a professional editing process (e.g., adding features such as introduction, subtitling, voiceover, etc.), as TV like (Machet, 2011). According to ATVOD (2011a),[19] the fact that videos are edited (opening sequence, filtered images, voiceover, interviews, on-screen presenter, etc.) often is a strong indicator of TV likeness. Nevertheless, barely edited footage (e.g., speeches and newsstyle footage) can still be considered TV like too if the form and content are comparable (ATVOD, 2010a). Additionally, ATVOD considers the following criteria to evaluate the TV-like characteristic of a service: the availability of a full-screen mode and the fact that videos are preceded by advertisements (2011a), episodic nature (2011c), self-contained narrative feature (2011b), end credits, soundtrack, title sequences, adopts dramatic/fictional conceits and so on (also see Ofcom, 2011a). The following are generally deemed to be irrelevant to assess the TV likeness of a service: length (ATVOD, 2010d) and prior broadcast (2011d). Two landmark cases are the BBC Food and *Top Gear* YouTube cases, in which ATVOD's scope determinations (ATVOD, 2011g) have been reversed by Ofcom. According to Ofcom, the video clips did not fulfil the "comparability requirement" and hence could not be considered as AVMS (Ofcom, 2013): they began and ended abruptly and were only parts of full-length television programmes. Ofcom acknowledged that the grouping of videos into playlists with the ability to "auto-play" made the content more comparable to linear television programme services but did not conclude, in the case at hand, that the auto-play function changed the fact that clips still began/ended abruptly without any "links" connecting them to each other. Video playlists are not TV like if they do not link the individual clips into a coherent whole (with a narrative, etc.).

A last case worth mentioning here is the one involving Playboy's Climax 3 Uncut and Demand Adult online services, in which Playboy argued that its online services could not possibly be considered as TV like; they contained content that is prohibited, and hence never shown, on broadcast television. Ofcom, however, ruled that the form and content of the programmes are required "to be 'comparable', not 'identical,'" and so confirmed ATVOD's view that Playboy's online services constituted on-demand programme services (Ofcom, 2011a).

General Public

One of the more straightforward criteria to identify an AVMS is that it has to be directed to the general public. Recital 22 of the directive specifies that the service in question needs to be "mass media." This means that the service is "intended for reception by, and . . . could have a clear impact on, a significant proportion of the general public."

To assess the general public requirement, one should look both at the intention of the service provider and the (actual and/or potential) availability of the service. According to the Belgian CSA, the actual number of people who are using the service (if any at all) seems—like in the field of intellectual rights—a priori less adequate than the *potential* number of users (Machet, 2012). Some member states apply a quantitative threshold as a "de minimis" rule. In Germany, for instance, when more than 500 persons cannot use a service simultaneously, it is excluded from the scope of regulation (Machet, 2011).

The fact that services require payment in order to be accessible does not exclude them from being qualified as an AVMS. Services that can only be accessed with a password or pincode are not necessarily excluded either (CvdM, 2011), as long as they are available to anyone who wants to access them under the generally applicable terms and conditions set by the provider.

The Austrian regulator RTR has been struggling to assess the "general public" criterion with regard to university VOD services (Machet, 2011). Also, broadcasting services in public places—but closed circuits—such as airports, public facilities or shops (so-called "in-store channels"), usually are not considered to fulfil the requirement (Council of the European Union, 2006; AGCOM[20]). The Belgian CSA (2011) did, however, suggest the exact opposite: all services accessible to the public are covered. This would also include railway stations as long as the content is not specifically targeted at the actual travellers/customers. An intentional element seems to be necessary in order to fulfil the general public requirement. But the "intention" of the service provider will often be hard to determine in practice. A useful criterion that was deployed at the time of the Television without Frontiers Directive is to determine whether the recipients are individually identified or identifiable (Contact Committee, 2008). Nevertheless, this test can be misleading with regard to services that are directed to the general public but can be tailored to specific individual needs (e.g., VOD offerings such as Netflix, LOVEFiLM, etc.). The CvdM (2011) tried to clarify this by stating that a VOD service should not be considered as an AVMS when it is exclusively intended to serve the interest of a limited group and has no profit goals or advertisement (e.g., video services for local churches, sports teams, schools, hospitals, etc.).

Inform, Educate, Entertain

To qualify as an AVMS, the service should be offered with the intention to "inform, entertain or educate." Due to its intentional broadness and vagueness, this criterion is likely to cover almost any information targeted to end users. The changing media landscape does not change the fact that media, whether old or new, is inherently aimed to inform, entertain or educate. One of the only issues to arise in this context is how to assess platforms that are mainly intended as a marketing platform. In the Netherlands, for example, concerns have arisen on VOD services used as a marketing tool by companies that traditionally do not provide media services at all (e.g., RaboSport. nl, redbull.com; see Betzel, 2011).

Electronic Communications Networks

In order to qualify as an AVMS, programmes need to be delivered over electronic communications networks within the meaning of Article 2(a) of Directive 2002/21/EC. Such networks include cable, microwave, satellite, Internet and mobile networks. This criterion is mainly intended to limit the scope to situations similar to the traditional broadcasting model of intangible content delivery. Cinema screenings and the rental and sale of DVDs are, consequently, excluded. But with ever-growing bandwidth, these last two businesses are gradually moving to the intangible sphere as well (e.g., both Netflix and Amazon are increasingly moving from tangible to intangible media).

CONCLUSION

Going back to our example of NMAtv YouTube, it could be argued that the criteria described in this section are fulfilled and that NMAtv—if it were based in the EU instead of Taipei—would fall within the scope of the AVMSD. As the BBC Food and *Top Gear* YouTube cases in the UK have shown, however, the issue of whether their video clips constitute "programmes" that are sufficiently TV like could give rise to discussion.

NMAtv is an excellent example of how the lines between services that *are* regulated vis-à-vis services that *are not* is gradually blurring. This raises fundamental questions about the future scope of digital audiovisual media regulation. Is the current definition of AVMS still apt to achieve the policy goals—in relation to cultural diversity, protection of minors, prohibition of hate speech, and so forth—that the current regulation attempts to pursue? Major challenges in our view follow from the growing use of automated selection tools and algorithms. As the European Commission stresses in its

Green Paper on Media Convergence, filtering and personalisation mechanisms have a clear potential for empowering citizens by allowing them to navigate efficiently through today's information overload and to receive tailor-made services corresponding to their individual needs. At the same time, this may decrease the role of the media as editors in the public sphere and strengthen the role of platform providers. As their influence on the de facto choice for citizens to access media offerings grows (e.g., by varying the prominence with which certain content is displayed), is it still fair to put the regulatory onus only on the "TV-like" AVMS providers who are held to have "editorial responsibility" in the traditional sense? As we noted in an older contribution, the providers of "intermediate functions" in the digital media value chain (i.e., intermediate between the editing and provision of content, on the one hand, and the provision of transmission networks and services over and via which that content travels, on the other hand) currently fall in between the AVMSD on the one hand and the electronic communications directives on the other hand (Valcke, 2008). It remains to be seen whether the Green Paper on Media Convergence will trigger (again) the debate on a fair allocation of responsibilities in the digital media value chain. In this debate, it is the role of academics to investigate more deeply the exact nature of the selection, filtering and organisation activities of different actors (including the citizens themselves when using technologies for personalised search) and assess which "editorial impact" should trigger specific obligations in order to achieve the policy goals that we still value in the digital media environment.

NOTES

1. The research for this contribution has been financed by the European Commission (in the context of *Experimedia,* a project under the Seventh Framework Programme; www.experimedia.eu), the Flemish Agency for Innovation by Science and Technology (IWT-SBO-EMSOC project; www.emsoc.be), and iMinds (www.iminds.be). The chapter was completed on 1 July 2013.
2. This merger resulted in viewing possibilities extending from TV sets with added Internet connectivity, through set-top boxes delivering video content "Over-the-Top" (OTT), to audiovisual media services provided via PCs, laptops or tablets and other mobile devices.
3. To a growing extent, consumers use tablets or smartphones while simultaneously watching TV—for instance, to find out more about what they are watching or to interact with friends or with the TV programme itself.
4. The chapter will not touch upon jurisdictional challenges in an online video-on-demand environment; for a discussion of those, see, for instance, R. Craufurd Smith (2011), pp. 263–285.
5. The AVMSD was the successor of the Television without Frontiers Directive (itself adopted in 1989 and amended a first time in 1997) and was codified in 2010.
6. Article 1(1)(a) AVMSD. The notion also includes audiovisual commercial communication (such as advertising, sponsoring, product placement, etc.).

7. On the condition that they are sufficiently "TV like," meaning that the non-linear service competes for the same audience as linear television broadcasts and that the nature and the means of access to the service would lead the user to reasonably expect regulatory protection (Recital 24 AVMSD; see also infra in the text).

8. The AVMSD motivates this distinction on the basis of the presumed higher impact on public opinion and lower degree of user control in the case of linear services (Recital 58).

9. NMAtv can be watched from YouTube: www.youtube.com/nmaworldedition; see also the website of Next Media Animation at www.nma.tv/about/.

10. Recital 21.

11. www.epra.org/attachments/portoroz-plenary-1-new-services-and-scope-presentation-by-marc-janssen.

12. Also check references to legal documents in http://epra3-production.s3. amazonaws.com/attachments/files/2011/original/Plenary%201_overview_ responses_questionnaire_publicversion.pdf?1340972148, p. 13.

13. See, for instance, the following decisions of the Dutch media regulator *Commissariaat voor de Media*: Ziggo on Demand (5 June 2012), and Younity Media B.V. (8 May 2012), available at its website: www.cvdm.nl/besluiten/. In another case, categorisation based on genre was also deemed sufficient (Filmotech Nederland, 5 June 2012).

14. www.digitaltveurope.net/26261/ofcom-refers-sky-and-viacom-dispute-back-to-vod-regulator and http://stakeholders.ofcom.org.uk/binaries/enforcement/ vod-services/bskyb-appeal.pdf.

15. Unless it clearly contradicts the facts, in which case the clause will not be deemed determinative.

16. www.zeist.allesvan.nl, www.cvdm.nl/content.jsp?objectid=12815.

17. www.ehbo.nl, www.cvdm.nl/content.jsp?objectid=12813.

18. Ofcom's decision in this case has led ATVOD to withdraw also its determinations with regard to websites of the *Sunday Times*, the *Telegraph*, the *Independent*, the *Financial Times*, the *Guardian*, the *News of the World* and *Elle*.

19. This decision is currently being reviewed after the initial decision was overturned by Ofcom. www.digitaltveurope.net/31224/atvod-ruling-overturned-on-appeal/; www.atvod.co.uk/news-consultations/news-consultationsnews/ 20121214-channel-flip-appeal.

20. See reference to Italy in the Comparative Background Document (by E. Machet) for the plenary meeting at the 35th EPRA meeting in Portorož, 2012), available from the website of EPRA (European Platform of Regulatory Authorities) www.epra.org/ (direct link: http://epra3-production.s3. amazonaws.com/attachments/files/2011/original/Plenary%201_overview_ responses_questionnaire_publicversion.pdf?1340972148), at p. 16.

REFERENCES

Audiovisual Media Services Directive: Directive 2010/13/EU of the European Parliament and of the Council of March 10, 2010, on the coordination of certain provisions laid down by law, regulation or administrative action in member states concerning the provision of audiovisual media services (Audiovisual Media Services Directive). *Official Journal of the European Union* (2010) L 95/1. Directive 2010/13/EU coordinates Council Directive 89/552/EEC of 3 October 1989 on the coordination of certain provisions laid down by law, regulation or administrative action in Member States concerning the pursuit of television broadcasting activities—commonly known as the "Television without Frontiers Directive" (*Official Journal of the European Union* (1989) L 298/23), as amended by Directive 97/36/EC (*Official Journal of the European Union* (1997) L 202/60) and Directive 2007/65/EC (*Official Journal of the European Union* (2007) L 332 /27.

Autorità per le garanzie nelle comunicazioni (AGCOM). (2010). *Web-radio and web-TV: F.A.Q.* Retrieved from www.agcom.it/default.aspx?message=contenuto& DCId=495

Authority for Television on Demand (ATVOD). (2010a). *BNPtv.*

———. (2010b). *Community channel videos.*

———. (2010c). *Coolroom.*

———. (2010d). *Elite TV.*

———. (2010e). *FilmOn.*

———. (2010f). *Paulraymond.com full length videos.*

———. (2010g). *Tesco entertainment.*

———. (2011a). *ChannelFlip.*

———. (2011b). *Formula 1 video.*

———. (2011c). *Golfbug.TV.*

———. (2011d). *Guidance on who needs to notify.* Retrieved from www.atvod. co.uk/uploads/files/Guidance_on_who_needs_to_notify_Ed3.1_Mar_2011.pdf

———. (2011e). *ITV Archive content on the Virgin Media platform.*

———. (2011f). *Sun Video.*

———. (2011g). *Top Gear YouTube.*

———. (2012). *Viacom channel providers' content on the Sky Anytime platform.* All retrieved from www.atvod.co.uk/regulated-services/scope-determinations

Betzel, M. (2011). Finetuning classification criteria for on-demand audiovisual media services: The Dutch approach. Regulating on-demand services in Italy. In S. Nikoltchev (Ed.), *IRIS special: Searching for audiovisual content* (pp. 53–62). Strasbourg: European Audiovisual Observatory.

Chavannes, R., & Castendyk, O. (2008). Art. 1 of the AVMSD (Definitions). In O. Castendyk et al. (Eds.), *European media law* (pp. 799–846). Alphen a/d Rijn: Kluwer Law International.

Contact Committee. (2008). Minutes of the 27th meeting of the contact committee established by the Television without Frontiers Directive, Doc CC TVSF (2008) 4. Retrieved from the European Commission's archived website on Audiovisual and Media Policies http://ec.europa.eu/avpolicy/index_en.htm (direct link: http:// ec.europa.eu/avpolicy/docs/reg/tvwf/contact_comm/27_minutes_en.pdf)

Council for Broadcasting and Retransmission (CBR). (2009). Rozsah pôsobnosti zákonač. 308/2000 Z. z. v súvislosti so zmenami zákona účinnými. Retrieved from the website of CBR www.rvr.sk/en/ (direct link: www.rada-rtv.sk/_cms/data/ modules/download/1265805698_Rozsah_posobnosti_zakona_c._3082000_v_ suvislosti_so_zmenami_ucinnymi_od_15._decembra_2009.pdf)

Council of the European Union. (2006). Proposal for a directive of the European Parliament and of the Council amending Council Directive 89/552/EEC on the coordination of certain provisions laid down by law, regulation or administrative action in member states concerning the pursuit of television broadcasting activities (Proceedings of the Audiovisual Working Party, 2005/0260 (COD), 6994/06). Retrieved from the Public Register of Council Documents http://regis ter.consilium.europa.eu/

Conseil Supérieur de l'Audiovisuel (CSA). (2011). *Consultation publique sur le périmètre de la régulation des services de medias audiovisuels.* Retrieved from the website of the CSA http://csa.be/ (direct link: http://csa.be/system/documents_ consultations_files/124/original/CAC_20110505_competence_materielle_ consultation_publique.pdf?1305801617)

————. (2012). *Recommandation relative au périmètre de la régulation des services de medias audiovisuels.* Retrieved from the website of the CSA http://csa.be/ (direct link: http://csa.be/system/documents_files/1713/original/CAC_20120329_recommandation_competence_materielle.pdf?1333030000)

Craufurd Smith, R. (2011). Determining regulatory competence for audiovisual media services in the European Union. *Journal of Media Law*, Volume 3, Number 2, December 2011, 263–285.

Commissariaat voor de Media (CvdM) *Veelgestelde vragen over (aanmelding van) commerciële mediadiensten op aanvraag.* Retrieved from www.cvdm.nl/praktisch/commerciele-mediadienst-op-aanvraag-aanmelden

————. (2011). *Beleidsregels classificatie commerciële mediadiensten op aanvraag.* Retrieved from www.cvdm.nl/dsresource?objectid=12335

Directive 2000/31/EC of the European Parliament and of the Council of June 8, 2000, on certain legal aspects of information society services, in particular electronic commerce, in the Internal market (Directive on Electronic Commerce). *Official Journal of the European Union* (2000) L 178/1.

EMR (Institut für Europäisches Medienrecht—Institute for European Media Law). (2012, August). Service "tvsme" of the newspaper "sme" is held to be an on-demand audiovisual media service. *Europäisches Medienrecht—der NEWSLETTER*, p. 27. Retrieved from www.emr-sb.de/tl_files/EMR-SB/content/PDF/EMR-Newsletter/EMR_Newsletter_2012-8.pdf

European Audiovisual Observatory and Direction du Développement des Médias (DDM) (France). (2009). *Vidéo à la demande et télévision de rattrapage en Europe.* Retrieved from www.ddm.gouv.fr/IMG/pdf/RAPPORT_VoD.pdf

European Commission. (2012). *First report from the Commission to the European Parliament, the Council, the European Economic and Social Committee and the Committee of the Regions on the application of Directive 2010/13/EU "Audiovisual Media Services Directive"—Audiovisual media services and connected devices: Past and future perspectives,* COM(2012) 203 final. Retrieved from EUR-Lex http://eur-lex.europa.eu/

————. (2013). *Green Paper on preparing for a fully converged audiovisual world: Growth, creation and values.* Brussels, April 24, 2013, COM(2013) 231 final. Retrieved from https://ec.europa.eu/digital-agenda/sites/digital-agenda/files/convergence_green_paper_en_0.pdf

Gianni, Origoni, Grippo, Cappelli & Partners. (2011). *The new resolutions of the Italian media authority on the audiovisual media services via the Internet.* Retrieved from www.gop.it/doc_pubblicazioni/59_a8uoa94lak_eng.pdf

Hermanns, O., & Matzneller, P. (2011). "Whose boots are moade for walking?" Regulation of on-demand audiovisual services. In Nikoltchev, S. (Ed.), *IRIS special: Searching for audiovisual content* (pp. 7–30). Strasbourg: European Audiovisual Observatory.

Janssen, M. (2012). *New services and scope: What's in, what's out revisited—the Belgian CSA recommendation,* 35th EPRA meeting, Portorož, 31 May 2012. Retrieved from the EPRA website www.epra.org/ (direct link: www.epra.org/attachments/portoroz-plenary-1-new-services-and-scope-presentation-by-marc-janssen)

Machet, E. (2012). *New media & regulation: Towards a paradigm shift? New services and scope: "What's in, what's out revisited."* Comparative background document to 35th EPRA meeting, Portorož. Retrieved from the EPRA website www.epra.org/ (direct link: epra3-production.s3.amazonaws.com/attachments/files/2011/original/Plenary%201_overview_responses_questionnaire_pub licversion.pdf?1340972148)

————. (2011). *Content regulation and new media: Exploring regulatory boundaries between traditional and new media.* Background document to 33rd EPRA meeting, Ohrid. Retrieved from the EPRA website www.epra.org/ (direct link: http://epra3-production.s3.amazonaws.com/attachments/files/102/original/ Ohrid_session1_revised.final.pdf?1327492407)

Metzdorf, J. (2012). Regulierung der elektronischen Presse in Großbritannien?—Ein Anwendungsbeispiel zum Erwägungsgrund 28 der AVMD-RL. In J. Taeger, *IT und Internet—mit Recht gestalten.* Edewecht: Olwir.

Ofcom. (2011a). *Playboy—Climax 3 uncut.*

———. (2011b). *Sun video.*

———. (2012a). *MTV Viva TV.*

———. (2012b). *Nickelodeon, Comedy Central and MTV content on Virgin Media.*

———. (2013). *Top Gear YouTube & BBC Food YouTube.* Retrieved from http:// stakeholders.ofcom.org.uk/enforcement/video-on-demand-services

Schulz, W., & Heilmann, S. (2008). *IRIS special: Editorial responsibility, notes on a key concept in the regulation of audiovisual media services.* Strasbourg: European Audiovisual Observatory.

Swedish Broadcasting Commission. (2012). *Tidningars tv-verksamhet omfattas av radio- och tv-lagen.* Retrieved from the website of the Swedish Broadcasting Commission www.radioochtv.se/ (direct link: www.radioochtv.se/ Om-oss/Press/Pressmeddelanden/2012/Tidningars-tv-verksamhet-omfattas-av-radio--och-tv-lagen/)

Valcke, P. (2008). In search of the audiovisual search tools in the EU regulatory frameworks. In S. Nikoltchev (Ed.), *IRIS special: Searching for audiovisual content* (pp. 65–78). Strasbourg: European Audiovisual Observatory.

Valcke, P., & Lievens, E. (2009). Rethinking European broadcasting regulation. In C. Pauwels et al. (Eds.), *Rethinking European media and communications policy.* Brussels: VUB Press.

Valcke, P., Kuczerawy, A., Lefever, K., Lievens, E., Stevens, D., & Werkers, E. (2010). The EU regulatory framework applicable to broadcasting. In L. Garzaniti & M. O'Regan (Eds.), *Telecommunications, broadcasting and the Internet. EU competition law & regulation.* 3rd ed. (pp. 263–330). London: Thomson Sweet & Maxwell.

Valcke, P., & Lefever, K. (2012). Media law in the European Union. In *International Encyclopaedia of Media Law.* Alphen a/d Rijn: Kluwer Law International.

Verweij, J. (2011). YouTube en de Richtlijn Audiovisuele Mediadiensten. *MediaForum,* Volume 23, Number 4, April 2011, 105–113.

Viola, R., & Cappello, M. (2011). Regulating on-demand services in Italy. In S. Nikoltchev (Ed.), *IRIS special: Searching for audiovisual content* (pp. 47–52). Strasbourg: European Audiovisual Observatory.

3 Making TV Accessible in the 21st Century

Peter Looms

INTRODUCTION

Television in the 21st Century

Following the appearance of TV as a medium in 1928, viewing television programmes was initially a *social* experience. For the first few decades, the TV television receiver itself was relatively expensive, and TV viewing was therefore a collective activity. The television signal was initially delivered to TV screens by terrestrial broadcasting on analogue networks.

Towards the end of the 20th century, TV sets became cheaper in relative terms. The distribution of TV via terrestrial broadcasting was joined by distribution over digital cable and satellite networks and then by networks using the Internet protocol. The number of available channels increased with the emergence of pay TV. The remote control became an important prerequisite of viewing. With more channels to choose from, the viewer could discover and select something to view without going over to the TV receiver to change the channel. Middle-class homes had two or more TV sets. Being able to watch TV content on small handheld devices moved into the mainstream.

The emergence of devices like iPods and streaming music services in the noughties also changed consumer attitudes to content and its delivery. Just before the turn of the century, Bill Gates (1999), in a keynote at Telecom '99 that talked about his company's mission, also foresaw major changes in media such as radio and television:

> Software will play a critical role in helping businesses and consumers gain universal access to their information," Gates said. "Microsoft's mission is to provide the technology and platform building blocks that will enable new services to be deployed on broadband networks and to integrate with the PC, television and telephone, as well as a new generation of intelligent devices. We intend to offer customers access to their information *any time, anywhere and on any device.*

The keynote signalled the roles of digitalization and convergence in making information—also audiovisual content—universally accessible.

In the 21st century, television continues to evolve from the appointment viewing of channels to the use of TV content on multiple platforms. The trend towards multiple screens—big stationary ones in the home and smaller, portable ones elsewhere—has become more accentuated. The mantra for TV content is now consumer convenience—anything, anytime, anywhere and on any device—which can be traced back to Bill Gates's keynote.

Take the case of TV in Hong Kong. There are still TV sets and remote controls in most homes with free-to-air TV from two main networks, TVB and ATV, cable TV and PCCW's now TV delivered using Internet protocols. But viewing patterns are now more diverse. A recent study by TNS suggests that in Hong Kong the average citizen has nearly two mobiles (including conventional phones, smartphones and tablets).

Gattuso (2012) makes the point that broadcasters currently play only a minor role in the delivery of television content to American homes:

> According to Nielson ratings, only 9.6 percent of U.S. households relied on over-the-air broadcasts last year. While broadcasters still maintain towers and beam signals over their federally licensed frequencies, very few Americans receive their television signals this way. Cable TV is now the most common delivery mechanism. But even cable faces significant competition in today's world. As of late 2010, cable TV served 60 percent of the 'multi-channel video programming distributor' (MVPD) market. Satellite providers DIreCTV and DISH Network accounted for another third, with offerings from telecommunications providers, such as Verizon's FIoS and AT&T's U-Verse, serving some 7 percent more.

In two other chapters in this volume, Robert Frieden discusses in depth the migration of TV content from channels to platforms in the U.S., and, using examples from Europe, Peggy Valcke and Jef Ausloos identify the challenges for media policy such changes make.

Young adults have never watched much TV. Today they are more likely to view TV-like content such as Psy's latest video on YouTube while on the move than to see TV at home, as many young adults who have moved away from their parents' homes do not have a TV set, preferring to use their laptops or tablets. Exceptions include major events such the Olympic Games or a blockbuster TV drama series where viewing of such events is still a social phenomenon.

The consequence of this focus on consumer convenience is a television world in which television content delivery is more fragmented. The number of television channels has increased, and these are delivered both in real time and asynchronously in the form of "catch-up," "over-the-top" (OTT) or on-demand services on multiple networks not only to television receivers but also to computers, smartphones and other mobile devices. Television content providers need production and distribution strategies such as Create Once, Publish Everywhere (COPE) to deliver television services in an economically sustainable fashion on the platforms consumers want to use (Looms, 2006). In terms of global availability and use, television continues to be the most widely used mass medium. What many academics and policymakers often overlook is that a sizeable minority of the global population encounter significant barriers when trying to use and enjoy TV. These barriers arise as the result of the mismatch between the design of television service and the capabilities of its users. According to estimates by the International Telecommunication Union this is at least one in six of the world's adult population. The rationale for making television accessible is the subject of the next section.

Television and Accessibility—The Case for Action

Television viewers have diverse requirements that are a reflection not only of their interests and needs but also of their physical, intellectual, social and cultural capabilities. The United Nations Convention on the Rights of Persons with Disabilities (CRPD) came into force in May 2008. Article 30(1)(b) states the following:

> Parties recognize the right of Persons with Disabilities to take part on an equal basis with others in cultural life, and shall take all appropriate measures to ensure that Persons with Disabilities: a) enjoy access to cultural materials in accessible formats; and b) enjoy access to television programmes, films, theatre and other cultural activities, in accessible formats.

> A forthcoming G3ict document looks into further detail at the CRPD, at the coverage of "broadcasting accessibility" and identifies stakeholders that will be required to comply:

> The implication of Article 30 is that metrics for television accessibility need to cover not only awareness of access service provision, but also use and benefit. Finally, article 9(2)(b) stipulates that States Parties to the Convention must "ensure that private entities that offer facilities and services which are open to or provided to the public take into account all aspects of accessibility for Persons with Disabilities"—this covers private sector broadcasters and producers of audio-visual content.

Whether a television programme is "accessible" in the general sense of the word depends on the interplay of the potential viewer and the television services and the kinds of task that he or she needs to carry out in order to watch television. This is summarized in Figure 3.1:

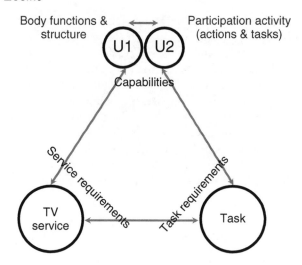

Figure 3.1   Two viewers watching television.

The two viewers (User 1 and User 2) have various capabilities that influence their use of a television service and the tasks they can carry out. Typical tasks related to television viewing include these:

Setting up the TV receiver: Both initially and "retuning" or installing updates during the lifetime of the TV receiver or a second-screen device
Discovering TV content: Using electronic programme guides (EPGs), spots and trailers or just zapping from one channel to the next
Selecting TV content: Deciding to view a specific program
Viewing TV: Watching TV and hopefully enjoying it
Talking about TV content: Both virtual and "presencial" communication in real time or asynchronously

Many of us assume that the prevalence of sensory impairments like deafness or blindness is quite small and that the viewing tasks listed here can be done by nearly everybody. This is not the case. Media decision-makers have an understandable tendency to overlook individuals who have cognitive impairments following illness or injury or to understate moderate or minor impairments affecting viewers, especially the elderly, for whom television is an important source of information and companionship.

That policymaker perceptions of the nature and size of the TV accessibility challenge may be wrong can be exemplified with reference to a specific case. In 2012, the Audience Research department of DR, a broadcaster in Denmark, conducted an interview survey with a representative sample of 1,004 Danes. Respondents were asked about their hearing (for example: "Can you hear when the doorbell rings?") and their views on TV audio. While this is not a comprehensive audiological study of hearing, it can be used as an indication of the respondents' perceptions of their hearing capabilities.

The study findings show that the following are true in Denmark:

About half of the adult population (53%) have "normal hearing."
21% report having hearing difficulties.
26% have what appears to be an undiagnosed hearing impairment.
30% of those older than 61 years acknowledged the existence of hearing problems.
15% of 40- to 60-year-olds and 9% of 12- to 39-year-olds have recognized hearing problems.
15% of those over 61 years old use a hearing aid.
Only 46% of those with recognized hearing problems are aware of the existence of and use captioning for the deaf and hard of hearing.

The impairment barriers to TV viewing mentioned in this study are broadly in line with earlier studies of accessibility such as Grundy and colleagues (1999)—the demographics of disability are quite stable.

When it comes to television, we can conclude that, even in small, affluent and well-educated countries such as Denmark, a significant minority has one or more disabilities. Some viewers are aware of their impairments while many others have not explicitly recognized their personal situation. Either way, disabilities of various kinds may make the viewing of television difficult or impossible. Regardless of the absolute numbers in question, television accessibility is an issue that needs to be addressed.

Where there are no good statistics on which to base TV accessibility actions, it may be necessary to conduct a study building on good practice such as the methodologies recommended by the United Nations Statistical Division (n.d.) Washington Group. Ambitions will depend on the resources available for this kind of research in the territory in question.

As the proportion of the world's population emerging from poverty increases, disabilities will still be with us, although there will be a gradual shift from functional impairments caused by accident or illness to age-related impairments. The key takeaway is that *all* of us are likely to have a disability-related problem watching TV at some point in our lives.

Television and Accessibility—An End-to-End Service

From an accessibility perspective, a television service consists of the following five components:

The television content itself: Television programmes organized temporally as channels

Access services such as closed captioning/subtitles, audio description and sign language interpretation to help individuals with various functional impairments

"Meta-content": Information about television programmes and channels in the form of EPGs, spots and trailers on television but also on other platforms (broadcaster websites, movie portals and other video portals such as YouTube; programme listings in newspapers and weekly magazines)

The television service interface: The means by which viewers discover, select, view and enjoy television content—typically a remote control device

Interfaces with other devices: For example, in the case of viewers with hearing impairments, wireless connections between a television receiver and the viewer's hearing aid allow the television audio to be received directly with the best possible quality; in the case of a viewer with visual impairments, there may be an interface to a screen reader to read aloud on-screen text

The design of these five components and the viewer's capabilities will have a direct impact on television viewing—the main tasks he or she carries out when watching TV. We can map accessibility actions to these five service components:

The intrinsic intelligibility of television content
Television access services
Television meta-content
The television service interface
Interfaces to other assistive technologies used by television viewers with functional impairments

The suggestion here is that to make TV accessible, one should focus on a television service end to end, all the way from planning, production and transmission to its use by the viewer. For each of these five service components, I will review what has currently been achieved to address television accessibility.

The Intrinsic Intelligibility of Television Content

The production of television content has undergone rapid changes in the last two decades as a consequence of digitalization and the availability of desktop production and editing systems. In principle, anyone with a laptop or a smartphone can make TV. Television news journalists increasingly do things that in the past were handled by trained cameramen, sound engineers and video editors. Such generalists are skilled in journalism and the narrative conventions of television but often have gaps in their knowledge about human perception—the working of human sight and hearing.

Judging from calls to broadcaster call centres and audience research on viewer complaints, desktop TV production can result in programmes where elderly viewers and those with hearing and sight impairments have difficulties understanding what is going on. Significant problems include these:

Viewer difficulties hearing what is said due to poor audio quality
Intelligibility problems caused by the use of sound effects or music in the background

Big jumps in loudness levels within and between programmes that cause discomfort to elderly viewers or even lead to their abandoning the viewing of a particular program

Internal reviews more than a decade ago at broadcasters such as the BBC (UK) and SVT (Sweden) have led to guidelines of best practice on audio to improve TV audio. This was followed by focused activities to build awareness and improve skills in television production planning (in-house and external), production and distribution.

Broadcasters in North America and Europe are now working to comply with technical recommendations and changes in television regulation that address the loudness issue (ATSC, n.d.). The Canadian Radio-Television and Telecommunications Commission (2012) ruled the following:

Effective September 1, 2012, Canadian broadcasters and television service providers (e.g., cable, satellite, and IPTV providers) must follow international standards for measuring and controlling digital television signals, and must ensure that TV commercials are broadcast at a similar volume to programs.

EBU (2010) mentions the EBU recommendation R128 that was the result of two years' work by the audio experts in the EBU PLOUD Group led by Florian Camerer of the Austrian broadcaster ORF. The new recommendation is accompanied by specifications for loudness metering, a loudness range descriptor, loudness test material and production and distribution guidelines.

R&D centres such as the Frauenhofer Institute in Germany and the NHK Research Center in Japan have come up with solutions for "clean audio" and customized user control over the clarity and delivery of speech on television and radio that are finding their way into digital television receivers and second-screen devices.

None of these measures need be particularly costly. Focusing on and optimizing the intrinsic usability of TV content makes a big difference to the viewing experience for users on the threshold of what they are capable of seeing or hearing.

Television Access Services

From a chronological perspective, the provision of access services can be divided into three main maturity phases:

From idea to proof of concept
From concept to service launch
From launch to mature access service provision

Each of these phases in the development of TV accessibility contains activities that typify the maturation process. The list has been derived using discussions of the process with practitioners with many years' experience in this field.

From Idea to Proof of Concept

Access services for television have been with us for longer than most of us realize. Getting the ideas in place and demonstrating proof of concept takes time. In some countries the case for such action is still not in place.

The introduction of subtitles and captioning predates television. According to Ivarsson (2004), the first example of what we now term "inter-titles"— texts, drawn or printed on paper, filmed and placed between sequences of the film—dates back to 1903. The jump from this to using captions— essentially intralingual subtitles—to help viewers understand the audio is not a big one.

According to Døvefilm (2013) the first known use of sign language interpretation in media was a film made by Viggo Chr. Hansen for a congress of the deaf community in Finland in 1929.

Audio description is a more recent development. According to the Audio Description Coalition (2013), Margaret and Cody Pfanstiehl of the Metropolitan Washington Ear collaborated with Arena Stage in Washington, DC, in 1981 to create and develop an audio description programme for live theatre performances.

The rationale for such access services has been in place for decades. Taking the first steps to apply this knowledge is not always easy.

From Concept to Service Launch

In a recent paper, Li and Looms (2013) explain the changes that have taken place in the way the term "accessibility" is used. The relationships among "digital literacy," "usability," "accessibility," "affordability" and "availability" are explained with reference to the accessibility "pyramid."

The impetus for introducing access services on television often comes from advocacy by national disability organizations. In countries like Spain or the UK, nongovernmental organizations (NGOs) like Organización Nacional de Ciegos Españoles, ONCE in Spain or The Royal National Institute of Blind People, RNIB and Action on Hearing Loss (formerly known as RNID in the UK) convinced public broadcasters to provide closed captioning, sign language interpretation or audio description for viewers who are deaf or blind.

Once the case for access services on television had been made and accepted by such broadcasters, national legislation, standards and regulation often followed.

Where the aim has been to provide captioning and description services on a permanent basis and to scale up provisions for both public and commercial broadcasters, self- and co-regulation is rarely sufficient. Even in cases where regulators such as USA's FCC prescribed the use of access services (such as the use of audio description with a limited number of TV programs), the mandated introduction of such an access service was initially challenged in the courts.

In 2001, the FCC implemented rules requiring major broadcast networks and cable companies in the top 25 television markets to provide 50 hours of described programming per quarter effective April 2002. In 2002, the U.S. Court of Appeals for the District of Columbia reversed the FCC ruling requiring audio description for television, finding that the FCC had acted beyond the scope of its authority in adopting those rules (Noix, 2013). Audio description was reinstated 9 years later on 25 August 2011 when the FCC adopted rules to implement the video description provisions of the Twenty-First Century Communications and Video Accessibility Act of 2010 (CVAA).

Similar formal and informal challenges to the legal basis of access service introduction took place in 2012 in the Czech Republic, Poland and Portugal.

The introductory phase of TV access services often contains a number of the following:

Open and subsequently closed captioning outside prime-time slots
Programming for the signing community scheduled during the day or late in the evening
A limited amount of audio description of fiction (films or TV drama series)
Audio subtitles (providing an additional audio channel where subtitles for programmes in foreign languages are read aloud in the official language)

From Launch to Mature Access Service Provision

The scaling up of access services and the achievement of a degree of service maturity contain a number of the following:

A gradual shift of focus from disability to accessibility recognizes that all of us in the course of our lives will have special needs. It extends target audiences for TV access services from individuals who are deaf or blind to include viewers with cognitive impairments and reading difficulties, to the very young and to adults with age-related impairments. In some cases, the focus on accessibility encompasses social and linguistic inclusion—making TV accessible to migrants and other ethnic groups.
A running-in period to reach targets for access services means that broadcasters with nationwide coverage and with a market share of over 1% may be given between 2 and 10 years to reach the final targets.
Mandatory targets may be set for specific (urban) areas and discretionary ones for the remaining areas, in the case of the United States.
Annual targets may be set that take into account first-time broadcasts and repeats, TV programming broadcast during primetime and peripheral slots as well as exemptions for certain content genres such as shopping channels or live programming. Captioning targets are often increased to 100% for preproduced output and repeats. Captioning of live TV programmes is then included.

A shift from "one-size-fits-all"—open captioning or signing language— to access services that viewers can choose to use and then customize.

Open sign language interpretation with signing for the deaf community in slots outside prime-time viewing.

Opt-in sign language interpretation of news and current affairs during primetime using a second signing channel, Internet delivery of the TV programme to computers only, or Internet delivery to "connected TVs" that have both broadcast and IP (Internet Protocol) connections.

Opt-in audio description can be provided for a limited proportion of television programming, increasing in some cases to about 20% of nationwide TV channel output. In countries such as Canada, there may be a TV channel dedicated to audio description.

Opt-in audio or spoken subtitles for some or all programming in foreign languages (for territories that use subtitles rather than dubbing to localize TV content) may be offered.

Metrics and key performance indicators (KPIs) for the measurement of access service provision, awareness and use can be used. AENOR (2012) and Ofcom (2013) contain further examples of recent work.

Mechanisms to automate the reporting of access service provision to the regulator to demonstrate compliance can be provided, an example of which is reported by Brady (2013).

This final phase of the maturity model can take 5 to 10 years.

The third focus area for TV accessibility is meta-content—information about TV content and TV accessibility.

Television Meta-Content

In a world where the choice of television programming is considerable, the viewer has to be able to find something he or she wants to watch and then select, use and enjoy that program.

Where the enjoyment of TV programming is dependent on the availability of an access service like closed captions, audio description or sign language interpretation, meta-content will have to facilitate these processes. If the EPG or programme listing does not mention the existence of closed captions or audio description (even if the access service is available), a viewer may choose not to watch the program.

The use of icons or abbreviations about the presence of access services is a central issue. Some widely used options to convey this kind of information include the following:

The numbers 888 on Teletext systems to indicate the availability of closed captioning

The use of letters to represent closed captioning (CC) and audio description (D) in the U.S. and comparable national abbreviations in other countries

The use of icons to represent the access service or its intended users

The use of a suffix to the channel name (DR1 *SYN*) to indicate the presence of a virtual DR1 channel that contains access services for those with visual and cognitive impairments

The organization of programmes in "access channels": a signing channel that contains programming from two or more competing channels for the signing community in Denmark; an AD channel on Canadian TV

Naming conventions give rise to serious communication challenges as TV accessibility provisions mature.

When the initial concern was to provide individuals who are deaf or blind with accessible TV, the use of icons that represent these two disabilities was acceptable.

With the shift in focus from disability to accessibility, however, a given service such as audio description or audio subtitles addresses the needs of *multiple* groups of users (elders who have hearing impairments, individuals with have cognitive impairments and those whose reading speed is low). A service icon for audio description that depicts a blind eye will not necessarily convey meaning ("this service is for you") to those with cognitive or reading impairments.

For this reason, the shift from phase 2 to 3 in the maturity model is a useful inflection point to consider icons that represent what the access service *does* rather than the intended *audience* of that service.

A related challenge is service awareness, the proportion of the population aware of the existence of a given access service. Building awareness is very different for closed captioning, which is available for most programs, and audio description, which is only available for a small percentage of television programming.

Audience research done on services for individuals who are blind or who have serious visual impairments reported as in Jakobsen and Studsgaard (2011) identifies some of the formal and informal communication networks that are required to promote the existence of a new service such as audio description. In the UK, the TV regulator Ofcom has required broadcasters to run campaigns to promote AD. Making a majority of the population (and the intended audiences for AD) aware of its existence has taken a number of years. Offering access services without making sure that people can find and benefit from them is a poor investment.

The Television Service Interface

Earlier in this chapter, there was a discussion of the interplay of the potential viewer and the television services and the kinds of task he or she needs to carry out in order to watch television.

Traditionally, the viewer of an analogue TV channel turned on the set and stayed with that channel or pressed a button to change to another. As the number of available channels increased, remote control devices allowed viewers to change the channel without having to go over to the set to press a button.

The transition from analogue to digital broadcasting required the use of a set-top box and, in some cases, the use of two remotes to handle interactions with both the TV and the set-top box.

The user interaction also changed. The viewer could now change channels by "zapping" (pressing the channel up and channel down arrow keys), by pressing the number keys or by selecting a channel from a list in the EPG and pressing "OK" to select that channel.

Furthermore, in order to customize the television receiver to always show closed captions or play the descriptions, viewers now have to learn how to set up the device (or find a family member or friend to do this for them).

For viewers unfamiliar with interface conventions from computers, learning to use a new TV service interface and "unlearn" their previous habits is a significant challenge.

An inspiring example of how to make the transition to digital television is the UK Help Scheme. It was "run by the BBC to help everyone who was eligible disabled, aged 75 or over, registered blind or partially sighted or anyone who had lived in a care home for 6 months or more with everything they needed to switch one TV to digital" (Help Scheme, 2012). As part of its remit, the Scheme worked with consumer electronics manufacturers to ensure the availability of digital television receivers that were easy to set up, use and retune. Considerable thought was put into the needs of elders when learning a new TV service interface in order to view TV content and access services.

For territories that have yet to go digital, the UK Help Scheme evaluation provides a wealth of practical information about the planning of such processes (Help Scheme, 2010).

While broadcasters increasingly promote accessibility by offering access services, viewers may need to use other assistive technologies when viewing.

An example is a hearing aid. Viewers with hearing impairments use them to compensate for hearing loss or the reduced ability to discriminate speech with background noise and competing speech sources. The use of wireless connections to hearing devices allows the direct transmission of audio information (speech, music, alarms, etc.) from the source to the ear, rather than using the built-in microphone of a hearing device. This reduces the level of disturbing background noise and competing sources, thus significantly improving the capability of hearing-impaired users to understand speech.

In his briefing document, Marcel Vlaming (2013) of the European Hearing Instrument Manufacturers Association (EHIMA) argues the case for global frequency allocations to allow for the wireless transfer of audio from television sets, mobile phones and public address systems in public areas to hearing aids, replacing the existing analogue options using induction coils that suffer from interference.

With the emergence of connected TVs, the use of synthetic speech (Text to Speech, or TTS) is now finding its way into mainstream digital television receivers. Viewers can set their TV to read aloud EPGs and, in the not-too-distant future, other kinds of on-screen text. To offer synthetic speech depends on clearly defined interfaces between the television service and these third-party assistive technologies either in the main screen or on a second screen (a smartphone or computer tablet). Looms (2013) provides examples of main-screen and second-screen solutions for TV accessibility.

Making television accessible is thus more than providing access services. As the review of television accessibility suggests, progress requires a number of carrots and sticks to promote change in the television "ecosystem" and consolidate achievements. Television is an end-to-end service that requires the concerted efforts of a number of stakeholders to make a difference. The final section will address the incentives and sanctions that drive television accessibility and suggest possible scenarios for this in the 21st century.

TELEVISION ACCESSIBILITY IN THE 21ST CENTURY—THE WAY FORWARD

Anecdotal evidence on accessibility at national, European and global levels suggests that the case for television accessibility is poorly understood.

Over the last two years, the author of this chapter has had the opportunity to discuss the issues with stakeholders in Europe, the Middle East, Latin America, India and South-East Asia. Putting together the case for making television accessible appears to be the first major prerequisite.

The Inclusive Design Toolkit of the University of Cambridge (UK) makes some suggestions about designing for accessibility and provides some basic, worldwide arguments for the case for inclusive design, including age variation (longer life expectancies and reduced birth rates), capability variation and a focus on simplicity. The toolkit also discusses the commercial incentives of inclusive design with reference to some case stories.

A different viewpoint on the drivers for improved television accessibility comes from the European Platform of Regulatory Authorities, EPRA (2013). Machet (2013) contains the results of a questionnaire survey of European television regulators. This comparative paper provides an overview on the general legal framework and broadcasters' obligations with regard to subtitling, signing and audio description for linear and on-demand audiovisual media services; on measures concerning the accessibility of end-user TV equipment; on the role played by broadcasting regulators in accessibility policies; and on funding issues. The paper documents that most European countries combine several legal instruments: legislation, specific access codes or rules, public service broadcasting contracts and rulings by the regulator.

Following off-the-record discussions with senior broadcast executives and engineers, a number of factors emerged that promote change management and drive the introduction of accessible TV. These have been organized in a SWOT diagram (see Table 3.1).

The consensus among respondents was that the key strengths of accessible TV are not S1 and S2, but improved satisfaction ratings (S3) and channel image (S4).

The main weaknesses were concerns to do with the capital and operational costs of offering access services (W1) and the need to do so on new platforms (W2). Such concerns are considerable for those who need to make investments in capital equipment (e.g., changes to their play-out centres to insert closed captioning and subtitles in dubbing territories). These concerns can be allayed by accessing reliable data on production and capital costs using a peer review by broadcasters from a neighbouring country.

A discussion of the UK digital television market focused on improvements in TV accessibility at major commercial broadcasters. The hypothesis that emerged is that action was taken because the opportunities (primarily O1) outweighed the threats (T1, T2 and T4). The threat of escalating costs and finding budgets to produce access services (T3) was raised. Commercial broadcasters in particular are concerned about the timing of increased regulatory demands. They are having to fine-tune their business models dependent on advertising to take into consideration the worst global economic crisis in the last 80 years.

Table 3.1   SWOT factors for accessible television

Strengths	Weaknesses
S1. Increased reach	W1. The cost of improved accessibility
S2. Increased share	outweighs the ratings benefits
S3. Improved satisfaction ratings among viewers with disabilities	W2. The cost of delivering access services on new platforms (additional broadcast
S4. Improved channel image (Corporate Social Responsibility, CSR)	and IP networks to TVs, PCs and mobile devices)

Opportunities	Threats
O1. Reduced program or channel churn	T1. The loss of a broadcast license as the result of noncompliance with
O2. Synergies (using subtitles and TTS to create access services for new groups)	regulator targets T2. Financial penalties as the result of noncompliance
O3. Public procurement rules (having to provide access services as a prerequisite for receiving public funding)	T3. Escalating costs of offering accessible TV
	T4. Increased competition for elder viewers from competing broadcasters offering access services

CONCLUSION—MAKING TELEVISION ACCESSIBILITY HAPPEN

The working hypothesis here is that the introduction of TV accessibility initiatives requires a stakeholder that can act as a catalyst for change. The stakeholder will have to piece together the arguments for action and list the consequences of inaction. The case for action should include not only the perceived needs of individuals with disabilities but also of all the key stakeholders who will be required to turn the accessibility vision into reality.

The catalyst will need all-round knowledge of television accessibility and will have to present a compelling case for action that uses examples of good practice (what works and why).

This catalyst may be one of the key stakeholders in television. In some cases, it could be the TV regulator that has a good sense of "television ecology" and has an understanding of which incentives and sanctions can be brought to bear. In territories with public service broadcasters, they may act as the catalyst. The history of TV accessibility suggests that state and public broadcasters in the past have been able to show proof of concept and blaze a trail for commercial stakeholders to follow. Disability organizations and even those active in international standardization can also play this role. Forthcoming statistical analysis of the United Nations (2006) Convention on the Rights of Persons with Disabilities by G3ict mentioned by Lebois (2013) at an International Telecommunication Union (ITU) workshop entitled "Making Media Accessible to All: The Options and the Economics" suggests that active disability organizations and stakeholders working on international media standards play critical roles.

At present in Argentina and China we are witnessing nascent TV accessibility initiatives that have catalysts in the public education system or at a university.

In conclusion, the key prerequisite of accessible television is the ability to put together a credible and compelling case for action. Such a case should outline a multi-stakeholder process where each stakeholder can contribute to accessible TV rather than defend the status quo.

REFERENCES

AENOR. (2012, May). *Subtitulado para personas sordas y personas con discapacidad auditiva. (Subtitling for deaf and hard-of-hearing people).* AENOR Asociación Española de Normalización y Certificación. UNE 153010 Norma española. Madrid, Spain.
ATSC. (2011 Recommended practice *Techniques for establishing and maintaining audio loudness for digital television.* Document A/85:2011, 25 July 2011. Advanced Television Systems Committee, Inc. Washington, D.C., USA. Retrieved from www.atsc.org/cms/standards/a_85-2011a.pdf
Audio Description Coalition (2013). *A Brief History of Audio Description in the U.S. Audio Description Coalition.* Audio Description Coalition. Retrieved from www.audiodescriptioncoalition.org/history.html

Brady, K. (2013). *Automated closed captioning and descriptive video compliance at Turner Broadcasting. Session: Access services—How can we produce them efficiently?* IBC 2013 Conference Proceedings. London: IBC.

Canadian Radio-Television and Telecommunications Commission. (2012). *Loud TV commercials.* Retrieved from www.crtc.gc.ca/eng/info_sht/g3.htm#ftn1; www.transedit.se/history.htm

Døvefilm. (2013). *Historie 1929–1962.* Retrieved from http://døvefilm.dk/

EBU. (2010). *Loudness.* EBU technical review. European Broadcasting Union, Geneva, Switzerland, Retrieved from http://tech.ebu.ch/loudness

European Platform of Regulatory Authorities (EPRA). (2013). *Round table on access to audiovisual media services for persons with disabilities.* Comparative background document. Revised public version, 8 July 2013. EPRA/2013/05. Retrieved from www.epra.org/news_items/access-services-what-role-for-the-regulator

G3ict (in press). *Model broadcasting accessibility policy.*

Gates, W. (1999, October 12). Keynote address. Telecom '99. Geneva, Switzerland.

Gattuso, J.L. (2012, November 6). Adjusting the picture: Television regulation for the 21st century. *Backgrounder, 2741.* Heritage Foundation. Retrieved from www.heritage.org/research/reports/2012/11/adjusting-the-picture-television-regulation-for-the-21st-century

Grundy, E., Ahlberg, D., Ali, M., Breeze, E., & Sloggett, A. (1999). *Disability in Great Britain: Results from the 1996/97 disability follow-up to the family resources survey.* Huddersfield, UK: Charlesworth Group.

Help Scheme. (2010). *Helping older and disabled people switch to digital TV: The Help Scheme story so far.* Switchover Help Scheme, The United Kingdom. Retrieved from www.helpscheme.co.uk/reports

Help Scheme. (2012). *About the Switchover Help Scheme: What was the Help Scheme?* Switchover Help Scheme, The United Kingdom. Retrieved from www.helpscheme.co.uk/helpscheme

Inclusive Design Toolkit. (2011). *1. Why do inclusive design: Overview. Inclusive design toolkit.* 2nd ed. Retrieved from www-edc.eng.cam.ac.uk/betterdesign/why/

Ivarsson, J. (2004). *A short technical history of subtitles in Europe.* Retrieved from www.helpscheme.co.uk/en/reports

Jakobsen, H.G., & Studsgaard, M. (2011, May). *Fjernsyn for blinde: En analyse af danske blinde og stærkt svagsynedes kendskab til eksistensen af, adgang til og nytte af synstolkning (Television for the blind: an analysis of awareness, take-up and use of—audio description among Danes who are blind or have serious visual impairments—Danish with a summary in English).* Master's thesis, IT University of Copenhagen, Denmark.

Leblois, Axel (2013). Oral contribution on Day 2. In unedited transcripts of 25 October 2013. ITU Workshop on Making Media Accessible to all: the options and the economics. 24–25 October 2013. Geneva, Switzerland, www.itu.int/en/ITU-T/Workshops-and-Seminars/mmaa/201310/Pages/default.aspx

Li, D., & Looms, P.O. (2013). Design models for media accessibility (媒体可及性的设计模型), *Journal of Designing in China, 1.*

Looms, P.O. (2013). TV in the 21st century—one screen or two? *RTHK Media Digest.* Hong Kong SAR, China. Retrieved from http://rthk.hk/mediadigest/20130205_76_122955.html

Looms, P.O. (2006). Public service media: All things to all people—on all platforms, anytime? In C.S. Nissen (Ed.), *Making a difference—public service broadcasting and the media landscape in Europe.* Published for the European Broadcasting Union. UK: John Libbey Publishing. New Barnet, Herts, United Kingdom.

Machet, Emmanuelle (2013) Editor. EPRA/2013/05 Working Group 3 Round Table on Access to Audiovisual Media Services for persons with disabilities Comparative background document, EPRA Secretariat. Strasbourg, France Revised public version—8 July 2013 Retrieved at www.epra.org/news_items/access-services-what-role-for-the-regulator

Ofcom. (2013, May 17). *The quality of live subtitling—improving the viewer experience*. Consultation document. Ofcom, UK. Available on OFCOM's website.

United Nations. (2006). *Convention on the Rights of Persons with Disabilities*. Retrieved from www.un.org/disabilities/convention/conventionfull.shtml

United Nations Statistical Commission. (n.d.). *Washington Group on disability statistics*. Retrieved from http://unstats.un.org/unsd/methods/citygroup/washington.htm

Vlaming, M. (2013). *Wireless access for hearing aids*. AVA-I-227. ITU-T Focus Group on Audiovisual Media Accessibility, Geneva, Switzerland.

4 Next-Generation Television and the Migration from Channels to Platforms

Rob Frieden

The ways to distribute video content to consumers have begun to diversify as the Internet becomes an increasingly significant and popular option for accessing new video content as well as material previously available only via broadcast, satellite and cable networks. A growing inventory of choices has become available thanks to technological innovations, such as the conversion from analog to digital media, faster transmission of content and a substantial reduction in the cost to store data files. A variety of new businesses seek to exploit the Internet's ability to serve as a single medium for a variety of previously stand-alone services delivered via different channels.

Viewers no longer need to tolerate "appointment television" access to content at a time prescribed by content creators or distributors and available only on a single broadcast, satellite or cable channel. Access is becoming a matter of using one of several software-configured interface options capable of delivering live and recorded content anytime, anywhere, to any device[1] and via many different transmission and presentation formats.

Video access will evolve from a linear, channel-based and medium-specific process to a platform[2] capable of providing consumers access to all kinds of content stored somewhere within the Internet cloud. The technological and business models for delivering video content have begun to assume that most consumers can and will use legal, questionable and even illegal ways to access content. This means that content creators and packagers can no longer rely on a single model of program delivery that locks viewers to channels-based[3] distribution technologies and various "windows" of access options[4] based on the elapsed time from initial release.[5] Instead consumers increasingly expect to have access at their convenience and on more flexible terms and conditions.

Internet protocol television (IPTV) and Over-the-Top television (OTT) refer to the ability of content creators and new or existing content distributors to provide consumers with access to video content via broadband links, in lieu of, or in addition to, traditional media. Currently content creators and distributors experiment with new Internet-mediated options (Hulu, 2012; Federal Communications Commission [FCC], 2012b, 2013), having perhaps reluctantly acknowledged that the status quo cannot persist in light of proliferating consumer self-help opportunities, many of which violate copyright laws and make it rather easy for consumers to access premium content for free, even soon after initial release.

The Internet offers many legitimate, questionable and absolutely illegal opportunities to access both amateur and professional video content via the broadband transmission of video files. Consumers can download video files in their entirety for subsequent replay or "stream" the same content via real-time delivery and conversion of bits into video and sound. IPTV also makes it possible to deliver live programming, including pay television sporting events. Consumers with access to high-speed broadband networks can launch applications and visit World Wide Web sites providing convenient techniques for acquiring movies and other premium content.

This chapter will examine the ongoing migration from channels to software-configured platforms for accessing video content. It will assess strategies of both market entrants and incumbents to use technological innovations for acquiring or maintaining market share. The chapter also will consider whether incumbents may overcome competitive threats by devising new ways to lock down content and prevent consumers from fully exploiting new options, even for lawful content sharing and recording.

Broadband Television

IPTV relies on broadband transmission networks to deliver video bitstreams to end users. This means that an existing broadband service subscription can provide users with access to increasingly diverse video content in addition to— in other words, "on top of"—existing services such as e-mail and the World Wide Web (Trope, 2005). Consumers must subscribe to fast, high-capacity broadband services because video service requires networks that can transmit content on an instantaneous "real-time" basis for immediate consumption or later playback. Even low-quality video files, which are highly compressed and have comparatively lower resolution, require broadband networks that can deliver traffic at rates exceeding 1 megabit per second (Netflix, 2012).

IPTV can enhance the value proposition offered by internet service providers (ISPs). Subscribers can increase their video content options thanks to the synergistic and serendipitous opportunities available from broadband networking. Internet protocols support the loading, switching and routing of different kinds of traffic via the networks that interconnect to provide a complete end-to-end link to the Internet cloud. This means that Internet routers can handle video traffic in much the same way as they manage other less bandwidth-intensive applications. So as long as the networks providing bitstream transmission can handle higher capacity streams and files, they can provide a medium for the delivery of video. IPTV refers to the ability of the Internet, and specifically its Internet Protocol addressing scheme and its Transmission Control Protocol traffic management formats,[6] to provide broadband users with user-friendly access to video content.

Many broadband subscribers of both wired and wireless services have discovered the benefit of using their subscription to access video. In doing so, these subscribers may increase substantially the total volume of content they download. Broadband carriers, particularly wireless operators, have become concerned that such downloading will trigger network congestion and exhaust existing capacity, requiring ever growing investment in transmission bandwidth. By offering subscribers unmetered, "all you can eat" (AYCE) service, broadband carriers have encouraged experimentation and access without regard to the operational and cost burdens imposed. Now many broadband carriers have abandoned AYCE pricing and offer metered service at different monthly rates based on the amount of permissible content downloading and bit transmission speed. In lieu of tiered service, many ISPs invoke the need to manage scarce transmission capacity as justification for deliberately slowing down ("throttling") the delivery of traffic to subscribers exceeding a quota of permissible downloading volume.

Prior to the elimination of AYCE service, ISPs branded the highest volume subscribers "bandwidth hogs" apparently in light of their ability to get more value and service than the ISPs intended or expected a subscriber to accrue. ISPs consider these heavy users as causing a problem instead of creating an opportunity. Heavy demand for data service contributes to the short-term potential for congestion and the need to increase transmission capacity. However, in the longer term subscribers' expanded demand for broadband provides ISPs with the enviable opportunity to serve a growing market rather than one that has become static or declining.

IPTV distribution includes three primary ways to deliver content: 1) simulcasting, the immediate, "real-time" streaming of programs also available at the same time via other traditional media, such as satellite, cable and broadcast television; 2) streaming, the incremental delivery of files containing video content so that the content gets displayed, but not stored, by consumers; and 3) downloading, the delivery of data filed that can be stored and viewed one or more times at the discretion of the consumer. Different commercial models have evolved to simulcast live content, stream content and offer file downloading. Incumbents recognize the need to offer more convenient access, but they do not want to make it possible for nonsubscribers to access the content or for subscribers to record and redistribute it. Bear in mind that fast broadband networks can distribute digital content quickly and repeatedly.

Evolving Trends in Video Distribution

Consumers now have added flexibility and choice made possible by the proliferation of broadband networks and three new content-display devices. In addition to the conventional television set, which delivers one of many channels in sequence, computer monitors, wireless smartphones and tablets offer a second-, third- and fourth-screen option. These video display media can include Internet-based content along with additional or duplicative content packaged by the carriers providing broadband access. Consumers appear willing to tolerate significant difference in the visual and audio quality of service between different-sized screens and also seem "technology agnostic" regarding which medium delivers the content.

Consumers have become less tolerant of attempts by content distributors, in particular, to restrict consumer access via multiple screens. They also have few qualms about accessing content that may violate copyright laws. A significant percentage of early adopters of new video access platforms may pursue illegal self-help options should content creators and distributors opt to impose a prohibition or restrictions on access to highly desirable, "must-see" television.

In conjunction with expanded display options, three models for video access have evolved:

1) Illegal, copyright-infringing access to content via efficient peer-to-peer file transfer, or other direct links, as well as real-time streaming of video content files and simulcasting of live television
2) New, lawful access to live television or video files via new intermediaries such as Amazon, Apple, Hulu, Joost, Netflix, Roku and YouTube
3) Efforts by incumbent broadcasters, broadcast networks, direct broadcast satellite (DBS) operators and cable television systems to offer new "television everywhere" options to paying subscribers, providing them additional access options via multiple screens with on-demand basis for content already distributed on an appointment-television basis

In the transition to platform-delivered access, incumbents and market entrants will compete for audiences. Market entrants will provide new, more flexible options that in turn will force incumbents to provide greater value and access options lest they lose market share. Heretofore content creators have explored new distribution options without abandoning traditional channels. Currently successful content creators appreciate that the status quo has generated substantial returns, largely because the models lock in and guarantee predictable, recurring payments from consumers (FCC, 2012a). For example the cable and satellite television model requires monthly subscription payments from subscribers who receive many channels, not all of which any single subscriber would want to pay for the opportunity to watch. By aggregating channels and prohibiting subscribers from choosing which individual channels they want on an individual, "a la carte" channel-by-channel basis, video content distributors can accrue higher revenues for more costly service tiers that package both desirable and unwanted channels. Sources of content appreciate that the aggregate revenues from an entire population of video subscribers will exceed the higher payments from a smaller subset of that population who select and pay for a specific channel of content. For example, ESPN accrues more revenue from a smaller per-subscriber payment applicable to every cable and satellite subscriber than from a higher per-subscriber payment applicable only to a la carte subscribers who specify the desire to receive ESPN.

Incumbent content creators and distributors appreciate that new distribution platforms can offer additional revenue-generating opportunities. However, the potential exists for these options not to accrue added revenues in light of the need to enhance the value proposition of monthly content subscriptions by offering greater flexibility for accessing and replaying content. In the worst-case scenario, a significant number of viewers can find ways to access content—even premium, pay-per-view offerings—at little or no cost because an unauthorized party has pirated the content. With lower cost or free access to desirable content, consumers may become more inclined to "cut the cord" and abandon subscriptions with existing intermediaries.

Incumbent distributors such as DBS and cable television operators risk "disintermediation"—in other words, elimination as middlemen in a chain of distribution if IPTV and other access options offer a better value proposition for access to desired content. Even if new distribution options impose pay-per-view charges, or monthly subscription rates, consumers might have available new, a la carte options that provide access to desired content with a much lower total out-of-pocket cost. The loss of access to even many channels may not matter if consumers had little interest in much of the content included in a tiered package of channels. Accordingly incumbent video distribution operators may have to respond to new access options with efforts to enhance the value proposition of their monthly and sizeable subscription charges based on an unmetered AYCE model.

Content creators may financially benefit from new distribution options and windows of availability, particularly if they achieve greater control over access and do not have to share as much revenue with distribution partners. However, the greater risk of piracy and strained relationships with long-standing distribution partners, such as DBS and cable television, also motivate content creators to experiment cautiously (Aldrich, 2007).

Illegal, Copyright-Infringing Models

The earliest video content access opportunities resulted from an adaptation of existing peer-to-peer file-sharing techniques such as BitTorrent that started as music-sharing sites. Because file-sharing software and the Internet generally make no distinction between file types, users found it easy to add video files. Similarly Internet protocols support the delivery of live video feeds and stored files. A variety of websites currently offer access to live television, including premium channels, as well as access to files of movies and television programs.

Absent a license to redistribute video content, along with the expected agreement to compensate the copyright holder, these sites violate the intellectual property of content creators and distributors. Ample case law supports the conclusion that web-based providers of access to content will incur liability for copyright infringement even though they did nothing more than provide the software that can configure direct Internet-routing links between one or more sources of the content and the recipient (MGM Studios, Inc. v. Grokster, Ltd.). Intermediaries that knowingly facilitate or induce copyright infringement bear the legal responsibility for damages caused by others. This means that web-based sites that help promote infringement will incur legal responsibility for the financial damages resulting from the distribution of file-sharing software or from offering a web-based platform for access to sources of copyright-infringing content.

Much of the IPTV content access opportunities currently available via the Internet violate the intellectual property rights of creators and their licensed distributors. Many content creators have refused to license access via Internet options because they consider the risk of lost revenues from piracy too great and too likely to exceed the potential for supplemental income.

New Legal IPTV Intermediaries

A growing number of incumbents have reconsidered their conclusion that they should try to thwart IPTV by refusing to offer content access alternatives. New and legal IPTV options, such as YouTube, have gained traction and visibility, thereby demonstrating that even amateur video can generate substantial audiences. Cautiously and incrementally content sources have explored directly distributing their content, via their own branded sites, or via new intermediaries such as Amazon, Apple, Hulu, Joost, Netflix, Roku and YouTube. Most broadcast networks and many cable/satellite networks now consider the web as offering an opportunity to reach more viewers, thereby generating higher market penetration and advertising revenues. These content sources typically provide access after initial distribution via traditional media outlets so that consumers do not abandon, or regularly substitute, traditional distribution intermediaries.

Incumbent content ventures can provide an interface between video content consumers and sources. By serving as an intermediary, cable and satellite television providers can enforce digital rights management[7] limitations on access, recording and redistribution as well as collect payments for premium content or superior access options. However, content creators can only go so far in their exploration because of existing and highly lucrative distribution contracts with incumbent media. While it might appear enticing to eliminate "middlemen" intermediaries, the proliferation of new ones evidences the resiliency and continuing viability of this model. Content sources will have to calibrate closely the blend of access options they offer directly, via incumbent outlets and via new intermediaries.

New Options via Incumbent Intermediaries

Broadcast, cable and satellite operators belatedly have recognized that IPTV will not go away. New distribution technologies generate threats to existing business models and greater risk to incumbents, but they also have the potential to help incumbents solidify their role as intermediaries by both content sources and end users. In light of vastly greater web-based content options, incumbent intermediaries now recognize that they must enhance the value and accessibility of the premium, "must-see" content they distribute. This translates into adopting new distribution options that provide subscribers with greater flexibility in terms of where, when, how and how often they can access content.

Content intermediaries have accepted the basic premise that they can no longer limit subscribers to one-time viewing of content, augmented by recording and playback of that one-time opportunity. This means that incumbents have to provide subscribers with new opportunities to access content via different devices, in both fixed and mobile locations. Television everywhere refers to the relaxation of access limitations by incumbent intermediaries so that duly authenticated subscribers, who prove their identity and status, can pass through firewall barriers to access files containing premium content, including episodes of programs already delivered at assigned times to conventional television sets. In other words, some incumbents have abandoned attempts to limit subscribers to appointment television or to the recording of content by devices controlled by and often leased from incumbents—for example, cable television set-top boxes and satellite receivers.

Subscribers to incumbent video program distribution services now can direct the carrier to save content for subsequent replay, a type of virtual video recording that replaces the need to have an on-premised digital video recorder (Cartoon Network et al. v. CSC Holdings). Additionally subscribers can access content for repeat viewing using different receiving and display devices that include multiple and geographically separated television sets, computers, smartphones and tablets.

Diverging Incentives and Increased Risks

Before the onset of new and experimental content distribution models, content creators and distributors had established a mutually beneficial model based on several sequential windows of access based on time since initial release and the willingness of consumers to pay for access. Movies followed a predictable track with initial access solely in theaters, followed by pay-per-view and other premium channel access, followed by release of a digital video disc (DVD), after which the content becomes less a lure for direct payments from consumers and more an advertiser-supported attraction typically first available on premium cable/DBS networks and subsequently on nonpremium, basic-tier networks, followed even later in time by broadcast television.

Cable programming has been tiered into categories of content access with premium content, such as movies and high-budget original programming, located on higher cost tiers, offered as a stand-alone premium channel, or even pay-per-view access (FCC, 2011). New distribution models provide consumers with access to some premium content earlier in time, on an a la carte, pay-per-view basis. Additionally some content creators have opted to provide access to even premium content, either via new access platforms operated by incumbent distributors or upon proof that the consumer already has paid for a subscription—for example, to a cable television operator.

Video program creators see new distribution platforms as possibly offering new revenue-growth opportunities and greater market penetration. However, content creators must operate with caution so that they do not lose control over access to their product and also do not harm the revenue stream flowing to traditional distribution partners. If a content creator decides to serve consumers directly via new distribution platforms, incumbent distributors might attempt to retaliate by favoring other content sources.

Content distributors want to maintain the highly profitable status quo, but the traditional locked-down, largely one-way distribution model based on their status as unavoidable intermediaries appears unsustainable in light of new options available to consumers. Incumbents have reluctantly concluded that they must provide greater access flexibility to subscribers, including the opportunity to watch the same content multiple times without additional payment. Incumbent video distributors so far do not seem to think it imperative to offer vastly more content, in addition to greater flexibility in accessing existing content. With the exception of a new cable television network managed by talk show host Oprah Winfrey, the industry has not introduced many new networks in the last few years. Likewise all of the top 20 networks, in terms of number of subscribers served, entered the market years ago (FCC, 2000; 2013).

As new access options provide both flexibility and more content, incumbents might recognize the need to increase options, despite having previously assumed that they need only serve as the gateway to currently designated must-see television. Consumers in growing numbers question a subscription model that regularly increases monthly rates well above general measures of inflation. Cable and DBS operators may have grown complacent that an AYCE model can remain dominant because consumers heretofore lacked options that offered the combination of must-see and niche content. Now the Internet operates as a medium for access to much of the same must-see television along with often free access to niche content.

EFFECT ON CONSUMERS

Consumers stand to benefit from proliferating video content access opportunities, with two caveats. First, the options cannot subvert existing and new payment models by offering free access to pirated content. Second, incumbents should not be able to collude with an eye toward preventing consumers from enjoying lawful alternative access opportunities. We can expect incumbent cable and satellite carriers to pressure content creators not to pursue options that eliminate them as intermediaries, whether through direct access or via replacement intermediaries. Likewise the possibility exists that incumbent intermediaries and content sources may seek to use new digital rights management techniques to reduce the opportunities subscribers have to copy and share content even in lawful ways (Frieden, 2008).

The copyright laws of many nations provide opportunities for copying and sharing content on a limited basis without liability for infringement. The concept of fair use refers to the ability of consumers, under specific and limited circumstances, to reproduce and share copyrighted content without securing consent of the copyright holder (von Lohmann, 2008; Tokson, 2009; Pote, 2010). The concept of fair use emphasizes that social benefits accrue from limited copying without significant financial harm to the content creator (Religious Technology Center v. Netcom; Sony Corp. of America v. Universal City Studios; Perfect 10, Inc. v. Amazon.com, Inc.).

Some of the technological innovations that make it possible to track consumer wants, needs and desires also provide ways to identify and block fair use opportunities. One such technology called deep packet inspection (DPI) provides a way to identify the content a specific subscriber is accessing. The power to track usage by subscribers can combine with the ability to block such access immediately. Fair use typically involves copying first and having to defend the copying later in court. With DPI content creators and distributors can block first and never have to pursue a judicial remedy (Armstrong, 2006). This means that even instances of fair use cannot occur because a carrier or content creator has opted to use techniques that block suspicious activity, regardless of whether it turns out to be an instance of fair use instead of piracy. End users will suffer from new content access options if incumbents can freely condition access based on their interpretation of what constitutes fair use. A limited view of this user right, backed up by technologies that can block access immediately, can further lock down content, rather than provide more diverse and lawful ways to enjoy it.

Effect on Advertisers

Next-generation television has a substantial and mostly positive impact on advertisers. The technologies that enable consumers to identify content based on specific interests also can provide advertisers the opportunity to understand more clearly consumers' interests and in turn to calibrate advertising based on such interests. Advertisers can target consumers for better calibrated commercial pitches using the same technology that enables consumers to specify their content interests.

Consider the parallel between the developing use of location-based advertising for wireless services and customized advertising based on consumers' content interests. In the former subscribers allow advertisers to calibrate messages based on location and analysis of what searches the subscriber undertook as well as what website he or she has viewed recently. For example someone searching for brewpub restaurants can trigger advertising for such restaurants located close by. For video content searches, simple analysis of web searches and content selections can help advertisers identify what products and services may be of interest to specific subscribers. For example, subscribers making frequent searches for content about bowling constitute ideal candidates to receive advertising for bowling alleys and purveyors of bowling accessories.

Advertiser-supported access to video content constitutes one of the major business models that span generations of technological innovations. Better targeting of messages can contribute to more effective advertising and the willingness of advertisers to pay more per targeted pitch. It appears that advertiser-supported access to content will continue to operate as augmented by more opportunities for a la carte access to, and payment for, content.

CONCLUSION

Demand for broadband Internet access will grow as consumers increasingly consider IPTV both a complement and an alternative to legacy video delivery technologies using satellite, cable and terrestrial wireless media. The allure of more flexible access to "must-see" television coupled with a vastly proliferating array of new, niche content enhances the value proposition of a broadband subscription. Additionally, flexible and more plentiful access to video content can further stimulate demand for broadband service by residents having inferior access or none at all. Carriers may face more strident demands and complaints if they cannot accommodate the growing demand for accessible, affordable and fast broadband service.

The perceived deprivation in not having broadband access perhaps will compound one's sense of deprivation and expectation that government should more aggressively abate the "digital divide." Even though video access may involve mostly entertainment content, a lower priority than the goal of providing access to "lifeline" services such as voice telephony, consumers denied proliferating video options may sense an equally stinging sense of loss. As residents of nations with commercially viable or subsidized broadband enjoy ever more content options, residents lacking broadband may sense they have fallen farther behind.

An expanding video divide will occur so long as broadband access opportunities are unequal, but also so long as content creators consider IPTV options worth pursuing. New video access opportunities cannot subvert existing or future business models that deliver sizeable financial rewards for creativity and popularity in content creation and for the ventures that deliver such content to consumers. The freedom to access content at anytime, anywhere, for multiple viewings, via an expanded array of devices using different delivery formats, surely promotes consumer welfare, flexibility and choice. However, these options should not expand the opportunities for piracy because commercial participants in the creation and distribution of content will not use new media without anticipating the opportunity for increased total revenues.

Even before the onset of Internet-mediated access to video content, individuals had some "free rider" opportunities to consume advertiser-supported content without buying the advertised products and services. The possibility exists that IPTV will offer even more free-rider opportunities, at least initially when content providers and distributors have not yet perfected a payment scheme and consider it advantageous to promote new Internet access opportunities by offering attractive content for free and with less advertising. When payment schemes apply and new intermediaries establish sustainable business models based on payments from both subscribers and advertisers, consumers should understand that using techniques to avoid payment by evading digital rights management safeguards will have an adverse impact on the incentive for ventures to continue offering IPTV options.

The duty to pay for content offered for compensation does not mean that content creators and distributors can avoid having to find ways to enhance the value proposition of what they offer. IPTV promotes greater competition for consumer payment and attention. Incumbent content creators have no right to expect that everything they offer qualifies as must-see video, nor do existing intermediaries have a right to expect that consumers cannot access content except through their distribution channel.

Distribution intermediaries in particular have to make their subscriptions worth the sizeable fees charged, particularly if new access opportunities offer cheaper access for the same content or a lower total out-of-pocket cost for the most desired content. Only recently has an economic downturn coupled with new IPTV options resulted in a small decline in viewership using traditional media, particularly by young viewers (FCC, 2012a). The urge to "cut the cord," or reduce one's cable or satellite bill, will become more compelling as new access opportunities develop and proliferate, even if they too require payment. A user-friendly interface, reasonable prices and conscientious customer service—all lacking to some extent among incumbents—can stimulate subscriber migration.

From a current vantage point, video consumers enjoy new opportunities to access long-successful content options, for example, sporting events, movies and blockbuster, mass-market programming, as well as new options. It would be premature to predict the demise of intermediaries and the rise of direct dealing between content source and consumers. However, electronic commerce conducted via the Internet demonstrates that while the viability of intermediaries remains strong, who operates as one and how they add value and justify their fees will be subject to change. The potential for significant change in the video marketplace appears quite real.

NOTES

1. "Consumers can access online video via multiple Internet-enabled devices, including computers, smartphones, tablets, gaming consoles, television sets, and other equipment" (FCC, 2013, ¶220).
2. "To respond to viewers' desire to view video programming in more places at more times, broadcast station owners [and other content distributors] have developed online and mobile media platforms, using their websites as extensions of their local brands" (FCC, 2012a, ¶203).
3. Currently broadcast, cable and satellite television operators transmit signals on specific frequencies using either wireless or closed-circuit channels. Content providers operating on one of the first channels in a linear sequence can benefit from frequent viewership by subscribers who "surf" channels in order. Additionally most content distributors organize content by category, thereby creating "neighborhoods" of channels with similar content (see FCC, 2011; FCC, 2012c).
4. "In recent years, some content owners have altered their business strategies with respect to the type of video content created, the timing of release of specific video content through the various delivery windows ('windowing'), and the prices charged for content in each window" (FCC, 2012b, ¶76, p. 8604). "In addition to distributing movies in theaters, producers sell rights to distribute them on DVDs, on demand, pay television services (e.g., HBO and Showtime), broadcast networks, and cable television networks. Likewise, television production companies have traditionally adhered to prescribed time gaps between the initial broadcast and cable distribution of a program series, DVDs, and syndication" (FCC, 2012b, n. 111).
5. Before the disruption caused by Internet-mediated access, content creators and distributors sought to create different sequential "windows" of access. Consumers seeking early access typically had to pay more than others willingly to accept a delay. For example, access to a movie followed a time-based sequence of windows starting at a theater, followed by video on demand via cable and satellite television, followed by rental access and placement on a premium television network such as HBO, followed by access on nonpremium channels and broadcast networks. The Internet makes it possible for impatient consumers to access premium content often early in the windowing sequence at little or no cost.
6. "The Internet is a vast network of individual computers and computer networks that communicate with each other using the same communications language, Transmission Control Protocol/Internet Protocol (TCP/IP). The Internet consists of approximately more than 100 million computers around the world using TCP/IP protocols. Along with the development of TCP/IP, the open network architecture of the Internet has the following characteristics or parameters: 1. Each distinct network stands on its own with its own specific environment and user requirements, notwithstanding the use of TCP/IP to connect to other parts of the Internet. Communications are not directed in a unilateral fashion. Rather, communications are routed throughout the Internet on a best efforts basis in which some packets of information may go through one series of computer networks and other packets of information go through a different permutation or combination of computer networks, with all of these information packets eventually arriving at their intended destination. 2. Black boxes, for lack of a better term, connect the various networks; these boxes are called 'gateways' and 'routers.' The gateways and routers do not retain information but merely provide access and flow for the

packets being transmitted. There is no global control of the Internet" (Trope, 2005, p. 4).
7. Digital rights management refers to the use of technological tools by copyright owners and distributors to regulate the uses of their works and, in particular, to restrict or prohibit copying.

REFERENCES

Aldrich, N. (2007). An exploration of rights management technologies used in the music industry. *Boston College Intellectual Property & Technology Forum.*
Armstrong, T. (2006). Digital rights management and the process of fair use. *Harvard Journal of Law & Technology, 20*, 49–121.
Cartoon Network v. CSC Holdings, 536 F.3d 121 (2d Cir. 2008).
Federal Communications Commission (FCC). (2000). *Annual assessment of the status of competition in markets for the delivery of video programming.* CS Docket No. 99–230, Sixth Report, 14 F.C.C.R. 978.
Federal Communications Commission (FCC). (2011). *Tennis Channel, Inc., Complainant v. Comcast Communications, Inc., LLC, Defendant.* Initial Decision of Chief Administrative Law Judge Richard L. Sippel, FCC 11D-01.
Federal Communications Commission (FCC) (2012a). *Annual assessment of the status of competition in markets for the delivery of video programming.* Fourteenth Report, FCC 12–81.
Federal Communications Commission (FCC) (2012b). *Annual assessment of the status of competition in markets for the delivery of video programming.* Notice of Inquiry, FCC 12–80.
Federal Communications Commission (FCC) (2012c). *Bloomberg L.P., Complainant v. Comcast Cable Communications, LLC, Defendant.* MB Docket No. 11–104, Memorandum Opinion and Order, DA 12–694.
Federal Communications Commission (FCC) (2013). *Annual assessment of the status of competition in markets for the delivery of video programming.* Fifteenth Report, FCC 13–13–99.
Frieden, R. (2008). Internet packet sniffing and its impact on the network neutrality debate and the balance of power between intellectual property creators and consumers. *Fordham Intellectual Property, Media & Entertainment Law Journal, 18*(3), 633–675.
Hulu. (2012). *Overview.* Retrieved from www.hulu.com/about/product_tour
MGM Studios, Inc. v. Grokster, Ltd., 545 U.S. 913 (2005).
Netflix. (2012). *How fast does my broadband Internet connection need to be to watch instantly?* Retrieved from https://signup.netflix.com/HowItWorks
Perfect 10, Inc. v. Amazon.com, Inc., 508 F.3d 1146 (9th Cir. 2007).
Pote, M. (2010). Mashed-up in between: The delicate balance of artists' interests lost amidst the war on copyright. *North Carolina Law Review, 88*, 639–693.
Religious Technology Center v. Netcom, 907 F. Supp. 1361 (N.D. Cal. 1995).
Sony Corp. of America v. Universal City Studios, 464 U.S. 417 (1984).
Tokson, M. (2009). The content/envelope distinction in Internet law. *William and Mary Law Review, 50*, 2105–2176.
Trope, K. (2005). Voice over Internet protocol: The revolution in America's telecommunications infrastructure. *Computer & Internet Lawyer, 22*(12), 1–15.
von Lohmann, F. (2008). Fair use as innovation policy. *Berkeley Technology Law Journal, 23*, 829–865.

5 New Media Policy
The Redistribution of Voice[1]

Amit Schejter and Noam Tirosh

Since its appearance in public life, the Internet has often been touted as more than a mere platform—instead, as an actual "game changer"—and its many applications are often referred to as "new media." Different constituencies, however, perceive its "newness" differently and see its "game-changing" capabilities in different contexts. Some see its data-mining potential as a marketing boon; others see it as a threat to traditional civil liberties. Some see its abundance of content as an opportunity to capitalize on the many different tastes consumers have, yet others see this richness of outlets as the demise of citizenry and solidarity. The goal of media policy, since its inception, has been to serve the public interest, and its challenge has been to balance between the principle of freedom of expression and the belief in the role of government as charged with identifying the public's needs and guiding the media to serve them. Media policy has also often been a balancing act between the need to promote government interests, the public interest and the demands of the commercial market. These oftentimes-conflicted missions have led to tensions between the commercial, civil, political and public actors in their desire to make policy and its outcomes serve their needs.

This chapter tries to expand theoretical approaches to the advent of "new media" by examining the components of what by now have become too often used, and too rarely thought about, terms—"new media" and "democracy"—in order to promote a comprehensive theoretical underpinning to the establishment of a public interest–serving public policy overseeing the development of future media technologies. We first try to understand what "newness" of the "new media" is relevant in order to change the way we think about media policy. Next, we seek to examine what elements of democracy currently missing from the regulation of existing media could be promoted with the introduction and proliferation of "new media," and as a result we propose what goals "new media policy" should aspire to reach. In this context we try to bridge the idea of democracy with the idea of social justice and to propose a theoretical framework that sees the need to overhaul the conditions for democratic participation utilizing corrective measures of distributive justice.

What's New about New Media?

There is probably no term more overused in the history of media research than "new media." So overused that recently the need rose to define "new new media" (Levinson, 2012)! Indeed, all media are new when they appear on the horizon and "old" by the time another newer medium appears. The description of a medium as new denotes that something in this medium is different and sets it apart from existing media. What characteristics make a medium new, and how are we to know which media we are currently discussing when describing "new media"? The technological determinist tradition identified different media characteristics as descriptors of their newness. The by-now classic classification first developed by Innis (1951) differentiated among media and described their development based on their bias toward space or toward time. McLuhan (1964/1994) added the distinction between media that he perceived as "hot" and media that were "cold." Meyrowitz (2010) distinguishes among the oral, scribal, print and electronic features of media and the eventual impact they have had on forms of interpersonal interaction and social organization.

The revolutionary media of the nineteenth century were the industrialized forms of the newspaper; the twentieth century saw the dominance of the telephone, radio and television. Four processes of contemporary "new media" characterize the early years of the current century: (1) the advent of digitization, (2) the popularization and commercialization of the Internet, (3) the introduction of the mobile-turned-smart-phone and (4) the convergence of the previous generation's media technologies, obscuring accepted and traditional differentiations between print and audiovisual media, between interpersonal and mass media and between what can be perceived as "infrastructure" and what is determined "content."

Every communication between and among humans can be broken down into the basic building blocks of "information theory" (Longstaff, 2002). Also known as the "mathematical theory of communication" (Shannon & Weaver, 1949), sender, receiver, coding, message and noise are present in any communication process. The study of communications, however, has transitioned from viewing a singular communication process to observing mass communications in which "production, reproduction, and multiple distribution of messages through technological devices" (Turow, 1990, p. 16) are involved and in which feedback and storage (Longstaff, 2002) are required elements in the process. A useful differentiation between media over time (the only way "newness" has a meaning) needs as a result to take into account changes in all of these elements: identities of senders and receivers, coding methods, typologies of messages, identification of different types of noise, production and distribution processes, speed and quality of feedback and storage capabilities.

When print media were the major means of mass communication, the process was characterized by very slow production and by high fixed costs.

These contributed to this "very old" media industry's disposition to gyrate toward high levels of concentration. Indeed, it could be very inexpensive to create content that is only print; however, the production process is slow, as is the distribution, and both are costly. To those who control the production presses and distribution channels, these characteristics provide much power. Except for times of extreme shortages caused by natural or political disaster, there are unlimited potential distribution channels, yet the high cost that maintaining them entails leads to the ease of controlling them. "Very old" media also operate with very little need for direct feedback to the content they produce and distribute. The only feedback its commercial form takes into account are sales. As a result, beyond avoiding censorship or other limitations on free speech, government policy to support such media can only come in the form of subsidies, which can be in a direct or indirect form and which were common practice in the United States in the early days of the republic (McChesney & Nichols, 2010) and still are across a number of European and Nordic countries (Murschetz, 1998; Picard, 2007).

Electronic media—radio and later television—were "new" in relation to print media upon their appearance in the first half of the twentieth century, and scholars named media such as cable television and video cassette recorders (VCRs) as "new media" in their scholarly work only two decades ago (Brown et al., 1990). However, by now all these audiovisual media are "old." In order to compare among the different generations, we will therefore name the print media "very old" and the current media "contemporary," rather than "new." Production in the "old media" world, just like in the "very old," was both slow and costly. As a result, the old media also tend to become more concentrated and held in the hands of a few that attempt to both expand their control and lower their costs through efficiencies. However, this first generation of electronic media were distributed to their audiences instantly, and in that they greatly differed from their predecessors due to the fact that the distribution was done electronically and that there are ways to collect almost immediate feedback at some level as it too can be sent electronically to the distributor.[2] The old electronic media developed very differently in Europe, in the United States and in the developing world. One characteristic common to the development of all the models is the fact that they were perceived to have a "powerful effect," probably far more than print. As a result, in the European tradition electronic media were concentrated in the hands of government-appointed "public" organizations whose goal was to "entertain, inform and educate" (Holtz-Bacha & Norris, 2001); in the developing world they simply remained in the hands of government (Schejter, 2003); and in the United States, at least until the 1980s, they were closely regulated for content (Pickard, 2011).

The transition of the Internet from an interacademic network to a commercial communication enterprise brought about the latest wave of references to the existence of "new media," which we call "contemporary." The characteristics of these media separate them from their predecessors along almost each of the elements previously identified. The Internet is a "global web of horizontal communication networks that include the multimodal exchange of interactive messages from many to many both synchronous and asynchronous" (Castells, 2007, p. 246). As such it can be described simultaneously as "mass communication," "multimodal" and "self generated in content, self directed in emission and self selected in reception" (p. 248) or "mass self communication" (p. 248). While some content may be slow to produce and labor-intensive, much if not the vast majority of content over the Internet is cheap and quick to both produce and reproduce. Both the fixed costs of content production and the marginal costs of reproduction are virtually nonexistent. Distribution over the Internet is instant, and the packet-based format of Internet traffic makes the traditional "channel" structure developed in the old electronic media world obsolete and the amount of content that can travel over the network virtually infinite. As for the feedback, it is immediate and personal and in fact can go directly and unmediated to the producer/distributor of content (whether a person or a corporation) from its consumer/receiver. Since its early days, the Internet was described as "interactive." While this characterization may have been questionable at the outset, the advent of more recent developments of the Internet renders it virtually interactive.

Interactivity in itself is not one-dimensional, nor is it static. While observing the development of online collaborative networks, Dutton (2008) identified the transition of interactivity from the mere "sharing" of content to "collaboration" in the creation of new content and further on to the actual "co-creation" of content. Communication networks in themselves have different characteristics that support this development. Each and every one of them—hypertextuality, user-generated content and online collaboration—can and probably may have been seen by observers as a characteristic creating yet another "new" medium. "Contemporary" media therefore are those in the "pre-collaboration" stage in which media allow for the "collaborative production of information products" (Cobo, 2012, p. 291).

However, as exciting and different as the "contemporary new media" seem to be, they too are controllable in at least three ways: First, while the Internet was designed to survive a military strike by not having a "center," it still requires a physical infrastructure, and the "pipes" through which it "travels" are notoriously limited and controlled by well-entrenched telecommunications semi-former or long-standing monopolies in some parts of the world or by governments in other. Second, due to its technological characteristics, the differentiation between the content carried over the network and the network's "infrastructure" is not as clear-cut as in the traditional audiovisual technologies. The Internet is a multilayered space. Beyond the physical copper, fiber or electromagnetic airwaves, the Internet protocols, operating systems, web browsers and "social media" applications can all be perceived as either content or "physical" infrastructure. Their regulation, thus, can be perceived as addressing or infringing upon both property and expression rights and thus raises concerns from a multitude of perspectives and allows stakeholders to muddle (or clear up) the technological differences and to manipulate the policy discourse in order to maintain existing power structures. Third, while the Internet gives the impression that it is a vast and uncontrollable multiarmed giant, recent revelations about the United States government obtaining direct access to the systems of the world's largest Internet giants (Greenwald & MacAskill, 2013; Roberts & Ackerman, 2013) prove the opposite. The sophistication of the Internet only allows for more rather than less surveillance of individuals and their privacy. The Internet is no longer the liberal alternative to the deepest fears of an Orwellian world that it was supposed to be.

What's Democratic about Democracy?

Naturally, since the transitions in the nature of media lend to the never-ending quest to control them, a discussion of the optimal structure and form of the relationship they have with governments requires an understanding of our concept of democracy. However, it was never easy to define "democracy" without reducing it into a set of formalistic procedures, a checklist of must-have mechanisms that determine whether a political regime is democratic or not. "One aspect of this is that primary use of the term [democracy] is to identify, not a distinct system of ideas, but a particular form of government, or a way of taking collective decisions" (Jay, 1984/1994, pp. 119–120). Yet democracy is first and foremost an idea, without which its formal characterizations are meaningless. Indeed, identifying democracy as a distinct system of ideas can be traced back to its interpretation among the Greek who coined the term. They understood democracy as a regime in which citizenship, access to public office and participation in public debates and decisions were widely shared among the many rather than exclusively the preserve of the few (Jay, 1984/1994, p. 120). This interpretation carries with it notions of equality, the need for due process for decision making and the acceptance of the rule of law as determined in the accepted formal proceedings. A significant turn in the understanding of democracy came with the acknowledgement that economies of scale require that representatives of the many make decisions in their name. The new challenge thus became to adhere to a standard immortalized in Abraham Lincoln's quest that government should be "of the people, by the people, [and] for the people." Rising to this challenge gave rise to different theories of democracy that tried to cope with the inherent democratic deficit of "representative" democracy and to redefine it as an idea and as an ideal system of control.

Held (2006) distinguished between four classical and five contemporary models of democracy (van Dijk, 1996). Among the classical models, he counted the Athenian classic democracy; the liberal protective democracy, which juxtaposes liberals against the absolutist state; the developmental democracy, which stresses the education of the citizenry; and direct democracy. Among contemporary models, Held (1987) counted competitive-elitist democracy, pluralism, legal democracy, participatory democracy and developmental autonomy. Applying democratic theory to media development, van Dijk (1996) differentiated among these latter five models along two dimensions of political democracy that he deemed relevant to the understanding of the role of media technologies in democracy. One continuum stretches between seeing the model as based on direct or representative democracy, the other on focusing the goal of democracy as lying between "opinion formation" and "decision making." For the context of this chapter, we perceive these two goals differentiating between recognizing theories of democracy as normative—and aimed at creating a knowledgeable and active citizenry—or descriptive—and aimed at assuring the system is functioning to reach decisions. Indeed, the latter cannot truly exist without the former, or more precisely, a system that does not make a normative choice ensuring freedom of expression cannot be perceived as a democracy.

One attempt to make a claim to the contrary was Zakaria's (1997) differentiation between "liberal" and "illiberal" democracies. Zakaria claims that if a country "holds competitive, multiparty elections" (p. 25), that is sufficient to label it as democratic, albeit "illiberal." However, even within this minimalist view of what a democracy means, he admits that "of course elections must be open and fair and this requires some protections of freedom of speech and assembly" (Zakaria, 1997). Yet once one accepts that even the minimalist view of a democracy requires the preservation of freedom of expression, when does "some" become "enough"? Who is to determine that point? And what level of free expression helps make the transition from "illiberal" to "liberal"? Thus even if one is willing to accept that democracy is first and foremost a system designed to make decisions, one cannot deny the need to ensure a minimal level of rights so that the decision making is meaningful. That minimal level includes free expression. This determination is crucial for the purposes of this chapter since expression is the matter that media carry; thus the maintenance of a democratic regime is rooted in the maintenance of a free media system.

"Free," however, is a notion arising from the "liberal protective" model (Held, 2006, p. 77), which juxtaposes government against individuals and analyzes the relationship between them as if the political were a separate and distinct sphere from the cultural, the economic and the private. It is insufficient in order to understand the role of media in maintaining and supporting democracy. A perspective that provides such support, taking into account the need to balance opinion formation and decision making in a democracy, is articulated by Habermas (1996), who asked not to dismiss the normative aspects of democracy on the one hand, but never to neglect, on the other, the "liberal" task to institutionalize procedures that will ensure the democratic process. The path to the Habermasian "essential" or "discursial" democracy passes through the constant maintenance of a vital public sphere—a sphere of human activity that provides "the conditions for creating citizens who are capable of exercising their freedoms, competent to question the basic assumptions that govern political life, and skilled enough to participate in developing social movements that will enable them to shape the basic social, political, and economic orders that govern their lives" (Giroux, 2011, p. 20). This kind of public sphere will create a "formative culture in which people are provided with the knowledge and skills to be able to participate in such a [democratic] society" (p. 17). Only by gaining these components would it be possible to maintain the democratic idea both as a normative ideology and as a formalized political system (Castoriadis, 1997). In the words of Habermas (1996), "there is a necessary connection between the deliberative concept of democracy and the reference to a concrete substantively integrated ethical community. Otherwise, one could not explain, in this view how the citizens' orientation to the common good would be at all possible" (p. 24).

Contemporary "New Media" and Democracy

It has long been established that the media have a role in maintaining and developing democracy both formally and substantially. But what role, if any, do contemporary media play in the protection and enhancement of democracy? One way to try and decipher this riddle is by observing the wave of protests, uprisings and contestations of authoritarian regimes and the neoliberal world order or the "market fundamentalism" (Giroux, 2011) that characterize the first decade of the twenty-first century. These social movements are often typified by the extensive use of contemporary and previously nonexistent media as well as of new information and communication technologies (ICTs) by the protesters, which led to nicknaming them with catch descriptions such as the "Twitter revolutions" or the "Facebook uprisings."[3] This phenomenon has supported the claim that the use of new ICTs in these public uprisings represents one of the main differences between contemporary protests and older social movements (Vicari, 2013). The visible presence of contemporary media devices among the various "Occupy" movement demonstrators has further strengthened the claim that media, "new media," democracy and democratization processes were all strongly connected not only in authoritarian and less than democratic regimes (Pearce & Kendzior, 2012; Diamond, 2010; Schmidt & Cohen, 2010; Nisbet, Stoycheff & Pearce, 2012; Groshek, 2009; Shirky, 2011; Benski, Langman, Perugorría & Tejerina, 2013; Gladwell, 2010; Tufekci & Wilson, 2012). However, it is accurate to say that the new debate over media and democracy interconnections only echoes a much more traditional discussion between "utopist" and "skeptic" approaches to the determinist connection often made between media and democracy.

Diamond (2010) incorporates the term "liberation technologies" when describing the information technologies of our era, which consist of all interrelated forms of digital ICTs ranging from the computer, through the

Internet and the mobile phone, to contemporary "social media," such as Facebook and Twitter. These "liberation technologies" have the ability to expand freedom whether it be of the political, social or economic flavor. Schmidt and Cohen (2010) argue that liberation technologies reshaped the sphere of social activity due to the fact that "any person via access to the internet, regardless of living standard or nationality, is given a voice and the power to effect change" (p. 1). Benski and colleagues (2013) use Said's (1996) concepts while claiming that the new ICTs are a tool that, in addition to enabling speaking truth to power, widely disseminates those "truths" and "counter-hegemonic" discourses to those negatively impacted by the rise of international neoliberalism. Thanks to these tools, they add, mobilizations in one place could inspire people in remote locations, and activists become capable of sharing tactics and coordinating actions worldwide.

However, in contrast to this "utopian" view, a vast literature claims the opposite, namely that democratization processes have not been contributed to, and will not be, by communication technologies. Groshek (2009) claims that "over the last hundred years, new communication technologies including telegraphs, telephones, radios and televisions have, in most cases, failed to fulfill their social potential" (p. 117). Gladwell (2010) adds that while "social media"[4] have the potential for challenging the existing social order more efficiently, they are not necessarily the "natural enemy of the status quo" (p. 49). These pre-collaborative contemporary media, in his eyes, are based on "weak ties" between imaginary "friends" or "followers" that are never enough to conduct political change. "In other words," claims Gladwell, "Facebook activism succeeds not by motivating people to make a real sacrifice but by motivating them to do the things that people do when they are not motivated enough to make real sacrifice" (p. 46).

An even more extreme form of "media skepticism" is employing the term "networked authoritarianism" (Pearce & Kendzior, 2012; MacKinnon, 2011; Morozov, 2011), which suggests that not only are digital communications not liberating, but in fact they can become the tool used by authoritarian regimes, which embrace and adjust them to their needs. This adjustment manifests itself when these regimes use new technologies in order to deepen their authoritarian control. Indeed, even a close analysis of recent social uprisings and a close investigation of the protesters' use of ICTs and contemporary media fails to answer whether there is an inherent connection between "democracy" and these media. Thus, for example, Vicari (2013), who examined contemporary media use among Italian protesters during the Occupy protests of 2011, found that although interactive media platforms were used extensively by the protesters, they operated "more as news media rather than truly interactional platforms for dialogical public sphere dynamics" (p. 487). The Spanish "15M" movement, another Occupy movement, used a complex combination of online activism and traditional forms of militant protest such as street demonstrations, public assemblies and camps that were characterized by "bodies being present in a spatial meeting place" (Perugorría & Tejerina, 2013, p. 437). A similar "dystopia" of contemporary media's essential role in recent social movements was demonstrated in the Tahrir Square demonstrations in Egypt in 2011, a prominent example of these social movements in the Arab world, in which the "complex intertwining of multiple online and offline spheres" (Tufekci & Wilson, 2012, p. 376) that emanate from three different components of the media ecosystem—Al-Jazeera satellite TV, rapid Internet diffusion that enabled extensive interactive media uses and cross-country spreading of mobile phone technologies—influenced and helped the revolution.

A more nuanced perception of the ties between contemporary media and democracy is thus called for. First, it is always preferable to examine relations between media environments and progressive social movements for change (Monterde & Postill, 2013), instead of focusing only on specific media platforms or devices (Tufekci & Wilson, 2012). Second, it is clear that contemporary media and especially collaborative platforms and applications (i.e., Facebook) have affected the means of collective action by canceling the binary choice between participating and not participating in collective action and by enabling a new role to formal organizations due to the new organizing abilities of these ICTs (Bimber, Flanagin & Stohl, 2005). Third, contemporary media function as democratic agents mainly in already democratic countries and still face major obstacles when acting as such in nondemocratic regimes (Nisbet, Stoycheff & Pearce, 2012; Shirky, 2011). Fourth, better than measuring media effects on democratic institutions in the short run, we should consider their contributions to society at large and to the public sphere. Years and decades can pass before it will be possible to measure democratic changes in these fields (Shirky, 2011). Indeed, Giroux (2011) accurately claims that "the conditions for democracy do not come easily and must be struggled over continuously . . . new media can play a crucial role both for and against that struggle" (p. 25).

Hence, it will be wiser to critically examine the ways in which contemporary ICTs and democracy are intertwined. At the same time, we should not neglect the efforts of finding out the ways contemporary media and their underlying communication systems contribute to a public sphere that is both distinctly different and at the same time offers "the promise of recasting modes of agency and politics outside of the neoliberal ideology and disciplinary apparatus that now dominate contemporary culture" (Giroux, 2011, p. 21).

CONCLUSION: IMPLICATIONS FOR CONTEMPORARY MEDIA POLICY

Can policy help contemporary media serve a "new democracy"? Perhaps not new in its underlying philosophical understanding of the term but rather new in its ability to unleash the potential new technologies offer?

It seems that the challenge of contemporary media policy, at least when it comes to its role in and relationship with democracy, is to serve as a tool strengthening democracy, and not only in its formal aspects, but more importantly in its substantial ones. As we have seen, the most substantial element of a democracy, even a democracy most narrowly defined, is the right for expression. For long, expression was defined in dichotomous terms: whether it was allowed or denied. The right for expression thus became synonymous with the right for "free expression," a negative right (Berlin, 1959) derived from the prohibition on government to obstruct it. A prime example of this policy is the First Amendment to the United States' Constitution, which prohibits the government from enacting laws abridging freedom of speech. This narrow interpretation has been challenged over the years with attempts to broaden it. One such attempt was introducing "social responsibility" of the media (Hutchins, 1947), another a "right of access" to the media (Barron, 1967) and yet another a right of access to the media's audiences (Napoli & Sybblis, 2007). What characterizes these more progressive approaches is that while they recognize that government is not the sole threat to free communications, they are still embedded in the old media paradigms (simply because contemporary media were nonexistent when these derivatives of the right to expression were conceived and developed). It is interesting to recognize that what these enhanced rights developed by media scholars, practitioners and critics decry is the inability of voices to be heard, despite the existence of the mass media. Individuals may be free to express themselves, but what they lack is the ability to have their voices heard where it matters: within (or over) the mass media. The challenge therefore is not for expression free of obstruction, but rather for expression devoid of opportunity.

At the same time, in each of their developmental stages, media technologies were designed, even by the most benevolent and well-meaning regimes, to serve a limited form of democracy, more often than not one that served the rulers no less than the ruled. In the "very old" print media days, the ease of controlling distribution and the high cost of production awarded very few policy options to government beyond restraining themselves from limiting the media. In the old electronic media era, we were witness to the controlled development of media outlets, again even in regimes perceived as democratic. The justification for this limitation may have been technological ("spectrum scarcity"), economic or cultural ("inform, educate and entertain"), but the results were similar to what had developed in the older media regime: access was limited to those in control of the communication process, whether they were commercial entities, governments or the "public." Since "natural" forces such as technology and economics could have justified this control of expression, the inability to reach an ideal from of democracy was seen as a necessary evil.

But contemporary media has the ability to overcome these obstacles and to provide an opportunity of voice to many more. This technological capability, the combination of the four "new media" characteristics—interactivity, mobility, abundance and convergence—allows us to make a conceptual leap: from discussing speech in terms of freedom to discussing speech in terms of equality. In the contemporary media era, therefore, the conversation about media policy makes a transition from a conversation about liberty to a conversation about social justice. And the implications for policy are substantial. Since democracy is about voice and contemporary media are about the creation of opportunity for more voices to be expressed than ever before, "new media policies" in a democratic regime need to focus on creating more opportunities for voices to be expressed. What needs to be done is give voice—and in a justice-centered conversation this means in particular giving voice to the voiceless, a redistribution of voice.

Already in the early days of the Internet, Van Cuilenberg and McQuail (2003) observed that despite political rhetoric, there is little emphasis on equality when it comes to Internet policy, and that the political drive to incorporate large swaths of the population in the network society is driven by commercial and surveillance interests rather than by a belief in "social equality." This tendency, notes McChesney (2009), "may prove to be a dubious contribution to the development of our species" (pp. 41–42). More recently Bertot, Jaeger and Hansen (2012) noted that it was those already technologically privileged who more often benefited from technological development. The combination of commercial interests governing policy and controlling existing limited channels of communications and the tendency of policy to serve the haves serves as further justification of the need to introduce a justice-focused policy to the development of media. Concentrating on remedial access reform on the one hand and on promoting policies that avoid blocking[5] the potential abundant number of voices on the other can and should be a good start in that direction.

NOTES

1. This study has been supported by a Career Integration Grant awarded by the Marie Curie FP7 program of the European Union and by the I-CORE Program of the Planning and Budgeting Committee and the Israel Science Foundation (grant no. 1716/12). Both authors contributed equally to this study.
2. Using this perspective, media such as VCR tapes, seen as "new" in comparison to television in the 1980s and 1990s, are actually "old" as they require physical distribution and the feedback to their content is yet again diffused and slow.
3. A random Google search of the term "Twitter revolution" came up with 861,000 responses.
4. Which in his terminology means collaborative and interactive Web 2.0 applications such as Facebook and Twitter.
5. Such policies are most commonly referred to as "universal access" and as "network neutrality"; however, explication of these terms would require a separate study.

REFERENCES

Barron, J. A. (1967). Access to the press: A new first amendment right. *Harvard Law Review 80*(8), 1641–1678.

Benski, T., Langman, L., Perugorría, I., & Tejerina, B. (2013). From the streets and squares to social movement studies: What have we learned? *Current Sociology, 61*(4), 541–561.

Bertot, J. C., Jaeger, P. T., & Hansen, D. (2012). The impact of polices on government social media usage: Issues, challenges, and recommendations. *Government Information Quarterly, 29*(1), 30–40.

Berlin, I. (1959). *Two concepts of liberty: An inaugural lecture delivered before the University of Oxford on 31 October 1958.* Oxford: Clarendon.

Bimber, B., Flanagin, A. J., & Stohl, C. (2005). Reconceptualizing collective action in the contemporary media environment. *Communication Theory, 15*(4), 365–388.

Brown, J. D., Childers, K. W., Bauman, K. E., & Koch, G. G. (1990). The influence of new media and family structure on young adolescents' television and radio use. *Communication Research, 17*(1), 65–82.

Castells, M. (2007). Communication, power and counter-power in the network society. *International Journal of Communication, 1*(1), 238–266.

Castoriadis, C. (1997). Democracy as procedure and democracy as regime. *Constellations, 4*(1), 1–18.

Cobo, C. (2012). Networks for citizen consultation and citizen sourcing of expertise. *Contemporary Social Science, 7*(3), 283–304.

Diamond, L. (2010). Liberation technology. *Journal of Democracy, 21*(3), 69–83.

Dutton, W. (2008). The wisdom of collaborative network organizations: Capturing the value of networked individuals. *Prometheus, 26*(3), 211–230.

Giroux, H. A. (2011). The crisis of public values in the age of the new media. *Critical Studies in Media Communication, 28*(1), 8–29.

Gladwell, M. (2010). Small change. *New Yorker, 4*, 42–49.

Greenwald, G., & MacAskill, E. (2013, 6 June). "NSA Prism program taps in to user data of Apple, Google and others." *Guardian.* Retrieved from www.guardian.co.uk/world/2013/jun/06/us-tech-giants-nsa-data

Groshek, J. (2009). The democratic effects of the Internet, 1994–2003: A cross-national inquiry of 152 countries. *International Communication Gazette, 71*(3), 115–136.

Habermas, J. (1996). Three normative models of democracy. In S. Benhabib (Ed.), *Democracy and difference: Contesting the boundaries of the political* (pp. 21–30). Princeton, NJ: Princeton University Press.

Held, D. (2006). *Models of Democracy.* 3rd ed. Stanford, CA: Stanford University Press.

Holtz-Bacha, C., & Norris, P. (2001). "To entertain, inform, and educate": Still the role of public television. *Political Communication, 18*(2), 123–140.

Hutchins, R. M. (1947). *A free and responsible press: A general report on mass communication: Newspapers, radio, motion pictures, magazines, and books.* Chicago: University of Chicago Press.

Innis, H. A. (1951). *The bias of communication.* Toronto: University of Toronto Press.

Jay, R. (1994). Democracy. In R. Eccleshall, V. Geoghegan, J. Richard, M. Kenny, L. Mackenzie & R. Wilford (Eds.), *Political ideologies—an introduction* (pp.118–152). 2nd ed. London: Routledge. (Original work published 1984)

Levinson, P. (2012). *New new media.* Cranbury, New Jersey: Pearson.

Longstaff, P. (2002). *The communications toolkit: How to build and regulate any communications business.* Cambridge, MA: MIT Press.

MacKinnon, R. (2011). China's "networked authoritarianism." *Journal of Democracy,* 22(2), 32–46.

McChesney, R. W. (2009). Public scholarship and the communications policy agenda. In A. Schejter (Ed.), . . . *And communications for all* (pp. 41–56). Lanham, MD: Lexington Books.

McChesney, R., & Nichols, J. (2010). *The death and life of American journalism: The media revolution that will begin the world again.* New York: Nation Books.

McLuhan, M. (1994). *Understanding media: The extension of man.* Cambridge, MA: MIT Press. (Original work published 1964)

Meyrowitz, J. (2010). Media evolution and cultural change. In J. R. Hall, L. Grindstaff & M. Lo (Eds.), *Handbook of cultural sociology* (pp. 52–63). New York: Routledge.

Monterde, A., & J. Postill (forthcoming). Mobile ensembles: The uses of mobile phones for social protest by Spain's indignados. In G. Goggin & L. Hjorth (Eds.), *Routledge Companion to Mobile Media.*

Morozov, E. (2011). *The net delusion: The dark side of Internet freedom.* New York: Public Affairs.

Murschetz, P. (1998). State support for the daily press in Europe: A critical appraisal Austria, France, Norway and Sweden compared. *European Journal of Communication,* 13(3), 291–313.

Napoli, M. P., & Sybblis, T. (2007). Access to audiences as a First Amendment Right: Its relevance and implications for electronic media policy. *Virginia Journal of Law & Technology,* 12(1), 1–31.

Nisbet, E. C., Stoycheff, E., & Pearce, K. E. (2012). Internet use and democratic demands: A multinational, multilevel model of internet use and citizen attitudes about democracy. *Journal of Communication,* 62(2), 249–265.

Pearce, K. E., & Kendzior, S. (2012). Networked authoritarianism and social media in Azerbaijan. *Journal of Communication,* 62(2), 283–298.

Perugorría, I., & Tejerina, B. (2013). Politics of the encounter: Cognition, emotions, and networks in the Spanish 15M. *Current Sociology,* 61(4), 424–442.

Picard, R. (2007). Subsidies for newspapers: Can the Nordic model remain viable? In H. Bohrmann, E. Klaus & M. Machill (Eds.), *Media industry, journalism culture and communication policies in Europe* (pp. 236–246). Koln: Halem.

Pickard, V. (2011). The battle over the FCC blue book: Determining the role of broadcast media in a democratic society, 1945–8. *Media, Culture & Society,* 33(2), 171–191.

Roberts, D., & Ackerman, S. (2013, June 7). US admits secret surveillance of phone calls has gone on for years. *Guardian,* p. 1.

Said, E. W. (1996). *Representations of the intellectual: The 1993 Reith Lectures.* New York: Vintage Books.

Schejter, A. (2003). Public broadcasting, the information society and the Internet: A paradigm shift? In M. McCauley, E. Peterson, L. Artz & D. Halleck (Eds.), *Public broadcasting and the public interest* (pp. 158–174). Armonk, NY: M.E. Sharpe.

Schmidt, E., & Cohen, J. (2010). Digital disruption. Connectivity and the diffusion of power. *Foreign Affairs,* 89(6), 75–85.

Shannon, C., & Weaver, D. (1949). *The mathematical theory of communication.* Urbana: University of Illinois Press.

Shirky, C. (2011). Political power of social media. Technology, the public sphere, and political change, *Foreign Affairs,* 90(4), 28–41.

Tufekci, Z., & Wilson, C. (2012). Social media and the decision to participate in political protest: Observations from Tahrir Square. *Journal of Communication,* 62(2), 363–379.

Turow, J. (1990). The critical importance of mass communication as a concept. In B. Ruben & L. Liverouw (Eds.). *Mediation, information and communication* (pp. 9–20). New Brunswick, NJ: Transaction.

Van Cuilenburg, J., & McQuail, D. (2003). Media policy paradigm shifts towards a new communications policy paradigm. *European Journal of Communication, 18*(2), 181–207.

Van Dijk, J. A. (1996). Models of democracy: Behind the design and use of new media in politics. *Electronic Journal of Communication/La Revue Electronique De Communication, 6*(2), n. 2.

Vicari, S. (2013). Public reasoning around social contention: A case study of Twitter use in the Italian mobilization for global change. *Current Sociology, 61*(4), 474–490.

Zakaria, F. (1997). The rise of illiberal democracy. *Foreign Affairs, 76*(6), 22–43.

Part II

Policy Issues

Country Case Studies

6 Policy Implications from the Changing Market Environment Including Convergence between Telecommunication Services and Broadcasting Services[1]

Yasu Taniwaki

The market environment surrounding the telecommunications and broadcasting services has been changing dramatically. This change can be divided into two perspectives. One is the horizontal integration of networks through breaking down walls created in the bundled relationships between transmission networks and information over the networks. The characteristics of networks defined by transmitted services have been gradually lost in line with the convergence between telecommunication services and broadcasting services. Thereby the rationale for regulations applied respectively for telecommunications and broadcasting services has been lost.

The other market change is an emergence of horizontally integrated business models. Especially, as represented by the mobile telecommunication service market, the previous business models led by common carriers have been replaced by those led by upper-layer players called OTT, or "Over-the-Top," players, including cloud service providers. As a result, regulatory authorities focusing on network layers to ensure fair and effective competition have been forced to modify competition policies. Simultaneously, business models led by upper-layer players create new values through collection, storage, analysis, and utilization of data, and these business models work most efficiently by taking best advantage of utilizing cloud services. Under these circumstances, from the perspective of competition policy and industry policy, the effectiveness of regulations and policies by each country has been limited, and more attention should be paid to global policy coordination.

Emergence of a Digital Ecosystem and Its Policy Implications

This chapter adopts the analytical framework of the four layers depicted in Figure 6.1. Here, the vertically integrated business models relate to the structuring of these four different layers, which include a terminal layer, a

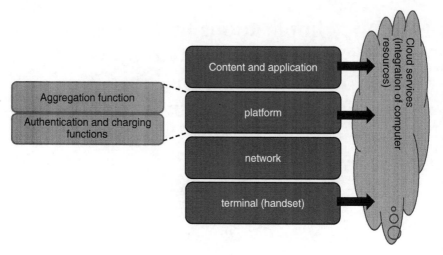

Figure 6.1   Layer competition model.

network layer, a platform layer, and a content and application layer. The following discussion covers the development of horizontal integration of networks, followed by the emergence of vertically integrated business models.

Development of Horizontal Integration of Networks

Networks previously deployed were built respectively by services, and relevant regulations were developed for each set of networks and service. In Japan, legal frameworks regarding information and communication technology (ICT) markets have been divided mainly into the Telecommunications Business Act (TBA) on telecommunications services and the Broadcasting Act on broadcasting services. In the case of the TBA, common carriers with a certain share of fixed subscriber lines are recognized as having market dominance, and obligations to open up their networks to competitive carriers are applied.[2] In addition, regulatory authorities should check that access charges or prices to lend their networks to other carriers are calculated appropriately, without any excessive profit being made. In addition to dominant regulations applied for fixed networks, there exist other dominant regulations applied for mobile networks, whose level of regulations remains lower than those for fixed networks based on the preposition that main lines for subscribers are fixed networks instead of mobile networks. The Broadcasting Act stipulates regulations such as the obligations of universal service provision, the political neutrality of content, and restrictions on media ownership.

However, as represented by factors such as the progress of fixed mobile convergence (FMC), which means the integration of fixed communication services and mobile communication services, and the increase of mobile devices as main lines, the rationale for making distinctions between fixed communication services and mobile communication services has been lost. Moreover, the transition from legacy networks such as public switched telephone networks (PSTNs) to Internet Protocol (IP)–based networks, as represented by facts such as the provision of broadcasting services by common carriers and the provision of broadband services by cable TV (CATV) operators, the government was forced to reconsider the market distinctions between telecommunications services and broadcasting services.

Development of Vertical Integration of Layers

The emergence of vertically integrated business models across the layers in Japan has been triggered by mobile Internet service launched by NTT DoCoMo in 1999 under the service name "i-mode." Under this business framework, common carriers decide the specifications of devices and procure mobile devices at once from vendors. These devices are sold via mobile device shops owned or entrusted to operate by common carriers. In addition, over these mobile Internet services, subscribers can purchase content and applications on the portal site operated by common carriers.

In this business model of mobile Internet service, platform functions include aggregation functions where common carriers collect content and applications, as well as functions of authentication and charging systems used by subscribers when purchasing content and applications. These platform functions have also been provided by common carriers, allowing common carriers to take the initiative to build up vertically integrated business models.

With the proliferation of smartphones and cloud services, however, mobile business models have been forced to change. In the case of business models structured by Apple, for example, Apple provides devices such as the iPhone and the iPad. Over these devices, Apple provides an authentication function of iTS (iTunes Store) based on the user's Apple ID. In addition, devices provided by Apple can use multicarrier networks, which means Apple's business model does not depend on networks operated by specific common carriers.

In the case of Google, many mobile devices embedded with open source operating system (OS) "Android" abilities have been introduced into the market, although devices with their own brand of Google have been limited. In addition, like at Apple, platform functions of authentication and aggregation have been developed by using the user's Google ID and providing Google Play as a platform to provide applications.

Considering these business models developed by Apple and Google, it is clear that vertically integrated business models led by common carriers have been replaced by independent networks operated by common carriers. In addition, three characteristics can be found in the latter business models.

First, in the latter business models, the ecosystem has teamed up with many players including vendors, common carriers, the community of application and content developers, cloud service providers, and the user community. It is especially important to point out that strengthening inter-dependency between service providers and users contributes to improve the value generated by this business model.[3]

Second, each layer except for the network layer has been empowered by cloud services, enabling them to provide services across national borders. This means this business model can be developed globally for less cost in comparison with vertically integrated business models led by common carriers.

Third, this business model allows service providers to collect a huge amount of personal data by taking best advantage of cloud services. This leads to the active usage of personal data as a marketing tool, which means personal data has become one of the most important management resources.

These characteristics make clear the importance of platform layers. Platform functions, in the previous vertical business models led by common carriers, have included authentication functions, charging systems, and aggregation functions. In the new vertically integrated business models, however, platform functions work as "gateways" to provide a variety of services using a huge amount of information resources stored in the cloud along with the progress of accessibility to information resources from any device and via any network. If this gateway is monopolized by a limited number of players, there is a possibility of making the market distorted by way of an overly dominant power, thus circumventing the healthy development of the information market.

In addition, in progressing the horizontal integration of networks for tele-communication services, and for broadcasting services, it might be possible to combine respective platform functions that were deployed separately in different service markets. Here, it becomes necessary to consider how to recognize market dominance beyond the existing legal market demarcations.

As reviewed earlier, the utilization of information resources has become the core of current business models, and many new businesses based on "big data" have been emerging. Under these circumstances, from the viewpoint of maintaining the openness of platform functions and promoting the healthy development of an information market, it is appropriate for a government to take several of the following approaches as policy options.

First, a government must ensure the openness of cloud services. Currently, cloud services have been provided with different data formats. However, as social and economic activities depend more on cloud services, the cloud service market will be transformed from the provision of silo-type cloud services to inter-cloud environments where a variety of cloud services are interconnected with each other. In this inter-cloud environment, the emergence of user "lock-in" by a specific cloud service provider stifles the healthy development of the cloud service market. Therefore, it is necessary for a government to take actions to keep open the cloud service environment.

Second, it is necessary for a government to promote the releasing of data, which leads to helping the information resource market flourish. For this, a government must make data owned by said government public and must release a common API (application programming interface) to allow any user in the private sector to utilize data both for profit, and for nonprofit, purposes. In the United States, the open data strategy has been in operation since 2009 (White House, 2009). In addition, the EU has also made public open data strategy in 2011, and specific projects are in progress (European Commission, 2011).

Third, new rules or frameworks on how to utilize personal data should be developed. Under the circumstance whereby a lot of personal data has been stored in the cloud, it is an important policy issue to consider how to ensure the balance between protection of privacy and the fostering of new businesses that utilize personal data. In 2011, the European Commission released a proposal on personal data protection (European Commission, 2012), and the procedure to legalize this proposal is in progress at the European Parliament. Following this action, in the United States, the executive branch of the White House has released the Consumer Privacy Bill of Rights, establishing new rules for personal data protection (White House, 2012).

Policy Issues Regarding Platform Markets

In the progress of the horizontal integration of networks and the vertical integration of layers, policy issues regarding platform markets can be summarized respectively from competition policy perspectives and also from industry policy perspectives.

Platform Layer and Competition Policy
From perspectives of competition policy, policy issues regarding the horizontal integration of networks can be discussed from the following two perspectives.

First, it is necessary for a government to review related regulations regarding telecommunication services, and broadcasting services, in response to the convergence of both services. In Japan, Internet Protocol television (IPTV) has entered into the takeoff stage in the market, where a more flexible provision of broadcasting services is on the upcoming policy agenda. This includes the collaboration of content transmission via legacy broadcasting networks and via the Internet as well as content viewing through multiple screens including smartphones and tablet PCs via wired and/or wireless networks. In this situation, however, telecommunication services are under the regulations of the TBA, although broadcasting services are under those of the Broadcasting Act. This legal framework could generate a conflict in the regulations under each act. Specifically, in the case of broadcasting companies planning to provide a platform business in collaboration with common carriers, it is unclear which act applies to this collaborative platform business.

Second, the status of dominant regulations should be reviewed. Current dominant regulations stipulated in the TBA are based on the market share of access (subscriber) lines, and dominant regulations are applied to designated dominant carriers. If dominant carriers abuse market dominant power at the platform layer, dominant regulations or rules of conduct are applied to these carriers. However, if OTT players abuse market dominance at the platform layer, no specific regulations can be applied, and this causes an inconsistency in the regulations for common carriers and for OTT players.

In addition, the prevention of market dominant power by common carriers in the TBA is ensured by the application of the rules of conduct relating to these common carriers who might have the capacity to control retail prices. Many business models structured by OTT players, however, have one of the characteristics where they provide services for free to users. OTT players recover this operational cost by way of an advertisement fee from advertisers, and the triangle model among OTT players, users, and advertisers has been established. In this business model, it is hard to identify the capacity of OTT players to control retail prices.

Third, it is hardly possible to identify market dominance only in domestic markets because vertically integrated business models have been provided globally. This situation leads to the necessity to introduce new analytical frameworks on how to define markets across international borders to recognize and designate market dominance.

With regards to policy issues including those described so far in this chapter, in June 2013, the government of Japan decided upon the Japan Revival Plan, which includes a whole list of policies to revive the Japanese industry and to create a new market (Government of Japan, 2013b).[4] This strategy says the review process of competition policies in the field of telecommunications markets will be launched in the summer of 2013, and specific issues to be considered will be listed by March 2014, followed by drawing up the policy conclusions by the end of 2014.

Platform Layer and Industry Policy

From the perspectives of industry policy, policy issues regarding platform layers represent three main issues—the promotion of open cloud, an open data strategy, and the development of new rules on personal data. The actions taken by the Japanese government can be summarized as follows.

First, it is necessary to establish an open cloud environment, whereby open cloud is a necessity in ensuring an open interface among different cloud services. Recently, cloud services have been introduced into mission critical areas such as public administration services, medical services, and financial services. Promotion for introducing cloud services can be realized through ensuring high levels of credibility and meeting requirements on reliability, responsibility, data quality, and security levels. This leads to the necessity of realizing an inter-cloud environment where a variety of cloud services are interconnected by broadband networks and where these cloud services are complemented by each other.

The standardization of interfaces for interconnecting different cloud services and network protocols, however, is still on the way at international fora such as the ITU (International Telecommunication Union). In June 2009, the GICTF (Global Inter-Cloud Taskforce) was established by common carriers, and by vendors and academia in July 2009, in collaboration with the Ministry of Internal Affairs and Communications (MIC). GICTF released a draft standard for inter-cloud services as a proposal for ITU-T (GICTF, 2012) and has been making contributions to global standardization activities.

Second, an open data strategy is one of the key policy issues to be promoted. In July 2012, ICT Headquarters[5] decided on the open data strategy (Government of Japan, 2012). This strategy was intended to encourage government agencies to make public data owned by the government with machine-readable formats such as CSV (comma-separated values) and to allow the private sector to use this data both for commercial and for noncommercial purposes. Based on this strategy, the Japanese government has been developing platforms for open data, including the establishment of copyright rules for open data, the establishment of data portal sites putting together data provided by different agencies, and the establishment of common API including standardization of data format and structure. The data portal site is scheduled to be in operation starting from April 2014.

Third, it is necessary to establish rules on how to deal with personal data. In April 2005, the Personal Data Protection Act took effect in Japan. This act stipulates that personal data is legally protected when a specific person is identifiable from personal data. ICT has allowed service providers, however, to provide services with better convenience through collecting and utilizing personal data such as location data, purchase records, and health records. Under these circumstances, it is necessary to change the concept of legally protected personal data, where personal data to be legally protected is specified by criteria as to whether or not personal data includes privacy.

However, the concept of privacy differs from person to person. This leads to two policy implications. One is the requirement to establish rules to get permission in advance from each person when utilizing his or her personal data. The other is the necessity to promote the development of PET (privacy-enhancing technologies) such as anonymity technology, which allows service providers to utilize personal data for business. In this case, there is a possibility of reidentifying a person through linking unidentified data with other personal data, which means it is necessary to establish rules to be able to collect and utilize personal data only under the conditions of prohibiting reidentification of personal data.

The government has launched a study at ICT Headquarters on a new legal framework to utilize personal data while ensuring privacy; the new framework, which includes the possibility of establishing a privacy commissioner system or independent regulatory authority, is to be considered, and aims at deciding policy directions by the end of 2013.

Consideration on personal data protection in the EU and the U.S. is focusing on consumer protection. At the same time, this implies that the policy to promote the utilization of personal data to create new businesses under the current environment is sufficiently protecting the privacy of citizens. Legal frameworks and policy approaches differ across different countries, although the EU, U.S., and Japan can share the policy direction on personal data to ensure the balance between utilization of personal data and privacy protection. Transborder data flow including personal data, however, has been increasing, which means any serious difference on personal data protection rules across said countries could stifle the smooth flow of data. In this context, the global coordination of rule making on personal data protection is required.

In addition, thanks to rapid technological innovation and business model innovation, the market structure in the ICT field has been changing dramatically. This implies the legal framework on personal data protection should have enough flexibility. For this, it is appropriate for a government to decide only basic principles on personal data protection, followed by specific rules decided and operated through a multistakeholder processes with participation from the private sector. In this coregulation[6] process, the government checks the conformity of specific rules developed by the private sector as toward basic principles decided by the government. In addition, it is appropriate for a government to have the legal power of policy enforcement to put administrative penalties on companies violating rules.

CONCLUSION

In June 2013, the Japanese government decided on a new ICT strategy (Government of Japan, 2013a),[7] whereby information resources are recognized as a national strategic resource, along with other resources such as human resources, natural resources, and financial resources. Based on this, the strategy focuses on utilizing information resources as much as possible by promoting the establishment of an open cloud environment, promoting an open data strategy, and renovating the legal framework on personal data protection. Promoting the emergence of new business models supporting economic growth requires the government proceed with relevant policies from two perspectives as follows.

First, it is necessary for a government to establish a competitive market allowing every citizen to obtain access to information with an "any device, any network" environment. This leads to a requirement for reviewing the framework of competition policy, where it is necessary to review new legal frameworks exceeding legacy market demarcations such as distinctions between telecommunication services and broadcasting services. It is also necessary to review the status of market dominance reflecting a new concept of market definition in the context of the globalization of the ICT market.

Second, creating new business thorough a mash-up of information requires a government to ensure the openness of platform functions. Specifically, by utilizing platform functions that become a gateway when utilizing information resources, a government must proceed with an open cloud policy, an open data strategy, and the establishment of personal data protection rules.

When considering the policy issues mentioned in this chapter, one of the most important things a government should consider is to realize globally coordinated rules. In the past, the WTO (World Trade Organization) has established global rules on the transborder flow of goods and services. Especially in the case of the liberalization of the trade in services, trade in telecommunication services was discussed, and a series of rules made contributions to a remarkable liberalization of the telecommunication service market and its rapid growth in market size. Simultaneously, the openness of platform functions helps the liberalization of transborder data flow, whereby global economic growth will be realized. In this sense, it is necessary for each country to share the importance of transborder data flow, which is placed as one of the pillars to measure market access to ensure a global free trade system.

NOTES

1. Opinions in this chapter belong to the author and do not necessarily represent the official stance of the government of Japan.
2. The Telecommunications Business Act (Government of Japan, 1985) defines "telecommunication service" as a service "intermediating communications of others through the use of telecommunications facilities, or any other acts of providing telecommunications facilities for the use of communications by others" (Article 1 (iii)). Based on this definition of "intermediating communications of others," Internet service providers (ISPs) are categorized as telecommunication service providers under the regulations of TBA.
3. With regards to interdependency between service providers and users, Organisation for Economic Co-operation and Development (OECD) (2013) offers the following explanation of the concept of "smart":

   An application or service is able to learn from previous situations and to communicate the results of these situations to other devices and users. These devices and users can then change their behavior to best fit the situation. This means that information about situations needs to be generated, transmitted, processed, correlated, interpreted, adapted, displayed in a meaningful manner, and acted upon. (OECD, 2013, p. 8)

4. The Japan Revival Plan decided by the Japanese government in June 2013 (Government of Japan, 2013b) contains seven plans to revive Japanese industries including the promotion of ICT-related investment, the specification of four strategic fields for creating a new market, and global strategy for newly created industries.
5. ICT Headquarters in Japan was established in 1999, based on IT Basic Law. The headquarters is chaired by the prime minister and its members are all

ministers, government CIOs (chief information officers), and several experts from the private sector. The role of the ICT Headquarters includes the compilation of ICT-related policies for developing the national ICT strategy of the government.

6. Ofcom (2008) defines regulations into three categories: (a) self-regulation enforced by the private sector on a voluntary basis, (b) coregulation enforced in collaboration between the private sector and the government, and (c) statutory regulation enforced by the government based on legislation.

7. ICT strategy decided in June 2013 (Government of Japan, 2013a) aims at realizing the most advanced ICT-utilization nation in the world within five years. To become an "information resource based nation," the strategy focuses on creating a new industry by taking best advantage of information and data owned by the public sector and the private sector. The strategy has three pillars: (a) the creation of new industry through the release of public data and the promotion of knowledge-based management in agriculture, (b) the realization of a safe and secure society through the accelerative introduction of ICT into medical, nursing, and health services and the revitalization of local communities by the power of ICT, and (c) the realization of one-stop administration services by providing e-government services and the reformation of administrative information systems.

REFERENCES

European Commission. (2011). *Open data: An engine for innovation, growth and transparent governance.* Retrieved from http://ec.europa.eu/information_society/policy/psi/docs/pdfs/opendata2012/open_data_communication/en.pdf

European Commission. (2012). *Proposal for a regulation of the European Parliament and of the Council on the protection of individuals with regard to the processing of personal data and on the free movement of such data (general data protection regulation).* Retrieved from www.europarl.europa.eu/document/activities/cont/201305/20130508ATT65776/20130508ATT65776EN.pdf

Global Inter-Cloud Taskforce (GICTF) (2012). *Intercloud interface specification draft (intercloud protocol, cloud resource data model).* Retrieved from www.gictf.jp/doc/GICTF_CloudIF_ResourceDataModel_WhitePaper_e_20120515.pdf

Government of Japan. (1985). *Telecommunications business act.* Retrieved from www.soumu.go.jp/main_sosiki_tsusin/eng/Resources/laws/pdf/090204_2.pdf

Government of Japan. (2012). *Open data strategy* (decided in July 2012 by IT Headquarters, available in Japanese). Retrieved from www.kantei.go.jp/jp/singi/it2/pdf/120704_siryou2.pdf

Government of Japan. (2013a). *Declaration on creating IT nation leading the world* (decided in June 2013 by the Cabinet, available in Japanese). Retrieved from www.kantei.go.jp/jp/singi/it2/kettei/pdf/20130614/siryou1.pdf

Government of Japan. (2013b). *Japan revival plan* (decided in June 2013 by the Cabinet, available in Japanese). Summary in English retrieved from www.kantei.go.jp/jp/singi/keizaisaisei/pdf/en_saikou_jpn.pdf

Organisation for Economic Co-operation and Development (OECD). (2013). *Building blocks for smart networks.* OECD Digital Economy Papers No. 215. Retrieved from www.oecd-ilibrary.org/docserver/download/5k4dkhvnzv35.pdf?expires=1370327781&id=id&accname=guest&checksum=C302CA562778F89387AB1845EB2E0C11

Ofcom. (2008). *Identifying appropriate regulatory solutions: Principles for analysing self-and co-regulation.* Retrieved from http://stakeholders.ofcom.org.uk/binaries/consultations/coregulation/statement/statement.pdf

White House. (2009). *Open government initiative.* Retrieved from www.whitehouse.gov/open/documents/open-government-directive

White House. (2012). *Consumer data privacy in a networked world: A framework for protecting privacy and promoting innovation in the global digital economy.* Retrieved from www.whitehouse.gov/sites/default/files/privacy-final.pdf

7 Reconsidering the Telecommunications and Media Regulatory Framework in Taiwan

Using the Newly Emerging Media as Examples

Yu-li Liu

With the development of digital convergence, new media platforms have rapidly emerged. The first was Internet Protocol television (IPTV), followed by mobile TV. One of the most recent was the "Over-the-Top" (OTT) video service. As Benjamin and colleagues (2012) point out, the Internet challenges the entire notion of video channels. Internet video is sometimes called OTT video because delivery is not tied to any particular legacy architecture. Users can access the content from any Internet-connected device and platform. Whenever a new technology or service emerges, the regulator needs to find out how to classify this new service. In the EU, the regulators are urged to use the "linear and nonlinear" classification to regulate different media. In Japan, the government has integrated four electronic media laws and has classified the audiovisual media into two categories: basic and general broadcasting. Both linear and basic media are more strictly regulated than nonlinear and general media. In the United States, newly emerging services such as OTT TV are considered to be information services; therefore, the Federal Communications Commission (FCC) does not have specific rules for them.

As is the case in other countries, Taiwan's communication laws also lag behind communications technology. Currently, four laws are related to converged media and services. They are the Telecommunications Act, the Radio and Television Act, the Cable Radio and Television Act, and the Satellite Broadcasting Act. When converged services such as IPTV emerged, the government did not know how to deal with them. After the converged regulator, the National Communications Commission (NCC), was established in February 2006, it took a full year to add some articles to the fixed line regulation in order to handle IPTV. However, the NCC realized that this was only a temporary measure. Like IPTV, OTT TV also raises new questions: Should the NCC govern OTT TV and legacy media with the same regulation, or should it regulate them differently? Which policy model or paradigm should the NCC adopt? Clearly, a new regulatory framework is needed to deal with the newly converged media services. This chapter aims to analyze the appropriate regulatory framework and regulations for the newly emerging media such as IPTV and OTT TV in Taiwan. The research methods employed include literature reviews and surveys.

Major Communication Law Paradigms in the World

Since the laws and regulations for media platforms have become outdated as a result of digital convergence, a revision of the regulatory framework is deemed necessary by many countries. There are currently two major paradigms for communication legislation in regard to convergence policy. The first is the United States' "silo" model of regulation. The second is EU's "horizontal" model of regulation.

The United States' Silo Model of Regulation

In the United States, different media are regulated differently, even if they deliver the same content, because there may be different social impacts based on the delivery technology. For instance, terrestrial broadcasters are more strictly regulated than cable television because they use the so-called "scarce spectrum," even though some critics have argued that spectrum is not scarce in the digital world (Benjamin et al., 2012). The Communications Act of 1934 has seven titles. Figure 7.1 illustrates that each title regulates different media or telecommunication carriers based on their technical characteristics, types of functions, and so forth. Therefore, this vertical approach is commonly referred to as the "silo model."

However, this approach faces challenges with the presence of digital convergence. Werbach (2002) argued that since convergence allows different platforms to provide similar services, viewers may now watch programs via the Internet that were once only available on cable TV. Different platforms

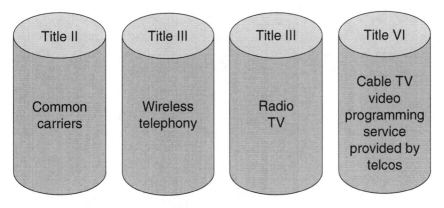

Figure 7.1   Silo model of regulation.
Source: Adapted from Whitt (2004) and the Communications Act of 1934

are becoming more and more difficult to distinguish from each other, and therefore a vertical approach may not be suitable anymore (Flew, 2012; Adler, 2013). Frieden (2003) also identifies four limitations with the silo approach. First, the distinctions between services can no longer be identified because of convergence. Second, the classification is not mutually exclusive as to the category in which a service belongs. Third, each category of service may have links with other categories. Finally, the silo approach inadequately considers the relationship between network architecture and the services provided to the users.

The EU's Horizontal Approach
The EU's regulatory framework for electronic communications can be considered to be a horizontal approach. In 2002, the EU adopted a new regulatory framework for electronic communications to encourage competition in the electronic communications markets (EU, 2002). The Framework Directive introduced technology-neutral definitions of "electronic communications networks" (ECN) and "electronic communications services" (ECS) as key concepts for delineating the scope of the electronic communications regulatory package (which covers, simply put, networks and transmission services).

With regard to content, electronic media are regulated by the Audiovisual Media Services Directive (AVMSD), which covers all audiovisual content irrespective of the technology used to deliver the content. The AVMSD makes a distinction between linear (television broadcasts) and nonlinear (on-demand) services. Linear service means that the service is for simultaneous viewing on the basis of a program schedule. Nonlinear service means that programs are viewed "at the moment chosen by the user and at his individual request on the basis of a catalogue of programs selected by the media service provider" (EU, 2010). The AVMSD applies only to providers under EU jurisdiction. It does not apply to content delivered over the Internet from countries outside the EU (Valcke & Lievens, 2009; Onay, 2009).

With the increasing popularity of and improvements to various handsets and devices, viewers may now access the same content over both linear and nonlinear platforms. The distinction between these two platforms is no longer obvious to the audience. In response to this change, the European Commission released a "Green Paper on Preparing for a Fully Converged Audiovisual World: Growth, Creation and Values" in April 2013. The objective of this Green Paper is to invite the stakeholders to share their views on the changing media landscape and Internet as well as the market conditions, interoperability and infrastructure, and implications for EU rules. The Green Paper (European Commission, 2013) addresses the issues in regard to the current regulation on audiovisual media content, as well as the preservation of creativity, cultural diversity, and consumer protection. It asks whether there is evidence of market distortion caused by the regulatory differentiation between linear and nonlinear services. Is there a need to adapt the definition of audiovisual media services (AVMS) providers or the scope of the AVMSD? In addition, in which areas could emphasis be given to self- and coregulation (European Commission, 2013)?

The Strength and Weakness of the Layered Model of Regulation

The layered policy model is a conceptual framework and can be used to provide a unified regulatory direction for the newly evolving media and services.[1] It is proposed by some U.S. scholars and experts who argue that current U.S. regulations are no longer appropriate for the converged services (Werbach, 2002). Some scholars may consider the EU's horizontal approach to be a kind of layered model. In fact, the EU framework is "a set of approved regulations that are being currently implemented by member states," whereas the layered model is "a tool to help policy makers establish a unified policy model" that facilitates "consistent, systematic treatment" of issues (Sicker & Mindel, 2002; Mindel & Sicker, 2006). When the idea of a layered model is used by policy makers, the layers vary from two to five layers (Cuilenburg & Verhoest, 1998). The two-layer model comprises infrastructure and content. The three-layer model adds a layer for service (Fransman, 2002; Liu, 2004).

The useful part of the layered model is that it provides a unified legal framework for the converged services. It can prevent the phenomenon that the same services provided by different technologies are regulated differently. It also encourages deregulation for the upper layers such as the content and application layer. The industry will have more flexibility in its management and can increase innovation and efficiency (Liu, 2004). For instance, if the broadcasters only want to be content providers, they do not need to build transmission towers. They can use others' facilities if they want. It is a so-called separation of transmission and content. The entry barrier for each layer is lower and easier than in the vertical structure. All the players can be innovative and flexible.

However, the defect of the layered model is that it is only a concept or framework and cannot solve all the problems the regulators and industry are facing every day. Sicker and Blumensaadt (2005) also point out the existence of various misunderstandings regarding the layered model. Nevertheless, the layered model can be regarded as a major paradigm shift from vertical to horizontal regulation (Liu, 2011).

Japan's New Approach

When the IPTV technology appeared, the Japanese government drew up a specific law that was referred to as the "Law Concerning the Broadcasting of Telecommunications Services" to regulate IPTV. In 2006, the Ministry of Internal Affairs and Communications (MIC) started to review the comprehensive structure to enable convergent services. Originally, it planned to integrate all the telecommunications laws and electronic media laws into one comprehensive law based on the layered model (Sugaya, 2009). However, in 2010, Japan decided to only merge four electronic media laws into one Broadcasting Act, under which broadcasters are categorized as either basic broadcasters or general broadcasters. Basic broadcasting means broadcasting using radio frequencies, such as terrestrial broadcasting, Broadcasting Satellite (BS) broadcasting (a Direct-to-Home TV service), and 110°E Communication Satellite (CS) broadcasting. General broadcasting covers broadcasting by means other than those specified for basic broadcasting, such as 124/128°E CS broadcasting, cable TV, and IPTV (Ministry of Internal Affairs and Communications [MIC], 2010).

Regulations Towards IPTV and OTT

Whenever a new technology or service emerges, the regulator needs to find out how to deal with that innovation. When IPTV services appeared in the market, various countries adopted different approaches to regulate IPTV (Tadayoni & Sigurdsson, 2006). In the United States, the Telecommunications Law of 1996 stipulates that the telecommunications service provider can provide video service via an open video system. However, some local governments think that if the telecom company wishes to provide the video service in the local market, it still has to apply for a franchise from the local government. Until now, the FCC has not made a decision on the legal classification of IPTV. In the case of the ruling for AT&T's IPTV service (U-Verse), the District Court reversed the ruling of Public Utility Control and decided that the IPTV service U-Verse was in fact a cable service and should therefore be subject to rulings related to franchise fees and other regulations under the 1984 Cable Act (Office of Consumer Counsel v. S. New Eng. Tel. Co., 2007).

Compared with the United States, the government of the United Kingdom seems to have different views. David Harrison, former head of broadcast and new media technology at Ofcom, said that if IPTV provides a video-on-demand service only, no regulation is involved. It will be up to the Authority for Television on Demand (ATVOD) (and ultimately Ofcom, as the appeal body) to decide.[2] If, on the other hand, IPTV carries channels, broadcast regulation can be applied. With regard to the Internet content, this is subject to self-regulation (Informitv, 2005).

In Japan, the Law Concerning the Broadcasting of Telecommunications Services was enacted in 2001 to allow telecommunications operators to multicast live channels. According to the law, registration is only needed for telecommunication operators to provide IP multicasting. In 2010, the IPTV law was integrated into the new Broadcasting Act. Under the new law, IPTV is deemed to be a general broadcaster similar to cable television. To obtain the license for a general broadcaster, the operator should register with the regulator.

Aside from IPTV, OTT services have also brought challenges to the regulators in many countries (Kim, Chang, & Park, 2012). Nowadays, users increasingly have access to content and choices via the OTT video platform, and entry barriers for users to be "prosumers" are relatively low. Content providers can increase the number of distribution channels to reach consumers via OTT platforms. To compete with the existing media platforms, the OTT service providers have to adapt their practices and strategies in the wake of copyright law and quality of service provisions.

If one takes the United States as an example, aside from stressing network neutrality to ensure fair competition in the market, there is no regulation governing OTT services. Countries such as Australia, New Zealand, and Japan are also leaning toward the American approach. These countries do not require licenses from OTT, and therefore they are more lenient when it comes to regulating the newly emerging services. However, child protection and indecent and unlawful content are still regulated to varying degrees in these countries (Peng & Cheng, 2013; National Communications Commission [NCC], 2013).

Compared with the United States, the EU's regulation is more strict when it comes to OTT services. Under AVMSD, on-demand services also have to respect the basic tier of obligations such as no incitement to hatred based on race, sex, religion, or nationality. When the media service provider selects the content and determines the manner in which it is organized, its service is subject to the AVMSD even if the content is delivered over the Internet. In most member states, this implies that registration will be required for the OTT service providers.[3] However, countries such as China and Singapore even require the OTT service providers to obtain licenses before entering the market (Peng & Cheng, 2013; NCC, 2013).

CASE STUDY: TAIWAN'S IPTV LAW AND POLICY

Which Law Applies to CHT's IPTV Service?

In Taiwan, before the Cable Radio and Television Act was revised in 1999, there was a ban on telecommunications and cable TV cross-ownership in Taiwan. After the ban was lifted, Chunghwa Telecom (CHT) thought about providing IPTV service, for which it adopted the name "multimedia-on-demand" (MOD). Since MOD was a newly converged service, when CHT wanted to provide the MOD service in 2001, there was much debate regarding how the MOD should be regulated. Which law could be applied to regulate the service? Was the IPTV a telecommunications service that was subject to the Telecommunications Law? Or was it a cable TV service subject to the Cable Radio and Television Act? Or should it be regulated by a new converged law?

The former telecommunications regulator, the Directorate General of Telecommunications (DGT), thought that, according to Article 2 of the Telecommunications Act, telecommunications referred to the "conveyance, transmission or reception of signs, signals, writing, pictures, sounds or messages of any other nature in a wired or wireless manner through the use of optical, electromagnetic systems, or other scientific products" (Telecommunications Act, 2007). CHT was a Type I telecommunications enterprise. Therefore, if CHT provided IPTV service, it should be subject to the Telecommunications Act. The DGT said that the government should give the new service some room to develop as long as it served the public interest. However, the former broadcasting regulator, the Government Information Office (GIO), contended that, according to Article 2 of the Cable Radio and Television Act, "cable radio and television" referred to the transmission of images and sound through cable for direct viewing and listening by the public. Therefore, regardless of the technology that CHT used for its MOD service, as long as it transmitted images and sound with a line (a cable), it should be within its jurisdiction and thus CHT needed to apply for a license for its MOD service. Obviously, the two government agencies had different points of view regarding how a new service like CHT's MOD should be regulated.

At the end of 2002, a technology committee within the Legislative Yuan instructed the GIO to let CHT provide its MOD service on a trial basis.[4] Following the requirement that it adhered to the Cable Radio and Television Act, CHT submitted a proposal in January 2003. It was finally issued a license by the GIO to operate in a few cities in February 2004.

Facing a Dilemma Caused by the Government Shares

If CHT's MOD service was considered to be a type of cable TV service, it had to abide by the Cable Radio and Television Act. CHT did not object to following the Cable Radio and Television Act as long as it could provide MOD service. However, the revised Articles 19 and 20 of the Cable Radio and Television Act had made it difficult to continue to provide the MOD service. In December 2003, the Legislative Yuan passed a resolution requiring the government and the political parties to dispose of their shares in all the electronic media by December 2005. Since 41% of CHT's shares at that time were still owned by the government, CHT faced a dilemma: it either had to dispose of its government share by the deadline or receive penalties, either in the form of fines or the revocation of its license from the regulator. Since the MOD service at that time only occupied a small part of CHT's business, CHT did not want to consider divesting all the government shares.

The New Regulator's Interpretation of CHT's MOD Service

According to the NCC Organization Act, the roles of the DGT and the GIO regarding telecommunications and broadcasting regulations were both replaced by the NCC after it was established in February 2006. For this reason the NCC had to decide whether CHT had violated the revised Cable Radio and Television Act.

New Service Versus Regulatory Parity

Faced with the issue of whether CHT needed to withdraw its government shares because of its MOD service, the NCC considered four relevant laws: the Cable Radio and Television Act, the Telecommunications Act, the NCC Organization Act, and the Fundamental Communications Act (FCA). If the NCC were to classify IPTV as a type of cable TV, the Cable Radio and Television Act would be applicable. Accordingly, this would force CHT to make a decision: to withdraw its government shares, to close its MOD service, to sell MOD to a third party, or to face the threat of its license being revoked. If the NCC were to classify IPTV as a telecommunications value-added service, the Telecommunications Law would be applicable. CHT would then be asked to open its platform to all the content providers and all the Internet service providers (ISPs). In addition, its MOD service would have to avoid being regarded as a cable TV–type of service.

The FCA was passed in January 2004. It established important and fundamental principles for all the telecommunications and electronic media laws. Article 16 of this act gave the NCC the authority to interpret the telecommunications and broadcasting laws based on the FCA if there was a conflict between the existing laws and the FCA. Even though the NCC seemed to have much leeway to interpret the laws in regards to new technologies or new services, it believed that the consistency of the government regulations was also important. For this reason it would not apply Article 16 capriciously of its own volition unless all the provisions of existing laws had been exhausted. When the IPTV issue was considered, there was a conflict between Articles 6 and 7 of the FCA. Article 6 of the FCA stipulated that "the government shall encourage new telecommunications technology and new service. Without proper reason, there should be no restrictions on the new technologies and new services. The interpretation of the telecommunications-related laws should not obstruct the development of the new technologies and new services" (Fundamental Communications Act, 2004). According to Article 6, it seemed that the NCC should encourage new services such as CHT's MOD service. Therefore, the NCC did not have to apply the Cable Radio and Television Act to a new service such as CHT's MOD.

However, Article 7 of the FCA stipulated that "the government shall avoid regulatory disparity among different transmission technologies. The allocation of the scarce resources can be exempted." Therefore, if CHT's MOD also provided channels to its subscribers like cable TV, it became a provider of cable TV–like services. Article 7 would mandate regulatory parity when the withdrawal of the government share was involved.

The NCC's Decision

Before the NCC made its decisions regarding CHT's MOD government share issue, it invited all the relevant telecommunication companies, cable TV associations, telecommunications and broadcasting scholars, and public interest groups to express their views in April 2007. Most of the telecommunications scholars urged the NCC to apply Article 6 of the FCA. The broadcasting scholars and the consumers groups emphasized that the NCC should encourage the development of different digital platforms and promote consumer choice in connection with TV services. The cable operators contended that Article 7 of the FCA was much fairer to the industry. They urged the NCC to fine CHT for its MOD service right away. They stressed that regulation parity was more important than the new service. After several meetings of the Commission and the working group meetings within the NCC, the NCC announced its decision in June 2007. It said that if CHT's MOD service opened up its platform completely, it would not be regarded as a cable system, nor would it have to withdraw its government shares as required by the Cable Radio and Television Act.[5] Having no other choice, CHT agreed that it would avoid the characteristics of cable TV such as the closed system from the head end to the consumers.

Accordingly, the NCC revised the Regulations for Administration of Fixed Network Telecommunications Business by adding Article 60-1 to regulate CHT's MOD. The NCC used the term "Multimedia Content Distribution Platform Service" (MCDP) to regulate CHT's MOD. It asked all the channel providers on CHT's MOD platform to obtain licenses pursuant to the Radio and Television Act, Cable Radio and Television Act, or Satellite Broadcasting Act. The MCDP has to abide by fairness and nondiscrimination principles when it rents its platform to the content providers. In addition, it cannot interfere with the channel provider's program planning, sales, and rates. As a matter of fact, before the NCC reached its decision, there were hot debates about how to deal with CHT's MOD issue in the Commission Meeting. The majority of the Commission accepted this open platform decision, but one commissioner contended that the NCC should pass a rule that could regulate all the IPTV service providers rather than only dealing with CHT's special case(Liu, 2007). After this decision, there was no legal definition for IPTV in Taiwan's telecommunications laws and regulations. Instead, the NCC created a new term for IPTV in Taiwan, which is referred to as MCDP. In other words, superficially, there is no IPTV in Taiwan. However, the IPTV service provider has to act as an MCDP by following the revised fixed network regulation.

The Regulator's Policy Toward OTT Video Services

By September 2013, the fourth-term NCC commissioners still had not formally dealt with the issues of OTT video services. Unlike the United States, the United Kingdom, France, and Korea, Taiwan's OTT video services have not been confronted by network neutrality issues. It is not clear whether any ISP has boycotted an OTT service in Taiwan. The only concern is that there is no content regulation for OTT TV. Furthermore, the content and shopping service providers on the OTT platform do not need to obtain licenses (NCC, 2013). For this reason, fair competition becomes an issue.

In Taiwan, the existing media platforms have to pay attention to the development of the OTT video because their ratings and revenues may decrease due to the newly emerging media platform. Since cable TV penetration exceeds 80%, content providers are afraid of being boycotted by the cable operators if they sell their content to other platforms such as IPTV or OTT. Therefore, the OTT video services might have difficulty acquiring good content for their viewers.

Like IPTV, OTT TV also faces the question: Should the NCC govern OTT TV and legacy media with the same regulation, or should it regulate them differently? In terms of regulating a newly emerging media like OTT video services, the NCC has not discussed this issue formally in its Commission Meetings. Currently, it holds the view that not all OTT content falls under its jurisdiction. OTT services can be divided into linear, nonlinear, within the country, and outside of the country. The NCC may regulate the OTT service providers located within the country. If the content delivered via OTT is linear, then the same regulations for cable TV shall apply. If the content delivered via OTT is nonlinear, the NCC may refer to the Protection of Children and Youths Welfare and Rights Act to see if there is any indecency or obscenity (NCC, 2013). As of now, the regulations regarding OTT video services are still vague in Taiwan.

Attempting to Add a Special Chapter to the Telecommunications Act to Cope with the Newly Emerging Media

In order to cope with the newly emerging media such as IPTV and OTT, the NCC proposed adding a special chapter to the Telecommunications Act. In this chapter, Type 1 and Type 2 telephone companies can provide audiovisual media services and value-added services. The NCC applied the layered model and tried to make the regulation equivalent to other media platforms. For instance, the channel providers on the audiovisual media service platform also have to apply for licenses in accordance with the Radio and Television Act and the Satellite Broadcasting Act. There should be no discrimination against those who want to use this platform. However, if the service such as OTT video service is not pervasive and does not guarantee quality of service, there is no need to obtain a license, and the service is not subject to any content regulation. Therefore only the general law applies. Self-regulation and coregulation mechanisms are encouraged for this type of OTT service. Some experts have criticized this special chapter for having neglected one thing, which is that some OTT service providers may not be telephone companies (Peng & Cheng, 2013). In this case, this special chapter cannot be applied to their practices. Therefore, this proposed chapter is not thoughtful and comprehensive.

Options for Accommodating Convergence in Taiwan: Separate Laws or Convergence Law

The Draft of the Telecommunications Administrative Act

In addition to IPTV, other converged services such as digital audio broadcast (DAB) have also encountered many problems caused by outdated legislation. For instance, the DAB operators could not provide data service unless they adhered to the Telecommunications Act. However, before the Telecommunications Act was revised, the DAB operators were not qualified to provide telecom service because they were considered to be broadcasters. These examples clearly show that the existing laws are outdated (Liu, 2011).

In order to cope with the convergence issues, the first-term NCC commissioners decided to integrate the Telecommunications Act and three broadcasting-related laws into one comprehensive law. The NCC adopted a three-layer framework that aims to offer consistent regulatory criteria to operators running comparable businesses, encourages flexible and creative business models, and represents a shift from vertical regulation to horizontal regulation. The three layers include the Content & Application Layer, the Service/Platform Layer, and the Infrastructure/Network Layer. The NCC finished its first draft of the integrated law and subsequently held two public consultations in September and November 2007 (Liu, 2013).

Stakeholders' Responses to the 2007 Converged Legal Framework

The NCC only gave the public two weeks to submit their opinions in response to the proposed converged law. The stakeholders all complained that the period was too short for public consultation. They said that the impact of the new law on the industry would be huge. The NCC should at least conduct a Regulatory Impact Analysis (RIA) before it introduced its converged law (Liu, 2011).

In the draft bill, the NCC only asked the service/platform providers to provide network interconnection. Most of the stakeholders suggested that the network layer should also bear the responsibility for network interconnection. In regard to the service layer, some stakeholders questioned the NCC as to why the telecommunications services and broadcasting services were still regulated differently within this layer. The public interest groups also voiced concerns about domestic and locally produced programs and media concentration issues. They opposed lifting the cross-media ownership restriction and relaxing foreign investment regulations for some media. In addition to the media sector, there was also concern over not regulating foreign investment within the network layer. The NCC explained that foreign owners could not take away the facilities in which they invest. When faced with convergence, most of the stakeholders were concerned with the definition of the market. What constituted the market was unclear in the draft. Some stakeholders also complained that there was too much delegation of power to the regulator. The articles of the comprehensive law should be very specific. The draft bill should not leave too much room for the regulator to interpret its stipulations (Liu, 2011; Chien, 2007).

Even though the draft was opposed and questioned by the telecom and media industries as well as academics, because of time constraints, the NCC submitted the draft of the converged law to the Executive Yuan in December 2007. It came as no surprise that the Executive Yuan returned the draft of the integrated law to the NCC in April 2008.

The Digital Convergence Development Policy Initiative

When the second-term NCC commissioners took office in August 2008, they only amended the separate laws. So the adoption of the draft comprehensive law was put off. In July 2010, the Executive Yuan announced the Digital Convergence Development Policy Initiative (DCDPI), which included three main objectives for development within the time frame of 2010–2015: (1) build a sound digital convergent environment, (2) provide good convergent services, and (3) promote cross-industry competition. The DCDPI evaluated the current situation from the market and regulatory perspectives and indicated that regulations for broadcasting and telecommunication services were outdated because the distinctions between different platforms were blurred by technology. Table 7.1 shows the inconsistent regulations between the Telecommunications Act and three broadcasting-related acts.

For instance, in terms of structural regulations, the minimum capital requirement is low for electronic media, but it is high for the major telecom business. The foreign investment limitation is stricter for electronic media, but it is more lenient for telcos. The government and the political parties cannot invest in electronic media, but there is no restriction on government ownership in telecommunications. Cable TV can only provide services in its designated area, but telephone companies can run at the national, regional, or local level. There are horizontal and vertical integration restrictions for cable TV, but there are no such restrictions for telcos.

With regard to behavioral regulations, terrestrial TV is vertically managed, but telcos like CHT cannot be involved in content production. The "must-carry" rule is applied to cable TV, but it cannot be applied to telcos' IPTV. There are two-tier rate regulations for cable TV, but the rate regulation only applies to Type 1 telcos and the dominant players. Cable TV has to reserve a channel for public access. IPTV does not have to provide public access to local people. However, there are interconnection and universal service obligations for Type 1 telcos.

Table 7.1 Comparisons between the electronic media laws and the Telecommunications Act

	Radio and Television Act, Cable Radio and Television Act, Satellite Broadcasting Act	Telecommunications Act
Structural Regulations	Minimum capital requirement is low.	Minimum capital requirement is high for the major telcos.
	More foreign capital restriction.	Less foreign capital restriction.
	Government and the political parties cannot invest in broadcasting- related media.	No restriction for government ownership.
	Cable TV can only provide services in its designated area.	Has national, regional, and local service.
	Has horizontal and vertical integration ownership restriction for cable TV.	No horizontal and vertical integration ownership restriction.
Behavior Regulations	Terrestrial TV is vertically managed.	Not involved in content production (refers to CHT's case).
	"Must carry" rule applies to cable TV.	No "must carry" rule for IPTV.
	Two-tier rate regulation for cable TV.	Only has rate regulations for Type 1 telcos and dominant players.
	Cable TV has to reserve a channel for public access.	There are interconnection, universal service obligations for Type 1 telcos.

Source: Digital Convergence Development Policy Initiative (Executive Yuan, 2010)

The DCDPI called for a two-stage regulatory revision to help promote the development of digital convergence. In the first stage (from 2010 to 2012), the NCC was to immediately amend the outdated articles of the Radio and Television Act, Cable Radio and Television Act, Satellite Broadcasting Act, and Telecommunications Act. These revisions were to be drafted by the NCC and sent to the Legislative Yuan for deliberation after being approved by the Executive Yuan. In the second stage (from 2013 to 2014), the NCC was to follow the layered regulatory model and complete a convergence regulatory framework. The resulting draft was to be passed by the Legislative Yuan by June 2014.

Since the revision of legislation is by nature a lengthy process, it requires more than one term of office for the commissioners to work it through. The second-term and the third-term NCC commissioners took office in 2008 and 2010, but they only focused on revising the separate laws. When the fourth-term NCC commissioners took office in 2012, they were still working on the amendment of separate laws. However, in July 2013, when the Executive Yuan reviewed the amendment of the Telecommunications Act presented by the NCC, Minister without Portfolio Simon Chang urged the NCC to submit a forward-looking integrated convergence law as indicated in the DCDPI to replace the current Telecommunications Act as well as three broadcasting-related acts. The NCC agreed to submit the draft bill of the convergence law to the Executive Yuan in February 2014 (Shih, 2013). As of October of 2013, the NCC has not released its draft bill for public consultation.

Stakeholder's Opinions Regarding the Converged Law

In early 2013, the author conducted two surveys on stakeholders' opinions on the convergence law and content regulation across different platforms. Respondents who took part in the studies were selected from telecommunications carriers, cable operators, channel providers, broadcasters, industry associations, experts, government officials, and scholars who were aware of the laws and government policy related to digital convergence. Each of the categories had 10 respondents. The first survey collected 79 valid samples. The second survey collected 69 samples because some telecommunication carriers were not considered to be qualified to answer the questions related to content regulation.

According to the survey results, 50.6% (40 out of 79) of the respondents would like to integrate the current laws, while 13.9% would like to amend the separate laws first and then integrate them. This means that 64.5% of the respondents favored an integrated law. Only 15.2% of the respondents suggested the amendment of separate laws. For those who agreed with the convergence law, 36% supported a two-stage amendment, and 36% supported a one-time amendment (see Table 7.2). In addition, 28% of the respondents thought that the government only needed to integrate the electronic media laws (Liu, 2013). In addition to the amendment of the convergence law, the author also asked the respondents whether they agreed that the content regulation across platforms should be consistent: 63% of the respondents agreed that the content regulation across platforms should be consistent, and 30% of the respondents disagreed. Most of the respondents preferred to adopt the EU's horizontal model for content regulation. Interestingly, most of the respondents felt that the Internet should be regulated; however, there was no clear consensus on the applicable laws.

Table 7.2 Stakeholders' opinions about the Converged Act

Questions	Options	Telecom	Cable	Channel	Radio & TV	Trade Association	Experts	Officers	Scholars	Total
How should the NCC amend the laws to accommodate convergence?	Amend separate laws	3	1	2	2	1	3	0	0	12
	Create new laws for the new media	1	0	0	0	0	0	0	2	3
	Merge current laws	5	6	4	3	7	6	4	5	40
	Amend separate laws and then merge	1	1	0	1	1	1	5	1	11
	Others	0	2	4	3	1	0	1	2	13
Options for the convergence law	Only merge 3 broadcasting-related laws	0	0	2	1	1	2	2	1	9
	Only merge 4 broadcasting-related laws	0	2	0	0	0	1	1	1	5
	Two stages: Merge 3 broadcasting-related laws, then merge Telecommunications Act	0	0	2	2	0	0	4	2	10

Two stages: Merge 4 broadcasting-related laws, then merge Telecommunications Act	4	0	0	1	1	1	0	1	8
Integrate 3 broadcasting-related laws and Telecommunications Act at one time	1	0	2	0	2	3	1	1	10
Integrate 4 broadcasting-related laws and Telecommunications Act at one time	0	1	0	0	1	0	2	0	4
Merge 6 laws at one time	0	0	0	0	0	0	0	0	0
Merge 7 laws at one time	0	1	0	0	0	0	0	0	1
Merge 8 laws at one time	0	2	0	0	0	1	0	0	3
Others	1	1	0	0	2	0	1	0	5

CONCLUSION

In recent years, the adoption of the layered policy model has become the regulatory trend for many nations. In order to cope with the impact of convergence on the communications laws and regulations, Taiwan's regulatory paradigm has also shifted from the United States' silo approach to the EU's horizontal approach. Although the NCC has announced that it will submit a comprehensive draft bill to the Executive Yuan by February 2014, it is speculated that the suggested deadline will be too tight to ensure that a comprehensive version of the law that can satisfy most of the stakeholders is drawn up.

The author suggests that the Radio and Television Act, Cable Radio and Television Act, and Satellite Broadcasting Act can be integrated first. Meanwhile, the government can think of how to merge the integrated broadcasting law with the Telecommunications Act. The merged draft law should be based on the policies and goals the government has been trying to achieve instead of just writing a new law. During the period in which the laws are amended, it is not necessary to add a specific chapter to the Telecommunications Act to regulate the newly emerging media. The articles of the specific chapter can be combined with those of the integrated broadcasting law. Both Japan and Korea have drafted specific acts to regulate IPTV, but after several years, Japan integrated its IPTV law into the converged Broadcasting Act in 2010. Unlike Japan and Korea, Taiwan has chosen to revise the fixed network regulation to let CHT provide its IPTV service to consumers. The regulator has determined that it will not write a new law for the new service.

Currently, even though the government in Taiwan wants to have a comprehensive convergence law, such drafting should not be rushed in order to meet an arbitrary deadline. Interaction with all the stakeholders is needed to find the most appropriate solution. The layered model emphasizes that the regulation should be consistent in the same layer no matter what technology the platform uses. However, since immediate regulatory parity is impossible, the suggestion is for Taiwan to take gradual steps in response to the changing and rapidly developing technology. Meanwhile, the balance of interests between different stakeholders can be harmonized if the regulator gives them enough time to react. If Taiwan adopts Japan's approach in amending the broadcasting-related laws, the regulator has to treat IPTV and cable TV equally because they are both considered to be "general broadcasting." In this case, the government has to reevaluate its policy of the nongovernment share in the media because CHT has government shares. Otherwise, CHT's MOD will face the same dilemma once more. With regard to the OTT video service, the NCC might consider the EU's AVMSD for reference purposes. At this stage, the NCC's preliminary thinking is that if the OTT video service is not pervasive and does not guarantee quality of service, it does not need to apply for a license. It should be subject to general legal provisions such as the Protection of Children and Youths Welfare and Rights Act. In other words, the regulation for the OTT service should only be kept to a minimum, and self-regulation should be encouraged.

NOTES

1. The earliest layered model is the Open System Interconnection Reference Model (OSI model), which is an abstract description for layered communications and computer network protocol design. It divides network architecture into seven layers: physical, data-link, network, transport, session, presentation, and application.
2. See chapter 2 of this book by Valcke and Ausloos, who discuss the interpretation by ATVOD and Ofcom (which do not always share the same views) of what constitutes an on-demand program service that falls within the scope of the broadcasting rules.
3. This is not the AVMSD imposing such registration requirement. Most member states require a license or at least a notification in order to be able to monitor the service's compliance with the rules in the AVMSD. See chapter 2 of this book by Valcke and Ausloos.
4. The Legislative Yuan, referred to as the "parliament," is one of the five branches of government in Taiwan.
5. The measures related to an open platform include the following:

(1) Allow all interested channels, video-on-demand (VOD), and application service providers to use CHT's MOD platform.
(2) Let the customers of other ISPs be connected with CHT's MOD platform.
(3) Allow other aggregators to use CHT's MOD platform.
(4) Let the customers of other fixed networks be connected with CHT's MOD platform.

Also, CHT has to change its business models. It cannot originate channels or manage channels. Other aggregators have the freedom to manage channels themselves.

REFERENCES

Adler, R. (2013). *Rethinking communications regulation.* Report of the 27th Annual Aspen Institute Conference on Communications Policy. Washington, DC: Aspen Institute.

Benjamin, S.M., Lichtman, D.G., Shelanski, H.A., & Weiser, P.J. (2012). *Telecommunications law and policy.* Durham, NC: Carolina Academic Press.

Chien, W.K. (2007). From the convergence of technologies to the convergence of regulations: Reviews of NCC policies. *Technology Law Review, 4,* 227.

Cuilenburg, J., & Verhoest, P. (1998). Free and equal access: In search of policy models for converging communication systems. *Telecommunications Policy, 22*(3), 171–181.

European Commission. (2013). *Green paper on preparing for a fully converged audiovisual world: growth, creation and values.* Brussels, April 24, 2013, COM(2013) 231 final. Retrieved from http://eur-lex.europa.eu/LexUriServ/LexUriServ.do?uri=COM:2013:0231:FIN:EN:PDF

EU. (2010). *Audiovisual media services directive.* Retrieved from http://eur-lex.europa.eu/LexUriServ/LexUriServ.do?uri=CELEX:32010L0013:EN:NOT

EU. (2002). Directive 2002/21/EC of the European Parliament and of the Council of 7 March 2002 on a common regulatory framework for electronic communications networks and services (Framework Directive). *Official Journal of the European Communities, L 108*, 33–50.

Executive Yuan. (2010). *Digital convergence development policy initiative*. Taiwan. Retrieved from www.ey.gov.tw/Upload/RelFile/26/75806/012916565471.pdf

Flew, T. (2012). Media classification: Content regulation in an age of convergent media. *Media International Australia, 143*, 5–15.

Fransman, M. (2002, October). Mapping the evolving telecoms industry: The uses and shortcomings of the layer model. *Telecommunications Policy, 26*(9), 473–483.

Frieden, R. (2003). Adjusting the horizontal and vertical in telecommunications regulation: A comparison of the traditional and a new layered approach. *Federal Communications Law Journal, 55*(2), 207.

Fundamental Communications Act (2004). Retrieved from NCC website, www.ncc. gov.tw/english/files/07090/17_366_070907_1.pdf.

Informitv. (2005). *IPTV world forum conference report*. Retrieved from http://infor mitv.com/news/2005/03/09/iptvworldforum/

Kim, Y., Chang, Y., & Park, M. (2012). Smart TV business regulation and collaboration among business operators and regulators: Focus on the case analysis of smart TV blocking and IPTV regulation process in Korea. *The 19th ITS Biennial Conference 2012*. Thailand: National Broadcasting and Telecommunications Commission of Thailand (NBTC).

Liu, Y.L. (Ed.) (2004). *Telecommunications*. Taipei: Yeh Yeh Book Publishing.

Liu, Yu-li (2007, January 30). The dissenting opinion of the MOD's platform solution. *The 139th NCC Commission Meeting Record*. Retrieved from www.ncc. gov.tw/chinese/files/07052/67_1463_070608_1.pdf

Liu, Y.L. (2011). The impact of convergence on the telecommunications law and broadcasting-related laws: A comparison between Japan and Taiwan. *Keio Communication Review, 33*, 43–67.

Liu, Y.L. (2013). *Law and policy research of digital convergence: Communications platforms and content-related issues* (2). Taipei: NSC Research Report. Unpublished report.

Ministry of Internal Affairs and Communications (MIC). (2010). *Broadcasting Act*. Retrieved from www.soumu.go.jp/main_sosiki/joho_tsusin/eng/Resources/laws/ pdf/090204_5.pdf

Mindel, J., & Sicker, D.C. (2006). Leveraging the EU regulatory framework to improve a layered policy model for US telecommunications markets. *Telecommunications Policy, 30*(2), 136–148.

National Communications Commission (NCC). (2013). *Report on content regulation for broadcasting services in Taiwan*. NCC internal document.

Office of Consumer Counsel v. S. New Eng. Tel. Co., 514 F. Supp. 2d 345, 351 (D. Conn. 2007).

Onay, I. (2009). Regulating webcasting: An analysis of the Audiovisual Media Services Directive and the current broadcasting in the UK. *Computer Law & Security Review, 25*, 335–351.

Peng, S.Y., & Cheng, C.Y. (2013). The study of regulation toward newly emerging media platforms—Using OTT TV as an example. *NCP Newsletter, 53*, 13–15.

Shih, H.C. (2013, July 7). Cabinet sends back NCC proposal after review postponed. *Taipei Times*. Retrieved from www.taipeitimes.com/News/taiwan/archi ves/2013/07/17/2003567301.

Sicker, D., & Blumensaadt, L. (2005). Misunderstanding the layered models. *Journal on Telecommunications and High Technology Law* (Fall), 44–111.

Sicker, D. C., & Mindel, J. (2002). Refinements on a layered model for telecommunications policy. *Journal of Telecommunications and High Technology Law*, 1(1), 69–94.

Sugaya, M. (2009). The transformation of telecommunication regulatory structure in Japan: Vertical and horizontal perspectives. *Keio Communication Review*, 31, 23–36.

Tadayoni, R., & Sigurdsson, H. M. (2006). IPTV market development and regulatory aspects. In T. Lu, X. Liang, & X. Yan (Eds.), *16th Biennial conference of the International Telecommunications Society: Information and communication technology (ICT)*. Beijing: China Institute of Communication.

Telecommunications Act (2007). Revised version. Retrieved from NCC website, www.ncc.gov.tw/

Valcke, P., & Lievens, E. (2009). Rethinking European broadcasting regulation. In C. Pauwels et al. (Eds.), *Rethinking European media and communications policy*. Brussels: VUB Press.

Werbach, K. (2002). A layered model for internet policy. *Journal on Telecommunications and High Technology Law*, 1(1), 37–67.

Whitt, R. S. (2004). A horizontal leap forward: Formulating a new communications public policy framework based on the network layers model. *Federal Communications Law Journal*, 56(3), 587–672.

8 Japan's Legislative Framework for Telecommunications

Evolution toward Convergence of Communications and Broadcasting[1]

Yoko Nishioka and Minoru Sugaya

Japan's legislation pertaining to communications and broadcasting was reorganized in 2011 in response to a significant structural change in the industry, namely, the convergence of communications and broadcasting due to technological innovation. Over the last 20 years, major countries around the world have reformed their legislative frameworks to respond to the development of this converging market. The United States originated an integrated legislative framework for communications and broadcasting, which was then reformed in order to promote competition between cable televisions and communications companies in 1996. The European Union (EU) introduced a layered structure in its legislative framework with accompanying regulatory coverage in 2003.

Japan followed these movements 8 years later. The reorganization of eight relevant acts regulating the field of broadcasting into four successfully changed the legislative framework from one with a vertical structure to one with a horizontal structure. This reorganization for institutional change, the first in 60 years since the enactment of the Broadcast Act, ended up being more limited in scope than had been expected initially.

There have been very few studies on the Japanese reorganization. Sugaya (2009) analyzed the draft law from the perspective of the policy's economic rationality and the media's social role, such as securing the freedom of speech. Liu (2011) conducted comparative research between Taiwan and Japan to examine possible impacts of legal reform on convergence in each country. There exists neither research concerning the reorganization in Japan itself, nor any on the Japanese telecommunications legislative framework from the viewpoint of institutional change.

The purpose of this chapter is to reveal the nature and background of institutional change on the legislative framework for telecommunications in Japan from the viewpoint of Comparative Institutional Analysis (CIA) under the New Institutional Economics (NIE),[2] which has been developed to analyze various economic institutions considering political and social aspects and applied widely (Aoki et al., 2012; Aoki & Rothwell, 2012). It is also useful in explaining institutional change regardless of whether the given research is comparative or not.[3] This chapter summarizes the institutional changes from the beginning of the legislative framework that was created by the current major laws (i.e., the Telecommunications Business Act and the Broadcast Act) and examines the detailed process and actual regulatory changes of the reorganization for convergence in order to determine the nature of the accompanying institutional change and its background.

ANALYTICAL TOOLS AND OUTLINE OF JAPAN'S LEGISLATIVE FRAMEWORK FOR TELECOMMUNICATIONS

Comparative Institutional Analysis represents one of two major approaches[4] of institutional theories under the analytical paradigm of the New Institutional Economics and views institutions as mechanisms that contribute to the "equilibrium of the game," evolving endogenously through the interactions of economic agents (Aoki, 2001). CIA is based on evolutionary game theory and thereby considers institutional change as a transition to a new equilibrium. This, in turn, explains many aspects of the mechanisms of institutional change; for example, institutions tend to resist change, referring to the fact that equilibrium has a tendency toward inertia.[5] In other words, institutions are durable, and institutional change usually progresses only gradually, as long as destructive events, such as war or revolution, do not occur.

CIA also explains that among multiple equilibria, equilibrium actually occurs with path dependence, as explained by evolutionary game theory. Moreover, initial conditions significantly affect subsequent directions, or paths of development. Therefore, historical analysis is important in institutional analysis to reveal its path dependence.

This chapter follows the approach of CIA, examining the historical development from the beginning of the history and change of specific institutions, treating the legislative framework as an institution, and paying special attention to the "durability" of institutions and their "path dependence."

The main players involved in this "game" of law making in telecommunications are politicians, bureaucrats at the Ministry of Internal Affairs and Communications (MIC), communications companies, and broadcasters with jurisdiction over telecommunications, including broadcasting and communications businesses. Over time, the MIC has developed information and communication technology (hereinafter referred to as ICT) policies and laws in a setting where bureaucrats, rather than politicians, usually prepare bills as the experts. They also assist the industry with publication of administrative ordinances if there are problems involving industry regulation or compliance. It is one of the prominent characteristics of the regulatory environment in Japan that there is no independent regulatory committee for telecommunications.

In Japan, the major communications companies are Nippon Telegraph and Telephone Corporation (NTT), KDDI Corporation (KDDI), and Softbank

Table 8.1   Relationship between major broadcasters and national newspapers

Major broadcaster (A)	National newspaper company (B)	Relationship between A and B, as of March 31, 2013
Nippon Television Holdings	Yomiuri Shimbun Holdings	B holds 14.27% ownership of A's stock
Fuji Television Network	Sankei Shimbun Co., Ltd.	Fuji Media Holdings, Inc. holds 100% of A's stock and 45.4% of B's
Tokyo Broadcasting System Holdings, Inc.	Mainichi Newspapers	B's president and representative director is a board member of A
TV Asahi Corporation	Asahi Shimbun Company	B holds 24.73% ownership of A's stock

Note: This table was created by data collected from the securities reports of the broadcasters or their holding companies, as of March 31, 2013. Fuji Media Holdings, Inc., 2013, p. 9–10; Nippon Television Holdings, 2013, p. 31; Tokyo Broadcasting System Holdings, Inc., 2013, p. 44; TV Asahi Corporation, 2013, p. 25.

Corp. (Softbank). As for broadcasting, there is National Broadcasters Association in Japan (NAB),[6] consisting of terrestrial and major satellite broadcasters and usually funded by major terrestrial broadcasters (205 in total as of April 2013), as well as the public broadcaster, Nippon Hoso Kyokai (NHK, Japan Broadcasting Corporation). It should be noted that each of the groups of major private broadcasters is financially connected with different national newspaper companies (see Table 8.1). Commentators of TV news are very often from parent newspaper companies, and together they have opposed any bills that represent a threat to mass media activities. For example, the Privacy Protection Bill and Protection of Human Rights Bill in 2002 were labeled as "mass media restriction bills" and were thoroughly criticized for their possible restrictions on mass media research, regardless of their substance.

Cable television usually retransmits terrestrial and satellite channels, with the exception of a very limited number of channels. The major free satellite channels were controlled by major terrestrial broadcasters, and there are also many small independent thematic channels.

TRANSFORMATION OF TELECOMMUNICATIONS REGULATIONS COMMUNICATIONS: GRADUAL MODIFICATIONS FOR INCREASING COMPETITION

Barriers to market entry were broken down in 1985, when the NTT Public Corporation was privatized by the enactment of the Telecommunications

Business Act and the NTT Act, which together replaced the Public Telecommunications Act. Specifying details of the communications business, Article 1 of the Telecommunications Business Act lists promotion of fair competition as one of its objectives.

New policy regarding entry into the regulated natural monopoly market has had two significant effects. The first was to activate the market with new entrants; consequently, the market price of long-distance communications fell, producing consumer benefits. The second effect was to decrease the internal reserves of NTT, although NTT was given the freedom to invest in any market outside of broadcasting. Overall, competition was introduced successfully into the communications markets, which was the policy of the then prime minister Nakasone, who, known for his leadership, privatized Japanese National Railways and Japan Tobacco and Salt Public Corporation at the same time.

Deregulation progressed, and NTT, which maintained market power after the introduction of competition, was eventually divided in 1999. In addition, still following international trends, deregulation progressed in the areas of rates and market entry,[7] including foreign ownership, in further promotion of competition in both fixed and mobile markets.

With the emergence of the Internet and competitive market structure changes, the role of platform such as Google has come to attract attention. Therefore, correctly addressing platforms in the legislative framework and regulations has become an issue in the transformation of communications regulation.

In sum, in the communications domain, after the introduction of competition by the Nakasone administration, deregulation has been progressing toward the pursuit of fair competition, along with global trends of deregulation and Internet business development including the emergence of platforms such as Google.

BROADCASTING: GRADUAL INTRODUCTION OF SEPARATION OF CONTENT AND TRANSMISSION WITH THE INTRODUCTION OF NEW BROADCAST SERVICES BY ADDING NEW ACTS

Broadcasting had been regarded as a special kind of wireless telecommunications of "the transmission of radio communications with the aim of direct reception by the public" (Ministry of Internal Affairs and Communications [MIC], 2010b) before amendment of the Broadcast Act in 2011. In other words, "broadcasting" was defined as using airwaves to send TV programs and includes both terrestrial and satellite broadcasting.

Due to the limited frequencies available for broadcasting, market entry has been regulated from the beginning, which led to the formation of an oligopolistic market. Entry into the market required a license from the government, which managed the entire spectrum, and those who obtained broadcast licenses were regulated as information providers with social influence. Technically, when a license came up for renewal, a new entrant could enter the market in place of an existing one. In practice, however, all licenses were actually renewed, thereby functionally limiting any possible competition.

In contrast, broadcasting regulations tend to reflect each country's history and culture. The broadcasting licensing system in Japan has been similar to the one in the United States, including the definition of broadcasting. In both countries, terrestrial broadcasting licenses have been granted to broadcasters as wireless stations.

This similarity is due to the history of the passage of the Broadcast Act. In 1950, 5 years after the end of World War II, three acts related to radio waves (the Broadcast Act, the Radio Act, and the Act for Establishment of Radio Regulatory Commission) were passed in Japan under the influence of the General Headquarters (GHQ) of the supreme commander for the Allied Powers, which considered media policy to be of importance. GHQ requested the Japanese government to enact the Broadcast Act under the new Constitution in 1946; it took more than 3 years to discuss and draft the bill between GHQ and the Japanese government (Murakami, 2008). With the passage of the three acts, the Wireless Telegraphy Act of the prewar period was abolished, and the Japan Broadcasting Corporation (a.k.a. NHK) and the Radio Regulatory Commission, which was an independent regulatory commission modeled after the U.S. Federal Communications Commission (FCC), were created.

The predecessor of NHK was reorganized into the current organization, and technology research was clearly designated as part of NHK's operation. The act also clarified the legal basis for private-sector broadcasting, and two private broadcasting stations, the first such stations in Japan, began operations in 1951.

The purpose of the Broadcast Act, which constitutes the foundation of the current broadcasting system in Japan, is to regulate broadcasting activities so that they contribute to public welfare and to promote their sound development, following three main principles: maximizing broadcasting coverage, securing freedom of expression through broadcasting, and contributing to the sound development of democracy through broadcasting. The Radio Regulatory Commission, which had been established to take charge of licensing and other operations, was abolished when the first television license was issued by the Ministry of Posts and Telecommunications, which became MIC after merging with the Ministry of Home Affairs.

As for content issues, through long discussion between GHQ and the Japanese government, the rules of editing programs that had been kept in the Broadcast Act[8] were decided and applied to new broadcast services with minor addition and modifications (Murakami, 2008). There was no penalty provided in the Broadcast Act even against those editing rules furthering the idea of autonomous content control by broadcasters themselves. Legal penalties on broadcasters' violations have only resulted in revocation or suspension of licenses by the Radio Act, chiefly for technical regulation of wireless radio stations; in reality, these are rarely executed (Shimizu, 2008). Ministerial ordinances, however, have been actual measures and are often criticized for their arbitrariness. However, setting up new penalties such as monetary punishment has been criticized as tightening regulations on freedom of speech and has not been realized (Murakami, 2010). This institutional arrangement, regulating broadcasters' business through the Broadcast Act and licensing including penalties through the Radio Act, is favorable to broadcasters and has been well accepted by them.

In 1959, responding to rising public concern about programs with low character among increasing numbers of broadcasters, the act was modified to require that any broadcaster publish their principles of editorial control over programs. It also then stipulated that any broadcaster must establish a broadcast programming council to examine whether its broadcast programs are "proper." In addition, broadcasters were asked to submit the proportion of programs by category in the renewal of their license. There have been no serious modifications regarding editing programs since then.

The Cable Television Broadcast Act came into effect in 1972, garnering attention because the original concept that broadcasting is a special telecommunications system was then extended to the area of wired telecommunications. Furthermore, it allowed for the separation of facility-based businesses (cable television broadcasting facilities) from services (cable television businesses), which had not been seen until this time in the terrestrial broadcasting business.

Based on cable television regulation, the license division of "trusting broadcasting" and "entrusted broadcasting" business was introduced for satellite broadcasting in 1989 and was especially aimed at broadcasting via communications satellite. An entrusted broadcaster operates a communications satellite business (transmission business), and a trusting broadcaster leases a communications satellite from an entrusted broadcaster and provides original programs while exercising editorial control (content business). Up to that point, the transmission division and content division had been integrated in terrestrial broadcasting; the introduction of this new regulation meant that the separation of content and transmission had been accomplished.

Furthermore, the 2001 Act Concerning Broadcast on Telecommunications Services amended the law to allow broadcasters to provide services over wired and wireless "communications" networks. Taking advantage of this new legislative environment, major communications companies began providing multichannel broadcasting services through Internet Protocol (IP) networks, one after another since 2002, and cable television operators started offering services through optical fiber networks (in much the same way as traditional cable television programs were transmitted).

As discussed earlier, since additional acts were formed for new media services, different acts and standards were applied to services that are almost the same to end users, such as cable television and IP broadcasting, which both use fixed lines. There was thus a problem that some of the operators entering the market were required to obtain a license, while others were only required to register.

In addition, SkyperfecTV emerged as a platform business for a multi-channel satellite broadcast service, although there is no regulation addressing this business configuration. SkyperfecTV works between a number of trusting broadcasters and customers as a central player. It selects channels to be placed into packages for customers, puts advertising to end users and marketing packages for trusting broadcasters, and collects fares of packages for trusting broadcasters.

Looking back on the history of broadcasting legislation, the original vertical legislative and business structure of terrestrial broadcasting introduced under U.S. influence has remained, as well as content regulation. At the same time as new broadcast services have emerged, new acts have been added, one after another, and have brought about separation of content and transmission in terms of the industrial structure.

Along with changes in the legislative framework, the industry changed as well. Content and transmission channels had actually become separated as technological innovations brought increasing flexibility for handling content. In other words, particular content could be delivered through different transmission channels and shown on different terminal devices. For example, the same television programs had come to be provided not only through broadcasting channels such as terrestrial broadcasting, satellite broadcasting, and cable television, but also through IP broadcasting on communication networks. Television programs can now be transmitted through mobile phone networks and watched on smartphones or through data communications networks and watched on tablet computers. For business, it is desirable to provide content through transmission channels and terminal devices for varied consumers' needs, depending on time and place. Also, the more variety of content delivered through the same transmission channel, the more attractive the service is to consumers. Clearly, the role of the platform as a mechanism for coordinating content and transmission channels has become significant.

EVOLVING DISCUSSION TOWARD A NEW LEGISLATIVE FRAMEWORK CONCEPTION OF THE INFORMATION AND COMMUNICATION ACT

The revision of the legislative framework originated as a bold proposal from the Round Table on Telecommunications and Broadcasting, a private discussion group assembled by the minister of the MIC at that time, Heizo

Takenaka, of the Koizumi administration (Liberal Democratic Party, LDP), which was known for advancing deregulation and structural reforms starting in 2006. The formation of the Round Table discussion group was a rare procedural step by political leadership; usually, it is the bureaucrats who take the leadership role in producing bills.

Discussion on the legislative revisions lasted for almost 5 years, as shown in Table 8.2. Before the Round Table started, Takenaka challenged the participants in a press conference with the questions: "Why can't we watch live television broadcasts on the Internet? Why isn't there a major company like Time Warner in Japan?" (MIC, 2005). The Round Table proceeded to comprehensively examine the convergence of telecommunications and broadcasting, the strengthening of competitiveness and "soft power," and other issues, without being limited by the boundary of the MIC. The final report of the Round Table in June 2006 (MIC, 2006) argued that fundamental reexamination of the vertical legislative framework was an urgent issue and advocated its reorganization into three layers (transmission, platform, and content). Free business operation remained hindered by artificial market segmentation because telecommunications and broadcasting were separated in terms of the legislative framework despite technological advancement in

Table 8.2 Important events in the process of reorganizing the legislative framework

Time period	Activities
January–June 2006	MIC minister Takenaka's informal panel, the Round Table on Telecommunications and Broadcasting
June 2006	Agreement between the government and the ruling parties on regulatory framework
August 2006–December 2007	Study Group on a Comprehensive Legal System for Telecommunications and Broadcasting
February–August 2008	Telecommunications Council on Comprehensive Legal System for Communications and Broadcasting
September 2009	Democratic Party of Japan's new administration takes power
March 2010	Reorganization of eight acts into four, by decision of the Cabinet
May 2010	The new Broadcasting Act submitted to the Diet by the MIC minister
November 2010	The new Broadcasting Act passed

their convergence. At that time, there were still as many as nine acts in place for regulating the telecommunications and broadcasting fields as a whole.

During the Round Table discussions, the NAB showed concerns about threats to existing business, such as possible IP network delivery of TV programs beyond existing broadcast areas, and possible separation of content and transmission, pointing out potential problems with broadcasting in times of disaster (National Association of Commercial Broadcasters in Japan [NAB], 2006a). Immediately after the Round Table report was published, the NAB announced opposing opinion on shifting to a layered structure that would lead to the separation of content and transmission (NAB, 2006b).

Meanwhile, the Round Table report went on to present the direction of reform on a wide range of issues such as improvement of the Copyright Act, which was a hurdle to the spread of IP multicast broadcasting; reexamination of relevant acts and regulations in order to promote greater competition in the telecommunications business (as well as in the reorganization of NTT); relaxation of the principle of excluding multiple ownership of the media; effective use of the broadcast spectrum; creation of an environment promoting free business operation in broadcasting (as well as the issue involving retransmission of terrestrial digital broadcasts in IP multicast broadcasting); and fundamental reform of NHK, which had experienced a series of scandals and was accused of being inefficiently managed (MIC, 2006).

The ruling party and the government, who originally had different ideas, reached an agreement that the discussion for new legislation was to be finalized by 2010, one year prior to the year that terrestrial analog broadcasting was scheduled to cease. In addition, it was agreed that the issue of possible restructuring of NTT would be reexamined in 2010 (Suzuki, 2006).

A series of discussions ensued by the Study Group on a Comprehensive Legal System for Communications and Broadcasting, which was organized by the MIC, and its final report in 2007 concretely conceptualized the "Information and Communications Act (tentative name)." The report advocated transformation of the legislative framework from the traditional vertical structure, where businesses were regulated according to types of media by separate acts such as the Broadcast Act and the Cable Television Broadcast Act, to a layered structure where regulations would be enforced separately for each of the content, platform, and transmission infrastructure layers (see Figure 8.1). The report also concluded that Japan should aim, simultaneously, to create the world's most advanced legislative framework by unifying the acts and regulations for telecommunications and broadcasting under a single framework (MIC, 2007).

In describing current conditions, the Study Group report discussed changes in media structure as seen in the emergence of consumer-generated media, or in the Internet performing the role of the media, which followed digitization in the field of broadcasting, a shift toward multichannels, and

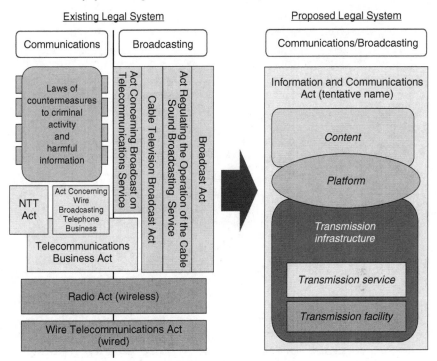

Figure 8.1 Schematic image of the reorganization of the telecom legislative framework.
Note: Modified from MIC, 2008.

the spread of IP and broadband networks. As for the convergence of telecommunications and broadcasting, the report emphasized progress made in terms of transmission channels, terminal devices, and business operators, stating that services that integrate telecommunications and broadcasting are expected to develop further, once the world's most advanced transmission infrastructure is created, along with the digitization of terrestrial broadcasting in 2011.

With regard to other countries, the report compared the EU's legislative framework consisting of a layered structure with the example of the United States, where the relevant acts and regulations are organized "vertically" for each type of media, under one legislative framework. From the standpoint of creating and promoting a unified European market, Europe had constructed a layered legislative framework based on technological neutrality. The regulatory package for electronic communications, which is relevant to the transmission layer, centers on ex-post regulation and is designed to promote free business operation. As for the content layer, the target of regulations has been expanded from television broadcasting to audiovisual media services (video services for the public, including content on the Internet).

The Study Group's proposal is considered to aim for the EU-style legislative framework in terms of its horizontal structure. It was proposed that content openly distributed on communication networks be categorized into "special media services," "general media services," and "open media content," according to the degree of its social influence. Broadcasters insisted on maintaining the integration of facilities and services, however, as well as on securing localism held by basic broadcasting—terrestrial broadcasting based on a balance of industrial promotion and a rich information environment to be developed for the public. At the same time, this segment expressed concern that the use of social influence as an indicator to categorize content in the possible layered system might strengthen government involvement through content rule making. In addition, broadcasters pointed out that setting a "common" minimum rule on illegal information could restrict free speech and expression on open media content (NAB, 2007a; 2007b).

MODIFICATION BY THE INFORMATION AND COMMUNICATIONS COUNCIL

After receiving the Study Group's report, the Ministry of Internal Affairs and Communications requested the Information and Communications Council to provide advice. The council submitted an advisory report in August 2009, after discussions lasting 1 1/2 years. Responding to the broadcasters' continued strong opposition, the advisory report proposed a substantial correction of course, although it supported the initially proposed layered structure. The report suggested keeping only existing "broadcasting" subject to regulation other than open media content, which means to continue to use a concept of "broadcasting" instead of "media service." At the same time, it concluded that broadcasters should be able to choose whether they provide broadcasting stations, services, or both (MIC, 2009).

START OF THE DEMOCRATIC PARTY OF JAPAN ADMINISTRATION

As a result of the Democratic Party of Japan taking power in September 2009, the bill was amended further, with the Democratic Party advocating a shift away from traditional bureaucrat-led government toward politician-led government. Minister of MIC Haraguchi took the lead on matters at this point.

Immediately after the change of administration, the Task Force on ICT Policy in the Global Era took up a reexamination of previous information and communications technology policies. The task force addressed issues regarding communications infrastructure, utilization, and international competition, including NTT issues, based on an agreement between the ruling party and the government in 2006.

In addition, as proclaimed in the Democratic Party's manifesto, a Japanese version of the U.S. FCC was proposed to resolve the contradiction that the broadcasting stations were supervised by the very government authorities that they were expected to monitor. The broadcasting industry strongly opposed this, however, claiming that the Broadcasting Ethics and Program Improvement Organization (BPO) already existed as the broadcasters' voluntary regulatory organization and that no new regulatory agency was needed. Also, some questioned the political neutrality of the FCC as a model for the proposed agency, pointing out that the majority of FCC commissioners were appointed by the president. The idea of the Japanese version of the FCC gradually lost support (Murakami, 2010).

Separately, Haraguchi insisted on including the basic principle of excluding multiple ownership of the media, which had been prepared only as a ministerial ordinance of the MIC, and noted that they must consider the difficult environment surrounding broadcasters, such as that faced by local broadcasters during the recession (MIC, 2010a).

After further discussions, the bill for amending a part of the Broadcast Act and other relevant acts was finally passed in November 2010.

PRIMARY CHANGES MADE IN THE REVISION OF RELEVANT ACTS

As a result of 5 years of discussion, the Cable Television Broadcast Act, the Cable Radio Broadcast Act, and the Act Concerning Broadcast on Telecommunications Services were integrated into the Broadcast Act; the Act Concerning Broadcasting Telephone Business was integrated into the Telecommunications Business Act; and parts of the Radio Act and the Wire Telecommunications Act were amended (see Figure 8.2). Although the initial plan to organize all related acts into one as the "Information-Communication Act" was not achieved, the reorganization of acts effectively realized a shift from a vertical to a horizontal framework in broadcasting.

The top layer is the content layer, including broadcast services. Broadcasting was redefined as "the transmission of telecommunications with the aim of direct reception by the public." Broadcasting was then classified into "basic broadcasting" and "general broadcasting," categorized by transmission channels. Basic broadcasting means broadcasting using radio waves of frequencies allocated either exclusively or preferentially to radio stations broadcasting pursuant to the provisions of the Radio Act, such as terrestrial broadcasting, Broadcasting Satellite (BS) broadcasting, and 110°E Communication Satellite (CS) digital broadcasting. General broadcasting means broadcasting other than basic broadcasting, such as 124/128°E CS digital

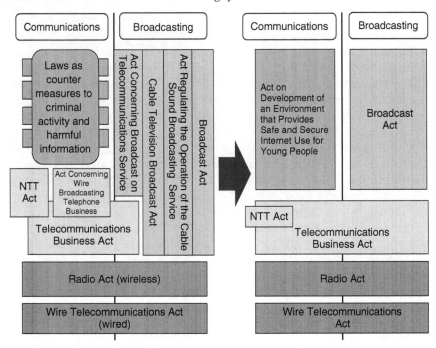

Figure 8.2 Change of legislative framework/overall institutional arrangements in telecommunications.
Note: Modified from MIC, 2008.

broadcasting, cable television broadcasting, and IP multicast broadcasting (MIC, 2011). Accordingly, the procedures for market entry for various broadcast services are now streamlined.

With this new layered framework, all broadcasters can choose whether to provide both content and transmission alone or to collaborate and divide those tasks among multiple broadcasters in an approach that was welcomed by local broadcasters who seek to streamline their business. Now, multiple local stations can share broadcast stations for transmission and thereby run their business more efficiently. As an exception, existing terrestrial broadcasters that provide basic broadcasting are allowed to continuously provide broadcast services with only transmission licenses issued under the Radio Act.

Revision of the Radio Act enables radio stations to be used for both telecommunications and broadcasting for effective use of the radio spectrum and flexible business operation, although the use of a radio station had been limited to either telecommunications or broadcasting. For example, a television station can take advantage of a radio wave used for broadcasting during the day and use it for telecommunications services during the night, such as for the transmission of information for digital signage.

Thus, the industry is basically prepared for the convergence, considering that separation of content and transmission was introduced to terrestrial broadcasters, even though it is not mandated. The legislative environment now allows for a competitive situation of a flexible combination of transmission and content if desired. Furthermore, the flexible use of radio stations for communication or broadcasting is a significant deregulation of the Radio Act, providing a competitive environment. On the other hand, the maximum stock ownership ratio of basic broadcasters by given person and juridical person or organization was relaxed from 20% to 30% for considering less competitive broadcasters in a changing business environment.

CONCLUSION

This chapter traced the historical development of the laws on communications and broadcasting in Japan and the reorganization process for the merging of those laws and legislative framework to meet the institutional and regulatory needs related to the technical and business convergence of the fields. In the domain of communications, successfully introduced market competition attributable to prime minister Nakasone through the Telecommunications Business Act and NTT Act paved the way to subsequent deregulation. Then, by modification of the acts, deregulation materialized, step by step, until a competitive communications market was created in Japan. On the other hand, in broadcasting, while maintaining the Broadcast Act created under the influence of GHQ, new acts were passed as new broadcast services emerged.

The reorganization after 60 years was a challenging attempt by the Koizumi administration, which also conducted other major deregulation attempts to put the vested interest group, terrestrial broadcasters, who have been main players and influential in the industry as well as in society, into the layered structure under development, which meant to take the vested interest away by dividing broadcast content and transmission channels. It was not fully completed as originally planned as, in the end, the vested interests of terrestrial broadcasters were maintained.

One of the reasons for this is that the LDP administration was overtaken by the Democratic Party in the middle of discussion, and political leadership did not work well. More importantly, broadcasters, who were the most involved players other than the LDP, were actually afraid of losing their vested interests, such as through regional oligopoly of the television market. Especially since separation of content and transmission represented a great threat to those who believed that license of radio waves for transmission was the key factor to maintain their vested interest, they continued to criticize the concept of a layered legislative framework, claiming that there were potential problems, such as with conducting broadcasts during disasters and with tightening content control.

Industry promotion and the creation of a free and safe information environment were both important principles for the reorganization of the telecommunication legislative framework in Japan. Democratic values, including freedom of speech, represented an important part of the latter, which was persuasive for opposing the separation of content and transmission.

These facts show that strong political leadership, which emerged in a few moments over time, accomplished substantial institutional change; otherwise, most institutional change initiated by bureaucrats was gradual. They also suggest that broadcasting institutions have more "durability" than communications institutions in terms of introducing competition, seemingly because terrestrial broadcasters, who are major players, were difficult to convince. One reason for this was the cross-ownership of broadcasting entities and newspapers, which could be used to create favorable public opinion for media companies, often referring to freedom of speech.

The institutional arrangement in the broadcast domain in 1950 under GHQ has brought path dependence to the development of broadcast institutions as the initial conditions of autonomous content control were given to broadcasters under the influence of GHQ, which intended to eliminate any military influence and establish a democratic media environment. The broadcasters were supposed to handle both functions of content production under the Broadcast Act and transmission of content under the Radio Act in the integrated manner. However, licenses and penalties were only given under the Radio Act. On the other hand, no legal penalties were given to broadcast businesses including content production. These initial conditions had been generally maintained, although later, ministerial ordinances were issued occasionally. Introducing a layered structure causing content and transmission to be regulated separately would result in direct regulation of broadcasters' business including content production, which is very likely to be unacceptable for broadcasters. Therefore, path dependence especially with the initial conditions worked on boosting the durability of broadcast institutions.

NOTES

1. In this chapter, the term "telecommunications" is used in a broad sense to include "communications" and "broadcasting," although "telecommunications" is often used to denote "communications" in government reports and the names of study groups.
2. Though there are not many studies based on NIE in the field of telecommunications, NIE can be an important analytical tool for this area (Just & Puppis, 2012).
3. Nishioka (2008) used some of analytical concepts of comparative institutional analysis to examine the life cycle of the international telecommunication regime, which was created in the era of telephones, as an institution and the role of international organizations, which changes as the cycle proceeds.
4. The other approach defines institutions as "exogenous rules of the game" (North, 1990).

5. Aoki (2001) provides detailed explanations of institutions.
6. The English name was changed to Japan Commercial Broadcasters Association (JBA) in April 2012 (JBA website, www.j-ba.or.jp/category/english/jba101004).
7. Regulations for communications companies by Type 1 and Type 2, which require government permissions, were replaced with a registration or notification system in 2004.
8. "(i) It shall not harm public safety or good morals; (ii) It shall be politically fair. (iii) Its reporting shall not distort the facts; (iv) It shall clarify the points at issue from as many angles as possible where there are conflicting opinions concerning an issue" (Broadcast Act, 2010).

REFERENCES

Aoki, M. (2001). *Toward a comparative institutional analysis.* Cambridge. MA: MIT Press.

Aoki, M., Austin, G., Abdi, A. A., Chaney, E., Choudhury, P., Gaiha, R., . . . Wong, R. B. (2012). *Institutions and comparative economic development.* Hampshire, UK: Palgrave Macmillan.

Aoki, M., & Rothwell, G. (2012). A comparative institutional analysis of the Fukushima nuclear disaster: Lessons and policy implications. *Energy Policy, 53,* 240–247.

Fuji Media Holdings, Inc. (2013). *Yuuka Shoken Hokokusyo* [Annual security report—72th Stage (2012.04.01—2013.03.31)]. Electronic Disclosure of Investors' NETwork (EDINET) of Financial Service Agency. Retrieved from http://disclosure.edinet-fsa.go.jp/EKW0EZ1001.html?lgKbn=1&dflg=0&iflg=0

Just, N., & Puppis, M. (Eds.). (2012). *Trends in communication policy research.* Bristol, UK: Intellect.

Liu, Y. (2011). The impact of convergence on the telecommunications law and broadcasting-related laws: A comparison between Japan and Taiwan. *Keio Communication Review, 33,* 43–67.

Ministry of Internal Affairs and Communications (MIC). (2005). *Takenaka Soumudaijin Kakugigo Kisyakaiken no Gaiyou.* [Summary of press conference of Minister Takenaka, December 6]. National Diet Library Archives. Retrieved from warp.da.ndl.go.jp/info:ndljp/pid/286922/www.soumu.go.jp/menu_news/kaiken/back_01/d-news/2005/1206.html

Ministry of Internal Affairs and Communications (MIC). (2006). *Tsushinn Hoso no Arikata ni Kansuru Kondannkai Houkokusyo* [Final report of the Round Table on Telecommunications and Broadcasting]. Retrieved from www.soumu.go.jp/main_sosiki/joho . . . /060606_saisyuu.pdf

Ministry of Internal Affairs and Communications (MIC). (2007). *Tsushinn-Hoso no Sougouteki na Houtaikei ni Kansuru Kenkyuukai Houkokusyo* [Final report from the Study Group on a Comprehensive Legal System for Communications and Broadcasting]. Retrieved from www.soumu.go.jp/main_content/000035773.pdf

Ministry of Internal Affairs and Communications (MIC). (2008). Study Group report: Final report from the Study Group on a Comprehensive Legal System for Communications and Broadcasting. *MIC Communications News, 18*(21). Retrieved from http://warp.ndl.go.jp/info:ndljp/pid/286922/www.soumu.go.jp/main_sosiki/joho_tsusin/eng/Releases/NewsLetter/Vol18/Vol18_21/Vol18_21.html

Ministry of Internal Affairs and Communications (MIC). (2009). *Tsushinn-Hoso no Sougouteki na Houtaikei no arikata—Toshin* [The advisory report to the minister regarding comprehensive legal system for communications and broadcasting]. Retrieved from www.soumu.go.jp/main_content/000035773.pdf

Ministry of Internal Affairs and Communications (MIC). (2010a, January 5). *Haraguchi Soumudaijinn Kakugigo Kisyakaiken no Gaiyo* [Summary of press conference of Minister Haraguchi after Cabinet meeting]. Retrieved from www.soumu. go.jp/menu_news/kaiken/23366.html

Ministry of Internal Affairs and Communications (MIC). (2010b). *Housouho no Ichibu wo Kaisei Suru Horitsuann no Gaiyou* [Outline of the bill of partial amendment of Broadcast Act]. Retrieved from www.soumu.go.jp/main_content/ 000058201.pdf

Ministry of Internal Affairs and Communications (MIC). (2011). *Broadcast Act, Act No.132 of May 2, 1950, Act No.65 of December 3, 2010*. Retrieved from www. soumu.go.jp/main_sosiki/joho_tsusin/eng/Resources/laws/pdf/090204_5.pdf

Murakami, S. (2008, June). Kennsyou: Kennsyou Hosoho "Banngumijunnsoku" no Keiseikatei [Verification: Creating process of the general standard for programming]. *Hoso Kenkyu to Tyousa*, 2008, 54–67.

Murakami, S. (2010, June). Hosokannrenhou Saihenn Nokosareta Kadai [Reorganization of broadcast related acts, remained issues]. *Hoso Kenkyu to Tyousa*, 2010, 68–79.

National Association of Commercial Broadcasters in Japan (NAB). (2006a). *Soumusyo "Tsuushinn—Hosono Arikata ni kannsuru Konndannkai" Tsuikashitumonn heno Kaito* [Response to additional question from "The Round Table on Telecommunications and Broadcasting" at MIC at April 11]. Retrieved from www.soumu.go.jp/main_sosiki/joho_tsusin/policyreports/chousa/tsushin_hosou/ pdf/060411_3_05.pdf

National Association of Commercial Broadcasters in Japan (NAB). (2006b). *Soumusyo "Tsuushinn—Hosono Arikata ni kannsuru Konndannkai" Hokokusyo ni taisuru Minnpourenn kaityuo komennto* [Chairman's comment on the report of "The Round Table on Telecommunications and Broadcasting" at MIC at June 6]. Retrieved from www.j-ba.or.jp/category/topics/jba100623

National Association of Commercial Broadcasters in Japan (NAB). (2007a). *Soumusyo "Tsuushinn—Hosono no Sogotekina Houtaikei ni kannsuru Kennkkyuukai" Tyuukann-torimatome ni taisuru ikenn* [Comment on "The Interim Report of Study Group on a Comprehensive Legal System for Communications and Broadcasting" at MIC at July 23]. Retrieved from www.j-ba.or.jp/files/ jba100647/20070723.pdf

National Association of Commercial Broadcasters in Japan (NAB). (2007b). *Soumusyo "Tsuushinn—Hosono no Sogotekina Houtaikei ni kannsuru Kennkkyuukai" Houkokusyo ni taisuru Minnpourenn Kaityou komennto* [Chairman's comment on "The Report of the Study Group on a Comprehensive Legal System for Communications and Broadcasting" at MIC at December 6]. Retrieved from www.j-ba.or.jp/category/topics/jba100655

Nippon Television Holdings. (2013). *Yuuka Shoken Hokokusyo* [Annual securities report—80th stage (2012.04.01–2013.03.31)]. Retrieved from http://disclosure. edinet-fsa.go.jp/EKW0EZ1001.html?lgKbn=1&dflg=0&iflg=0

Nishioka, Y. (2008). *Kokusai Denkitushinn Shijyou ni okeru Seido no Keisei to Henka—Udekitsushinn kara Internet Governance made* [Institutional formation and change in the telecommunications market]. Tokyo: Keio University Press.

North, C.D. (1990). *Institutions, institutional change and economic performance*. New York: Cambridge University Press.

Shimizu, N. (2008, November). Johotsushinnhoukoso to Hosokisei wo meguru Ronngi [Discussion around information-telecommunications act and broadcast regulations]. *Reference, 2008*, 61–76.

Sugaya, M. (2009). The transformation of telecommunication regulatory structure in Japan: Vertical and horizontal perspectives. *Keio Communication Review, 31*, 23–36.

Suzuki, Y. (2006, October). Tsushinn to Houso no Yugo wa Dou Giron Saretanoka? [How has convergence of telecommunications and broadcast been discussed?]. *Hoso Kenkyu to Tyousa*, 2006, 14–31.
Tokyo Broadcasting System Holdings, Inc. (2013). *Yuuka Shoken Hokokusyo* [Annual securities report—86th stage (2012.04.01–2013.03.31)]. Retrieved from http://disclosure.edinet-fsa.go.jp/EKW0EZ1001.html?lgKbn=1&dflg=0&iflg=0
TV Asahi Corporation. (2013). *Yuuka Shoken Hokokusyo* [Annual securities report—73th Stage (2012.04.01–2013.03.31)]. Retrieved from http://disclosure.edinet-fsa.go.jp/EKW0EZ1001.html?lgKbn=1&dflg=0&iflg=0

9 The Impact of Digital Convergence on the Regulation of New Media in Korea
Major Issues in New Media Policy

Euisun Yoo and Hyangsun Lee

Digital convergence driven by the rapid development of digital technology and Internet communications has caused substantial changes in the media environment and our way of life. Traditional media have been digitized, and digital content travels all over the world on digital networks, being offered through various platforms and consumed using new and diverse devices. This chapter provides an overview of the impact of digital convergence on both the new media environment and media regulations, specifically focusing on major pending policy issues that affect business and content regulation, respectively.

First, the chapter discusses major changes in media regulatory systems, particularly those driven by the convergence of broadcasting and telecommunications. It reviews the background for the recent adoption of a dual regulatory system for media businesses, with the Ministry of Future Creation and Science (MFCS) and the Korea Communications Commission (KCC) participating. This dual system was an attempt to overcome the limitations of the KCC-only system in promoting both the media industry and technology to the utmost degree in the convergence era. It also considers emerging conflicting issues caused by digital convergence, which requires that current content regulatory systems be modified.

The chapter then reviews the major pending policy issues in media business regulation and content regulation, which have become the focus of policy interest as digital convergence progresses. First, the issue of media ownership regulation is considered, and the media diversity index that was recently developed by the Media Diversity Committee is introduced. It also examines the issue of retransmission compensation for terrestrial TV broadcasts by pay-TV operators, an issue that has compounded as more and more convergent media platforms emerge. Next, net neutrality is considered, focusing on its increasingly complicated management resulting from accelerated convergence in services among network providers, platform providers and content providers.

Finally, changes in content regulation in the era of digital convergence are discussed, focusing on regulations governing news impartiality and virtual child pornography. Regarding news impartiality, the chapter considers how the changes in media environment could obscure traditional medium-specific review standards and the necessity of employing horizontal regulatory schemes. In relation to virtual child pornography, a growing issue given digital technology, the chapter considers its distinction from "real child pornography" and explores whether differentiated regulatory standards should be adopted.

Change in Regulatory Systems

The amendment to the Government Organization Act, proposed by the newly launched Park Geun-Hye administration, recently passed in the National Assembly. One noteworthy change is the adoption of dual systems for media business regulation in Korea: one for the fast-paced development of technology and its related industries; the other for the protection of the public interest when developing relevant policies. The amendment gave rise to the MFCS, which will deal with ICT and broadcasting-telecommunications convergence issues focusing on the promotion of technology and its related industries.[1] The necessity of the creation of the MFCS was widely agreed upon in that focused governmental support and assistance for the digital media sector is critical in vitalizing the Korean economy in the convergence era.

While the MFCS was created to promote the ICT and broadcasting and telecommunications industries, the focus of the KCC, as a collegiate regulatory agency, was narrowed to the regulation of broadcasting and telecommunications operators in order to protect the public interest. The KCC was created in 2008 to respond to the need to integrate regulatory bodies for broadcasting and telecommunications, in line with media convergence. The original KCC role included the promotion of technology and its industries. This has now been transferred to the MFCS after many years of debate on the effectiveness of a consensus-based "commission" system in promoting technology and industry in the media convergence era. The major difficulties in arranging jurisdictions between the MFCS and the KCC involve how to appropriately demarcate the area between industry promotion and regulation, especially when the traditional sectors of broadcasting and telecommunications have been integrated at a significant level. Now that the roles of the MFCS and the KCC have been decided, however artificial and arbitrary the division may have been, Korea has entered the stage of another regulatory experiment for the media sector.

In terms of content regulation, the Korea Communications Standards Commission (KCSC) was also launched in 2008. The KCSC integrated the review functions of the Korea Broadcasting Commission for broadcast content and the Korea Internet Safety Commission for Internet content. While the KCC was established as a central government agency in charge of general broadcasting and telecommunications policy and administration, the KCSC was created as a statutorily independent agency in charge of content review with particular sensitivity to how content regulation and the existence of a governing regulatory agency affect freedom of expression (Lee, 2012). Although content-regulatory bodies were merged into the KCSC, different review standards have been applied to broadcasting content and Internet content. However, as digital convergence has proceeded further and further, the necessity of a system to appropriately deal with convergent content (i.e., broadcasting programs offered through Internet sites and including video on demand (VOD), Internet TV or Internet radio programming, etc.) has become obvious. Particularly, the KCSC is now in the midst of heated debates about the scope of media and types of channels to which its traditional regulatory standards for broadcasting, which are based on public interest principles, should be applied.

The Press Arbitration Commission (PAC), an independent statutory agency for ADR (alternative dispute resolution), settles disputes concerning reputation, rights or other legal interests violated through any press report or medium by any press organization, and so forth.[2] The PAC's purpose is to save the conflicting parties time, money and energy by allowing them to settle their differences out of court. As digital convergence has advanced, the jurisdiction of the PAC, which had mainly dealt with conflicts involving news reports by print media, has continued to expand to include broadcasting and online newspapers. In 2009, "Internet news services," such as portal services that intermediate news articles originating from other news organizations, were included under the PAC Act category "press, etc." This change followed prolonged debates on the concept of "press" (Lee, 2008).[3]

Major Issues in New Media Policy

Ownership

Promoting diversity is an essential media policy goal to ensure that the public be exposed to multiple views regarding issues of public interest. Diversity is achieved through the appropriate regulation of ownership concentration, which creates effective media market competition. However, as digital convergence advances, regulation of ownership becomes increasingly complex. Defining a relevant market and determining significant market players have become more and more difficult due to a significant level of convergence among mediums and services. As in many countries, there have been attempts in Korea to create new rules and standards for ownership regulation that appropriately reflect these changes.

One such attempt was a reshuffling of media ownership regulations in 2009. This substantially relaxed entry barriers among media and services and allowed a higher degree of vertical and horizontal integration among media companies. This was also a response to the demand that ownership regulation be redesigned so domestic media firms could gain sufficient strength to compete with gigantic global media conglomerates as media increasingly globalized and the stage for competition extended beyond domestic borders (Kim, 2009).

Media ownership regulation is governed by the Monopoly Regulation and Fair Trade Act and the Broadcasting Act in Korea. Particularly, Article 8 of the Broadcasting Act, as amended in 2009, specifies ownership ceilings for a broadcasting business operator, considering its special sociocultural and economic influence when it is vertically or horizontally integrated with other media firms as a result of media convergence. Paragraph 2 of the article[4] specifies that "no one may own in excess of 40/100 of the total stock or equity shares of a terrestrial broadcasting business operator or a program-providing business operator engaged in general programming or specialized programming of news reports." Paragraph 4 of the article stipulates that "in cases where the subscription rate[5] is 20/100 or higher for a daily newspaper, the corporation owning the newspaper shall not concurrently run a terrestrial broadcasting business or program-providing business engaging in general programming or specialized programming of news reports." Furthermore, via Article 35–4, the act established the Media Diversity Committee as a statutory institution to promote diversity of public opinion through media. One of the major tasks of the Media Diversity Committee was to develop an aggregated impact indicator among media—that is, a diversity index applicable to the Korean context as a criterion to determine the appropriate level of ownership regulation for media companies in a converged market (Yoo, 2009). After a few years of studies, the committee developed a formula to calculate the aggregate impact among media. (Refer to Table 9.1).

This formula was developed with reference to Germany's KEK model and the United States' diversity index. Through an extensive survey in 2010, the Media Diversity Committee determined each medium's weighted impact on public opinion as follows: TV—1, Radio—0.3, Newspaper—0.4, Internet—0.6. Article 69–2 of the Broadcasting Act stipulates that "the audience share of

Table 9.1   Suggested equation for aggregate impact among media

$$TI = \sum_{I=1}^{n}(W_i \times \sum S_i)$$

Here,

TI = aggregate impact among media

$\sum S_i$ = each medium's market share (i.e., viewing rate, subscription rate)

W_i = weighted impact of each medium relative to TV's impact, which is set at 1
   = the amount of use of each medium x each medium's attributes influencing public opinion

(attributes: audiovisual appeal, degree of dealing with news and current affairs, use convenience)

Source: Korea Telecom, 2012

a broadcasting business operator shall not exceed 30/100 . . . The audience share of a broadcasting business operator . . . shall be determined by summing up the audience shares of related parties to the audience share of the broadcasting business operator." It also prescribes that "the subscription rate of a daily newspaper shall be converted into audience share at a certain ratio as prescribed by Presidential Decree, and added to the audience share of the relevant broadcasting business operator." However, the weighted impact of Internet portals remains unresolved. Figure 9.1 shows an example of how to estimate a media corporation's influence on public opinion (see Figure 9.1).

Suppose that a TV operator owns radio, newspaper and Internet companies and the coverage (reach)[6] of each is 15%, 10%, 10% and 5% respectively. Applying a weighted impact to each medium (TV—1, Radio—0.3, Newspaper—0.4 and Internet—0.6), the aggregate influence of the media corporation on public opinion is 25%. The law requires that a media corporation should not be allowed to own additional media firms when the aggregate influence of a corporation is larger than 30%. Therefore, the media corporation in this example may own more media companies since its aggregate influence is less than 30%.[7] As in the case of the German KEK, which has been deliberating on whether to consider Internet portals as agenda setters of public opinion, Korea's Media Diversity Committee has been contemplating whether Internet portals have the editorial power to influence public opinion.

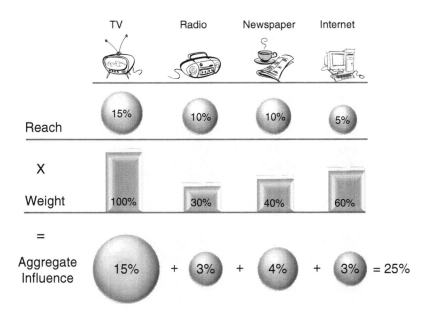

Figure 9.1 An example of how to estimate a media corporation's influence on public opinion.

Retransmission of Terrestrial TV Broadcasts

For many years, there was no charge for a pay-TV channel to retransmit terrestrial TV signals to viewers in Korea. It was considered to benefit both terrestrial and pay-TV operators. Terrestrial TV operators did not have to worry about losing audience share because people in fringe areas used pay TV as a means to watch terrestrial TV. (The direct reception rate of terrestrial TV signals is relatively small in Korea because more than 70% of the land is mountainous.) Pay-TV operators benefited from retransmitting terrestrial TV signals, charging subscription fees to viewers who mainly wanted to watch terrestrial TV programs.

However, as new digital-based platforms emerged, terrestrial TV began to lose its dominance, with the average viewing rate and subsequent advertising revenue continuing to lessen. Another problem terrestrial TV operators are facing is that pay-TV operators become increasingly formidable competitors as they use diverse business models with digital content, such as VOD services, running diverse premium channels, utilizing interactive services and so forth.

Confronting the problem of diminishing advertising revenue and the enormous cost for a transition to digital TV, terrestrial TV networks have been desperately looking for additional sources of revenue. Retransmission compensation from pay-TV operators emerged as one such source, since terrestrial TV programs are still popular and essential in the pay-TV market. Surveys show that a significant number of Korean viewers subscribe to pay TV mainly to view terrestrial TV programs. Currently, more than 80% of terrestrial TV viewing takes place through pay-TV platforms, such as cable TV, satellite broadcasting, Internet Protocol TV (IPTV) and so on. The first targets terrestrial TV operators aimed at in order to levy retransmission compensation were IPTV providers, which are Korea's three major telecommunications service operators. The gross revenue of telecommunications operators is 10 times bigger than that of broadcasters. Since the telecom operators started the IPTV business when the pay-TV market was saturated with cable and satellite TV, they desperately needed a stable provision of terrestrial TV programs for "killer" content. Therefore, they willingly accepted terrestrial broadcasters' demand of 280 Korean won ($0.25) for cost per subscription (CPS) (E-Daily, 2009). This became a precedent rate that terrestrial TV broadcasters also applied to other pay-TV platforms, such as cable and satellite.

Retransmission compensation is a major pending issue, particularly between terrestrial TV broadcasters and cable TV operators. Currently, cable TV is the dominant pay-TV platform in terms of subscription rates: cable TV enjoys about 15 million households as subscribers, while satellite TV has 4 million and IPTV has 7 million households, respectively. (The number of IPTV-satellite hybrid service subscribers is about 2 million households; see E-Daily, 2013; MediaUs, 2013). If terrestrial broadcasters keep demanding 280 won for CPS, cable TV operators will have to pay about $135 million every year to the three major terrestrial TV broadcasters. Cable TV operators argue that such a demand is absurd considering that they previously never paid a single dollar to terrestrial TV broadcasters. They say they are entitled to charge broadcasters for the transmission of their broadcasting signals to such a large number of viewers, helping broadcasters maintain their audience share and allowing them to charge more for advertising.

Sharp confrontations from both sides have characterized the past few years. While broadcasters threatened cable TV operators with not allowing the retransmission of broadcast TV signals unless cable TV operators paid 280 won for CPS, cable TV operators said they would blackout the signals if broadcasters continued to coerce them. Finally, terrestrial TV broadcasters brought this matter to court by suing major cable TV operators that relay digital broadcast TV signals for infringing on their right of simultaneous relay. Article 85 of the Copyright Act stipulates that broadcasting organizations shall have the right to send out their broadcasts simultaneously.

The Seoul Central District Court ruled in 2009 that cable TV operators infringed on terrestrial TV broadcasters' right of simultaneous relay. The court rejected cable TV operators' argument that relaying broadcast TV signals is a simple assisting action based on the fact that cable TV operators made use of digital TV broadcasts in various ways and that they charged more than real expenses for the relay to subscribers to make profits. The court also rejected cable TV operators' request to impose statutory licenses for the retransmission of terrestrial TV signals in that statutory licenses should be applied restrictively only in limited cases, as prescribed in the Copyright Act (Seoul Central District Court, 2009). Article 51 (Broadcasting of Works Made Public) of the Copyright Act stipulates that "where a broadcasting organization which intends to broadcast a work already made public for the sake of the public benefit has negotiated with the owner of the authors' property rights but failed to reach an agreement, it may broadcast the work by obtaining approval of the Minister of Culture, Sports and Tourism . . . and paying to the owner of the authors' property rights or depositing a sum of compensatory money according to the criteria determined by the Minister."

The Central District Court also ruled in a related case in 2010 that terrestrial TV broadcasters did not breach the principle of faith and trust, given that digital-based media businesses are substantially different from analog-based businesses. The court explained that both the principle of faith and trust and implied consent only work within the context of a possible business coexistence and with the assumption of not doing harm to each other (Seoul Central District Court, 2010). That is, in the case of a digital-based business, unlike an analog-based business, expecting cooperative behavior between the two sides for coexistive purposes is not natural from a business perspective. In fact, cable TV operators have already become formidable competitors against terrestrial TV networks in terms of program diversity, resolution quality, on-demand services and so forth. The Seoul Higher Court confirmed lower court decisions using the same logic that the lower courts relied on (Seoul Higher Court, 2011).

In spite of the courts' decisions, confusion and conflict remain, given the complexity of the retransmission issue. Many scholars and commentators suggest that it may not be desirable to deal with the issue only from a copyright standpoint and that this issue needs to be managed comprehensively by referring to constitutional law, broadcast law, civil law and fair trade law.[8] One of the keys to resolving this dispute may be expanding the scope of must-carry channels and adjusting the level of retransmission compensation. According to Article 85(f) of the Copyright Act, KBS1 (a Korea Broadcasting System channel that is not supported by advertising) and EBS (the Korean Educational Broadcasting System) are statutorily designated must-carry channels to which simultaneous relay broadcasting rights are not applicable. Currently, there is a debate about whether to expand the number of must-carry channels to the other two major Korean broadcast networks. The KCC continues to conduct studies and hold seminars and hearings on this matter.

In spite of efforts to resolve it, the retransmission issue may be fast approaching a stage where regulation in the traditional sense may not work anymore. New forms of digital television services are fast emerging, and service convergence keeps progressing in the market. Recently, one of the major cable TV operators abruptly made a contract with terrestrial TV operators to pay them CPS for their new N-screen service at the same rate received by IPTV operators.

Net Neutrality

Recently in February 2012, KT (a major Korean telecom service provider and IPTV operator) blocked Internet access to Samsung Smart TVs, urging one of the nation's largest smart TV manufacturers to pay the cost of network use. KT's rationale was that doing so would protect Internet users from a possible network traffic jam[9] caused by smart TV use (see Figure 9.2).

Figure 9.2 shows that the amount of traffic caused by transmission of music videos or movies is likely to cause heavy traffic jams at the beginning of streaming. Based on this data, KT argued that increases in smart TV operators would negatively affect the market in the near future. KT said Samsung was free-loading and profiting using KT's Internet network. Samsung counter-argued that KT's blocking of Internet access was a violation of net neutrality, stressing the fact that no country has ever imposed a financial burden on TV manufacturers for Internet traffic. Although KT ended the blockade five days later following the mediation of the KCC, this incident accelerated debates on how an Internet network should be managed and who should be most responsible for the cost of Internet traffic.

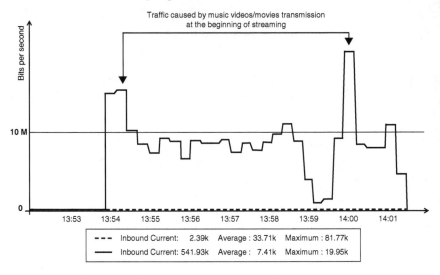

Figure 9.2   The impact of smart TV on Internet traffic.

As digital convergence has driven exponential increases in the use of audiovisual content, linear or nonlinear, through the Internet, network neutrality has become one of the most controversial policy areas. The principle of network neutrality states that all content, applications and services should be treated equally on the Internet by network operators to promote innovation at the end of the network. This argument has been vehemently challenged by those who believe that Internet regulation relying strictly on this principle would hinder the development of networks, which are essential resources for the development of a digital economy and culture (Pfister, 2007; Wu & Yoo, 2007; Yoo, 2007).

Many countries, including the U.S. and most EU nations, have been very cautious about strict enforcement of a net neutrality regulation, leaving room for a flexible interpretation of net neutrality in the market. In the era of digital convergence, when innovation in digital technologies and related business models occurs in a rapid and perpetual manner, it is very difficult to predict the direction in which the market and industry will develop. Therefore, governments try not to intervene too early. Rather, they take the position that interested parties be allowed to resolve conflicts by themselves in the market. This has been true in Korea as well. The KCC has refrained from employing mandatory regulations. Instead, it began to run an Advisory Committee on Net Neutrality Policy in February 2012 and later adopted guidelines focusing on the maintenance of transparency and reasonableness in traffic management and consumer protection.

The KT and Samsung dispute over smart TV access to the Internet, which seemed a very serious deadlock between the two sides, unfolded in an unexpected way when the line between smart TV and IPTV started to collapse as a result of service convergence. KT is preparing to provide IPTV on Samsung Smart TVs as an application, giving KT a boost in its competition with cable TV providers and allowing the smart TV manufacturer to offer a wider range of content. Meanwhile, telecom operators in Korea have begun confronting major Internet portal service providers—such as Naver, Daum and Google—urging them to share the cost of Internet traffic (Kyungjae, 2012). It will be very interesting to see how this confrontation unfolds.

News Impartiality

The Constitution of Korea protects freedom of speech and the press in Article 21. Although regulation of speech and the press is made possible through additional constitutional clauses that specify exceptions to the protection,[10] media content regulation has caused serious conflicts from time to time between speakers and regulators. This has been especially true of political content, such as news reports and content related to current affairs, since the protection of political points of view is essential to promoting democracy.

Historically, print media, notably newspapers, have enjoyed the greatest freedom of expression on the grounds that they are privately owned and the entry barrier to the market is low. In contrast, terrestrial broadcast news reports have experienced relatively stricter regulation due to the unique characteristics of terrestrial broadcast media, which use spectrums, scarce public resources, and are considered to be uniquely pervasive and available to children. Article 6 of the Broadcasting Act of Korea requires that a broadcast news report should be impartial and objective. The KCSC reviews terrestrial broadcast news reports using rules and standards it created based on the article.

However, the justifications for regulating terrestrial broadcasts (spectrum scarcity and unique pervasiveness) do not work well in the era of digital convergence when terrestrial broadcast content is transmitted through various types of networks and platforms. Therefore, debates arise on whether to apply review standards for terrestrial broadcasts to other media or whether to relax review standards for terrestrial broadcasts to the level used for other media. The KCSC has applied the Rules on Broadcast Review to terrestrial broadcasts and cable and satellite broadcasts. When reviewing programs, the KCSC has the discretion to consider differences in the professionalism and diversity of each medium and channel.

Problems in terms of content regulation occurred when IPTV services were launched. There had been a prolonged debate on whether IPTV should be regulated as broadcasting or telecommunications. The solution was to create an act separate from the Broadcasting Act for IPTV (the Internet Multimedia Broadcasting Act) that reflected the hybrid nature of IPTV as a convergent medium. According to the IPTV Act, content review standards for existing broadcasting services should apply only to linear broadcasting of IPTV. However, the legislation created a loophole for the regulation of nonlinear broadcasting of IPTV. Currently, nonlinear IPTV broadcasting programs can only be regulated by Article 44–7 (Prohibition on Circulation of Unlawful Information) of the Network Utilization and Information Protection Act as information publicly available through the Internet rather than as broadcasts.

As digital convergence proceeds, one of the most controversial issues in terms of content regulation is how webcasting, such as Internet TV or radio, should be regulated. In a legal sense, webcasting is considered a supplementary telecommunications service rather than a broadcasting service in Korea, however large the audience size and however large the influence a service could exert on public opinion. Internet broadcasting can only be regulated by Article 44–7 (Prohibition on Circulation of Unlawful Information) of the Network Utilization and Information Protection Act, which applies significantly relaxed standards that only assess the illegality of the information in question.

Recently, during election season for public officials, including Seoul City mayor, one webcasting program called "Naggomsu," providing a review of current affairs by three liberal hosts, earned enormous popularity, enjoying hundreds of thousands of followers. Although there were many complaints filed to the KCSC that the hosts made various unconfirmed, politically biased statements, there was no legal basis on which the KCSC could begin a review proceeding based on public interest and impartiality standards. Only when the hosts' comments were considered defamatory could the hosts be sued by alleged victims.

Broadcast content is increasingly distributed through the Internet, which is classified as a telecommunications network under the traditional vertical regulatory framework. Under the traditional framework, the conduit for distribution is considered a decisive criterion for regulatory standards for content. In Korea, a regulatory reshuffling that organizes the whole system into horizontal frameworks has long been discussed. Under a horizontal framework, factors such as the nature of the content (i.e., audiovisual or text, feature length or short clips, linear or nonlinear) and its potential influence on audiences need to be considered as criteria upon which more reasonable and consistent content regulatory systems may be based.

Virtual Child Pornography

With the proliferation of wireless Internet and smart media devices, increasingly easy access to and distribution of obscene material has become a serious social problem. Child pornography is at the center of these concerns in that the production and consumption of child pornography is believed to be closely related to crimes of predatory child sexual abuse. Therefore, child pornography is strictly regulated both domestically and internationally. As more and more child pornography crossed borders through the Internet, the need for international cooperation to regulate it was well recognized by the international community between the late 1990s and early 2000s. As a result, cooperative international regulatory systems are well established, and rules and standards in the area of child pornography are well harmonized among countries (Lee, 2013).

As digital technologies rapidly develop, virtual child pornography—computer-generated images and other realistic visual representations of the sexual exploitation of children—plays a more and more significant role in child pornography. Many countries included virtual child pornography in the scope of child pornography, and many international agreements recommend that virtual child pornography be regulated as the equivalent of real child pornography, which uses real children in sexual depictions. The major justification for the regulation of virtual child pornography is that the distinction between real and virtual child pornography becomes increasingly difficult to detect due to technological developments. The observation that virtual child pornography is often used as bait by child sexual offenders to lure children is another justification for its regulation (Cisneros, 2002; Mota, 2002; Poborilova, 2011).

Korea joined the international trend of regulating virtual child pornography by amending the definition of child pornography in Paragraph 5 of Article 2 of the Act on the Protection of Children and Juveniles from Sexual Abuse in September 2011 as follows:

> Original definition: "the term 'child or juvenile pornography' means the <u>depiction of children or juveniles</u> doing an act specified in subparagraph 4[11] or engaging in any other sexual act in the form of film, video, game software, or picture or image, etc. displayed on computers or other communication media."
>
> Amended definition: "the term 'child or juvenile pornography' means the <u>depiction of children or juveniles, or of persons or expressions that can be recognized as children or juveniles</u> doing an act specified in subparagraph 4 or engaging in any other sexual act in the form of film, video, game software, or picture or image, etc. displayed on computers or other communication media."

Since the adoption of the amendment, there has been a sharp increase in the arrest or prosecution of alleged perpetrators accused of the distribution, consumption/use or simple possession of virtual child pornography. However, the problem in the regulation of virtual child pornography is that the definition is obscure and overbroad. Therefore, legitimate content, such as movies with artistic value[12] or audiovisual material with educational or scientific value, could be included in its scope. There has also been a big controversy over (1) whether erotic descriptions of animated characters should be regulated using identical criteria and (2) whether the harsh provision that punishes the simple possession of virtual child pornography should also be applied to the completely private possession of privately produced materials using only fictional characters. As technology for cloud computing develops, not only downloading files on one's computer but also watching streaming files retrieved from a cloud service platform will need to be examined as an action of simple possession in a legal sense (Lee, 2013).

It seems that the issue of virtual child pornography will remain one of the major policy controversies for a considerable period of time in Korea until more detailed rules, standards and guidelines are established through in-depth legal, academic and social discussions.

CONCLUSION

Regulation always lags behind the development of technology and consequent changes in industry, as well as their effect on people's behavior. This is especially true in the era of digital convergence. Changes in digital technology tend to be geared toward the seemingly automatic propagation of subsequent technological developments that lead to various behavioral changes in media consumption and business operations. Such changes include the acceleration of media service convergence and globalization, media ownership concentration, the emergence of diverse new media service platforms and extreme competition among them, the proliferation of digital content across media, the phenomenon of a real-world increasingly defined by a virtual world and so forth. Comprehending the meaning of these changes and coming up with regulatory solutions to deal with them comprehensively and effectively seems implausible. Therefore, regulatory policies in the era of digital convergence tend to be fragmented, incomplete and apt to change.

For these reasons, the best regulatory strategy in an era of digital convergence may be to carefully observe changes in technology and the market and intervene at the necessary minimum at the right moment and in the right spot. That is to say, regulators need to refrain from acting too proactively to keep from hindering innovations and distorting the market. They are, rather, required to be sensible coordinators among competing interests at various levels.

In this chapter, we discussed meaningful changes in the Korean media industry in relation to digital convergence. Regulatory schemes that can comprehensively and neatly manage such changes do not seem to be available, in spite of prolonged discussions since regulatory bodies for broadcasting and telecommunications physically merged in 2008 in response to digital convergence. Since then, many problems and issues have appeared and have been discussed in the search for solutions. There have been two different types of regulatory response: (1) proactively amending existing rules or laws to the necessary degree as a means to facilitate the market for effective competition or to fill in gaps in existing regulations that were created by technological advances; (2) taking a wait-and-see position and letting the market deal with problems, with regulators mediating through guidelines or supporting with professional studies. The modification of ownership rules and the creation of the media diversity index are examples of the first type of response, while what the KCC did with regards to retransmission of broadcasts and net neutrality issues are the second type of response. In terms of content regulation, virtual child pornography regulations seem to be an example of the first type of response, while news impartiality regulations may be of the second.

Digital convergence has brought revolutionary changes in broadcasting and telecommunications. The line between the two has blurred to a significant level, and print media firms, such as newspapers and magazines, are increasingly joining broadcasting and telecommunications businesses. In the not-too-distant future, it will become meaningless to classify media sectors into broadcasting, telecommunications or pure print media. While the vertical "silo" model, a traditional regulatory framework, is fast losing its utility, a new horizontal regulatory model is considered an effective alternative to cope with the changes caused by digital convergence. However, the change from a vertical regulatory model to a horizontal regulatory model at a macro level cannot by itself offer a comprehensive solution for the complex problems resulting from digital convergence. Along with a paradigm shift in the regulatory framework at the macro level, the first and second type of regulatory responses discussed in this chapter will continue, at the micro level, to address the various aspects of change resulting from digital convergence.

NOTES

1. Article 28, the Government Organization Act.
2. Article 1, the Act on Press Arbitration and Remedies, Etc. for Damage Caused by Press Reports.
3. Article 2(18), the Act on Press Arbitration and Remedies, Etc. for Damage Caused by Press Reports.
4. Article 8, Paragraph 2, The Broadcasting Act.(Memo: This should be an endnote No. 5. I have put a footnote because I am not allowed to put an endnote in this file. Please rearrange endnotes for the whole manuscript.)
5. This refers to the ratio of households that subscribe to a paid daily newspaper for a given period out of total households.
6. Market share for TV viewing = viewers' TV watching hours for each channel / total viewing hours for all channels

   Market share for radio listening = number of audience members per channel / sum of audience number for all channels
   Market share for paid daily newspaper = number of paid subscriptions per newspaper / number of paid subscriptions for all daily newspapers
   Market share of TTS (total time spent) for each website = TTS for each website / TTS for all websites

7. $(15\% \times 1) + (10\% \times 0.3) + (10\% \times 0.4) + (5\% \times 0.6) = 25\%$
8. The Monopoly Regulation and Fair Trade Act.
9. It is believed that smart TV causes 5 to 15 times more traffic than IPTV.
10. Freedom of speech and the press may be restricted in cases where speech "violates the honor or rights of other persons or undermines public morals or social ethics" or when "necessary for national security and the maintenance of law and order for public welfare" (Article 21(4) and 37(2) of the Constitution).

11. Those are (a) sexual intercourse ; (b) pseudo-sexual intercourse using parts of the body, such as the mouth and anus, or implements; (c) touching or exposing the whole or part of the body, which causes sexual humiliation or repugnance of ordinary people; and (d) masturbation.
12. Recently, there was a court decision that depictions of sexual acts in a film by an of-age actress who played the character of a minor were not a violation of the virtual child pornography provision (Suwon District Court, 2013).

REFERENCES

Cisneros, D. (2002). "Virtual child" pornography on the Internet: A "virtual" victim? *Duke Law & Technology Review, 19,* 1–13.
E-Daily. (2009, January 16). *Retransmission disputes between terrestrial broadcasters and cable TV operators.* Retrieved from http://showroom.edaily.co.kr/news/Read.asp?newsid=02250086599398376
E-Daily. (2013, May 6). *KT emerging as a powerful player in the pay TV market.* Retrieved from www.edaily.co.kr/news/newsRead.edy?SCD=JE31&DCD=A00503&newsid=02407526602806296
Government of Korea. *The Act on the Protection of Children and Juveniles from Sexual Abuse,* as amended by Act No. 11690, March 23, 2013.
Government of Korea. *The Broadcasting Act,* as amended by Act No. 12093, August 13, 2013.
Government of Korea. *The Copyright Act,* as amended by Act No. 11903, July 16, 2013.
Kim, N.D., Lee, J.W., Whang, Y.S., & Kim, D.G. (2012). A study on the development and utilization of a cross-media summated influence index. *Broadcasting & Telecommunication Policy Study,* 12-Promotion-042, KISDI.
Kim, T.O. (2009). Major issues with and content of the amended Media Law. *Journal of Law & Economic Regulation, 2*(2), 182–186.
Korea Telecom (KT)(2012). *The impact of smart TV on Internet traffic.* Internal report.
Kyungjae, M. (2012, May 3). *3 major telco surge portal services to share cost for Internet traffic.* Retrieved from http://news.mk.co.kr/newsRead.php?no=267766&year=2012
Lee, D.C. (2008). Discussions of the legal regulation of news portals: Focusing on the reform bills of the Newspaper Law and the Press Arbitration Law. *Korea Law Review, 30,* 1–25.
Lee, H.S. (2012). Paradigm changes in Internet content regulation: A study on the adoption of co-regulatory systems. *Korean Journal of Broadcasting & Telecommunication Studies, 26*(4), 215–264.
Lee, H.S. (2013). Regulation of virtual child pornography in the digital era: A comparative exploration and its implications for our society. *Korean Journal of Broadcasting & Telecommunication Studies, 27*(2), 227–268.
MediaUs (2013, May 6). *IPTV subscribers exceed 7 million.* Retrieved from www.mediaus.co.kr/news/articleView.html?idxno=34009
Mota, S.A. (2002). The U.S. Supreme Court addresses the Child Pornography Prevention Act and Child Online Protection Act in Ashcroft v. Free Speech Coalition and Ashcroft v. American Civil Liberties Union. *Federal Communications Law Journal, 55,* 85–98.
Pfister, F.W. (2007). Net neutrality: An international policy for the United States. *San Diego International Law Journal, 9,* 167–211.
Poborilova, M. (2011), Virtual child pornography. *Masaryk University Journal of Law and Technology, 5*(2), 241–253.

Seoul Central District Court. (2009). 2009 Ka Hap 3358, decided on Dec. 31, 2009.
Seoul Central District Court. (2010). 2009 Ga Hap 132731, decided on Sept. 8, 2010.
Seoul Higher Court. (2011). 2010 Na 97688, decided on July 20, 2011.
Suwon District Court. (2013). No 1215, decided on June 27, 2013.
Wu, T., & Yoo, C. (2007). Keeping the Internet neutral? Tim Wu and Christopher Yoo Debate. *Federal Communications Law Journal, 59*, 575–592.
Yoo, C. (2007). What can antitrust contribute to the network neutrality debate. *International Journal of Communication, 1*, 493–530.
Yoo, E. S. (2009). Media diversity: Policy implications and means to achieve it. *Journal of Broadcasting Research, 69*, 42–68.

10 Fine-Tuning the Competition

The Case of Singapore's Cross-Carriage Rule in Ending Content Exclusivity

Mabel Tan and Peng Hwa Ang

Singapore is known for a few things. It is a hot, muggy country almost year-round, its citizens are passionate "foodies" who will take great pains to ensure the quality of food and its civil servants are passionate about efficiency, as evidenced from the airport. Less well-known is that Singaporeans are also passionate about football, or what is known as soccer.

That passion is best captured by how the Singapore pay-TV operators handle the exclusive broadcast rights of the English Premier League (EPL). In 2006, the incumbent rights holder, StarHub, outbid the new entrant, SingTel, to maintain exclusive broadcast rights of the EPL. But it could only do so at the cost of raising the monthly subscription price for EPL from S$15 (US$12.25) before the higher bid to S$25 (US$20.50) in 2007 after the successful but higher bid. In 2010, SingTel, which had been struggling to capture a critical mass of viewers, struck back. It wrested the coveted exclusive multiyear broadcast rights away from StarHub by bidding more than US$250 million, compared with the previous estimated bid of US$150 million in 2006. For SingTel, the move was a "game changer" indeed as it did achieve its goal of garnering a critical mass of subscribers to turn its IPTV business toward the path of profitability. But for subscribers, this meant an increase of another S$25 to watch the EPL on the new platform.

Singapore is not unique in experiencing the ill effects of escalating content costs. Such price wars have become a worldwide phenomenon in many markets where liberalisation has seen competing pay-TV operators competing fiercely for sought-after content. The 2010 bid, however, made Singapore one of the most expensive places in the world to watch the EPL. More significantly, it was yet another battle lost to consumers in the escalating war between the pay-TV operators as they fought for market share.

Having witnessed the exponential fee increases at these bidding auctions, and the consequent price hikes suffered by its citizens, the Media Development Authority of Singapore set a global first in March 2010 when it imposed a "cross-carriage rule": any pay-TV operator who procures exclusive content must allow that content to be "cross carried" on its rivals' pay-TV platform in its entirety, at the same price and package conditions as its own subscribers on its platform.

This was a first in many regards. It was a significant shift in policy paradigm in the small country with a strong free market approach to business. So strongly has it toed the free market line that it is consistently ranked among the freest economies in the world (Heritage Foundation, 2010). It was also the first content-access regulation to be imposed on the pay-TV industry in Asia, an industry heavily dependent on foreign imported programming in ready-packaged channels and premium content such as "live" sports events and movies.

In defending the new policy, the media regulator Media Development Authority of Singapore focused the issue on the problem of high exclusive content where "more than 90 (pay-TV) channels (in Singapore) are available exclusively at one place. No other country in the world has that" (Chai, 2010b). An official response by its acting minister revealed that the number of exclusive content agreements more than doubled from 2005 to 131 in 2010 since SingTel's entry into the pay-TV market (Ministry of Information, Culture and the Arts [MICA], 2010).

This chapter examines the issues and the policy response in Singapore and analyses the effectiveness of its objectives in light of the evidence in the 2 years since the cross-carriage rule took effect. Singapore's policy solution will be reviewed and compared against other regulatory measures in the United States and Europe, with a discussion of how the formative policy may be further enhanced in its relevance and application for other similar pay-TV markets in Asia and beyond.

The Problems in Singapore's Pay-TV Market

The Side Effects of Liberalisation?
Singapore had joined the global movement to deregulate and liberalise its national telecommunications industry from the early 1990s. In April 2000, the country ended the telecommunications duopoly held by Singapore Telecommunications Ltd ("SingTel") and StarHub Pte Ltd ("StarHub"), which until then were the only fixed-line and cable network respectively. With compensation at S$1.2 billion (US$1 billion) paid to both companies for the loss of the duopoly, the government also awarded to SingTel an additional licence for the country's second pay-TV network, operationalised as an IPTV (Internet Protocol TV) platform in 2004 (Ittogi & Lazim, 2004).

This coincided with the formation of the Media Development Authority in Singapore (MDA) in 2003 to become the umbrella authority for both promoting and regulating the media industry. Hitherto, its predecessor, the Singapore Broadcasting Authority, had the role of regulating the broadcast media. MDA acts as the sectoral competition regulatory authority for the media industry within its Code of Practice for Market Conduct ("Code"), which specifies the rights and obligations of participants of the industry, including the definition and abuse of market power by dominant players (Ittogi & Lazim, 2004).

Liberalisation of the telecommunication and pay-TV industry was widely touted to bring the benefits of competition to its citizens. Singaporeans, however, saw a jump in the costs of their key content such as EPL. Thanks to fierce competitive fervour, the rights holder, StarHub, increased its bidding fee in 2006, raising monthly subscription to the prized EPL programme from S$8 (US$6.50) to S$25 (US$20.50) (Cotta, 2009).

Media reports speculated that the bidding fee had increased from the estimated US$60 million previously to US$150 million in 2006. It was obvious that the higher costs could not be recouped in spite of the higher subscription prices for the 3-year period on StarHub's sports subscriber base. StarHub therefore raised the price to its basic channel packages between 2006 and 2009 even as many of these flagship channels in education (Discovery, National Geographic), kids (Disney, Nickelodeon), news (CNN, Bloomberg), entertainment (MTV, Star World) and movies (HBO, Star Movies, Cinemax) remained exclusively on its platform. That is, even those who did not want to view the EPL but merely to continue with the same channels they had would now have to pay the higher basic package fee.

The price war intensified in the following season, with SingTel winning the exclusive rights for EPL by bidding between US$250 million and US$280 million in 2010. This meant that over a period of 6 years after deregulation in 2004, competition between the pay-TV operators had more than tripled the estimated costs of the rights as well as the retail subscription costs to one pay-TV channel alone.

Counter-Competitive Consumer Welfare

The resultant cost increases experienced by its citizens extended beyond the direct price increase of the sports programming. As the EPL programming swung over to SingTel, consumers felt coerced to have to sign up to both pay-TV networks in order to maintain the same suite of programming across the key genres in entertainment, news, sports and movies. What was previously available only on StarHub, as the monopoly, now needed two subscription packages and two set-top boxes to enjoy. This subjected viewers to a higher level of minimum sign-up fees, subscription packages and the technical challenges of having to deal with different platforms and operating systems on their TV. The consumer predicament conflicted with the notion that competition was intended to bring about greater choice, if not lower costs.

These issues were compounded by the fact that many of StarHub's existing pay-TV subscribers were "locked in" to minimum contractual periods as part of its aggressive, preemptive marketing prior to 2006. These customers were enticed with generous premiums such as the (then) latest Xbox consoles and HD TV sets offered as part of their contract renewals for between 1 and 3 years. Termination of the contracts meant incurring high penalty charges (Bahrawi, 2007).

Adding insult to injury was the poorer performance quality of SingTel's new IPTV platform, which suffered repeatedly from latency issues and compromised the viewing experience especially for the prime EPL "live" matches. The final few minutes of the final match froze, to the frustration of subscribers (Chong, 2012). The confluence of all these issues led to a public outcry that compelled the media regulator, MDA, to act.

Us-Versus-Them Culture

The two leading telecommunications and pay-TV operators in Singapore, StarHub and SingTel, engage in sharply antagonistic competition. As both were once monopoly players in fixed-line and pay-TV services respectively, liberalisation saw each one going head-to-head with the other in the strategy for "triple play" of mobile, broadband and pay-TV services.[1] Both operators are known to employ sales campaigns against each other through competing road shows, premium giveaways and promotions in their contest for subscribers and market share.

In contrast, Hong Kong's pay-TV industry has four operators with varying degrees of market share and content niches and a range of customer options from bundled tier packages to a la carte subscriptions. Given the symbiotic relationship between sports and pay TV, the level of competitive bidding for the crown-jewel EPL is also active, and the exclusive rights were won by the new entrant PCCW's now TV in 2006 only to be regained by the incumbent iCable in 2010. Bidding costs went up, but on a lesser scale from US$200 million to US$260 million in the same period for a territory of 7 million (compared with US$150 million to US$280 million for a population of 4.5 million in Singapore).

So is this a case of the culture of cut-throat competition among Singapore's duopoly contributing to an average annual pay-TV bill of US$424 compared with Hong Kong's US$218 and its four networks (Cable and Satellite Broadcasting Association of Asia [CASBAA], 2011)? Or is this an economic consequence of a duopoly market structure in Singapore versus the multifirm oligopoly structure of four firms in Hong Kong?

The Policy Solution—The Cross-Carriage Rule 2010

Deterrence Against Content Exclusivity

The problems and issues highlighted here culminated in the policy response of the new cross-carriage rule in March 2010 (Media Development Authority of Singapore [MDA], 2010). The rule is targeted only at exclusive channel or content agreements. Under it, the exclusive content operator ("Supplying Qualified Licensee") bears the costs of transmission of its exclusively contracted content ("Qualified Content") on its rival's network (the "Receiving Qualified Licensee"). It makes clear that the "Supplying Qualified Licensee must enter into a customer service arrangement" with subscribers on the other, rival platform in a direct customer relationship and pay "all incremental costs directly incurred by Receiving Qualified Licensee in providing its Subscribers with access" (Media Develoment Authority of Singapore Act, Chapter 172, 2010).

This clearly sets out the deterrent effect the code is expected to bring onto the pay-TV operators in the Singapore market. The partiality in the code was subsequently mitigated through a Variation of Code of Practice in July 2011, which sets out the "Pricing of Costs of Cross-Carriage" including clear charging methodology and costs standards, limiting the amount that could be exacted for the transmission of content by the receiving operator.

The intended outcome of the cross-carriage rule is to dissuade pay-TV operators from pursuing exclusivity as a marketing strategy because such content will no longer be exclusive to them and unavailable to the competition. The rule assumes that the content owners selling their rights nonexclusively will operate in classical profit-maximisation behaviour and seek to exploit rights across as many pay-TV operators and subscribers as possible. The hoped-for behaviour of profit maximisation through maximising rights exploitation should then slow if not thwart the ill effects of the price wars and consequent fee increases from exclusive rights' bidding.

Policy Objectives

Enhancing Content Access

Under the cross-carriage rule, any exclusive content, whether linear, non-linear or as part of bundled package, must be offered "at prices (including all applicable discounts and promotions), terms and conditions that are the same as the prices, terms and conditions at which the Supplying Qualified Licensee provides such content to Subscribers on its own platform" and at service levels "at a level of quality that is not inferior . . . or any act that may diminish, impair or otherwise degrade the viewing or customer service experience" as its own subscribers.

This is intended to bring about greater choice and uniform pricing of exclusive programming. Media statements by MDA said that lower prices were not the objective of the regulation, but primarily "to facilitate greater consumer access to pay TV content," where "consumers will no longer require multiple set top boxes or have to switch pay TV retailers just to enjoy exclusive content" (2010).

Promoting Innovation

In its public statement, the MDA said: "Cross-carriage was introduced to rectify the high degree of content fragmentation in the Singapore pay-TV market, and shift the focus of competition from an exclusivity-centric strategy to other aspects such as service differentiation and competitive packaging" (MDA, 2012b). The statement reiterates and clarifies the second intent of the rule: to foster innovation as a key aspect of growth in the industry. The cross-carriage rule excludes other technological platforms, notably as SingTel and StarHub both own and operate fixed-line, mobile and broadband network services. This means that other technological platforms may have exclusive content.

This is important in view of the extensive investment that the Singapore government has made towards the island's next-generation fibre optic network to the tune of S$1 billion (US$820 million), to be ready by 2015 (Infocomm Development Authority of Singapore [IDA], 2009). One of the key propositions of the open-access fibre optic network is to promote the growth of "interactive IPTV services." In the duopoly industry dominated by SingTel and StarHub, the cross-carriage rule is also intended to remove the bottleneck of high costs to acquire the driver content necessary for new entrants to enter into the nascent IPTV platform.

In MDA's communication, the cross-carriage rule was also posited for "potential pay TV retailers" because "it reduces the high barriers to entry where more content is available for acquisition" (MDA, 2012a). This also seemed consistent with the relatively low requirement of 10,000 subscribers in order to qualify as a Receiving Qualified Licensee to any exclusive content signed as part of the cross-carriage rule.

Increasing Media Plurality and Diversity

The policy intent then is to encourage plurality in the sector by fostering conditions such that new IPTV entrants may be able to compete on the new next-generation fibre optic network and increase diversity—not of content necessarily, since much of pay-TV programming is foreign imported in the country, but a diversity of new service options, technologies and innovation. The cross-carriage policy framework, however, contradicts that policy intent because it assumes that any such exclusive, "killer content" will not, or cannot, be sublicensed to rival operators as part of the rights acquired. By directly eliminating any possibility of sublicensing, and therefore requiring that exclusive content be carried in its entirety in the same form, package and terms, it precludes any alternative subscription options other than those of the exclusive content operator alone.

Does this show a lack of faith in the ability of the pay-TV operators for fair negotiation and sharing of content, given the antagonistic history between StarHub and SingTel? Or is this based on a flawed presumption that sublicensing is not an option from the rights owners of sought-after content such as the EPL?

Reactions and Evidence 2010–2012

The following discussion looks at the reactions from the varied stakeholders and the evidence in Singapore for a preliminary assessment of the effectiveness of the new policy.

Reactions to Rule

The business models and content offerings of the pay-TV industries are similar across Singapore, Hong Kong, Taiwan, Malaysia and Thailand. The Cable and Satellite Broadcasting Association of Asia (CASBAA) was concerned that other governments would follow suit and so drive down the prices of all exclusive content by removing their exclusivity. They argued that the rule violated the Free Trade Agreement that Singapore had signed with the United States, the dominant supplier of programmes, although in the case of EPL, the source was the UK (Chai, 2010a).

Objectives Met

The new cross-carriage rule seemed to have achieved the intended effects to force the incumbents to look beyond content exclusivity as the only basis of competition; it has also spurred innovation in new technological and service options for customers, expanded the operators' added value in the packaging of their own branded channels and brought about a broadened content offer.

Evidence of Innovation

The UEFA (Union of European Football Associations) Euro2012 TV coverage was lauded by the MDA as the "significant milestone" of the implementation of the cross-carriage rule (MDA, 2012a). StarHub secured the exclusive rights to the league, and its package of Euro2012 programming was extended not only to SingTel's mio TV subscribers at the same package and costs, but was also unbundled from its basic and sports tiers as an a la carte channel for new subscribers. This is a marked departure of the stance of the operator who had, until then, insisted that all subscribers adhere to its pyramid subscription levels of minimum "basic" tiers before customers were able to subscribe to a "premium" sport tier as a multichannel bundle, never as a single-channel a la carte option of its own.

Further, the exclusive content operator StarHub also rolled out its 23-channel "TV Anywhere" service, where dual- or triple-subscription customers of its pay-TV service may enjoy their TV programming over StarHub's mobile and/or broadband platforms at no additional charges. This enhances the viewing experience and utility of its programming and testifies to the expressed intention of the regulator for competition to shift away from content exclusivity to "service differentiation and competitive packaging" (MDA, 2012b).

The pay-TV operators have attempted to differentiate themselves by adding new capabilities. Where the operators have traditionally relied on simple retransmission of ready-made channels, both are now packaging and branding their own sports channels. StarHub created its own Football Channel in addition to its SuperSports 1 and 2, and SingTel added its mio Sports channel respectively. StarHub even ventured further into content production with its first 24-hour, "live" reality-format talent competition called the Sunsilk Academy Fantasia.

Broadened Content Offering

The number of new and nonexclusive channels between the two operators also increased in the 2 years since cross-carriage took effect. Both operators pursued new and niche programming on their networks in a bid to continue to differentiate their offerings and attract subscribers. Previously unexplored genres such as dialect language programming were launched on both networks. Another significant landmark was the renewal of the FOX network on a nonexclusive basis, bringing the network's 40 channels across both StarHub and SingTel in 2012. These included leading channels such as National Geographic, MTV, FX, and so on.

Unexpected Outcomes

The new policy, however, also produced some unexpected effects. While reducing prices was unequivocally stated not to be an intended outcome of the cross-carriage rule, the continual steep rises in the costs of sporting content was nonetheless a disappointing outcome. The exclusive UEFA Euro2012 on StarHub, which was the first exclusive content to be subjected to the cross-carry obligation, costs three times more to its subscribers at $65 compared with the previous season's $20. Was the 2.4 times increase over 3 years "excessive"? Arguably, it was not, because the football World Cup's subscription rate went from $15 in 2006 to more than $90 in 2010—a six-fold increase over 4 years—before the cross-carry rule was effected. On the other hand, it may also be argued that this is comparing apples and oranges because the World Cup is the pinnacle of football.

The first exclusive UEFA Euro2012 by StarHub since the cross-carriage rule took effect was also the only one to be cross-carried on rivals' platforms since then. Subsequent leagues followed a trend of nonexclusive agreements where flagship sporting events were available only on a single pay-TV operator, with StarHub offering the Bundesliga and J-League and SingTel being the only one to offer the FA Cup, Italian Serie A and the UEFA Champions League. Key sport leagues matches were being signed and offered only by a single operator in the market, albeit on a nonexclusive basis. Being nonexclusive meant that the cross-carriage rule did not apply. Ironically, the nonexclusive sports programmes still required subscribers to sign up for dual subscriptions and set-top boxes in order to enjoy the full suite of football events. The new nonexclusive arrangement therefore harks back to the days of the pre-cross-carriage rule and contradicts the objective of the cross-carriage rule.

That consumers were left with no choice but to commit to dual subscriptions is evidenced by the increase in total pay-TV subscriptions, which rose from 694,000 in 2009 to 900,000 in 2012. In the country with approximately 1 million households, the increase is mostly attributed to double subscriptions per household. Indeed, most of the increase in subscriber numbers belonged to SingTel, which seemed to have achieved its strategic intent in leveraging the key sporting events to drive subscriptions while StarHub's subscription base remained essentially flat. SingTel's total subscriber numbers increased from 100,000 in end-2009[2] to more than 300,000 in 2011,[3] while StarHub's total pay-TV subscriber numbers remained between

539,000 and 545,000[4] in the same period. The outcome suggests that Sing-Tel achieved its aim of obtaining a critical mass of viewers who would make its pay-TV business viable. It also suggests, however, that StarHub has been able to hold its own against the competition. The benefit to business begs the question as to the effectiveness of the cross-carriage rule in promoting consumer interests: "nonexclusive" content continues to require dual subscriptions, and price increases continue unabated, with operators and content owners seemingly determined to have the previous arrangement of preferred, single relationships.

Given the popularity of football, it is counterintuitive that the competing pay-TV operator did not, or could not, come to an agreement with the rights owners for nonexclusive rights to broadcast the same leagues as its competitor. Yet the trend persists, with the next three seasons of EPL 2013–2016 announced to be nonexclusively signed to SingTel ("SingTel secure EPL broadcasts rights," 2012). Indeed, the latest EPL agreement points to preferential relationships of the content owners, as the rights owner FAPL (FA Premier League) deviated from "all past practices" and awarded the rights to SingTel without a tender process, which had hitherto always been used historically. The closed-door nature of the manner in which the rights were awarded implies that negotiation was far from arms-length between the rights owner and its preferred pay-TV operator. Because the rights are nonexclusive, the cross-carriage rule does not apply. That is, SingTel has no obligation to provide access to its content to StarHub subscribers. In other words, it is back to the original situation of subscribers having to subscribe to SingTel's service to watch EPL. Unless, of course, StarHub also negotiates for the right to carry the EPL. As StarHub has a larger subscriber base, it would in all probability have to more than match SingTel's price. It would make Singapore among the most expensive places to view the EPL.

The MDA's response was to postulate that the situation may "indicate hard bargaining by both sides as they seek to discover a sustainable price for content in the Singapore market; in other words, that they are rational players operating within a clear framework of rules established by the regulator" (MDA, 2012b). This seems to point to the faith that the regulator has in the rational behaviour of the pay-TV operators and their ability to negotiate and abide by the fair rules of the game. While such a belief would appear rational, it also leaves open the inevitable conclusion that the regulator may have a flawed presumption that the option of sublicensing rights was not possible or reasonable to expect of the content owners.

Policy Comparisons and Discussion

How does Singapore's cross-carriage rule compare with other established regimes in ensuring access of content?

The U.S. model of access regulation is largely based on antitrust, where laws are designed to prevent specific instances of abuse of market power from vertically integrated media conglomerates against smaller or new market entrants in pay TV. The focus is on media powerhouses with extensive vertically integrated operations across content production, programme networks and pay-TV retail operators. Under the 1992 Cable Act, the Federal Communications Commission (FCC) imposed the "program access rules" (Cable Television Consumer Protection and Competition Act, 1992) on cable operators who own programming networks and forced them to sell these channel networks to pay-TV rivals. The intention was to prevent market foreclosure by these conglomerates who wield significant power through the ownership and operation of leading programme channels. This rule was extended twice since 1992 and ended in 2012, during which period Time Warner was required to offer its CNN network, and Comcast its Golf Channel, to smaller, rival satellite operators in the U.S. The "program access rules" were lauded by the FCC to be "one of the true success stories of the 1992 Cable Act" and were credited with paving the way for smaller satellite operators such as DirecTV and EchoStar, who "just would not exist" without them (Hearn, 2007).

In Europe, the pay-TV industry is also similarly concentrated, with significant market power in the hands of a few large media networks. BSkyB, for example, has leveraged on its first-mover advantage and amassed packaging capabilities and financial muscle and attracted regulatory attention. Its ability to buy up exclusive rights in the premium content markets for movie titles and sporting leagues, and in turn to package and brand them as part of its own channel networks for exclusive retailing, meant that smaller competitors were denied access to such premium content, and their survival was threatened.

Europe was the forerunner of pay-TV price wars in many respects, where the contest for exclusive sport content saw an astronomical rise in the value of these live event rights. Media rights for EPL rose from €280 million in 1992 to more than €2.5 billion in 2006 in UK alone (Lefever & Van Rompuy, 2009). In the coverage of EU intervention in ensuring access to sport content, Lefever and Van Rompuy reported that "no digital pay-TV package has been launched which did not include live football as part of its content." The high costs of live sport rights deemed as "stand-alone driver content" for new pay-TV operators resulted in significant barriers of entry for new entrants, which ultimately affects consumer welfare.

Singapore's pay-TV market shares certain similarities with the EU industry in spite of the wide size disparity. Being the first-mover meant that StarHub was able to leverage on the increasing subscriber base as adoption took off and build its capabilities in the packaging of its own branded channels, SuperSports 1 and SuperSports 2, a close parallel to BSkyB's own Sky Sports 1 and 2. Further, it packaged a third in-house channel, the Football Channel, in 2006 with the exclusive EPL rights as a direct preemptive move against the anticipated competition that SingTel would bring. The EU market is also dominated by a duopoly structure, where the two largest, BSkyB and Vivendi, dwarf all other competitors in size and financial strength.

Recognising that sport constitutes a "stand-alone driver content" for new media operators, the European Commission's Article 81 EC of the EC Treaty (Treaty Establishing the European Community) is one of the main antitrust provisions to ensure that content access is not unduly restricted by anticompetitive agreements. In the UK, "OFT concluded that BSkyB had a market power in the wholesale market of premium contents distribution" in 1995, and the additional regulatory pressure resulted in BSkyB's undertaking to make its branded channels available on a nondiscriminatory wholesale offer to other downstream competitors" (Nicita & Ramello, 2005). This is commonly referred to as a "must-offer" condition on the incumbent pay-TV operator BSkyB, who must make its EPL channels (Sky Sports 1 and 2) available to retail rivals across the spread of technological platforms whether satellite, cable or IPTV. A salient difference in the policy framework and effect was that these BSkyB programme channels were sublicensed to competitors (i.e., on a wholesale basis), who were then free to price and package these as part of their own larger bundled or as a la carte offerings to subscribers. On the other hand, Singapore's cross-carriage rule limited other downstream competitors from being able to offer the exclusive content as part of their own product mix and instead relegated them to the role of an operator billing on behalf of the exclusive content pay-TV operator. The marketing and economic obstacles in the cross-carriage rule are significant.

Further, the EU institutions have also investigated the potential anticompetitive effects of joint selling, particularly the possibility of market foreclosure when "rights were sold on an exclusive basis in a single bundle to a single broadcaster per territory, foreclosing competitors from accessing these rights for three years or more" (Lefever & Van Rompuy, 2009). This was exemplified in the European Commission's decision in its UEFA Champions League Decision (in 2003), where the competition review pressured the rights owner to modify the conditions of its sale and segment the media rights for the League into 14 smaller subpackages to be sold to multiple parties, across different technological platforms including mobile and the Internet. This general approach was subsequently adopted in later cases involving the German Football League and FAPL, where the "Commission imposed a no single buyer obligation . . . in order to prevent all rights packages being sold to the dominant pay TV operator in the UK, BSkyB" (Lefever & Van Rompuy, 2009).

These cases offer some interesting insights to the case of Singapore given the differences in regulatory perspective and execution. These policy options are discussed next.

Policy Options

"Must Cross-Carry" Versus "Must Offer"

The cross-carry rule builds upon the public interest paradigm of the "must-carry" obligations of the pay-TV operators (where pay-TV operators are

obliged to carry, at no additional costs, broadcasts of local free-to-air channels or national programmes deemed constructive to community or social
cohesion), with the regulator stating clearly its objective to negate the need
for multiple set-top boxes in order to enjoy premium content and, in so
doing, protect the consumer interests.

Unlike Europe, anti-siphoning measures in Singapore to prevent the
monopolisation of certain nationally significant programmes by pay-TV
operators to the exclusion of free-to-air TV do not apply to much of the
premium content in contest, particularly the football and sporting leagues
of high popular appeal. MDA's anti-siphoning lists of Category A and B
programming were opened for public consultation (MDA, 2012c) in a bid
to expand the sport categories of interest to the country. The criteria and
definition of "national significance" for anti-siphoning, however, meant that
the imported foreign sporting leagues were necessarily out of consideration.

To meet the policy objectives of promoting innovation and consumer
access, defined as the ability of consumers to choose between different service options for the same programming across different pay-TV operators
and platforms, it is proposed that the cross-carry rule be amended to allow
the possibility of wholesale sublicensing instead of carriage on-behalf alone.
Both the U.S. and EU have used wholesale sublicensing to prevent content
foreclosure by significant market incumbents. Doing so will allow smaller,
new market entrants the ability to sublicense the "driver content" at determined, wholesale rates and include these as part of their own bundle of
offerings on pay TV or new mobile and Internet platforms. This will mitigate the bottleneck of high content acquisition costs for smaller or new
entrants and will encourage more diverse service options and platforms.
Consumer choice can then be defined as the ability to choose between different operators, service packages and platforms instead of merely subscribing
to the same package terms offered by the dominant, exclusive content operator on competing networks.

Competition Review

In addition to reviewing the buying positions of such "driver content," the
EU example in critically scrutinising selling positions should also be further
considered. This is relevant especially given the dominant market position
of these upstream firms, such as the Football Association Premier League
and the Champions League, where these firms own a relative monopoly of
rights to the EPL and soccer programming worldwide.

The dominant monopoly seller will always prefer an exclusive contract
to maximise its total revenue. This is especially pertinent in situations where
payment is a lump-sum basis (as is the case for most sporting rights) and the
downstream firms believe that the rights will be granted exclusively to only
one player (i.e., the other firm loses all access to content). Economic mod-
elling suggests that the seller always maximises payoff when it is allowed

to create an all-or-nothing scenario for the sale of its rights on a lump-sum basis as this allows it to exploit the negative externality in the market suffered by the losing market players and consumer welfare (Armstrong, 1999).

The cross-carriage rule in Singapore offers an interesting twist. On the one hand, it illustrates the point that sports rights holders continue to prefer to sell their rights to a single pay-TV operator. On the other hand, the rule makes it financially rewarding for the rights holders to sell on a contractually "nonexclusive" basis through negotiations. Such a nonexclusive negotiated sale would not make sense in the absence of the cross-carriage rule.

The ability of the dominant upstream rights seller to extract huge payoffs is based on the condition that it is able to commit to an all-inclusive sale to one versus the other downstream player—in other words, each pay-TV operator believes that it will lose all access to the content, and therefore each is willing to pay large sums to keep the content from the other operator (Armstrong, 1999). This illustrates the dynamics of a duopoly market structure in particular, as is the case in Singapore, against the multifirm structure in Hong Kong with four pay-TV operators. Duopolies where two similarly large, established players fight tooth and nail for market share may perceive greater potential gains or losses in the competition for the key rights, as opposed to a multifirm industry where market share is more widely distributed. This may explain the smaller fee increases in Hong Kong and the seeming contradiction that the pay-TV operators in Singapore were willing to bid for these exclusive rights at a loss. Armstrong's model also showed that pay-TV operators will not be inclined to share the exclusive content rights as this will result in a lower profit level. Though its fee increases are moderate relative to Singapore, Hong Kong has also experienced active counter-bidding between its two largest pay-TV operators. The incumbent iCable had regained EPL after it lost to PCCW's now TV in 2006 and had been willing to pay 30% more to outbid its rival.

The EU has used its antitrust provisions in Article 81 to scrutinise the possible anticompetitive effects of such sale agreements. In particular, the EC recognised that overly restrictive terms of sale, which controlled trading conditions, bias the sale of a total exclusive bundle of rights to a single party. The European Court of Justice's review of the UEFA Champions League sale of rights in 2003 forced the revision of terms where the total bundle of rights was broken into different packages to be sold separately, including new media rights over mobile and Internet (Lefever & Van Rompuy, 2009).

In Singapore, this may be particularly difficult to implement as the small country may not have the number of buyers to warrant the sale of different package rights and platforms. This poses a chicken-or-egg dilemma as new entrants without the opportunity to bid for smaller rights packages are denied access, which will continue to keep the industry limited to its large incumbents.

It is proposed that terms of sale be subject to a level of scrutiny by MDA, who is also the sectoral competition authority, so as to mitigate the unhealthy bias towards a single buyer of all rights to the sought-after content. For example, examining the conditions of sale to ensure wholesale, sublicensing rights are mandated, and that rights packages are auctioned through a public tender process, will ensure that implicit or collusive attempts towards a single buyer are reduced.

CONCLUSION

For all its limitations, the cross-carriage rule is nonetheless a progressive step in recognising the need for regulating content access in order to promote consumer interests and innovation. The acting minister of information, culture and the arts, Lui Tuck Yew, said in his 2010 explanatory statement that the MDA thought that the situation of high content fragmentation was unlikely to "self-correct in the future" and that the cross-carriage rule was one of the "steps need(ed) to be taken to address this market failure" (MICA, 2010). In the 2 years since the passage of the cross-carriage rule, pay-TV operators in the country have extended themselves beyond simple channel retransmission of imported content by developing new packaging capabilities, service technologies over new media and broadened content genres.

While the acknowledgement of "market failure" was a good starting point, this chapter contends that the cross-carriage rule fell short of addressing the failures fully. First, the focus on extending exclusive content agreements across platforms was myopic as it could not promote the service and technology differentiation sought by the regulator by limiting subscription only to that of the exclusive content operator. Rather, a mandatory sublicensing of a "must-offer" regime similar to the model applied in Europe by the UK may spur the active innovation desired by allowing access to the premium content to give smaller or new entrants the ability to package a diversity of service packages over different platforms to compete effectively with the large incumbents.

Further, the market imbalance caused by a single monopoly seller of such premium content rights such as the EPL must be examined. It is proposed that the terms of sale be reviewed to counter the natural bias of the monopoly seller to extract large payoffs from an all-or-nothing sale to a single pay-TV operator. This requires a further shift in policy paradigm to one of proactive regulation to ensure that premium contents are not "locked up" through a single, total and exclusive package of rights to the exclusion of all other market players to a single pay-TV operator.

The case of Singapore's new cross-carriage rule will yield insights to other countries as the same issues of deregulation and liberalisation of the "natural monopoly" of the incumbent pay-TV operator pose the same quandary of how smaller or new entrants can access the premium content necessary for subscriber acquisition to start with. This chicken-or-egg dilemma is a real danger that may forestall the growth and development of an integrated info-communications industry that technological convergence can bring to nations' economies.

Similarly, the arguments contained herein may offer other countries who are witnessing the same phenomenon of "price wars" for premium content an insight into the expanded role that access regulation may play in correcting the market power of a monopoly upstream seller.

These are especially pertinent questions for developing economies as they look to mature their telecommunications, media and pay-TV industry in the next lap of global competition. Without this, they may find themselves locked in a competitive spiral of David-versus-Goliath battles and crippling price wars that impoverish their emerging info-communications industry and consumer welfare alike.

NOTES

1. In Singapore, "quad play" is not usually referred to as a fixed or land line—in other words, fixed telephone line use has been steadily declining in the country with more than 150% mobile phone penetration. Hence, "triple play" is emphasized in the country instead.
2. Subscriber numbers of SingTel mio TV as of December 2009 from its press release: http://info.singtel.com/node/6661.
3. Subscriber numbers of SingTel mio TV as of November 2011 from its press release: http://info.singtel.com/node/10074.
4. StarHub TV's subscriber numbers taken from its *2011 Annual Report*, page 5: https://events.miraqle.com/_Resource/_Module/gZSLLgdlcU638zpQWaY GmQ/StarHub-AR-2011/index.html.

REFERENCES

Armstrong, M. (1999). Competition in the pay-TV market. *Journal of the Japanese and International Economies, 13*(4), 257–280.

Bahrawi, N. (2007, June 13). With higher charges, StarHub should let viewers opt out: Case. *Channelnews Asia.* Retrieved from www.channelnewsasia.com/stories/singaporelocalnews/view/281876/1/.html

Cable and Satellite Broadcasting Association of Asia (CASBAA). (2011). A regulatory regime index for Asia Pacific multichannel television. *Regulating for Growth 2011.* Retrieved from www.casbaa.com/rfg2011

Cable Television Consumer Protection and Competition Act (1992). 106, S. 12, Pub. L. No. 102-385 § 628, 1460 Stat.

Chai, W. (2010a, October 8). Broadcast group wants pay-TV policy revoked. *Business Times.* Retrieved from www.asiaone.com/News/The%2BBusiness%2BTimes/Story/A1Story20101008–241391.html

Chai, W. (2010b, June 24). Why MDA stamped out TV "exclusives." *Business Times.* Retrieved from www.asiaone.com/News/The%2BBusiness%2BTimes/Story/A1Story20100624–223675.html

Chong, M. (2012, May 14). SingTel apologises for mio TV service disruptions. *Channel NewsAsia.* Retrieved from www.channelnewsasia.com/stories/singaporelocalnews/view/1201197/1/.html

Cotta, I. D. (2009, September 29). SingTel, StarHub submit bids for rights to broadcast EPL matches. *Channelnewsasia.com*. Retrieved from www.channelnewsasia.com/stories/singaporelocalnews/view/1008142/1/.html

Hearn, T. (2007, November 9). FCC extends program access rules. *Multichannel News*. Retrieved from www.multichannel.com/content/fcc-extends-program-access-rules

Heritage Foundation (2012). *Index of economic freedom*. Retrieved from www.heritage.org/index/country/singapore

Infocomm Development Authority of Singapore (IDA). (2009). *StarHub's nucleus connect selected as next gen NBN OpCo*. Retrieved from www.ida.gov.sg/About-Us/Newsroom/Media-Releases/2009/20090403155250

Ittogi, J., & Lazim, S. (2004, October 4). Media and telecommunications: Singapore law and regulatory framework. *Law Gazette*. Retrieved from www.lawgazette.com.sg/2004-10/Oct04-feature.htm

Lefever, K., & Van Rompuy, B. (2009). Ensuring access to sports content: 10 years of EU intervention. Time to celebrate? *Journal of Media Law, 1*(2), 243–268.

Media Development Authority of Singapore (MDA). (2010). *Media market conduct code revised to better serve consumers and create more opportunities for industry growth*. Retrieved from www.mda.gov.sg/Documents/PDF/Press%20Release.pdf

Media Development Authority of Singapore (MDA). (2012a). 3 things you should know before UEFA EURO 2012. *Media Exchange*.

Media Development Authority of Singapore (MDA). (2012b). *Cross-carriage rules achieving intended outcome*. Retrieved from www.facebook.com/notes/media-development-authority-singapore/mda-cross-carriage-rules-achieving-intended-outcome/372722252810505

Media Development Authority of Singapore (MDA). (2012c). *Proposed revisions to the anti-siphoning list and definition of delayed broadcast*. Retrieved from www.mda.gov.sg/Reports/ConsultationReports/Documents/Anti-Siphoning%20Public%20Consultation.pdf

Media Development Authority of Singapore Act (Chapter 172), S 148 2.7 (2010).

Ministry of Information, Culture and the Arts (MICA). (2010). *Committee of supply debate on driving innovation, productivity and competition for a vibrant economy*. Retrieved from www.mci.gov.sg/content/mci_corp/web/mci/pressroom/categories/speeches/2010/speech_by_mr_lui_tuck_yew_at_the_committee_of_supply_debate_on_driving_innovation_productivity_and_competition_for_a_vibrant_economy.mnews.publiccomm.html

Nicita, A., & Ramello, G. (2005). Exclusivity and antitrust in media markets: The case of pay-TV in Europe. *International Journal of the Economics of Business, 12*(3), 371–387.

SingTel secure EPL broadcasts rights for 3 more seasons. (2012, October 10). *Today Online*. Retrieved from www.todayonline.com/Hotnews/EDC121010–0000170/SingTel-secure-EPL-broadcasts-rights-for-3-more-seasons

11 Inverse Intranet
The Exceptionalism of Online Media Policies in China

Miklos Sukosd

The People's Republic of China (PRC) hosts a unique online system, a national "inverse intranet" that was developed as a distinct unit within the global Internet. The Chinese Communist Party (CCP) achieved this "intranet" using a double-pronged strategy: *control* and *growth*. Government exerts strong control over access, online content, and ownership of online companies. Meanwhile, it blocks access to key foreign websites, thus creating a huge market for domestic online services. To cultivate politically acceptable content, the CCP established a plethora of state-owned news portals (i.e., the People's Daily, Xinhua News Agency, and CCTV) and co-opts privately owned commercial websites to advance the Party line. As a result, successful Chinese companies now dominate the domestic online market and collaborate with state agencies to censor content. China's "intranet" policies have enabled the CCP to exert strict political control, minimize public discontent, and encourage a booming online economy. These policies may also be seen as the constituting elements of Internet sovereignty, creating a strictly Party-controlled, state-centered information regime. This presents a robust alternative model to the original, U.S.-based Internet, pointing to the power of a national government in reshaping what was once envisioned as borderless, global network commons based on free speech.

Since China's first Internet connection in 1994, a self-sufficient, gated digital universe has emerged within the global Internet. The country boasts the world's largest online population—564 million at the end of 2012 (China Internet Network Information Center [CNNIC], 2013), roughly 22% of all Internet users worldwide.[1] China's online community is almost double the United States' population (314 million) and larger than the total population of the 28 member states of the European Union (508 million). China's web footprint is also growing. The country hosted 2.68 million websites in 2012 (CNNIC, 2013), a dramatic increase from 694,000 in 2005 (CNNIC, 2006).

China's "intranet" has also become an economic juggernaut. Online advertising revenue in China jumped from RMB 6.07 billion (USD 988 million) to RMB 51.19 billion (USD 8.34 billion) between 2006 and 2011 (Wang, 2012). Total revenue from the Internet sector hit RMB 200 billion

(USD 32 billion) in 2010, and the Development Plan for the Internet during the 12th Five-Year Period expects it to reach RMB 600 billion (USD 97 billion) by the end of 2015 (Ministry of Industry and Information Technology, 2012). Leading domestic players such as Tencent, Baidu, and Sina are among the world's fastest growing, most profitable Internet companies (Table 11.1).[2]

China's "intranet" is defined by the nation-state within the World Wide Web. The so-called "Great Firewall" blocks access to undesirable foreign websites and services, allowing domestic websites and services to dominate the Chinese market. Of all page views within China, 96% go to Chinese-hosted websites (Roberts, 2011). Domestic entrepreneurs have aggressively adapted the principles and technological solutions of leading global online services. Chinese equivalents (or near-equivalents) have been developed for Facebook (Renren; formerly Xiaonei), Twitter (Sina Weibo), YouTube (Tudou; Youku), Amazon (Dangdang), e-Bay (Taobao.com), Groupon (Meituan), and many other global services.

Table 11.1   Key Chinese Internet content companies listed on stock exchanges

Company	Type	Exchange	Market capitalization (USD, billion)
Tencent	Web portal, social network,	Hong Kong	50 (HKD 391.75 billion)
Baidu	Search engine	Nasdaq	39.27
Netease	Web portal	Nasdaq	6.94
Sina	Web portal, microblogging	Nasdaq	3.74
Youku	Online video	New York Stock Exchange	2.28
People's Daily Online	News website	Shanghai	1.8 (RMB 11.8 billion)
Sohu	Web portal, social network	Nasdaq	1.46
Renren.com	Social network	New York Stock Exchange	1.3
Dangdang	Online bookstore	Nasdaq	0.32
Phoenix New Media (ifeng)	Web portal	New York Stock Exchange	0.28
Jiayuan	Social network	Nasdaq	0.2

Note: Price as of October 19, 2012
Source: Nasdaq.com, Sina.com, ThomsonOne

Researchers and critics have coined different terms to characterize China's Internet. Jack Qiu (1999) argues that the CCP imposes regulatory control and uses network technologies to separate "domestic cyberspace" from "foreign cyberspace." Within domestic cyberspace, he further distinguishes between "open arena of apolitical discussion and the taboo area of nonofficial OPC [online political communication]" (p. 2). Veteran reporter Michael Schuman (2011) describes China's Internet as the "second version of Internet," a product of "all sorts of methods of controlling what people can read, say and access on the web."

This chapter conceptualizes China's Internet as an "inverse intranet" with limited access from inside to the external world. In the original organizational context, intranets are defined as "the application of Internet technology for a prescribed community of users" (Dasgupta, 2001). They use TCP/IP (Transmission Control Protocol/Internet Protocol) protocol to allow computers to communicate, restricting external access with passwords and firewalls. Staff members working outside the organization may be able to access the intranet using a virtual private network (VPN).

Intranets were originally designed to facilitate information sharing within an organization while blocking outsider access. The opposite happens with China's domestic "intranet." China's "Great Firewall" limits domestic access to key foreign websites from the inside out. However, external, foreign Internet users may access China-hosted content from abroad. This is why the specific notion of "*inverse* intranet" was developed. Only Chinese netizens with access to foreign VPNs can "climb the wall" from the inside out. By conceptualizing the online space of the PRC as an "inverse intranet," this chapter does not suggest that the Chinese web fits all technological characteristics of an intranet (in fact, China's "intranet" does not prevent foreign users from accessing mainland-based websites). Nor does it indicate that the China's "intranet" has no blind spots for information spillovers. Instead, the technological metaphor of "inverse intranet" enables us to capture the key feature of China's Internet—that is, the peculiar combination of control and growth—and the strategic intent behind China's unique online regulation.

China is not completely alone in consciously creating a national "inverse intranet" system. Widely seen as "the worst Internet black hole" in the world (Zeller, 2006), North Korea has a national intranet called "Kwangmyong," launched in 2000 by the Pyongyang-based Korea Computer Centre. As a true intranet, Kwangmyong offers no links to the outside world. However, a privileged few close to the country's top leadership can enjoy unfettered Internet access via satellite link to servers in Germany. In April 2012, Iran also announced plans to build a nationwide intranet. American websites such as Google, Hotmail, and Yahoo would be blocked and replaced (Gayathri, 2012). For example, a national search engine called Ya Haq (Oh Just One) would supplant Google (Paul, 2012). Iran's strategy seems to follow the Chinese model.

Nonetheless, China's "inverse intranet" is perhaps the most sophisticated among its peers. It not only keeps major Western online services at bay, but also manages to meet the growing demands of over half a billion domestic netizens. In this sense, the Chinese leadership strategically and successfully built the structure of the country's "inverse intranet" by implementing exceptional online policies.

To explore how this exceptional "inverse intranet" was built, this chapter is organized into six sections. Sections 1–2 sketch out the evolution of China's Internet regulation regime since 1994, highlighting the increasingly centralized regulatory framework that underpins the "inverse internet" strategy. Sections 3–5 demonstrate how specific policies of the double-pronged "inverse intranet" strategy—control and growth—have been developed in three online sectors: online news, online entertainment, and social media. The final section concludes that China's "inverse intranet" strategy epitomizes the concept of Internet sovereignty, presenting alternative policies and structural model to the "original," U.S.-based Internet. It is also noted that the "intranet" strategy is fraught with difficulties. The control over netizens is by no mean total, and the growth plan that favors state-owned players may not support the long-term vibrancy of the Chinese online world.

Early Internet Regulation in China Between 1994 and 2000

China's early Internet regulations were fragmented. Rather than treat the Internet as a media platform, early policies focused on technological and security issues (Xu, 2005).

Before 1994, China's Internet regime featured competing government ministries (Tan, 1999). The dominant player was the Ministry of Posts and Telecommunications (MPT), the regulator of China's telecommunications services. However, MPT's authority was challenged by the Ministry of Electronics Industry (MEI), the regulator of manufacturing of information-technology products. Other government agencies involved in Internet regulation were the Ministry of Broadcast, Film & TV (MBFT, on content) and the Ministry of Public Security (MPS, on security). The State Council, China's cabinet, relied on these agencies to formulate Internet policies.

In 1994, the Chinese government created the Joint Conference for the Informatization of the National Economy to coordinate between the State Council and individual ministries. In 1996, the Joint Conference reorganized into the Information Technology Development Leading Group (ITDLG) under the State Council (Dai, 2000). ITDLG intended to formulate and implement regulations on China's information industry including the Internet (Tan, 1999). However, just as the Joint Conference, the Leading Group remained a transitional task force. In March 1998, MPT and MEI merged into the Ministry of Information Industry (MII), which then absorbed ITDLG. MII became China's primary regulator of telecom and Internet sectors until the MII became the Ministry of Industry and Information Technology (MIIT) in 2008.

In 1996, ITDLG issued the Interim Regulations on Management of Computer Information Network—International Connection (Order 195), which required all traffic to computer networks outside China to transmit through MPT-maintained gateways. The order prohibited any individual or institution from using other gateways without prior government approval.

This decree helped centralize China's global Internet access system (Table 11.2) into the "intranet" format. Currently, MIIT (formerly MII) maintains

Table 11.2   Interconnecting networks in China

Name	Operator	Nature
ChinaNet	China Telecom, The Ministry of Information Industry	For-profit
China Science and Technology Network (CSTNet)	Chinese Academy of Science	Non-profit
China Education and Research Network (CERNet)	The State Education Commission	Non-profit
China Network Communications Network (CNCNET)	China Netcom	For-profit
China International Economics and Trade Network (CIETNET)	The Ministry of Foreign Trade and Economic Cooperation	For-profit
China Unicom Public Computer Interconnection Network (UniNet)	China Unicom, The Ministry of Information Industry	For-profit
China Mobile Network (CMNET)	China Mobile, The Ministry of Information Industry	For-profit
ChinaSat Net (CSNET)	China Satellite Communications Co., Ltd	For-profit
China Railway Communication Net (CRCNET)	China Railway Communication*	For-profit
China Great Wall interNET(CGWNET)	The People's Liberation Army	Non-profit

Source: Compiled by the author from Wong & Nah (2005)

*China Railway Communication was acquired by China Mobile in 2008. It is now a wholly owned subsidiary of the latter.

at least six international gateways, in Beijing, Shanghai, and Guangzhou. Total international bandwidth reached approximately 1.3 million Mbps by the end of 2011 (CNNIC, 2012). The second tier of service providers are "interconnecting networks" with direct global interconnection through international leased lines.[3] There are 10 principal interconnecting networks in China. The largest network, ChinaNet, has more than 53 million subscribed users.[4]

The third tier of service providers is made up of "access networks," similar to Internet service providers (ISPs) in the West. They are not directly linked to the global Internet and must obtain a linkup business permit. Any Chinese company, after meeting certain requirements, can be licensed as an ISP. However, they are prohibited from establishing direct international connections through foreign ISPs.

At the bottom of the Internet structure are those users who obtain Internet access indirectly, from the second-and third-tier providers. All Internet users must register with the local public security bureaus within 30 days of obtaining an Internet connection.

Control has been the key theme of China's Internet regulation since the mid-1990s. From the beginning, the CCP exerted a tight grip on Internet gateways, restricting citizens' access to the global Internet. The heavy-handed control of the gateways echoes the CCP's longstanding information control regime (Sukosd & Wang, 2013), and is also reminiscent of the physical border control system by the Great Wall in imperial China. In the digital era, the Great Firewall system provides the infrastructural basis for the emergence of the "inverse intranet."

Regulatory Regime for the "Inverse Intranet" Since 2000

Since 2000, the CCP gradually incorporated the Internet into media communications policies. Efforts to streamline convoluted digital media policies advanced China's "inverse intranet" framework.

The Chinese government increased, intensified, and broadened the scope of Internet legislation since 2000. Six major regulations on Internet content were promulgated in 2000 alone (Cheung, 2006). As of 2006, there were 16 government ministries with some Internet regulatory oversight (Wei & Wang, 2007). Their functions still overlap and sometimes contradict. In 2011, the Chinese government established the State Internet Information Office (SIIO) to strengthen management of information online. SIIO is headed by officials from at least three agencies responsible for different aspects of the Internet. The State Council Information Office's current and vice directors take corresponding positions at the SIIO, while the vice ministers of the MIIT and MPS join as vice directors. SIIO supervises management of the Internet, handling approval of websites related to online news reporting and investigating/punishing websites that violate laws and regulations.

The establishment of the SIIO added a new coordinating body to China's Internet regulation (Figure 11.1). MIIT takes responsibility for licensing and registrations of all ISPs. MPS handles matters of the Internet security, including the monitoring and filtering of undesirable content. Ministries led by the Publicity Department of the CPC (also known as the Central Propaganda Department) oversee the production of online news and other content (Cao, 2007).

The CCP has been fine-tuning its Internet regulation since 2000. The key efforts include consolidating regulatory institutions and their division of labor, strengthening Internet legislation, and centralizing the regulatory framework. The Party extended its regulatory power to all vital aspects of the Internet—from infrastructure and content to online security. The depth of control is exceptional, laying a solid foundation for the development of the "inverse intranet." In the next sections I show how the Janus-faced policy of control and growth has been implemented in three online areas: news, entertainment (video-sharing sites and Internet Protocol television, or IPTV), and social media.

Online News

Control and growth of the online news industry illuminate China's "inverse intranet" policies. On the control side, the CCP set extensive licensing requirements to control the entry barriers to online news. As a result, only state-sanctioned players are granted entry into this arena. On the growth side, the CCP took a selective approach, prioritizing state-owned news websites over privately owned commercial portals. It gave state-owned websites the exclusive right to news gathering while relegating commercial portals to a secondary role as news aggregators.

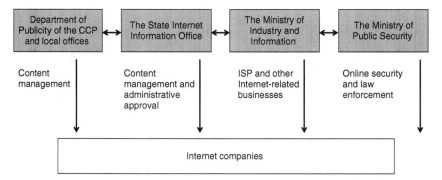

Figure 11.1   The regulatory regime in digital media sectors.
Source: Compiled by the author from Zheng (2007)

Licensing Requirements for Online News Providers

Online news has been a key instrument for disseminating the CPP's message and guiding public opinion in cyberspace since 2000. The State Council Information Office (SCIO) and MII issued the Interim Regulations for Administration of Websites' Engaging in News Publication Services to strengthen control of online news services in November of 2000. In September 2005, the two agencies jointly promulgated the Regulations for the Administration of Internet News Information Services, in which they set entry requirements for would-be online news providers and specified a wide range of forbidden content.[5]

The 2005 regulations distinguished between three types of online news providers:

- **Type 1:** Online news providers established by news organizations; post news in addition to information already published/broadcasted; provide bulletin board services on current political affairs and transmit messages to the public on current political affairs.
- **Type 2:** Online news providers established by non-news organizations; post information carried elsewhere; provide bulletin board services on political affairs and transmit messages to the public on current political affairs.
- **Type 3:** Online news providers established by news organizations; post information already published/broadcasted.

Both Type 1 and 3 are websites set up by state-owned news organizations. The difference is that Type 1 provides additional, original news on top of what is originally carried in the paper; Type 3 just copies to its website what is published in the newspaper. Type 2 (private commercial) news providers are largely restricted to carrying news from state-owned news organizations, essentially banned from gathering news independently. With respect to establishment requirements, Type 1 and Type 2 news providers require approval and licensing by SCIO. Type 3 providers (providing basically online archives) need only file for the record (*bei'an*) with the State Council.

Regarding the participation of private investment in online news services, domestic private companies are allowed to establish Type 2 news entities. However, the financial threshold is very high. The minimum registered capital amounts to RMB 10 million (USD 1.6 million). Online news providers in the form of Sino-foreign joint ventures or wholly foreign-owned enterprises are banned. The State Council must review collaboration between domestic online news providers and foreign companies for security reasons.

Online News Policy Priority: State-Owned News Websites

The CCP's online news policy seeks to reinforce and support state-owned news websites. In May 2006, the General Office of the CPC Central Committee and State Council issued the National Informatization Development Strategy (2006–2020), which declared "strong, influential and coordinated key websites" an objective for national and provincial-level state-owned media outlets.

Four months later, the government unveiled the Outline of the Plan for the Culture Development in the 11th Five-Year Plan Period, which reiterated the goal of establishing world-class "Internet media groups." (General Office of the CPC Central Committee and the State Council, 2006)[6] In June 2010, at the end of the 11th Five-Year Plan, Wang Chen (then director of SCIO) wrote about the ideal Chinese Internet structure in one of the Party mouthpieces, *Guangming Daily*. According to Wang, the CCP endeavors to establish "key [state-owned] news websites" as the "backbone" of the Internet industry. "Commercial portals" and "other types of websites" should cooperate with these key websites to build a "healthy online culture" (Wang, 2010).

State-owned news websites can be further divided into three groups. The first group includes news websites run by key national media organizations including People.com.cn (by the *People's Daily*), Xinhuanet.com, and CCTV.com. The second group comprises provincial-level news websites such as Qianlong.com in Beijing or Eastday.com in Shanghai. Provincial-level Party news organizations run some of these websites. For instance, the *Dazhong Daily*, the mouthpiece of Shandong Party Committee, operates dzwww.com. Some are local joint ventures. A consortium of media organizations in Beijing (the *Beijing Daily*, Beijing People's Radio and Beijing TV, etc.) founded Qianlong.net. The third group includes online editions of other state-owned media outlets.

Secondary Online News Providers: Private Commercial Portals

Privately owned commercial portals qualify as Type 2 online news providers. They can only aggregate news information from state-owned media. The 2005 decree defines news information as "the current political affairs, including reports and debates on public affairs such as politics, economics, military affairs and foreign policy as well as breaking social events" (SCIO & MII, 2005).

In 2010, an official with the General Administration of Press and Publication stressed in an interview with the *People's Daily* that major commercial websites are not eligible for press cards and therefore have no right to carry out interviews (Liu, 2010). In practice, commercial websites offer non-political news. Sina.com and Netease.com carry more self-produced news and user-generated content than the official Xinhuanet.com (Zhou, 2012). Most commercial self-produced news, however, is related to sports, entertainment, science, and technology. With riskier political and social news, they rely almost exclusively on official news sources.

In discussing the political function of commercial portals, Kalathil (2003) argues they play a disruptive role in elevating sensitive local stories to the national level. Their commercial impulse to aggregate provocative stories might appear to provide political coverage; however, major portals proactively align themselves with CCP propaganda imperatives. Baidu established a Party branch as early as 2005. It now has 1,080 Party members (Chen, 2012). In October 2011, the Party acknowledged the "constructive role" of commercial portals in cultural reform (Zhan, 2011).

Online Entertainment

The development of online entertainment also exemplifies China's "inverse intranet" strategy. Entrepreneurs and venture capitalists drove early development of China's online video-sharing sites. By 2007, the CCP stepped in to limit private ownership and ban foreign participation in this sector. Stringent rules of licensing and content production were implemented to ensure that only qualified video-sharing sites play the game. Global video websites were banned.

In addition to these control measures, the CCP make strenuous efforts to encourage the growth of online entertainment, as evidenced by the case of IPTV. As part of the so-called "tri-network convergence," IPTV receives strong policy support, reflecting the CCP's strong intention to keep pace with new digital technologies. Yet in practice, the development of IPTV has been overshadowed by the conflicting interests between government agencies within the Internet regulatory framework.

Video-Sharing Websites

China's earliest video-sharing websites emerged in 2005. Tudou.com is an acclaimed pioneer, founded by former Bertelsmann executive Gary Wang Wei in April 2005. Wang claims his inspiration came from iPodder. After reading a report on the *New York Times* about the popularity of podcast *The Dawn and Drew Show*, he quit his job to launch a Chinese podcasting platform. Five months after its establishment, Tudou had drawn approximately 50,000 registered users (Xinhua News Agency, 2005). In December, Wang raised USD 500,000 from the U.S. private equity firm IDG. A second round of financing followed in May 2006, generating USD 8.5 million from three venture capital funds.

Chinese Internet entrepreneurs flocked to launch other YouTube lookalike sites in 2006 and 2007. More than 200 such video-sharing sites proliferated by the end of 2006 (*China Business*, 2006). Although viable business models had yet to be established, investors rushed to the start-ups. In the first half of 2007 alone, capital raised by major Chinese online video sites totaled USD 100 million (*People's Posts and Telecommunications News*, 2007). Notable from this period was Youku.com, a YouTube imitator launched by Victor Koo in June 2006. The Hong Kong–born, U.S.-educated entrepreneur has extensive links with both Chinese Internet companies and U.S. venture capitalists. Youku quickly completed several rounds of financing while building strategic partnerships with domestic Internet giants Baidu and Sohu. By mid-2007, the site had amassed 4.5 million users, overtaking Tudou as the market leader.

However, daunting regulatory challenges face privately owned online video companies in China. As early as 2004, the State Administration of Radio, Film and Television (SARFT) promulgated the *Measures for the Administration of the Publication of Audio-Visual Programs through the Internet or other Information Network* to regulate the online video sector. Under Article 6 of this regulation, anyone who wishes to broadcast audiovisual programs via the Internet must apply for an audiovisual transmission permit. The document guided digitization of state-owned television stations; it still did not specify rules for user-generated video sites. Since user-generated sites also fall under the jurisdiction of MII, enforcement of SARFT regulation had been lax.

Regulators in China began consolidating control of user-generated video sites in 2007, after clips mocking original works (or *e'gao*) became hugely popular. Propaganda officials considered the clips to be ideologically dubious.[7] In December 2007, SARFT and MII jointly issued the Regulations on Online Audio-visual Services (commonly known as Document No. 56), which came into effect as of January 2008. This document formally establishes SARFT as the key regulator of online videos, especially with respect to content and security issues. Accordingly, MII plays a supporting role in other regulatory matters. In CCP propaganda jargon, the policy requires online video sites to maintain "correct direction [of public opinion]" and encourage healthy online culture. The regulations emphasize licensing requirements for online video sites:

1) Anyone who wishes to provide online audio and video services shall obtain an "Online Audio-Visual Broadcasting License" from SARFT. Only state-owned or state-controlled entities can apply.
2) Anyone who wishes to provide online radio or television services discussing current political affairs must also obtain a "Radio and Television Broadcasting License" or an "Internet News and Information Service License."
3) Anyone who wishes to engage in online audiovisual hosting, interviewing, or reporting must also obtain a "Radio and Television Broadcasting License" or "Internet News and Information Service License."

Under Article 15 of Document No. 56, "state-owned strategic investors" are encouraged to invest in online audio and video companies. State-owned enterprises receive preferential treatment, becoming the driving force of China's online video industry in place of private companies backed by venture capital.

Document No. 56 triggered widespread concern among private video-sharing sites. Considering domestic ownership requirements, many feared their services would be labeled as illegitimate. In February 2008, SARFT and MIIT held a joint press conference to answer questions about the regulations. They clarified that online video websites that predated the regulations could apply for a license to continue operation, provided they had not violated any laws.

Sites established after the release of the regulations would be subject to the new ownership requirements. For the founders of domestic video-sharing sites, this clarification provided relief. However, foreign video sites were less fortunate. Regulators showed no leniency to foreign video-sharing sites that transgressed Party line. Notably, YouTube was blocked in March 2009 on allegation that it contained a fabricated video uploaded by supporters of the Dalai Lama.

Increasingly stringent content regulation followed Document No. 56. In 2009, SARFT issued the Notice on Strengthening Content Management of Online Audio-visual Programs, which specifies 21 prohibited content items in addition to the original forbidden content defined in the 2007 regulations. Some of these prohibited content items include taboo subjects related to violence, pornography, terrorism, gambling, and superstitious factors. Others are intended to maintain a positive image of the Party and state organizations (e.g., banning content with "imagery maliciously derogating the People's Army, the Armed Police, Public Security and the judiciary"; see State Administration of Radio, Film and Television [SARFT], 2009). Still others are deliberately broad and vague, subject to the interpretation of the government (e.g., "audiovisual programs and films, television programs and deleted extracts of which the dissemination was prohibited by the SARFT" and "those violating the spirit of relevant laws and regulations"; SARFT, 2009).

Self-censorship on the part of online video sites has became commonplace. Major video-sharing sites have established sizeable internal censorship teams to squelch politically sensitive material and sexual content. Youku reportedly employs hundreds of workers to operate a sophisticated monitoring system (*Economist*, 2011). In-house censors screen video clips by sampling and examining screenshots at various specified intervals (*Deutsche Welle*, 2012). Online video companies must accept self-censorship as a prerequisite for their business survival. As Victor Koo defended Youku's censorship practices, "when dealing with this environment, you have to be ready to work within the rules" (Pierson, 2010).

IPTV

To discuss China's IPTV, it is necessary to understand the so-called "tri-network convergence," a broader policy initiative with which IPTV is closely associated. "Tri-network convergence" is aimed at promoting convergence of telecommunications, cable TV, and the Internet into a single digital platform.

Network convergence in China is not simply a technological shift, but also involves breaking the regulatory barriers that separate the telecommunications, Internet, and broadcasting sectors. Although dis-cussions about tri-network convergence cropped up in both telecoms and broadcasting industries in the late 1990s (Shi, 2010), the well-known Document No. 82 in 1999 effectively prohibited broadcasting organi-zations and telecoms operators from entering each other's realms.[8] In the early 2000s, the government began to push for the convergence of different networks. It formally put network convergence on the policy agenda in the 10th and 11th Five-Year Plans starting in 2001.

Central planning set the path toward convergence but failed to dismantle barriers between regulatory agencies. In fact, the prospect of tri-network convergence remained rather dim in the mid-2000s, primarily due to the turf war between MII (the regulators of telecommunications and Internet networks) and SARFT (the regulator of cable TV networks). MII forbade cable network operators from offering telecoms and Internet services while SARFT, citing Document No. 82, kept telecoms operators away from IPTV business. Both intended to gain more terrain for their own business but were unwilling to open the market to each other (Zhang, 2003).

In 2008, the State Council took the first step to break the regulatory barriers by promulgating the Notice on Policies to Encourage the Develop-ment of Digital TV (commonly known as Document No. 1). The document encouraged broadcasting organizations to run IPTV service via telecoms networks and value-added telecoms services through cable networks. Mean-while, it allowed telecoms operators to construct digital access networks and digital head-end platforms.

In 2010, the State Council accelerated the progress of tri-network con-vergence by issuing the Notice Concerning Issuing the General Plan to Move Forward Tri-network Convergence (Document No. 5). The notice further specifies the reciprocal opening of the telecoms markets and the radio and TV transmission markets.[9] In addition, it sets a timetable for tri-network convergence. From 2010 to 2012, a trial program would be conducted to connect the broadcasting and telecoms networks.[10] Basic architecture for overall integration of the three networks would be implemented from 2013 to 2015.

As a form of online entertainment, IPTV stands out as one of the key areas of the tri-network convergence in China (alongside mobile TV and digital TV; see Wei, 2010). Telecoms operators and broadcasting groups are avid supporters of IPTV since they regard it as an engine of future growth. But the government remains cautious. Operation of IPTV service entails as many as four licenses: Online Audio-Visual Broadcasting License; Internet Culture Operation License; ICP License; and License for Value-added Tele-communication Service. In 2005, Shanghai Media Group launched China's first IPTV service with the approval of SARFT. As of the end of 2010, seven media organizations had obtained IPTV licenses from SARFT, including six state-owned media organizations and one private company.[11] Foreign investment, again, is prohibited.

In July 2012, SARFT also issued Notice Concerning Questions Relating to IPTV Integrated Broadcast Construction in an attempt to centralize IPTV platforms in China. In May 2013, SARFT brokered a deal between BesTV and CNTV, the online TV service operated by CCTV. The two sides established a joint venture named "Aishang Dianshi Media" (literally, "Fall in Love With TV") with registered capital of RMB 50 million (USD 8 million), in which 55% comes from CNTV and 45% from BesTV (*Marbridge Daily*, 2013). Under the agreement, BesTV's IPTV platform will function as a backup platform of the national integrated platform built and operated by CNTV.

Despite policy impetus, regulatory barriers remain entrenched. Currently, SARFT reserves content production as its exclusive right, while MIIT refuses to give Internet gateways to SARFT. In some places, healthy collaboration is achieved between broadcasting authorities and telecom operators in offering IPTV services, as demonstrated by BesTV, the IPTV arm of Shanghai Media Group. How to promote this cooperation nationwide remains an open question.

Social Media

Social media policies provide the latest example of building China's "inverse intranet" strategy. Similar to the case of video-sharing sites, private start-ups initiated China's social media platforms in 2005. Instead of banning private investment in this nascent sector altogether, the CCP implemented regulations and censorship to put the development of social media within the orbit of the Party state. Chinese users' access to global social media sites as well as corporate entry to Chinese domestic markets by global social media companies were prohibited. Domestic microblogging platforms were subjected to several layers of stringent censorship.

Social Networking Sites

Two of China's earliest social media networks went online in the second half of 2005. Taking inspiration from Myspace, entrepreneur Pang Sheng-dong launched 51.com in August 2005. The site was originally positioned as a blogging and online dating platform. Four months later, Wang Xing, a Chinese-born, American-educated computer engineer, founded Facebook-like Xiaonei. Both sites quickly attracted legions of users. In May 2006, 51.com raised USD 4 million during its first round of venture capital funding from Sequoia Capital, the backer of Google and Yahoo (VentureData, 2006). Xiaonei was less fortunate in venture capitalist funding, despite rising popularity among college students. In October 2006, Wang sold the burgeoning site to Internet entrepreneur Joe Chen for USD 2 million.

Numerous Facebook-like start-ups were founded in the wake of 51.com and Xiaonei. Many captured venture capitalist backing despite uncertain commercial models (Table 11.3). Networking sites boomed in 2008,

Table 11.3   Chinese social network sites with venture capital investment

Name	Date of establishment	Venture capital investment
51.com	August 2005	Sequoia Capital, SIG, Intel Capital, Redpoint Ventures
Xiaonei (renamed Renren in 2009)	December 2005	Softbank, JOHO Capital LLC, SBI Holdings
Yeejee.com	2005	IDG Venture Capital
Zhanzuo.com	April 2006	Sequoia Capital
Ifensi.com	November 2005	SK Telecoms
Mayi.com (closed in July 2010)	2006	HongdingVenture Capital
360quan.com (closed in July 2010)	July 2007	Koolanoo Group
Kaixin001	2008	North Light Venture Capital

Source: Compiled by the author

illustrated by the meteoric rise of Kaixin001.com. Established by former Sina engineer Cheng Binghao in early 2008, the site offered a variety of social games such as Friends for Sale and Happy Farm. An astounding 50 million users registered on the site within a few months. In September 2008, Kaixin001 received a USD 4–5 million investment from Northern Light Venture Capital, a leading China-focused venture capital firm.

Early government policy toward social media appeared relaxed between 2006 and 2008. Moreover, the government allowed American social networks to enter China on a case-by-case basis. Myspace China was established in 2007, a joint venture between Myspace.com, IDG VC, and China Broadband Capital Partners. However, the relaxed government attitude toward foreign social networks was fleeting. In 2009, when the CCP clamped down after the ethnic unrest in Xinjiang province, Facebook, Twitter, and YouTube lost government approval.

Microblogging Sites
China's microblogging sites developed slower than social network sites. The first group of microblogging services emerged in 2007. A noticeable pioneer was Fanfou.com, a clone of Twitter established by Wang Xing, founder of Xiaonei. The site drew more than 1 million users within two years' time (*Memeburn*, 2011). But in 2009, the site was shut down because of sensitive information published about the Xinjiang riots. It would not return for more than a year.

Other new microblogging sites were undeterred by Fanfou's temporary closure. The leading commercial portal Sina launched Sina Weibo in August 2009. Conceived as a hybrid service between Twitter and Facebook, the site pursued a strategy of courting celebrity users and soon scored a phenomenal success (DeWoskin, 2012). In November 2009, three months after its establishment, it had 1 million registered users. The tally hit 300 million by February 2012 (Xinhua News Agency, 2012), and the popularity of microblogging keeps growing.

Leading microblogging sites must vigorously self-censor. On the one hand, a large number of sensitive keywords that cannot be included in posts are defined by the authorities. This "prepublication" censorship means that the service prevents posting if one tries to cover sensitive topics with these keywords included. On the other hand, postpublication censorship removes messages that are considered politically incorrect later. Sina Weibo supposedly hires 1,000 "information security" editors to delete politically sensitive posts and comments (Weisberg, 2012). Personalized and targeted forms of censorship (e.g., targeting activists and online public opinion leaders with large number of followers) are also practiced. In May 2012, Sina Weibo also introduced a point-based system called "Weibo Credit" to manage user behavior. Each user is awarded a starting score of 80 points, which can be deducted for online comments that are judged to be inappropriate (Chin, 2012). Deductions cover a wide range of activities, including, but not limited to, spreading "untrue information," harassment of others, and promoting cults and superstitions. When a user reaches zero, his or her Weibo account will be canceled. The system also punishes those using homonyms (e.g., referring to the dissident artist Ai Weiwei as "love the future" in Chinese) to bypass censorship (Wines, 2012).

Frenzy surrounding microblogs also provided online propaganda opportunities for Party and government officials. In 2009, Yunan province launched the first government microblog feed, "Weibo Yunan." By the end of 2012, 170,000 government microblogs existed (Xinhua News Agency, 2013). New online control methods emerged, too. In December 2011, authorities in Beijing, Guangzhou, and Shenzhen required new users of microblogs to register with their personal details including names, ID numbers, and even telephone numbers. Failure to register could result in losing account privileges.

CONCLUSION

> Active use, vigorous development, and scientific management
> —President Hu Jintao on the principles of the
> Internet development in 2007[12]

The formation of the "inverse intranet" system in China did not take place by chance. It followed a centralized Internet regulatory regime dominated by two broad strategies: maintain political control and stimulate economic growth (Figure 11.2). Along with established policies—licensing, limitations on foreign and private content and service providers, preferential treatment to key party-state news providers, layers of censorship, and filtering—the government also occasionally cracks down on politically sensitive websites and individual netizens.

On the one hand, the strategy to achieve control consists of three structural components: a) limiting access to the global Internet (infrastructure); b) restricting foreign investment and independent private companies (market entry); and c) censoring domestic online content and filtering access to foreign sites and services (content regulation). On the other hand, growth strategies pursued by the government are highly selective. The government seeks to establish the dominance of state capital in all areas of the Internet industry while permitting a limited proportion of private ownership and co-opting private companies in some sectors.

Control and growth are interlinked strategies that enable China's "inverse intranet." Control strategies keep foreign services and content at bay while ensuring the political correctness of domestic sites. But without attractive substitutes for global services and content, users largely confined to China's "intranet" would eventually lose interest in domestic offerings. Growth strategies therefore help China's state-owned media companies and closely cooperating Internet entrepreneurs to cultivate homegrown substitutes for foreign services and content.

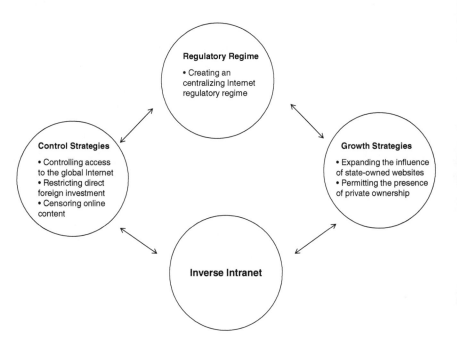

Figure 11.2   China's intranet strategies.

It is worth noting that China's grand "intranet" strategy was not hatched by any prophetic propaganda official. On the contrary, Chinese digital media policies responded to unexpected developments in the global and domestic Internet industries. Licensing and other regulatory systems were typically implemented in successive waves after certain disruptive phenomena alarmed regulators.

The success of China's resulting "inverse intranet" provides a prime example of what the Chinese government called "Internet sovereignty" (Information Office of the State Council, 2010). Put forward in response to China's dramatic encounter with Google, the concept originally implied that all foreign IT companies operating in China must abide by China's laws. However, Internet sovereignty should not only be viewed as a legal concept.

The present exploration of the specific policies of the "inverse internet" strategy provides another absorbing approach to Internet sovereignty. In fact, the digital policies analyzed here constitute practical building blocks of an actually existing Internet sovereignty system that may be seen as a strictly Party-controlled, state-centered information regime. Internet sovereignty in this sense presents a robust alternative model to the U.S-based Internet, pointing to the power of a national government in reshaping what was once imagined as borderless Internet, a global network commons based on free speech (Shackelford, 2013).

The analysis of specific digital policies also shows that China's authoritarian government, and propaganda apparatus, are much more resilient and adaptive than is often understood by Western observers. Moreover, while the legal concept of Internet sovereignty, originating from China, is echoed by Russia and other authoritarian governments, further comparative research could demonstrate to what degree their specific online policies also follow or diverge from the pattern of the PRC.

At the same time, China's "intranet" strategies are not omnipotent. Governments' online information control can never be total. Politically sensitive social media posts spill over regularly, especially during times of political unrest or natural disasters, and creative netizens invent new linguistic tactics to circumvent censorship. Also, growth strategies that favor state capital may not provide sustainable long-term development. State-sanctioned favoritism could eventually stifle innovation, impede competition, and lead to stagnation behind the Great Firewall.

ACKNOWLEDGEMENTS

This work was supported by a grant of the General Research Fund (GRF) of the University Grants Committee in Hong Kong ("Measuring Media Pluralism in Asia: Case Studies of Hong Kong and China," project # 105000097). I am grateful to Lake Wang (senior research assistant, Journalism and Media Studies Centre, The University of Hong Kong), who contributed greatly to the project.

NOTES

1. The number of Internet users worldwide was about 2.7 billion as of March 2013, according to Internet World Stats. Please see: www.internetworldstats. com/emarketing.htm
2. Some have used the variable interest entity structure to seek foreign investment and launch initial public offerings in overseas stock exchanges. A variable interest entity (VIE) involves contract agreements that allow foreign investors' control over companies operating in China that they do not actually own. It has been a popular structure for foreign investment in sectors restricted from foreign investment.
3. Interconnecting networks are also called backbone Internet service providers (ISPs); access networks are also known as last-mile ISPs.
4. This figure is cited from the website of China Telecom: http://en.chinatelecom. com.hk/DtView.do?method=a2&aid=26233.
5. For a useful English-language summary, see Deacons (2006).
6. In 2009, 10 news websites were selected as the pilots of the institutional reform in the online news sector. These government-owned websites will be transformed into shareholding companies in the coming years. The 10 websites include three at the national level (People's Daily Online, Xinhua.com, and CCTV. com) and seven provincial-level sites (Qianlong.com, Eastday. com, Enorth.com, Voc.com, Dzwww.com, ZJol.com, and Newssc.net).
7. A case in point is *The Bloody Case Caused by a Steamed Bun,* an online parody of the blockbuster *The Promise.*
8. Document No. 82, or the *Opinions on Strengthening the Management of Radio and TV Network Construction*, was jointly issued by SARFT and MII.
9. For an English version of the notice, please see: http://chinacopyrightand media.wordpress.com/2010/01/21/state-council-notice-concerning-issuing-the-general-plan-to-move-three-network-integration-forward/.
10. In 2010, 12 cities were chosen for the trial, including two municipalities, Beijing and Shanghai, and four provincial capitals, Harbin, Nanjing, Hangzhou, and Wuhan. In December 2011, Miao Wei, minister of MIIT, said the government would expand the pilot projects to more cities.
11. They are Shanghai Media Group, CCTV, Southern Media Corporation, China Radio International, Jiangsu TV, Wasu, and privately owned Huaxia Network.
12. For a highlight of Hu's speech, please see: http://news.xinhuanet.com/politics/ 2007-01/24/content_5648188.htm

REFERENCES

Cao, S.M. (2007). Promoting a healthy Internet culture with the innovative spirit (以创新的精神大力发展传播健康向上的网络文化). Retrieved from http://news. xinhuanet.com/theory/2007–05/17/content_6107612_3.htm

Chen, N. (2012). Baidu's practices of building Party branch (商业网站党建工作的百度实践). *Beijing CPC Member Newsletter* (北京支部生活), *3, 58–59.*

Cheung, A.S.Y. (2006). The business of governance: China's legislation on content regulation in cyberspace. *International Law and Politics, 38,* 1–37.

Chin, J. (2012). Censorship 3.0? Sina Weibo's new "user credit" points system. *Asia Wall Street Journal.* Retrieved from http://blogs.wsj.com/chinarealtime/2012/05/29/ censorship-3-0-sina-weibos-new-user-credit-points-system/

China Business. (2006, December 4). Venture capital pulls back (风险投资正在收手). Retrieved from www.dowjones.com/factiva/

China Internet Network Information Center (CNNIC). (2006). *The 2005 report on online information sources.* Retrieved from http://oi.pku.edu.cn/document/20111111160443621583.pdf

China Internet Network Information Center (CNNIC). (2012). *China Internet development report 2011.* Retrieved from www.cnnic.cn/research/bgxz/tjbg/201201/P020120118512855484817.pdf

China Internet Network Information Center (CNNIC). (2013). *China Internet development report 2012.* Retrieved from www.cnnic.cn/hlwfzyj/hlwxzbg/hlwtjbg/201301/t20130115_38508.htm

Dai, X. (2000). Chinese politics of the Internet: Control and anti-control. *Cambridge Review of International Affairs, 13*(2), 181–194.

Dasgupta, S. (2001). *Managing Internet and intranet technologies in organizations: Challenges and opportunities.* Hershey, PA: Idea Group Publishing.

Deacons (2006). *China: Regulations on online news providers.* Retrieved from www.worldservicesgroup.com/publications.asp?action=article&artid=1196

Deutsche Welle. (2012, July 10). Is the strengthened control of online video site aimed at eliminating vulgar content? (加强视频审查旨在打击低俗?) Retrieved from www.dw.de/%E5%8A%A0%E5%BC%BA%E8%A7%86%E9%A2%91%E5%AE%A1%E6%9F%A5%E6%97%A8%E5%9C%A8%E6%89%93%E5%87%BB%E4%BD%8E%E4%BF%97/a-16086133

DeWoskin, R. (2012, February 17). East meets Tweet. *Vanity Fair.* Retrieved from www.vanityfair.com/culture/2012/02/weibo-china-twitter-chinese-microblogging-tom-cruise-201202

Economist. (2011, July 30). An internet with Chinese characteristics. Retrieved from www.economist.com/node/21524821

Gayathri, A. (2012, April 9). Iran to shut down Internet permanently; "clean" national intranet. *International Business Times.* Retrieved from www.ibtimes.com/articles/325415/20120409/iran-internet-intranet-censorhip-freedom-tehran-google.htm

General Office of the CPC Central Committee and the State Council. (2006). *Culture Development Program during the National 11th Five-Year Plan Period.* Retrieved from http://news.xinhuanet.com/politics/2006-09/13/content_5087533.htm

Information Office of the State Council. (2010). *The Internet in China.* Retrieved from http://english.gov.cn/2010–06/08/content_1622956_3.htm

Kalathil, S. (2003). China's new media order: Keeping the state in. *Pacific Review, 16*(4), 489–501.

Liu, J. (2010). The institutional predicament of self-produced news facing commercial portals: An analysis of the coverage of the Lu You's ectopic pregnancy (商业网站自制新闻面临的制度困境:试析"陆幽宫外孕"传闻中商业网站的新闻报道). *Journal of International Communication, 6,* 27–33.

Marbridge Daily. (2013, May 18). *BesTV, CNTV Establish IPTV JV.* Retrieved from www.marbridgeconsulting.com/marbridgedaily/2013-05-20/article/66164/bestv_cntv_establish_iptv_jv

Memeburn. (2011, November 30). Chinese Twitter clone Fanfou makes a comeback. Retrieved from http://memeburn.com/2010/11/chinese-twitter-clone-fanfou-makes-a-comeback/

Ministry of Industry and Information Technology. (2012). *The development plan for the Internet during the 12th five-year period.* Retrieved from www.miit.gov.cn/n11293472/n11293832/n11294072/n11302450/14579003.html

Paul, R. (2012, April 10). Iran moving ahead with plans for national intranet. *Ars Technica.* Retrieved from http://arstechnica.com/tech-policy/2012/04/iran-plans-to-unplug-the-internet-launch-its-own-clean-alternative/

People's Posts and Telecommunications News. (2007, December 19). The profit model of online video sites begins to take shape (网络视频盈利模式初显). Retrieved from www.dowjones.com/factiva/

Pierson, D. (2010, February 14). The man behind the Chinese equivalent of You-Tube. *Los Angeles Times.* Retrieved from http://articles.latimes.com/2010/feb/14/business/la-fi-himi-koo14-2010feb14

Qiu, J. (1999). Virtual censorship in China: Keeping the gate between the cyber-spaces. *International Journal of Communications Law and Policy, 4,* 1–25.

Roberts, H. (2011). *Local control: About 95% of Chinese web traffic is local.* Retrieved from http://blogs.law.harvard.edu/hroberts/2011/08/15/local-control-about-95-of-chinese-web-traffic-is-local/

Schuman, M. (2011, October 26). Can China's economy thrive with a cen-sored Internet? *TIME.* Retrieved from http://business.time.com/2011/10/26/can-chinas-economy-thrive-with-a-censored-internet/

Shackelford, S. J. (2013, January 10). The coming age of Internet sovereignty? *Huff-ington Post.* Retrieved from www.huffingtonpost.com/scott-j-shackelford/inter net-sovereignty_b_2420719.html

Shi, T. Y. (2010, April 11). Without the integration of interests and institution, tri-net convergence is just a myth (沒有利益和体制的融合,三网融合只是个传说). *People.com.cn.* Retrieved from http://media.peoplecom.cn/GB/22114/70684/199892/12412472.html

State Administration of Radio, Film and Television (SARFT). (2009). *Notice on strengthening content management of online audio-visual programs.* Retrieved from http://chinacopyrightandmedia.wordpress.com/2009/03/03/sarft-notice-concerning-strengthening-internet-audiovisual-programme-content-management-2/

State Council Information Office & Ministry of Information Industry. (2005). *Reg-ulations for the Administration of Internet News Information Services.* Retrieved from www.lawinfochina.com/display.aspx?lib=law&id=4569&CGid=

Sukosd, M., & Wang, L. (2013). From centralization to selective diversification of the media field in China: A historical analysis of media structure and agency 1949–2013. *Journal of Media Business Studies, 10*(4), 83–104.

Tan, Z. X. (1999). Regulating China's Internet; convergence toward a coherent reg-ulatory regime. *Telecommunications Policy, 23,* 261–276.

VentureData. (2006, May 17). *Sought after by $ 4 million venture 51.com 5 years to be listed.* Retrived from www.venturedata.org/?i167867_Sought-after-by-$4-million-venture-51.com-5-years-to-be-listed

Wang, C. (2010). Pushing the development of Internet culture with Chinese char-acteristics (大力推動中國特色網絡文化繁榮發展). *Guangming Daily.* Retrieved from http://media.people.com.cn/GB/40606/11892995.html

Wang, F. X. (2012). Report on the development of online advertising in 2011. In Yin Yungong (Ed.), *The Bluebook of New Media* (pp. 267–279). Beijing: Social Sciences Academic Press.

Wei, L. P. (2010). The development and challenges of tri-network convergence (三網融合的發展與挑戰). *Huawei Technology* (華為科技), *48,* 4–6

Wei, L. R., & Wang, R. (2007). An analysis of Chinese Internet regulatory institu-tion (中國的互聯網管理體制分析). *China New Communications* (中國新通信), 32–35.

Weisberg, J. (2012, May 28). Hairy eyeball. *Slate.* Retrieved from www.slate.com/articles/news_and_politics/the_big_idea/2012/05/sina_weibo_han_han_and_chi-nese_censorship_beijing_s_new_ideas_for_cracking_down_on_debate_and_dis-sent_.html

Wines, M. (2012, May 28). Crackdown on Chinese bloggers who fight the cen-sors with puns. *New York Times.* Retrieved from www.nytimes.com/2012/05/29/world/asia/china-cracks-down-on-its-cagey-web-critics.html

Wong, J., & Nah, S. L. (2005). *China's emerging new economy: The Internet and e-commerce.* Singapore: Singapore University Press.

Xinhua News Agency. (2005, September 6). *Podcast: A new Internet force* (播克: 网络新力). Retrieved from http://news.xinhuanet.com/newmedia/2006–02/27/content_4233387.htm

Xinhua News Agency. (2012, February 29). The number of registered users of Sina Weibo surpasses 300 million. Retrieved from http://news.xinhuanet.com/tech/2012-02/29/c_122769084.htm

Xinhua News Agency. (2013, March 27). *China has over 170,000 government microblogs.* Retrieved from http://english.cpc.people.com.cn/206972/206978/8188760.html

Xu, W. (2005). *Chinese cyber nationalism: How China's online public sphere affected its social and political transitions.* Unpublished doctoral dissertation, University of Florida, United States.

Zeller, T. (2006, October 23). The Internet black hole that is North Korea. *New York Times.*

Zhan, X. (2011). Commercial websites should be at the cutting edge of the construction of online culture (商业网站要站在网络文化建设前沿). *Young Journalists* (青年记者), *34*, 94.

Zhang, J. H. (2003). Network convergence and bureaucratic turf wars. In Christopher Hughes and Gudrun Wacker (Eds.), *China and the Internet: Politics and the digital leap forward.* London: Routledge.

Zheng, Y. N. (2007). *Technological empowerment: The Internet, state, and society in China.* Stanford, CA: Stanford University Press.

Zhou, Q. (2012). A survey of news sources used by domestic commercial portals (国内商业门户网站新闻来源状况调查). *Today's Mass Media*, *3*, 38–40.

Part III
Marketing Strategies

12 Digital Media and the Roots of Marketing Strategy

Robert G. Picard

The rise of digital distribution platforms is creating a range of opportunities for all types of media companies to expand their operations and their contacts with customers. But they should also induce companies to rethink their content products, their presentation, and their entire way of doing business if they are to gain the greatest benefits from the new environment. This will require reconsideration of their business models and the fundamental marketing elements associated with their products.

Unfortunately, many media companies are approaching digital platforms as if they were just another place in which to make their offline product available or just another part of their portfolios of operations (Picard, 2005). Newspapers are putting their papers or the contents of their papers online. Magazine publishers are making their publications available on tablets. Broadcasters are making video clips from their shows on mobile phones. Motion picture owners are streaming their films through video on demand via cable and game consoles.

Although these developments move the firms into digital markets, these activities should only be initial steps in embracing digital media, and managers must be thinking strategically about the future and what their companies need to be doing now to renew and transform their entire way of doing business if they are to exploit other types of opportunities available in the digital media environment (Küng, 2008; Picard, 2010). The contemporary media environment involves not just technological changes, but fundamental changes in the information and entertainment people need, how and when they use it, and how it is financed. Consequently, the strategies and operations of media companies must transform to accommodate these changes (Picard, 2004; Albarran, Chan-Olmsted, & Wirth, 2005).

MARKETING STRATEGIES FOR MEDIA COMPANIES

To achieve success companies need to create strategies that do more than extend the existing strategies of their offline products (Young, 2010; Kerin, Hartley, & Rudelius, 2012). This is especially true of legacy media operating in digital media. If all they do is move their newspaper, magazine, broadcast, or other content online, or make it available on television, tablets, or mobile phones, they are not adding additional value or effectively using the capabilities of the new platforms, and they are missing opportunities to employ new price strategies and improve their revenue streams.

This is one of the reasons why many players, although enjoying the new revenue streams, remain unsatisfied with the level of returns they are receiving from digital media. This is especially true for the newspaper industry, which speaks of swapping print dollars for digital dimes.

In order to find ways to increase the value of their products and their financial returns, managers at the very least need to revisit the classic four *P*'s of marketing—product, price, place, and promotion—in considering strategies for products on digital platforms (Cohen, 2006; Kotler & Armstrong, 2011). Two of the four *P*'s of marketing—product and price—need substantial attention from companies in order to achieve success. Without reconceptualising how the two factors are applied in their businesses, media firms will be unable to achieve the benefits they want from the digital opportunities.

There is a need to think critically about how established products are repositioned in the contemporary environment (Trout & Rivkin, 2009), and instead of approaching digital activities as merely new places to distribute existing content, digital media activities need to be approached as new products on new platforms.

This means they need to be fully reconceptualized and that the basic elements of their business models and the fundamental issues of the product need to be focused upon (Chan-Olmsted, 2005). The ways content are presented and experienced on computer screens, tablets, and smartphones need to differ from the offline content and uses. The functionalities of the platforms for interaction, personalization, search, sharing, and contribution need to be exploited or they will not meet consumer expectations and produce the results desired. Each needs to provide some unique content, different content options, and new ways to interact with content.

Providing 19th- and 20th-century content that was created based on processes, traditions, and technologies of the offline environment cannot be expected to be successful in the digital environment where customers have different expectations of products, interaction, and control. To date, few legacy media companies have responded well to digital platforms. The greatest organizational changes have occurred in news organizations that have integrated print, broadcast, and digital operations. The primary changes have involved reorganizing internal processes through which they produce their products and finding ways to integrate newsrooms (Küng, Picard, & Towse, 2008; Quinn, 2013), but the content products themselves remain relatively unchanged across platforms. Part of the reason is that digital media require new ways of gathering, processing, and disseminating content (Deuze, 2013).

Price strategies in the digital age also need to be carefully attended to, and consumers' acceptance of pricing practices and payment systems needs to be considered. The traditional commercial mass media business model of keeping consumer price low to aggregate mass audiences and then relying on advertisers to pay most of the cost does not work well in the digital environment. Consequently, the public is going to have to bear more of the cost of digital content, and media firms must invest more in marketing activities to show the value of the product and induce consumers to purchase.

The public is not willing to pay for content they can receive free elsewhere and is not willing to pay more merely to obtain what they have been receiving offline. That means product development and innovation are crucial activities of legacy media companies moving on digital platforms. If public acceptance of pay in digital systems is to grow, media company products must be perceived to have value, to provide something different, to have advantageous features and characteristics not available in the offline content, and to be unique compared to other providers of news, information, and entertainment.

Merely trying to capture more digital revenue is not enough. In industry association meetings around the globe, publishers and broadcasters are discussing the need to generate new revenue from digital operations. But focusing on revenue is the wrong way to seek success in the digital environment. Instead, publishers and broadcasters need to focus on customer needs and uses of digital media and how they can make their content and interactions with the public more valuable. If they get the value proposition and configuration right, if they establish new customer interactions and relationships, the revenue issue will take care of itself. Business development activities that focus on the company and its revenue needs are destined to fail because of inattention to the customer that supports the company and fulfils its revenue needs.

Media enterprises that use the full capabilities of digital media to provide new types of value to consumers should be able to command not merely a similar price, but a price that is higher than that for offline content. This occurs because the digital environment offers many more ways to serve customer needs and to interact with them in ways that were never possible in the offline environment. It allows many types of option pricing for access to different types and amounts of content. It allows consumers to tailor content more to their liking.

The good news is that there is increasing willingness among the public to pay for digital new and information products and that consumers have increasing experience with payments for news: 10% of digital users have paid for news in nations with heavy digital uptakes, and willingness to pay is 14% overall and19% among heavy news consumers. Overall, 23% expect the lack of free quality news will lead them to pay in the future (Reuters Institute for the Study of Journalism, 2013).

These developments are helping digital start-ups make progress in attracting audiences and payments (Schaffer, 2010; Grueskin, Seave, & Graves, 2011, Bruno & Nielsen, 2012). However, getting the formulas right requires breaking from the mental mind-sets of past operations about the nature of the news and information provided, the structures of organizations, and its financing (Picard & Naldi, 2012). Some larger legacy players, including financial papers such as the *Wall Street Journal* and the *Financial Times*, national leaders such as the *New York Times* and the *Times of London*, and other specialized news players such as the *Economist*, are now gaining substantial portions of their income from digital news. Subscription and single-pay services for newspaper content online are growing rapidly with about 40% of U.S. newspapers, 60% of UK papers, and 80% of Canadian newspapers now charging for some digital news distribution.

Nevertheless, the growth of payments is not producing the levels of revenue or profitability desired by many news providers. The fundamental challenge is that the digital products are not yet well-enough conceived and designed to produce those results.

If media companies continue approaching their content as fully finished, static products that are merely to be consumed by users in the digital environment, they will never employ the functionalities of digital media and leave open a huge opportunity gap for new players to create malleable content that can be influenced and altered by users, employed in new ways, and able to generate new value.

Because legacy media have viewed digital media merely as a platform, significant new players have been created and are controlling infrastructure services and presentation technologies that could have been established by legacy media. Had they moved earlier to establish their own joint services, music and video firms and publishers would not be struggling with Apple and Amazon overprices for distribution of their products. Only now are a few media firms trying to overcome the distribution bottlenecks of Amazon, Apple, and Google by establishing their own initiatives such as Next Issue and engaging with alternative players such as Spotify and Press + and Piano Media. Had they thought more about different ways of presenting content in digital forms, legacy media companies might own technologies of social magazines such as Flipboard, Newsmix, Currents, and Pulse. These kinds of activities would have help reduced digital costs and brought in new revenues of their own.

Had they understood the critical role of infrastructures for digital distribution, they might have owned and influenced the capabilities of technology so that it was able to provide better functions than those being offered in most locations, and they might have become profit centres rather than operating cost centres.

As media firms move forward in digital products, it is crucial that they not merely respond to advances in digital media but actually take part in and guide its development. The idea that research and development in digital media should be done by others and that then media firms merely use it for their content purposes is a strategy *not* to harvest the value of digital media and puts content firms at a disadvantage in employing and benefiting financially from innovations. Media firms need to think not only of opportunities for their content products, but from the entire structures of how they will do business in digital media.

The strategic decisions and needs facing companies today require media companies to go back to the basics of business development and marketing strategy and not to think of marketing in narrow terms of advertising, promotion, and personal marketing. They need to shift from a company and content distribution focus to a customer and opportunity focus.

Media companies must become much more entrepreneurial and must rethink their entire businesses—not merely try to shift the existing businesses to the digital market. It is inevitable that some media companies will successfully transform themselves and that others will fail and disappear. Those who cannot find ways to create desirable products that serve customer needs, to create value above that of their competitors, and to be more than they are today will languish.

The media companies as we know them today were created in response to the fundamental needs of society to monitor events, to hold power to account, to entertain, and to express, but their current forms and activities should not be considered perpetual. The existing firms have been with us for only a short period of human existence and were created in response to technological and social developments that changed society and its communication needs.

CONCLUSION

We are now in the midst of a period of change in which technology and social developments are altering the ways we live and our fundamental communication needs. These changes are part of a broader transformation to a postindustrial society that has profound and is affecting all aspects of social life. Digitalization is creating a new type of society based on networks that alters the roles and potential of individuals, work, companies, and nations. This new environment requires that media companies take an entirely new look at their roles and functions, the value of their products and services, and their relationships with customers (Picard, 2010).

The transformational technologies underway are having profound economic effects, and, as past appearances of such general-purpose technologies have shown, such effects are not always beneficial to existing companies (Lipsey, Carlaw, & Bekar, 2006), create instability until new norms and practices of operation are established (Spar, 2003), and require the establishment of business and political legitimacy to survive (Aldrich & Fiol, 1994). We are now in the midst of the transformational period working out these practices and how the technologies will serve public needs.

The needs for information, for holding power to account, for entertainment, and for expression remain in place, but the ways in which these are accomplished need not remain static. New techniques for storytelling, for making information available, and for its presentation will need to be pursued. If media companies merely try to transfer the ways they have done things in the past to this new environment, they will become superfluous and will rapidly disappear into the annals of history.

The challenge for media managers, then, is to be thinking forward and differently about the methods of the fundamental contributions of their firms. That can only happen effectively if they completely reconceive their products and operations and start asking the fundamental questions posed within business model and marketing analysis.

REFERENCES

Albarran, A. B., Chan-Olmsted, S. M., & Wirth, M. O. (Eds.) (2005). *Handbook of media management and economics*. New York: Routledge.

Aldrich, H., & Fiol, C. (1994). Fools rush in? The institutional context of industry creation. *Academy of Management Review, 19*(4), 645–670.

Bruno, N., & Nielsen, R. K. (2012). *Survival is success: Journalistic online start-ups in western Europe*. RISJ Challenges. Oxford, UK: Reuters Institute for the Study of Journalism, University of Oxford.

Chan-Olmsted, S. (2005). *Competitive strategy for media firms: Strategic and brand management in changing media markets*. New York: Routledge.

Cohen, W. (2006). *The marketing plan*. 5th ed. New York: Wiley.

Deuze, M. (2013). *Media work*. Cambridge, UK: Polity.

Grueskin, B., Seave, A., & Graves, L. (2011). *The story so far: What we know about the business of digital journalism*. New York: Columbia University Press.

Kerin, R., Hartley, S., & Rudelius, W. (2012). *Marketing*. 11th ed. Columbus, OH: McGraw-Hill/Irwin.

Kotler, P., & Armstrong, G. (2011). *Principles of marketing*. 14th ed. Upper Saddle River, NJ: Prentice Hall.

Küng, L. (2008). *Strategic management in the media: Theory to practice*. London: Sage.

Küng, L., Picard, R. G., & Towse, R. (Eds.). (2008). *The Internet and the mass media*. London: Sage.

Lipsey, R, Carlaw, K., & Bekar, C. (2006). *Economic transformations: General purpose technologies and long term economic growth*. New York: Oxford University Press.

Picard, R. G. (2004). Environmental and market changes driving strategic planning in media firms. In Robert G. Picard (Ed.), *Strategic responses to media market changes* (pp. 1–17). Jönköping, Sweden: Jönköping International Business School, Jönköping University.

Picard, R. G. (Ed.). (2005). *Media product portfolios: Issues in management of multiple products and services*. Mahwah, NJ: Lawrence Erlbaum.

Picard, R. G. (2010). *Value creation and the future of news organizations: Why and how journalism must change to remain relevant in the twenty-first century*. Lisbon: Media XXI.

Picard, R. G., & Naldi, L. (2012). "Let's start an online news site": Opportunities, resources, strategy, and formational myopia in startups. *Journal of Media Business Studies, 9*(4), 47–59.

Quinn, S. (2013). *Knowledge management in the digital newsroom.* New York: Focal Press.

Reuters Institute for the Study of Journalism, University of Oxford. (2013). *Reuters Institute digital news report.* Oxford, UK: Reuters Institute for the Study of Journalism, University of Oxford.

Schaffer, J. (2010). *New voices: What works.* J-Lab: The Institute for Interactive Journalism. Retrieved from www.kcnn.org/WhatWorks/introduction/

Spar, D. (2003). *Ruling the waves: From the compass to the Internet, a history of business and politics along the technological frontier.* New York: Mariner Books.

Trout, J., & Rivkin, S. (2009). *Repositioning: Marketing in an era of competition, change and crisis.* Columbus, OH: McGraw-Hill.

Young, A. (2010). *Brand media strategy: Integrated communications planning in the digital age.* New York: Palgrave Macmillan.

13 Digital Media, Electronic Commerce, and Business Model Innovation

Richard A. Gershon

Digital media represents the artistic convergence of various kinds of hardware and software design elements to create entirely new forms of communication expression (Gershon, 2013a; 2011). From electronic commerce (Amazon.com, Google) to music and video streaming (Apple iTunes, Pandora, and Netflix), digital media has transformed the business of retail selling and personal lifestyle. Digital media is at the heart of today's communication revolution. We have entered the era of personalization where iPod users personalize their music listening and newspaper readers customize their news selection via their Apple iPad or Kindle e-Reader (Gershon, 2013a).

Business model innovation involves creating entirely new approaches for doing business. Business model innovation is transformative; that is, it redefines the competitive playing field by introducing an entirely new value proposition to the consumer (Osterwalder & Pigneur, 2010, p. 23). In the book *Blue Ocean Strategy*, business authors Kim and Mauborgne (2005) make the argument that in order to create new growth opportunities, innovative companies create an entirely new market space. They use the metaphor of red and blue oceans to describe the market universe. *Red oceans* are all the industries in existence today (i.e., the known market space). Direct competition is the order of the day. The goal is to grab a bigger share of the existing red ocean market. In contrast, *blue oceans* describe the potential market space that has yet to be explored. Competition is irrelevant because the rules of the game are waiting to be set.

This chapter represents a unique opportunity to look at the importance of innovation and innovative thinking to the long-term success of today's leading media and telecommunications companies. Specifically, it addresses two important questions. First, what does it mean to be an innovative media business enterprise? Second, how has digital media and business model innovation been used to transform the field of electronic commerce? The term *electronic commerce* (EC) represents the ability to sell goods and services electronically via the Internet. The combination of intelligent networking and advancements in computer and communication technology has created a vast global playing field where buyers and sellers from different countries around the world are free to participate. Special attention is given to three media companies: Apple, Inc., Netflix, Inc., and Amazon.com. These companies were selected because they introduced a unique business model that fundamentally changed the competitive business landscape following their respective product launch. In short, they were absolute game changers.

WHY IS INNOVATION IMPORTANT?

Innovation is important because it creates a competitive advantage for a company or organization (Hamel, 2006). Successful innovation occurs when it meets one or more of the following conditions. First, the innovation is based on a novel principle that challenges management orthodoxy. Second, the innovation is systemic; that is, it involves a range of processes and methods. Third, the innovation is part of an ongoing commitment to develop new and enhanced products and services. There is natural progression in product design and development (Hamel, 2006). See Table 13.1.

MEDIA INNOVATION METHODS AND APPROACHES

While most organizations recognize the importance of innovation, there is a wide degree of latitude regarding the method and approach to innovation. For some business enterprises, innovation is the direct result of a triggering event; that is, a change in market conditions or internal performance that forces a change in business strategy (Wheelen & Hunger, 1998). Both HBO's HBO Go service and Amazon's Prime Instant Video, for example, are strategic responses to the online video success achieved by Netflix. For

Table 13.1 Successful innovation: Feature elements

The innovation is based on a <u>novel principle</u> that challenges management orthodoxy.	**Apple:** Personal computer, the *iPhone*, and smartphone design **Google:** Key word search and the principle of micromarketing
The innovation is <u>systemic</u>; that is, it involves a range of processes and methods.	**Amazon.com:** Direct-to-home sales delivery, global inventory management, cloud computing, 24/7 customer support **Netflix:** Online video rental, global inventory management and television/film video streaming
The innovation is part of an <u>ongoing commitment</u> to develop new and enhanced products and services.	**Apple:** iPod, → iTunes, → iPhone, → iPad

Source: Adapted from Hamel (2006)

other companies, innovation is deliberate and planned. It is built into the cultural fabric of a company's ongoing research and development efforts. Such companies display a clear and discernible progression in the products they make (Gershon, 2013a). This can be seen in the method and approach adopted by Apple, Inc. starting with the Apple iPod and continuing forward with the iTunes music store, the iPhone, and the iPad (Lashinsky, 2011). See Table 13.1.

SUCCESSFUL BUSINESS MODEL INNOVATION

Successful innovation is not a guarantee of success. Rather, it is an opportunity (Davila, Epstein, & Shelton, 2006). As Hoff (2004) notes, "Inspiration is fine, but above all, innovation is really a management process" (p. 194). There are no shortcuts when it comes to innovation. Putting the right structures, people, and processes in place should occur as a matter of course—not as an exception (Collins, 2001). Part of the management challenge is learning how to work with a large assemblage of highly creative people. The task is to manage the dynamic tension between creativity and value capture. By value capture, we mean the ability to transform creative concepts into commercial realities. As Davila, Epstein, and Shelton (2006) point out, "how your organization innovates determines what it will innovate" (p. 28). Early in the project design process, a successful business model innovation should address five basic questions.

1) **How will the firm create value?** This first question concerns the value proposition to the consumer. The term "value" refers to the unique or specialized benefits derived from the product/service offering (Osterwalder & Pigneur, 2010). Consider, for example, the value proposition of being able to purchase a book or music via the Internet. From a planning standpoint, the firm starts with a clear understanding of the product/service mix. The level and type of innovation should match the company's larger overriding strategy. There should be a clear alignment of goals within the organization around the proposed innovation strategy.

2) **For whom will the firm create value?** This question focuses on the competitive environment in which the firm competes. Who is the target audience for the proposed product design or service? Such considerations as audience composition, geographic location, user technology, and proficiency level can have a significant impact on strategy approach, resource requirements, and the nature of the product/service that is offered to the consumer (Morris, Schindehutteb, & Allen, 2005). Netflix, for example, had to consider technology skill level as one important metric when it designed its Internet-based e-commerce service. Failure to adequately define the market is a key factor associated with business failure.

3) **What is the firm's internal source of advantage?** The term "core competency" describes something that an organization does well. The principle of core competency suggests that a highly successful company is one that

possesses a specialized production process, brand recognition, or ownership of talent that enables it to achieve higher revenues and market dominance when compared to its competitors. Core competency can be measured in many ways, including the following: brand identity (Disney, ESPN, CNN); technological leadership (Apple, Microsoft, Sony); superior business process logistics (Amazon.com, Netflix); manufacturing and production (Samsung, LG, Philips), and excellent customer service (Disney, Amazon.com, Dell Computers). Dell Computers was established by Michael Dell in 1984 and has grown to become one of the world's preeminent manufacturers of desktop and laptop computers. Dell builds computers to customer order and specification using just-in-time manufacturing techniques. They streamline the production process and thereby eliminate the need for stocking unwanted and unnecessary product inventory. Dell has built its reputation on direct sales delivery to the end consumer combined with strong customer support (Kraemer & Dedrick, 2002).

4) **How will the firm make money?** The financial business model provides the inherent logic for earning profits (Morris, Schindehutteb, & Allen, 2005). The financial model must take into consideration the strategy rationale for making money. The ESPN cable sports network, for example, has two distinct revenue streams. First, ESPN makes money though the sale of national advertising. Second, ESPN makes money through a licensing fee arrangement whereby it charges the cable operator an estimated $4.60 every month per subscriber for the right to receive the ESPN service (Gershon, 2013b). Alternatively, when the Apple iTunes Music Store began, it was designed to make money for Apple via the sale of iPods. Today, iTunes earns an estimated 20% for each downloaded song.

5) **How will the firm position itself in the marketplace?** This question asks us to consider how the new business start-up plans to position itself within its external competitive environment? Specifically, the new business start-up must determine how it plans to achieve an advantage over all would-be competitors (Amit & Zott, 2001; Porter, 1985). This idea is closely related to the firm's internal source of advantage (as listed earlier). The challenge for the business start-up is to identify specific methods and approaches that will provide competitive advantage. Consider, for example, Korea-based Samsung Corporation. Samsung has proven to be the organizational master in fast and efficient (almost military-like) production. Samsung has focused on superior manufacturing rather than original research and development. The company has learned how to manage and work through the highly volatile world of commoditized consumer electronics products. Speed is the key to all perishable commodities from mobile phones to digital television sets.

As Chang (2008) points out,

> . . . unless a firm comes up with its products quicker than its competitors, it is doomed to the hellish competition of commodities. Samsung Electronics has aggressively invested in product and process technology

so that it can beat its competitors to market and capture price premiums before its offerings become commodities. (p. 45)

Being First to Market

Being first to market presents significant opportunities for the organization when it comes to business model innovation. At the same time, being first to market is not without its challenges. The organization is having to create an entirely new market that, heretofore, does not exist. Consider, for example, the challenges of being Apple and convincing the general public about the value of an iPad computer tablet. This was a reasonable challenge given Apple's past success with its iPod and iPhone product offerings. Conversely, imagine the challenges faced by Sony Corporation in the late 1980s when it tried to persuade America's television-viewing audience about the benefits of high-definition television 10 years before the general public, television stations, and regulatory structures were in place to realistically consider it (Nathan, 1999).

Being first to market presents enormous opportunities for an organization that is able to establish a clear and recognized product/service before anyone else. All future competitors are faced with the task of having to compete with a well-established company possessing enormous brand recognition. In this chapter, we consider three such companies: Apple, with the iTunes Music Store; Netflix, with online video rental; and Amazon.com, with online retail shopping (see Table 13.2). Each of these companies fully utilized the power of the Internet and intelligent networking as the basis for their business model design. Once introduced, Apple, Netflix, and Amazon. com each achieved a distinct competitive advantage by becoming the undisputed market leader in their respective area of electronic commerce.

BOUNDARY SPANNING

In his book *Where Good Ideas Come From: The Natural History of Innovation*, author Steven Johnson (2010) describes what he calls "the adjacent possible."

We are often better served by connecting ideas than we are protecting them . . . Good ideas . . . want to connect, fuse, recombine. They want to reinvent themselves by crossing conceptual borders. (p. 22)

Table 13.2　Select examples of business model innovation and electronic commerce

▪ Apple	Launched iTunes, the first sustainable EC music service
▪ Netflix	Created the first successful EC on-line video rental service
▪ Amazon.com	Created the first successful EC business model specializing in the delivery of books and other retail items

I refer to this as boundary spanning. The term "boundary spanning" means finding complimentary (or adjacent) areas that add value to one's current business or organizational enterprise. The term was first coined by Tushman (1977) for the purpose of describing the challenges associated with internal organizational boundaries. The Center for Creative Leadership defines boundary spanning as the ability to establish direction, alignment, and commitment across boundaries in service of a higher vision or goal (Yip, Ernst, & Campbell, 2011). From a business model perspective, boundary spanning means the creative next step—that is, finding the natural extensions and partnerships that will add value to an organization's current set of product offerings. Highly innovative companies force themselves to create newer and better products and challenge the competition to do the same.

The Apple iPod and iTunes Music Combination

Few companies are so closely identified with the strategy, vision, and aesthetic tastes of one person. Apple is one such company and is a direct reflection of its cofounder, Steve Jobs. Throughout its history, Apple has a long record of approaching product design by paying close attention to detail. This is reflected in a striving for perfection in both product design as well as looking at entirely new ways to make products more user-friendly and useful. For Steve Jobs, one way to accomplish this was to have end-to-end software and hardware control for every product that Apple makes. Taking an integrated approach was a central tenant of Apple's basic design philosophy.

> We do these things not because we are control freaks. We do them because we want to make great products, because we care about the user and because we like to take responsibility for the entire experience rather than turn out the crap that other people make. (Isaacson, 2011, p. 35)

The blending of hardware and software can be seen in the design and development of the Apple iPod and the iTunes Music Store. The iPod is a line of portable music players designed and marketed by Apple. The first line was released on January 9, 2001. Though several different MP3 portable music players preceded it, the iPod's debut clearly represented a superior design. The iPod's simple interface design as well as the ease of loading music were unparalleled (Young & Simon, 2005). The original iPod held 1,000 songs. On April 28, 2003, Apple first launched the iTunes Store with the goal of providing digital music for people to buy online and download. In order to create the iTunes Music Store, Steve Jobs had to convince the industry's major music distributors to buy into the iTunes music concept. It was a formidable challenge given the reluctance of various music distributors to share their software products using an otherwise untested e-commerce system approach (Lashinsky, 2011).

The iTunes Music Store business model fundamentally challenged some basic assumptions involving traditional music sales and retailing. It introduced a different value proposition to the marketplace—namely, convenience, affordability, and customization. Consumers could now personalize their music playlists by simply choosing from a list of more than 200,000 songs. Individual songs could be downloaded via the Internet using an MP3 file-sharing software. Users were charged $0.99 per individual song. This, alone, represented a major departure from having to purchase a complete CD album containing multiple songs the user may or may not have wanted (Young & Simon, 2005).

The combination of the Apple iPod and the iTunes Store created the first sustainable music electronic commerce (EC) business model of its kind. Today, iTunes has become a lot more than music sales and distribution. iTunes has evolved into an electronic commerce network that manages various types of mixed-digital media files (photos, videos, music, podcasts, etc.) between the iTunes host site and the user's personal computer, smartphone, MP3 player, and/or portable tablet. The iTunes Store allows the user to purchase, organize, store, and play back various types of mixed-media files to any of these devices.

Netflix

Netflix is an online subscription-based DVD rental service. Netflix was founded by Reed Hastings in 1997. The story goes that Hastings found an overdue rental copy of *Apollo 13* in his closet and was forced to pay $40 in late fees. The business that emerged from Hastings's frustration was a rental company that uses a combination of the Internet and the U.S. Postal Service to deliver DVDs to subscribers directly. Netflix was founded during the emergent days of EC when companies like Amazon.com and Dell Computers were just beginning to gain prominence. Netflix offers the public a cost-effective and easy-to-use EC system by which consumers can rent and return films.

UNDERSTANDING THE EXTERNAL COMPETITIVE ENVIRONMENT

Netflix was conceived at a time when the home video industry was largely dominated by two major home video retail chains—Blockbuster Video and Hollywood Video—as well as numerous "mom-and-pop" retail outlets. Companies like Blockbuster fully recognized that renting a movie was largely an impulse decision. Having access to the latest movie was a high priority for most would-be renters. Market research at the time showed that new releases represented over 70% of total rentals (Shih, Kaufman, & Spinola, 2007).

The challenge for Hastings was whether he wanted to duplicate the traditional brick-and-mortar approach used by such companies as Blockbuster. The alternative was to utilize the power of the Internet for placing video rental orders and providing online customer service (Gershon, 2013b). Early on, Netflix focused their efforts on early technology adopters who had recently purchased DVD players. In contrast, most video rental store outlets were still using VHS cassette tapes (Shih, Kaufman, & Spinola, 2007).

Netflix and Business Model Innovation

There are four issues that are central to the Netflix business model. The first is product inventory. Netflix was able to contract with all major U.S. studios and select international studios for the rights to use their movie inventory as part of their program service. The second issue is delivery time, which it considers to be a key measure of customer satisfaction. Netflix made the decision to partner with the U.S. Postal Service (USPS) to deliver DVDs to its online subscribers. DVDs are small and light, enabling inexpensive delivery and easy receipt by virtually all U.S. customers.

Neflix offers its customers a great value proposition—namely, unlimited DVDs for a fixed monthly price. In practical terms, the average consumer may receive two to five DVDs in a week's time depending on the particular service plan as well as personal viewing habits. The general perception is that Neflix provides greater value to the consumer when compared to traditional video rental stores, which charge by the individual DVD rental unit. Netflix offers consumers greater convenience in the form of "no late fees." The subscriber is free to hold on to a specific video as long he/she wants (e-Business Strategies, Inc., 2002). Second, Netflix has developed a highly sophisticated enterprise resource planning system that enables the company to offer subscribers both good selection as well as fast turnaround time. Netflix has harnessed the power of the Internet to create a virtual organization. The company maintains a set of centers that serve as hub sites for DVD collection, packaging, and redistribution. The company adopted the easily recognizable red Netflix envelope and presorts all outgoing mail deliveries by zip code, thus cutting down sorting time by the USPS (Shih, Kaufman, & Spinola, 2007).

Third, a big part of Netflix's success is the direct result of personalized marketing, which involves knowing more about the particular interests and viewing habits of one's customers. Netflix fully utilizes a proprietary software recommendation system. The software recommendation system makes suggestions of other films the consumer might like based on past selections and a brief evaluation the subscriber is asked to fill out. The proprietary recommendation software system has the added benefit of stimulating demand for lesser known movies and taking the pressure off recently released feature films where demand sometimes outstrips availability (Gershon, 2013b). The focus on lesser known films is in keeping with Anderson's (2006) "long tail" principle. Fourth, Netflix has adapted to changing technology by offering a *Watch Instantly* feature that enables subscribers to stream near-DVD quality movies and recorded television shows instantly to subscribers equipped with a computer and high-speed Internet connectivity. Long term, Netflix is positioning itself to a future whereby the company will transition from direct-to-home DVD mail delivery to an instantaneous online communication system. This is video-on-demand in the truest sense of the term. The challenge is that other broadcast/cable television program producers, including HBO, Hulu, and YouTube, are positioning themselves to do the very same thing in direct competition with Netflix. In response, Netflix is undertaking the production of television and film programs that are exclusive to Netflix.

Amazon.com

Amazon.com is a transnational media and electronic commerce company headquartered in Seattle, Washington. Company founder Jeff Bezos incorporated the company in July 1994. Today, Amazon.com is the largest EC retailer in the world. In 1994, Bezos resigned his position as vice-president at D.E. Shaw, a Wall Street firm, and moved to Seattle. He began to work on a business plan that would serve as the blueprint for what would become Amazon.com. The basic idea was to create a mail-order catalogue, albeit electronically using the Internet and the power of intelligent networking (Brandt, 2011).

Amazon.com started with online books given the large worldwide demand for literature, the low price points for books, and the large number of titles available in print. At the time, there did not exist any significant mail-order book catalogs. The reasoning was simple. To build a substantial mail-order catalog covering books in all areas of arts, sciences, and humanities would require an encyclopedia-like publication. And it would be too expensive to mail. The solution, of course, was the Internet, which is ideally suited for organizing and displaying a limitless amount of information. It so happens that Bezos attended the American Booksellers annual convention, where he learned that books are among the most highly databased items in the world. Most of the world's publishers have their works fully listed in CD-ROM format. Bezos reasoned that such information could be organized and put online. Within its first two months of operation, the company was selling and distributing books in all 50 states as well as 45 countries. While the largest of America's bookstore chains might carry upwards of 200,000 titles, an online bookstore can offer several times that since it does not require the same level of warehouse space when compared to a traditional retailer (Ramo, 1999).

From the beginning, Bezos took a careful and long-term view of his business. He did not expect to make a profit for several years. His slow growth approach caused stockholders to complain about the company not achieving profitability fast enough to justify the level of investment. Amazon, for its part, survived the dot-com crash at the start of the 21st century and went on to achieve profitability by the end of 2001 (Matthews, 2012). Two years earlier, *Time* magazine named Bezos its Person of the Year, recognizing Amazon's success and contributions in helping advance the principle of electronic commerce. According to Walter Isaacson, former managing editor for *Time*:

> Bezos is a person who not only changed the way we do things but helped paved the way for the future . . . E-commerce has been around for four or five years . . . but 1999 was a time in which e-commerce and dotcom mania reached a peak and really affected all of us. ("Man of the Year," 1999)

Two decades later, Bezos presides over an EC company that has redefined online shopping for billions of people worldwide. The value proposition for all would-be Amazon customers is exchange efficiency, which can be translated in one of three ways: selection, convenience, and low prices. It is central to the Amazon business model and philosophy. To accomplish that, Amazon has become a master of supply chain management and enterprise resource planning.

Amazon and Supply Chain Management

Supply chain management (SCM) is a complex business model that takes into consideration the entire set of linking steps necessary to produce and deliver a product to the end consumer. SCM philosophy is grounded in the belief that everyone involved in the supply chain is both a supplier and customer and requires access to timely, up-to-date information. The goal is to optimize organizational efficiency while meeting the needs of both suppliers and customers. Information is key. To that end, a critical element of any SCM methodology is the ability to share timely information across the entire supply chain system. A well-designed SCM system gives automated intelligence to an extended network of suppliers, manufacturers, and distributors, as well as a host of other trading partners (Tarn, Razi, Yen, & Xu, 2002).

Amazon and Boundary Spanning

Amazon employs a multilevel e-commerce strategy. In its formative years, Amazon focused on business-to-customer (B-to-C) electronic commerce.

The challenge was to become more fully diversified in terms of product and service offerings. In time, they incorporated customer reviews and leveraged such information as a way to sell more products and services as well as improve the customer experience. Amazon is a highly innovative company and has adopted the principle of boundary spanning in three specific ways. Each area is a natural extension of what Amazon already does.

Amazon Web Services: Amazon Web Services is a collection of cloud computing services offered by Amazon.com via the Internet. The expression "putting something on the cloud" refers to the idea of storing information and data on a remote host site. Amazon's most daring strategy is its foray into business-to-business services. In recent years, Amazon has greatly expanded its cloud computing services by leasing out server capacity in its large data centers around the world so that small businesses do not have to make large upfront investments in computing infrastructure (Matthews, 2012).

Amazon Marketplace: Amazon has also greatly expanded its third-party marketplace, where merchants all over the world can set up their own virtual stores on Amazon.com and sell their products alongside Amazon's—all the while leveraging Amazon's large customer base and credit card–processing capability. Both retailers and individual sellers utilize the Amazon.com platform to sell goods. Large retailers like Nordstrom and Target use Amazon.com to sell their products in addition to selling them via their own websites.

Amazon Kindle: In November 2007, Amazon launched its Amazon Kindle, an e-book reader. Today, most analysts agree that Amazon probably sold its original Kindle hardware at breakeven or a small loss to subsidize media sales. With the original Kindle, Amazon pioneered the sale of digital books, and as a result owns over 90% of their distribution. By July 2010, Amazon e-book sales for its Kindle reader outnumbered sales of hardcover books for the first time ever. In September 2011, Amazon announced its entry into the computer tablet market with the introduction of its Kindle Fire, which runs on the Android operating system. The Amazon Kindle is much more than an e-reader. It represents the foundation for an entire media ecosystem (Matthews, 2012). Specifically, the Kindle Fire is a computer tablet, a media store, and a platform for digital media sales as well as a publishing imprint. The goal is to make all of Amazon's digital media product offerings part of the Kindle ecosystem. This includes: 1) digital books, 2) MP3 music and software products, 3) Internet video streaming (Amazon Instant Video), 4) software apps, and 5) advertising. The Amazon Kindle is a decade-long investment in media planning, product design, development, and distribution.

DISRUPTIVE EFFECTS ON THE MARKETPLACE

In this chapter's final section, we consider how the diffusion of such technologies and services into the marketplace has transformed/disrupted the competitive playing field. In 1942, Joseph Schumpeter (1942) introduced the principle of *creative destruction* as a way to describe the disruptive process that accompanies the work of the entrepreneur and the consequences of innovation. In time, companies that once revolutionized and dominated select markets give way to rivals who are able to introduce improved product designs, offer substitute products and services, and/or lower manufacturing costs. Disruptive technologies, by their very definition, introduce a whole host of intended and unintended consequences on the marketplace. One of the accompanying rules of creative destruction is that once a technology or service has been introduced, there is no going backward. Technology advancement is seemingly one directional.

Each of the business models discussed in this chapter has been a major game changer and has set into motion a variety of unintended consequences that have affected the larger competitive landscape as well as individual rival companies. Let us briefly consider each.

Apple

The debut of the Apple iPod had a devastating effect on the sales and distribution of the Sony Walkman portable CD player. Prior to its launch, the Sony Walkman was the established brand leader in the field of portable music players. With its catalog of music and foundation in electronics, Sony had the tools to create a version of the iPod long before Apple introduced it in 2001. Yet Sony was not prepared to move quickly enough and adjust strategy in order to preserve market leadership in the area of portable music. Instead, Sony focused on its now-defunct mini-disk technology. More importantly, Sony missed the MP3 revolution. Sony failed to grasp the importance of the user experience in terms of obtaining, organizing, listening to, and sharing music. By leveraging the power of the Internet and a digital lifestyle, Apple let music lovers browse and download a song or album in a fraction of the time it had previously taken to record music onto a Sony Walkman tape or CD (Gershon, 2013a). Moreover, Apple took a page out of the Sony's playbook by redefining the principle of portability in a whole new way by allowing music owners to place an entire music collection onto a simple device that could fit into one's coat pocket. Sony was caught flat-footed. It was adhering to an old industrial model where the emphasis was on stand-alone products sold in great volume (Hartung, 2012). Within three years, Sony's market share of portable music players fell dramatically.

The combination of the Apple iPod and the iTunes Music Store was the marriage of media and computer technology. It has forever changed the business of music sales and retail distribution. No longer would consumers have to purchase an entire CD in order to get the one or two desired songs from an album playlist. The success of iTunes coupled with the devastating effects of digital piracy caused CD sales to fall dramatically. Between 1995 and 2005, the CD market fell 25%. This, in turn, has had a major effect on so-called brick-and-mortar music retail store outlets. Gone are the custom retail stores like Tower and Virgin Records in what Keen (2007) calls "the day the music died." Keen laments the fact that blogging about music is no substitute for the high-touch experience of talking about music with music people and professional staff. Keen also points out that the music industry itself has become increasingly embattled. Many of today's music artists are discovering that Internet fame does not translate into the sort of sales and worldwide recognition once enjoyed by earlier generations of musicians.

Netflix

Blockbuster Inc. (currently Blockbuster LLC) is an American-based DVD and videogame rental service. Prior to 2009, it was the world's largest video rental movie service. Because of competition from Netflix (and to a lesser extent Redbox), Blockbuster has sustained significant revenue losses in recent years. The company filed for bankruptcy just shy of its 25th anniversary on September 22, 2010. In retrospect, it seems clear that the practice of driving to a store to rent a movie was a business model destined to fail as the Internet became more of a factor in the world of electronic commerce. Blockbuster was the right technology for the time. It was a 20-year interim technology that provided a practical solution in meeting the needs for home television viewing. For years, business analysts and professional observers have recognized that Blockbuster was a flawed business model that would be difficult to sustain in the wake of advancing technology ("How Blockbuster Failed," 2010).

For Blockbuster, creative destruction came in the form of Netflix, which offered consumers better value and convenience. Netflix was able to offer its customers a wider selection of films to choose from as well as an increased number of DVDs per week for a fixed monthly fee. In addition, customers could hold on to a film as long as they liked without risking a penalty fee for a late return. A common complaint with Blockbuster was the experience of being charged a fee for a late return. A second complaint with the company was the experience of renting an unfamiliar movie and being dissatisfied with the viewing experience later on. In contrast, Netflix utilizes a proprietary recommendation software that makes suggestions to users based on past selections as well an online evaluation form. To that end, Netflix is better able to personalize the television/film viewing experience for the viewer.

Amazon.com

Amazon.com is the world's largest EC retailer and America's 15th largest retailer in general (Matthews, 2012). Amazon's success has set into motion two disruptive effects. The first pertains to the collecting of taxes. How does a national or state government oversee the collecting of taxes by a company that operates virtually and without borders? Critics point out that Amazon realizes an unfair pricing advantage on goods and services (when compared to traditional retailers) since they have not historically collected sales taxes from the states in which they operate. To date, Amazon collects sales taxes from customers in only nine U.S. states. This is beginning to change. Amazon is under increasing pressure to begin collecting state sales taxes in states in which they do business. Several states have passed or are considering a so-called "Amazon tax" designed to compel Amazon (and other EC merchants) to collect local sales tax from consumers who purchase their products. The U.S. has no federal EC sales tax. In most countries where Amazon does business, a sales tax or value-added tax is uniform throughout the country, and Amazon is obliged to collect it from all customers.

The success of Amazon.com has created a second disruptive effect as well. It pertains to the problem of showrooming, whereby consumers use the local retail store for examining merchandise and gathering information (without purchasing it) and then place an order online for the same item. At first glance, this seems like a fairly innocuous practice. But upon closer examination, the problem of showrooming undermines the basic foundation of traditional retailing. Amazon (and other EC sellers) are typically better able to offer lower prices than their brick-and-mortar counterparts, because they do not have the same overhead cost. Showrooming can be costly to retailers, not only in terms of lost sales, but also due to many indirect costs associated with product display, including professional staffing, inventory management and storage, pricing and labeling, damage caused to store samples by consumers, and so forth.

CONCLUSION

Apple, Netflix, and Amazon.com each introduced a unique business model that fundamentally changed the competitive business landscape following their respective product launch. Each company was first to market and thereby established a market presence and brand recognition that would make them difficult to compete against in the future. The Apple iPod/iTunes music combination created the first sustainable EC music business of its kind. It changed music sales and retail distribution forever. Netflix was the first company to engage in the field of online movie rentals. Netflix has become the undisputed leader in EC video rental and the online streaming of featured television/film entertainment. Amazon.com took the early lead in EC development. Today, the company has become the face of electronic commerce with a worldwide presence.

What each of these companies share in common was a business model innovation that required a deep understanding of the Internet and the power of intelligent networking. What gives any network its unique power and intelligence are the people and users of the system and the value-added contributions they bring to the system via critical gateway points (Gershon, 2011). As intelligent networks grow and evolve, they often exhibit self-learning qualities in what Monge, Heiss, and Magolin (2008) describe as *network evolution*. This is a crucial element in helping us to understand why such companies (and their corresponding networks) improve over time. Apple, Netflix, and Amazon.com have each developed an algorithmic recommendation software that speaks to the power of customized media use. Each of the three companies discussed in this chapter were absolute game changers and had a transformative effect in the field of electronic commerce. They have given us an early preview of what it means to be a virtual company operating in a 21st-century global economy.

REFERENCES

Amit, R., & Zott, C. (2001). Value creation in e-business. *Strategic Management Journal, 22*, 493–520.

Anderson, C. (2006). *The long tail: Why the future of business is selling less of more.* New York: Hyperion.

Brandt, R. (2011). *One click: Jeff Bezos and the rise of Amazon.com.* New York: Penguin Books.

Chang, S. J. (2008). *Sony vs. Samsung: The inside story of the electronics giants' battle for global supremacy.* Singapore: John Wiley & Sons.

Collins, J. (2001). *Good to great.* New York: Harper Collins.

Davila, T., Epstein, M., & Shelton R. (2006). *Making innovation work.* Upper Saddle River, NJ: Wharton School Publishing.

e-Business Strategies, Inc. (2002, October). Netflix: Transforming the DVD rental business. *Published Report*, 1–10.

Gershon, R. (2011). Intelligent networks and international business communication: A systems theory interpretation. *Media markets monographs,12.* Pamplona, Spain: Universidad de Navarra Press.

Gershon, R. A. (2013a). Digital media innovation and the Apple iPad: Three perspectives on the future of computer tablets and news delivery. *Journal of Media Business Studies, 10*(1), 41–61.

Gershon, R. (2013b). *Media, telecommunications and business strategy* (2nd ed.). New York: Routledge.

Hamel, G. (2006, February). The what, why and how of management innovation. *Harvard Business Review*, 72–87.

Hartung, A. (2012, April 4). Sayonara Sony: How industrial, MBA-style leadership killed a once great company. *Forbes.* Retrieved from www.forbes.com/sites/adam hartung/2012/04/20/sayonara-sony-how-industrial-mba-style-leadership-killed-once-great-company/2

Hoff, R. (2004, October 11). Building an idea factory. *Business Week*, 194.

How Blockbuster failed at failing. (2010, October 11). *Time*, 38–40.

Isaacson, W. (2011). *Steve Jobs.* New York: Simon & Schuster.

Johnson, S. (2010). *Where good ideas come from: The natural history of innovation.* New York: Riverhead Books.

Keen, A. (2007). *The cult of the amateur.* New York: Random House.

Kim, W., & Mauborgne, R. (2005). *Blue ocean strategy.* Boston, MA: Harvard Business School Press.

Kraemer, K., & Dedrick, J. (2002). Dell Computer: Organization of a global production network. Retrieved from www.crito.uci.edu/GIT/publications/pdf/dell.pdf

Lashinsky, A. (2011). The decade of Steve. In *Fortune: The legacy of Steve Jobs 1955–2011.* (pp. 10–15). New York: Fortune Books.

Man of the year: Jeff Bezos. (1999, December 20). *Wired*. Retrieved from www.wired.com/techbiz/media/news/1999/12/33176

Matthews, C. (2012, July 16). Will Amazon take over the world? *Time*. Retrieved from http://business.time.com/2012/07/16/will-amazon-take-over-the-world/

Monge, P., Heiss, B., & Magolin, D. (2008). Communication network evolution in organizational communities. *Communication Theory, (18)*4, 449–477.

Morris, M., Schindehutte, M., & Allen, J. (2005). The entrepreneur's business model: Toward a unified perspective. *Journal of Business Research, 58*, 726–735.

Nathan, J. (1999). *Sony: The private life*. New York: Houghton-Mifflin.

Osterwalder, A., & Pigneur, Y. (2010). *Business model generation*. Hoboken, NJ: John Wiley & Sons.

Porter, M. (1985). *Competitive advantage: Creating and sustaining superior performance*. New York: Free Press.

Ramo, J. C. (1999, December 27). Jeffrey Bezos: 1999 person of the year. *Time*. Retrieved from www.time.com/time/subscriber/article/0,33009,992927,00.html

Schumpeter, J. (1942). *Capitalism, socialism and democracy*. New York: Harper & Row.

Shih, W., Kaufman, S., & Spinola, D. (2007, November). Netflix. *Harvard Business School Case Study Series* (9-607-138), 1–15.

Tarn, J. M., Razi, M., Yen, D., & Xu, Z. (2002). Linking ERP and SCM systems. *International Journal of Manufacturing Technology & Management, 4*(5), 420–439.

Tushman, T. (1977). Special boundary roles in the innovation process. *Administrative Science Quarterly, 22*(4), 587–605.

Wheelen T., & Hunger, D. (1998). *Strategic management and business policy*. Reading, MA: Addison Wesley Longman.

Yip, J., Ernst, C., & Campbell, M. (2011). *Boundary Spanning Leadership*. Greensboro, NC: Center for Creative Leadership.

Young, J., & Simon, W. (2005). *iCon: Steve Jobs*. New York: John Wiley & Sons.

14 Cross-Media Marketing Strategies

Bernd W. Wirtz, Philipp Nitzsche,
and Linda Mory

The competitive landscape of the media industry is characterized by increasing penetration movement with innovative information and communication technologies and ongoing industry convergence. Two major processes determine the development of competition in the field of electronic media and communications. First, especially in the Internet sector, a greater number of enterprise formations in the sense of Schumpeterian pioneering companies are reported. Examples of this development are companies such as Facebook, eBay and Google. On the other hand, fundamental processes of transformation of value chains in the information and communication sector can be observed.

In this environment, there is a significant repositioning of established media companies, which is characterized by a change in the current value-added structures and competitive strategies (Wirtz & Kleineicken, 2000, p. 290). The repositioning and the change in value-added structures let transnational media and Internet companies arise. Transnational media companies encounter on the acquisition of ownership interests vertically and laterally into new (media) product offering areas and merge economic activities in various media markets (Wirtz, 1994, p. 164).

In this context the lateral or even multilateral expansion of media distribution to various media channels or media market segments is referred to as cross-media. Cross-media management is the strategic foundation for integration efforts of companies in the media sector. Nowadays hardly any media company can do without an adequate cross-media strategy and a focused cross-media management. This is particularly true for large transnational media companies that dominate the industry in many submarkets today.

After the emergence of transnational media companies in the mid-1990s was affected by mega-mergers with vertical orientation, or rather by the advance of telecommunications providers in the media industry in the late 1990s, in the light of the increasing commercialization of the Internet, especially, the emergence of transnational media and Internet companies can be observed.

On one side, traditional media companies are trying to increase their position in the Internet sector through corporate investments or the acquisition of ownership interests. For example, in 2000 Pearson Plc. acquired National Computer Systems Inc. (NCS). This acquisition has enabled Pearson to become a leading transnational provider of educational materials and to distribute its own content on the various Internet-based systems of NCS as well as to create new personalized teaching courses (Business Wire, 2000). On the other hand, Internet companies penetrate into the realm of traditional media. The most prominent example in this context is the acquisition of Time Warner by AOL.

Fundamentals of Cross-Media Management

In recent years, the development and design of multichannel strategies in the media sector has experienced an increasing importance (Müller-Kalthoff, 2002, p. VII; Vogelsberg, 2006, p. 359; Jakubetz, 2008, p. 11). In the course of time, both in business practice and in the literature, the term "cross-media" has been established. Here, cross-media is primarily associated with generating competitive advantages in the context of convergence trends in the media industry. In particular, the future success of traditional media companies is often linked with the use of cross-media strategies to a high degree.

Thereby, the terms "cross-media" and "cross-media management" are often used without being clearly defined. This diverse/heterogeneous understanding of the term has been reinforced, above all, by the fact that the term "cross-media" has acquired a high relevance in various media or business disciplines. Especially within transnational media management, distribution marketing and communication marketing, the concept of cross-media management plays an important role. Whereas media management has a significantly more nuanced understanding of the concept, within marketing the multichannel use for various marketing activities is in the focus of attention.

In addition, from an interdisciplinary perspective, in the literature and practice it can be observed that cross-media is often too limited to the digitization of media content for distribution via online channels. Although the modern information and communication technologies exercise a decisive influence on the cross-media concept, it also includes the integration of traditional media forms and channels outside the emerging online media. It is therefore necessary for a cross-media analysis to take on the widest possible perspective of consideration. Cross-media as a comprehensive management approach therefore requires a unified understanding of the concept. In this context, cross-media should be defined as referring to a concept for the use of at least two media channels for marketing media products.

Moreover, the functional management term of the cross-media concept should be picked up and extended by the aspect of corporate management. Thereby, corporate management can be understood as a purposeful, formative intervention in the value-creation process of companies (Macharzina & Wolf, 2008, p. 35). Thus, cross-media management has a particular instrumental character since it aims at monitoring corporate long-term goals.

Thereby, cross-media management covers both the strategic and the operational level. Here, strategy is to be understood as "a planned set of measures of the company to achieve its long term goals" (Welge & Al-Laham, 2003, p. 13). In contrast, operational management is carried out under a short-term time horizon. Cross-media management is concerned, as is general media management, with the strategic and action-oriented options in respect to the sales of media products with special emphasis on the media-specific environment. Cross-media management can be defined as encompassing all purposeful activities of planning, organization, implementation and control in the marketing of media products through various media channels (Wirtz, 2011).

Manifestations of Cross-Media

In the media sector, different growth strategies can be observed. Regarding a systematization of the concept, it makes sense to rely on established growth approaches since cross-media strategies are special cases of general growth strategies. An early and very popular approach to the systematization of such strategies was established by Ansoff (1965). This approach is very suitable for the present context since the various strategy alternatives are presented in a product-market matrix. The so-called Ansoff matrix differentiates by existing and new markets, as well as existing and new products. Within cross-media systematization, it is necessary to extend the original matrix.

Further, it can be distinguished whether the new media market or the new media product is similar to an existing market or product. Media markets, which can be described in this context also as media industry or distribution channel, are for example the book market and the TV or newspaper market. In this context, media products or media formats are understood as text contributions (book text or edited text), images, audio contributions or audiovisual materials.

In an existing media channel, with the same form of media, a higher market penetration can be achieved through single media penetration. A similar media product, such as a book text and an editorial text (but in the same medium), based on the product policy, can be referred to as single media differentiation. If the product expansion is an entirely new media format—for example, an audio contribution in regular textual online environment—one can speak of single media diversification. Here, it should be noted that each of these forms of growth only extends to one media channel and thus cannot be assigned to cross-media.

If a new channel is used in addition to an existing media channel, this can be referred to as cross-media growth. When talking about the same or equal media product, it can be referred to as lateral cross-media; in the

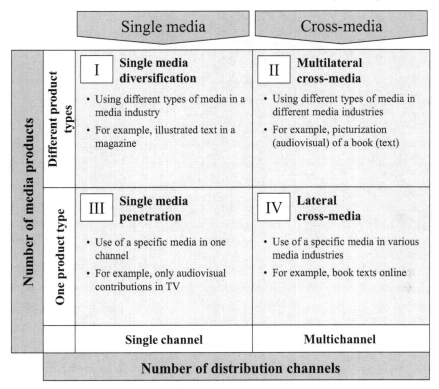

		Single media	**Cross-media**
Number of media products	**Different product types**	**I** **Single media diversification** • Using different types of media in a media industry • For example, illustrated text in a magazine	**II** **Multilateral cross-media** • Using different types of media in different media industries • For example, picturization (audiovisual) of a book (text)
	One product type	**III** **Single media penetration** • Use of a specific media in one channel • For example, only audiovisual contributions in TV	**IV** **Lateral cross-media** • Use of a specific media in various media industries • For example, book texts online
		Single channel	**Multichannel**
		Number of distribution channels	

Figure 14.1   Manifestations of cross-media in dependence of the media channels.

case of a similar or new media product, it can be referred to as multilateral cross-media. In this context, mainly the presence of several media distribution channels is crucial. Based on multichannel marketing, one can speak of a media multichannel strategy. Figure 14.1 displays the different growth strategies depending on the number of media products and the number of distribution channels. The various forms of cross-media and related strategies are presented later.

Causes and Catalysts of Cross-Media

The causes and catalysts that have led to the development of cross-media marketing of content (and still press ahead this trend) can be divided into market- or environment-oriented and business-related aspects. Within the market- and environment-oriented causes, the already described industry convergence on the media, communications and information markets and the growing penetration of the media markets with innovative information and communication technologies plays a central role.

From this, three market-related drivers or catalysts can be derived: digitization, the industry convergence and the changing usage patterns of the recipients. With digitization, which today encompasses all types of traditional media formats, particularly lower costs for porting of content to new media channels have emerged. This is mainly due to the much lower cost of adapting efforts for the cross-channel utilization of media formats. Thus, for example, a digital picture can be utilized in a book, a magazine article and an online channel with little extra effort.

Only the proceeding, fast-moving industry convergence and the possibilities of innovative information and communication technologies have led to the availability of new channels and to the absorption of these channels in transnational cross-media strategies. The pressure on traditional media companies to use new digital channels was significantly increased by new market entrants, especially from the electronic business sector. An example is the online video platform Hulu, with which many traditional media companies have created an additional marketing channel on the Internet.

The third market-related aspect is the change in recipient behavior. It can be observed that user preferences have moved toward new marketing channels in many industries. To an increasing degree, this leads to substitution of traditional media channels through new media channels. Furthermore, it appears that nowadays users even expect additional content via online channels in traditional channels. Even within windowing (the extension of value chains through the marketing on different distribution channels) and versioning (the differentiation of media products), user preferences have changed so that recipients prefer a stronger multichannel use.

The central business-related drivers and catalysts are as follows: higher revenue opportunities, lower marketing costs and a more efficient brand transfer. In this context, the higher revenue opportunities arise especially through multiple use of media content. Very often, these have very high first copy costs but can be distributed through digitization in a cost-effective way on different channels. Per additional media channel, there is additional revenue potential to cover the high first copy costs.

Decreasing marketing costs arise primarily from the economies of scale and interconnection/integration effects that transnational media companies can achieve through the use of cross-media. These interconnection effects or composite effects occur when there is a coordinated, cross-media channel use beyond the boundaries of individual marketing channels. This aspect plays an important role, especially in the distribution of media content as well as product development.

The third superordinate, business-related driver for cross-media marketing within media management represents brand transfer. Branding is a very complicated and cost-intensive marketing activity. Within cross-media management an established brand can be expanded to new channels with relatively little adjustment and coordination needs.

An example is the Harry Potter book series. The strong trademark Harry Potter allowed an efficient secondary use as a film and furthermore as a computer game. In doing so an established brand message could be reverted to. Figure 14.2 illustrates the market- and business-related drivers and catalysts of cross-media.

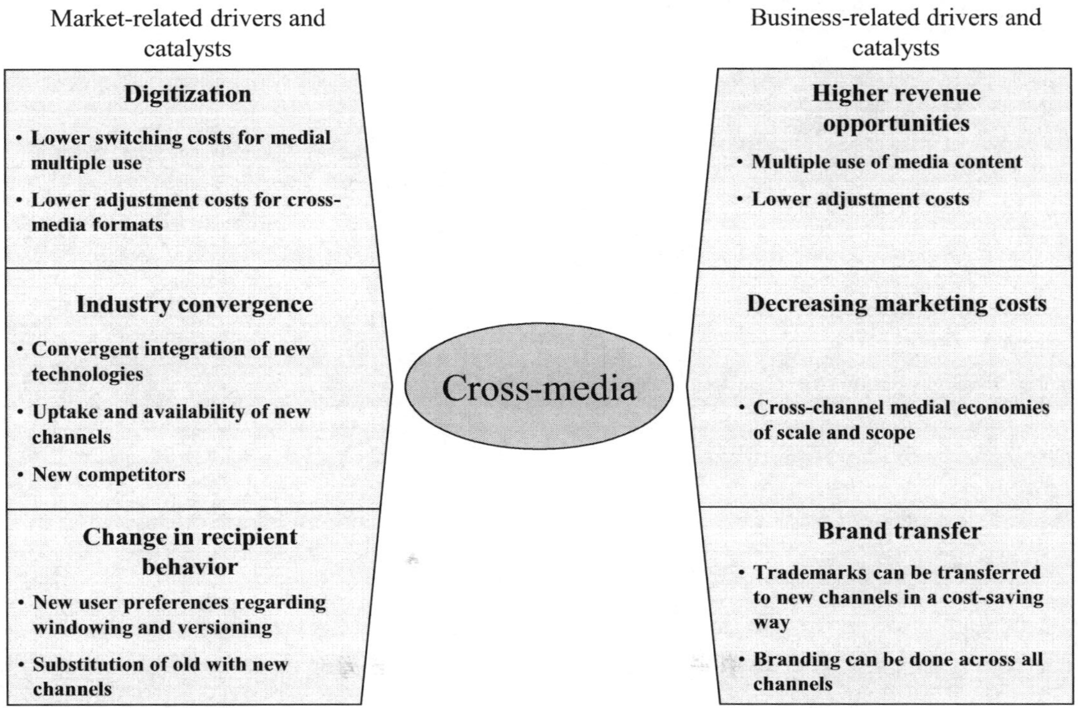

Market-related drivers and
catalysts

Business-related drivers and
catalysts

Digitization

· Lower switching costs for medial
multiple use

· Lower adjustment costs for cross-
media formats

Industry convergence

· Convergent integration of new
technologies

· Uptake and availability of new
channels

· New competitors

**Change in recipient
behavior**

· New user preferences regarding
windowing and versioning

· Substitution of old with new
channels

Cross-media

**Higher revenue
opportunities**

· Multiple use of media content

· Lower adjustment costs

Decreasing marketing costs

· Cross-channel medial economies
of scale and scope

Brand transfer

· Trademarks can be transferred
to new channels in a cost-saving
way

· Branding can be done across all
channels

Figure 14.2 Drivers and catalysts of cross-media.

Cross-Media Potentials, Strategies and Processes

In recent years, with the increasing importance of cross-media management, various cross-media strategies have emerged. Basically, the strategy alternatives can be distinguished based on the number of repurposing as well as the company-specific coordination of media formats and channels. Using these cross-media strategies as well as general approaches of strategic management, key cross-media processes can be identified. First of all, however, a fundamental understanding of the interaction between media channels and media formats and the resulting cross-media potentials is necessary.

Potentials of Cross-Media

The systematization of cross-media approaches has shown that the combination of media format and media channel is one of the central challenges of cross-media management. Media channels (in the broadest sense also referred to as branch channels) are the book market, the market for newspapers and magazines, the radio market, the TV market, the film market and the online market. In the cross-media context, in terms of potential and adaptation effort estimations, it makes sense to differentiate between a stationary and a mobile online market.

In this context media format is understood as text contributions, images, audio contributions or audiovisual material. Due to the significant differences, in production and scope, among others, the text format is also to be subdivided into book texts and edited texts. Thereby any combination of media formats and media channels has its specific characteristics that are of major importance for implementing a targeted cross-media management. Overall, a number of different combination possibilities emerge. For these characteristics the adaptation effort and the potential can be estimated.

The adaptation effort can generally be ascribed to the similarity of the combination to the original repurposing combination, including classical repurposing combinations, such as "book text" in a book. The more alike the target channel of a media format to its original using channel, the lower the adaptation effort. For example, a book contribution can easily be reprinted as a serial story in a daily newspaper.

The film version of the same work, such as a TV series, is considerably more elaborate and consequently associated with significantly higher costs. An exception in this context is online formats. In principle, all media formats can be adjusted to the online environment through digitization. Since nowadays the majority of the content is already produced digitally, the adaptation effort required for these channels is often comparatively moderate.

The potential of a combination of media format and media channel depends not only on the similarity of the channels but on other factors as well. Both development trends in the media industry (for example, toward online channels) and media format-specific characteristics need to be noted.

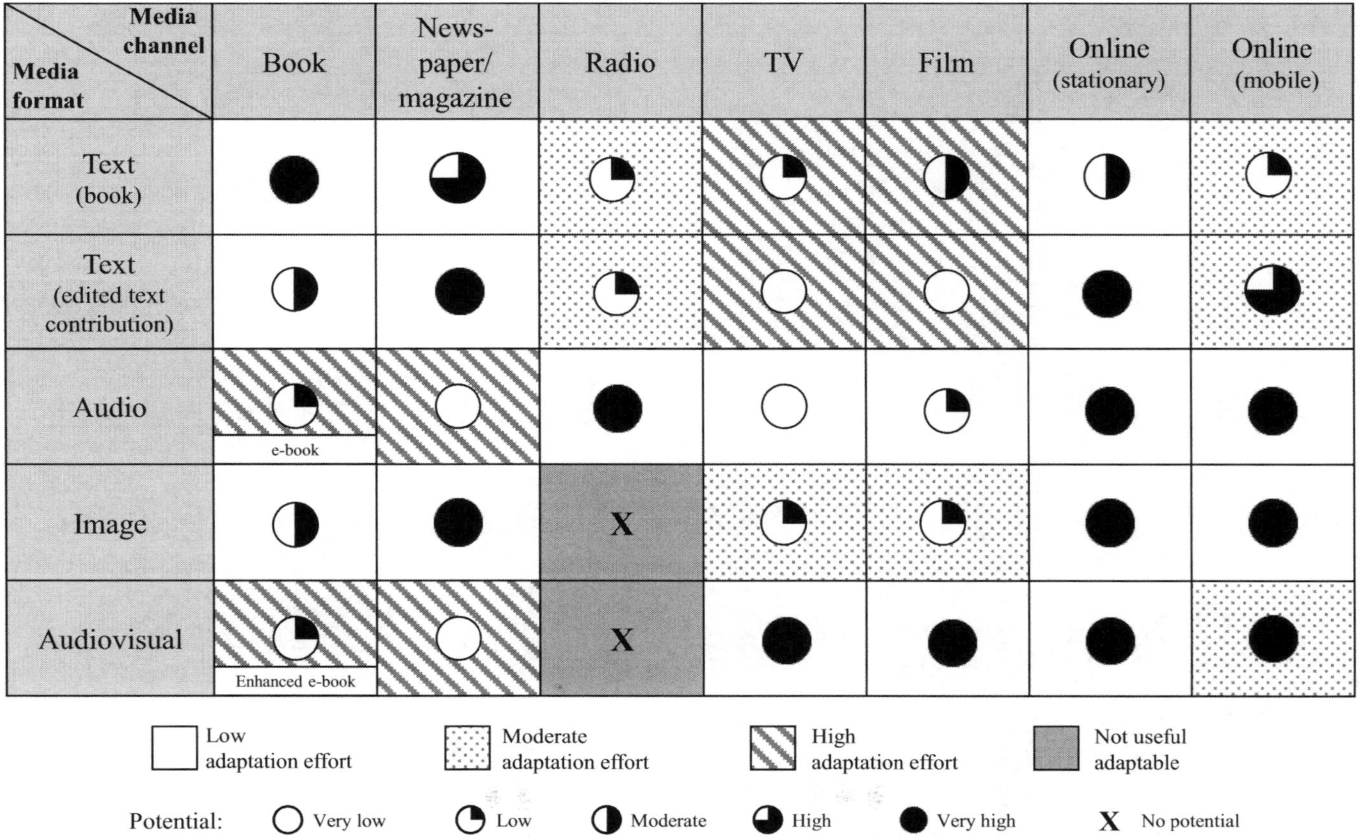

Media format \ Media channel	Book	News-paper/magazine	Radio	TV	Film	Online (stationary)	Online (mobile)
Text (book)	Very high	High	Low	Low	High	Moderate	Low
Text (edited text contribution)	Moderate	Very high	Low	Very low	Very low	Very high	High
Audio	Low (e-book)	Very low	Very high	Very low	Low	Very high	Very high
Image	Moderate	Very high	X	High	Low	Very high	Very high
Audiovisual	Low (Enhanced e-book)	Very low	X	Very high	Very high	Very high	Very high

Adaptation effort:
- Low adaptation effort (white)
- Moderate adaptation effort (dotted)
- High adaptation effort (hatched)
- Not useful adaptable (grey)
- X No potential

Potential:
○ Very low   ◔ Low   ◑ Moderate   ◕ High   ● Very high

Figure 14.3 Cross-media adaptation effort and potential.

For example, the transmission of audio content on TV is possible without increased effort.

Nevertheless, for this combination of pure audio format and audiovisual medium, no cross-media potential can be identified. Figure 14.3 shows possible combinations of media format and media channel and evaluates them according to their adaptation efforts and the possible cross-media potential. It should be noted that within the media channel book, audio books and also e-books are subsumed. All other digital formats are assigned to the online distribution channels.

It is apparent that in traditional media channels, away from the original repurposing combinations, there is limited cross-media potential. The various text formats can be utilized within the print media channels relatively easily and with medium to high cross-media potential. Moreover, the book text has cross-media potential in terms of radio utilization (as a reading) and for the TV or film market (as a script for a movie or a series). However, the relatively high adaptation effort must be considered. The media format image has cross-media potential in the media channels TV and film as an imagery for marketing purposes.

However, both the stationary as well as the mobile online channel offer high to very high cross-media potential. All media formats, with restrictions regarding the book text format, can be perfectly transferred to the online channel. Whereas the stationary online channel is already fully established as a repurposing channel, the mobile online channel is still in its development phase. The sharp rise in performance of mobile devices and the steady increase in bandwidth for the mobile Internet provide for rapid development toward a full-fledged cross-media channel.

Cross-Media Strategies

In the context of cross-media strategies, the number of used repurposing stages and the company-specific coordination of the media formats and channels are of special importance. Based on these criteria, various strategic alternatives can be identified. First, in this context, a distinction should be made based on the number of stages of the cross-media marketing chain. It should be noted that one can only speak of a cross-media strategy if at least two different channels are used.

Therefore, the simplest form represents the two-stage cross-media strategy. Through intelligent use of channels, transnational media companies can expand the multichannel utilization up to five channels. This can be illustrated by the example of book text as the original media format. The classical first utilization is the printed book, which can also include special formats such as audio books. Another utilization channel, and thus the basis for a two-stage cross-media strategy, represents the film. Herewith, book text (or mostly a modified version in the form of a script) is used as a template for a film adaptation. This is usually followed by a broadcast on

TV as a third utilization channel. As part of the windowing, the extension of the value chain for media content, the specification of the channel (for example, pay TV and free TV) and the sequence and timing also play an important role.

Here it should be noted, however, that the typical sequences of channels have experienced increasing changes in recent years. This mainly concerns the temporal dimension of the cross-media repurposing. The use of content in different channels is converging. So nowadays, very often there is less time between the broadcast of a film in cinemas and broadcasting it on pay TV. With new channels in some cases, even the complete elimination of temporal utilization windows can be observed.

Therefore, the cross-media repurposing does not need to be linear. The fourth repurposing stage, the online publication of the book text (for example, on a website), is conceivable after the TV broadcast as well as together with the book publishing. Moreover, a book text can easily be utilized as a serial story in a magazine and thus a fifth repurposing stage can be developed. In this case, a five-stage cross-media strategy is present.

Furthermore, cross-media strategies can be differentiated by the type of channel coordination. In principal, three different coordination forms are possible from which three types of strategies can be derived: the isolated cross-media strategy, the combined cross-media strategy and the transnational cross-media strategy. The three types of strategies differ in terms of their design, their requirements toward the enterprise and its coordination.

The isolated cross-media strategy is characterized by the fact that the various media channels are completely independent of each other in terms of coordination, and their control is channel immanent. Therefore, a channel-specific management is required. Usually a lead channel structure is existent, that is, a media channel is superior to the other channels. The isolation of the channels in the context of this cross-media strategy can go as far as that competition between the channels is existent. This is, for example, the case with a publishing company who markets digital versions through an online channel in addition to the classic book.

Within the combined cross-media strategy, the various media channels are partially coordinated with each other, and the control is still channel immanent. This leads to a situation in which the media channels mesh with each other and support each other in competition, a so-called coopetition among the channels. Mostly within this strategy type there is a higher level channel; however, the management is usually across the channels. An example of this strategy is the German public broadcaster ARD, where content is exchanged between TV, radio and online.

In a transnational cross-media strategy, all media channels are fully coordinated with each other and controlled across channels. The media channels are usually managed in a way so that they complement each other and that

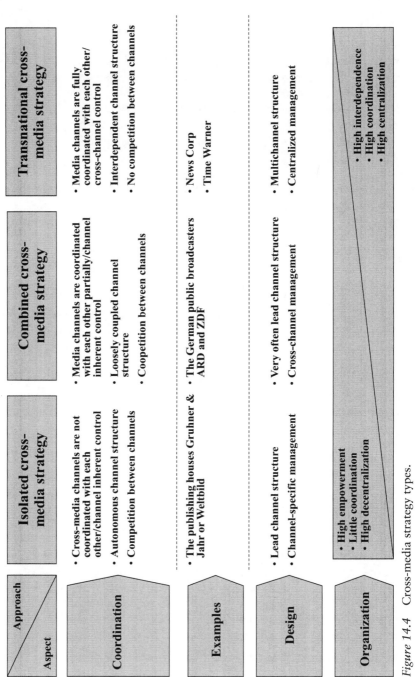

Approach / Aspect	Isolated cross-media strategy	Combined cross-media strategy	Transnational cross-media strategy
Coordination	• Cross-media channels are not coordinated with each other/channel inherent control • Autonomous channel structure • Competition between channels	• Media channels are coordinated with each other partially/channel inherent control • Loosely coupled channel structure • Coopetition between channels	• Media channels are fully coordinated with each other/cross-channel control • Interdependent channel structure • No competition between channels
Examples	• The publishing houses Gruhner & Jahr or Weltbild	• The German public broadcasters ARD and ZDF	• News Corp • Time Warner
Design	• Lead channel structure • Channel-specific management	• Very often lead channel structure • Cross-channel management	• Multichannel structure • Centralized management
Organization	• High empowerment • Little coordination • High decentralization		• High interdependence • High coordination • High centralization

Figure 14.4 Cross-media strategy types.

no competition between the channels arises. This requires a high degree of central control of the activities. In recent years, a clear trend toward integration of different media channels in the sense of a transnational cross-media strategy can be observed. Especially international media groups such as Time Warner and News Corp are using this strategy.

The demands on the organization change depending on the used cross-media strategy. Whereas the isolated cross-media strategy requires a high empowerment of individual channel management, there are high interdependencies between the various media channels within the transnational strategy. Also, the coordination effort and the degree of centralization increase with growing channel integration. Figure 14.4 illustrates the strategy types of cross-media management.

Process of Cross-Media Management
The process of cross-media management is divided into four areas that build on each other to show the entire course of an idealized development of medial multichannel systems. The cross-media management process is predominantly oriented to the general procedure of the planning process in the context of strategic marketing. The result of this are the initial strategic situation of the company, market segmentation as well as the strategy definition in medial multichannel systems.

Strategic decisions are long-term oriented and will help secure or even expand the competitive advantage of the company. The planning process for cross-media strategy development begins with a general business analysis to identify the company's own strengths and weaknesses as well as the opportunities and threats of the environment and thereby to obtain a complete overview of the initial situation. This situation analysis is particularly important for a medial multichannel strategy in order to understand the specific requirements for the cross-media management and if necessary adapt the target definitions and planning processes.

Building on the strategic initial situation, a segmentation of the market takes place in order to achieve a target group–specific, successful handling of the market. For this purpose a variety of potential segmentation criteria (geographic, sociodemographic, behavioral, psychographic and benefit oriented) are used. On the basis of the market segmentation, the definition of the company's individual cross-media strategy takes place.

The process of cross-media management is completed with the design of cross-media systems and is based on a four-step planning process. The first step is determined regarding potential media channels based on the market segmentation strategy and the strategy definition. Following, the form of the cross-media system is determined for the differentiated configuration of the channels. Here, core activities are the determination of the media stage number, the media positioning and the determination of the medial degree of differentiation.

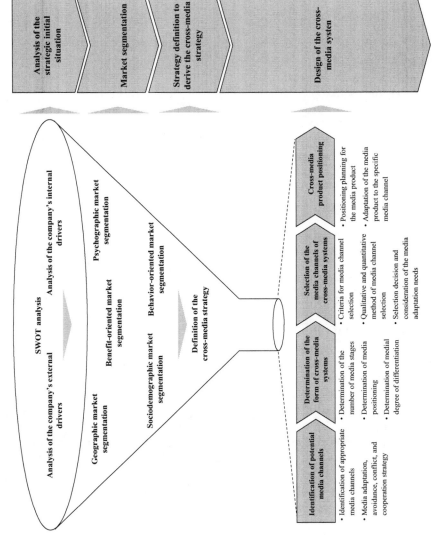

Figure 14.5 Processes of cross-media management.

The third step of the design process is concerned with the identification of specific requirements to the media channels in order to carry out a specific channel selection on this basis. The design process is completed with the cross-media product positioning. In the process the channel-dependent positioning planning for the media product is created. Furthermore, the adaptation of the media product to the media channel needs to be carried out. Figure 14.5 illustrates how the master planning process compresses to the design process of the cross-media system.

CONCLUSION

As highlighted in the previous section of this chapter, cross-media has become a new and important field of media management. A major reason for this is the digital revolution and with it the convergence of media markets. In this digital age of convergence of media markets, cross-media marketing strategies are a key for success of companies in the media sector.

All in all, cross-media is referred to as the lateral or even multilateral expansion of media distribution to various media channels or media submarkets. In this regard, cross-media management is the strategic foundation for integration efforts of companies in the media sector. Nowadays, hardly any media company can do without an adequate cross-media strategy and focused cross-media management. However, the success of cross-media management depends on many factors. Many of these key success factors have been highlighted in the previous chapter but are summarized in the following in an aggregated form.

A basic prerequisite for the implementation of a cross-media strategy and thus a key to the success of cross-media management is the availability of multiple channels. Although one can already speak of cross-media when there are two channels available, with each additional channel new advantages arise that sometimes scale disproportionate to the number of channels (such as economies of scale).

However, each additional channel increases the coordination effort. Therefore, channel adjustment is an additional important factor for a successful cross-media management. This is especially true for coordinated and transnational cross-media strategies. The success of cross-media management also depends crucially on the sharing of channels and resulting synergies. First, co-branding should be mentioned; it allows the transfer of a trademark to another channel or the synchronous brand development for multiple channels. Since branding is a lengthy and often expensive process, co-branding, as part of the cross-media management, has a high success meaning—in other words, is a major success factor.

The success factor cross-selling/cross-promotion is closely related to the co-branding. Here, a media channel is used for cross-media marketing of new media products. This results in considerable sales growth potentials.

Further, various media channels can be bundled by companies for joint marketing. The so-called bundling of services is an important success factor in establishing new channels and the enforcement of a transnational cross-media strategy. In the media bundling of services, different media formats are combined in media offer packages.

Another success factor is called windowing or versioning of media products through various media channels. The right design repurposing windows and the creation of market- and segment-specific product versions are particularly important and critical to success when using many channels (up to five-stage cross-media strategy).

Moreover, multiple customer loyalty can be identified as a key success factor of cross-media management. Only if customers can be attached to the company via the boundaries of singular channels can a cross-media marketing strategy be established. In this context the channel-customer fit is of considerable importance. The planning of the target group channel design is therefore an important step in the cross-media management process.

REFERENCES

Ansoff, H. I. (1965). Checklist for competitive and competence profiles. *Corporate strategy*. New York: McGraw Hill.

Business Wire. (2000). *Pearson PLC to acquire National Computer Systems, Inc.* Retrieved from www.thefreelibrary.com/Pearson+plc+to+Acquire+National+Computer+Systems,+ Inc.-a063763571

Jakubetz, C. (2008). *Crossmedia*. Konstanz: UVK Verlagsgesellschaft.

Macharzina, K., & Wolf, J. (2008). *Unternehmensführung: Das internationale Managementwissen. Konzepte—Methoden—Praxis*. Wiesbaden: Gabler.

Müller-Kalthoff, B. (2002). *Cross-media management*. Berlin: Springer.

Vogelsberg (2006). Crossmedia. In O. Altendorfer & L. Hilmer (Eds.), *Medienmanagement* (pp. 359–381). Berlin: Springer.

Welge, M., & Al-Laham, A. (2003). *Strategisches management*. 4th ed. Wiesbaden: Gabler.

Wirtz, B. W. (1994). *Neue Medien, Unternehmensstrategien und Wettbewerb im Medienmarkt, Eine wettbewerbstheoretische und -politische Analyse*. Frankfurt am Main: Peter Lang.

Wirtz, B. W. (2011). *Media and Internet management*. Wiesbaden: Gabler.

Wirtz, B. W., & Kleineicken, A. (2000). Geschäftsmodelltypologien im Internet. *Wirtschaftswissenschaftliches Studium, 29*(11), 628–635.

15 Marketing Communications with Networked Consumers and Negotiated Relationships

Edward C. Malthouse and Don Schultz

Marketing, and particularly marketing communication (marcom), has experienced dramatic transitions over the last 60 years. From the dependency on mass media to the development of data-based systems, to today's digitally driven, interactive approaches, marcom has evolved based on new approaches and methodologies that were not even imagined six decades ago. As we will explain, marketers must operate in a world of networked consumers and negotiated relationships. The evolution has been driven by technological innovations (Achrol, 1991), social and political developments (Thorson & Moore, 1996) and economic shifts that have occurred around the world (Vargo & Lusch, 2004).

In this chapter, we outline, in broad strokes, the transition that has occurred in marcom in three phases based on observable marketplace changes (Kitchen & Schultz, 2009). We explain and illustrate why the changes occurred and the effect they have had on how marcom is researched, developed and implemented (Schultz, Kerr, Kim & Patti, 2007). Most of all, we use this transition as a springboard to identify a new marcom research agenda.

The Development of Customer-Focused Marketing

What we call modern marketing emerged quite rapidly following the end of World War II (Kotler, 2002). Building on a base of industrialization and manufacturing, the initial implementation of customer-focused marketing was based on producing as many products as quickly as possible to fill the voracious consumption appetites of product-deprived consumers around the world. The top part of Figure 15.1 illustrates the relationship between the maker/seller and the customer during this phase. This is called the *acquired relationship phase* because marketing firms acquired their relationships with customers through media and distribution channel partners.

The most important point about this phase is that the marketer controlled the entire system, ranging from identifying which products were to be produced, to how they would be distributed, to the price that would be charged, to the promotion and brand communication of those products through mass media and sales promotion. Tools were developed to manage

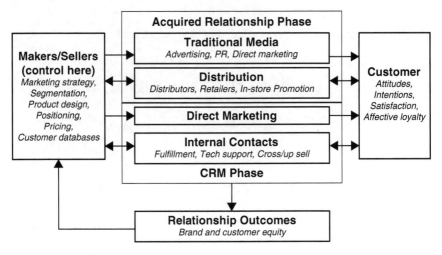

Figure 15.1 The acquired relationship and customer relationship management (CRM) models.

customers, such as a marketing strategy, segmentation, product design, positioning and pricing, which all helped the marketer control the relationship with the customer. Products were made available through marketer-dictated distribution systems—for instance, wholesalers, distributors, retailers and the like—that followed the dictates of the manufacturer (Day, 1994). Even in-store promotion was controlled by the marketing organization through the use of deals and discounts made available to the channel partners. The primary tools used by the marketing organization were traditional media such as print, broadcast and out of home advertising (Schultz, Barnes, Schultz & Azzaro, 2009).

Thus, by controlling the information systems, the marketer was able to dictate products and conditions to pliable customers. Since it was not easy for customers to acquire additional information on products from nonmedia sources, and, since much of the product information was distributed through free entertainment systems such as radio, television, newspapers and magazines, customers had few alternatives but to accept the conditions imposed by marketers (Schultz et al., 2009).

This model worked well, but marketers, operating in a competitive marketplace, needed to continually develop new approaches and methodologies that would give them a competitive edge. That quickly came in the 1970s and 1980s in the form of technology, primarily the development of digitalization and computational capabilities.

Evolving to Customer Relationship Management

By controlling all the marketplace communication and distribution systems, marketers increasingly dominated the marketplace. Success brought forth a rash of new products and innovations, all of which added to the marketer's dominance. Since information and information technology were responsible for much of the marketer's success, the drive to develop even more dominant technologies was soon on. First came computers, which, when connected to retail tills, gave marketers insights into consumer behaviors that they had never had before (Humby, Hunt & Phillips, 2004). Next came CRM (customer relationship management), where the marketing organization captured various levels of customer information, most often the customer's actual marketplace behaviors, which they then used to build more targeted marcom models and approaches. Many of these CRM approaches were initially developed from work done by direct marketers that was later emulated and extended by service organizations such as banks, airlines and hospitality organizations (Blattberg, Glazer & Little, 1994). Thus, the marketer's systems moved from mass to the individual and extended the marketer's control over the marketplace.

The bottom part of Figure 15.1 illustrates the approach. The model maintained the basics of mass marketing such as marketer-controlled traditional media and distribution channels, but added direct marketing, first through mailing systems and later through the telephone and eventually other electronic forms (Mehta & Sivadas, 1995). These new direct marketing systems extended the marketer's array of resources. Concepts such as test and control mailings, predictive analytics and scoring models (Malthouse, 2003) and customer segmentation and personalization improved the marketer's ability to discriminate among and between customers. Concepts such as lifetime value provided marketers with clear insights into the financial value of customers and enabled them to focus resources on best ones. Marketers added distribution channels with call centers, fulfillment facilities, technical support and customer service. Thus, marketers knew what customers were doing, what they were responding to and the value of those responses; customers were still mostly in the dark about what marketers were doing and why they were doing it. This period of the late 1980s and early 1990s was likely the high-water mark of traditional marketer-controlled marketing.

CRM was all to the benefit of the marketer. While it was termed "relationship marketing," the relationship was entirely controlled by the marketer. The system worked quite well for marketers until the middle 1990s and still works under certain conditions. Things began to change, however, when the first commercial uses of the Internet and the World Wide Web appeared (Ho, 1997). These new, interactive communication systems changed traditional marketer-controlled marketing forever. Even today, marketers still want to control the marketing system, but when customers get information and marketplace knowledge, marketers lose control.

Networked Customers and Negotiated Relationships

With the development and diffusion of new information technologies, traditional marketing and marcom has been changed forever. In this networked and negotiated relationship system (Figure 15.2), the marketer will continue

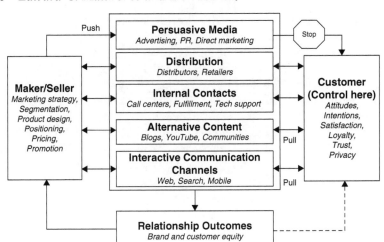

Figure 15.2   Networked consumers and negotiated relationships.

to develop products and services. They may continue to advertise and promote them in traditional media and with direct marketing (arrow A) and distribute them through mass distribution channels (arrow B) as well as through internal distribution channels (arrow C). That will be much like what has gone before. But the marketer no longer has the nearly complete control they enjoyed in the past over the messages, offers or even information about the products they are trying to vend.

It is important to note the role of the World Wide Web, search engines and now mobile devices. These technologies enabled customers to sort through, evaluate and make decisions based on information ranging from product descriptions to retail pricing to customer-generated evaluations of products and services (Nel, van Niekerk, Berthon & Davies, 1999). These developments have had much to do with the well-publicized "shift of marketplace power" (e.g., Deighton & Kornfeld, 2009; Hennig-Thurau et al., 2010). Mobile communication forms have enabled customers to access marketplace information anywhere at any time, thus breaking the tether of the broadcast signal, the cable wire and the Ethernet cord (Krause & Magedanz, 1996).

Customers are now networked. The system is no longer linear and direct, from marketer to customer. It is networked where multiple voices, both from the marketer and, more importantly, from other consumers, are all interconnected. This network model changes the marcom system, which has historically been based on a linear "stimulus-response" model (Lavidge & Steiner, 1961). The marketer sent out stimuli, in the form of messages and incentives, and consumers responded. In a network model, there are few loci of control. This obviates many of the traditional marketing concepts and approaches and is largely due to social media (Scott, 2007). With the rise of electronic systems such as Facebook, YouTube, Twitter and the like, customers can now talk back to marketers, ask questions, challenge claims and the like. Historically, marketers spoke and customers were supposed to listen and respond. Now customers can communicate with other, like-minded customers all over the world. That is, customers can create their own marketing and brand contact systems, either positive or negative, and share them with others or, indeed, the world. It is a system marketers can't control. More loss for the marketer, more gains for the customer.

Marketers are not the only ones adjusting to networked consumers. Social media and the existence of consumer networks have been credited with enabling the uprising against the 2009 Iranian election (e.g., Humphreys, 2010) and more recent uprisings in Egypt, Turkey and Brazil.

Relationships are now negotiated. That means when customers gain control of marketplace information, they become able to negotiate channels, pricing, terms and incentives—in short, the whole range of formerly marketer-controlled activities that determined the marketplace value of offers and product bundles (Tuli, Kohli & Bharadwaj, 2007). Today, it is not unusual for a consumer to walk into an electronics store, armed with a mobile device, view the retailer's offerings and prices and immediately compare and contrast them with what is available across the street. In these instances, which are becoming more common, the seller must either negotiate with the buyer or lose the sale.

Another important difference between the networked-negotiated model and earlier ones is that the continual pushing of controlled brand messages at customers and prospects is no longer as effective as it was in the past. Consumers are armed with technologies such as DVRs and spam filters and can shut out messages at will ("stop" sign impeding the flow through arrow F in Figure 15.2). They now seek out information and relationships with marketers of their choice through search or other interactive means.

As the bottom dashed arrow from the "Reciprocal Relationship Outcomes" box indicates, marketers must expand their focus beyond measures of value that benefit only the organization, such as customer lifetime value and customer and brand equity. They must move away from the view that they create the ongoing brand relationships to one where it is understood that relationships must be negotiated and reciprocal (Aggarwal, 2004). That means there must be value to the customer and the marketer if relationships are to be built. For marketers, this likely means rethinking many of the traditional, marketer-controlled CRM models that have developed over the last 30 years or so (Malthouse et al., 2013). In particular, key performance indicators such as lifetime value (Malthouse, 2013) must be reconsidered to include measures of value to the customer as well.

The traditional approaches used in the first two phases of marketing will continue to be useful and relevant, particularly in markets where information technology is less developed or where consumers are still learning how to be consumers (Schultz, 2012). The ability of makers/sellers to direct information to specific groups of customers and prospects, thus moving them out of the mass market and into identifiable segments to which relevant marketing materials can be delivered, will continue to evolve over time. Interestingly, it is often in the emerging markets where networked-negotiated relationships will likely become most prevalent.

When consumers have interactive capabilities, they quickly learn to use them to level the playing field with even the most sophisticated marketing organizations. Examples where this is occurring abound in Korea, China, India, Brazil and other markets (Mathews, 2009). Therefore, we argue the real challenge in this networked-negotiated marketplace will occur primarily in emerging markets. It is in those markets where the new interactive technologies are developing most rapidly (Schultz et al., 2009). Indeed, it may well be these new markets, which are often considered to be less developed by traditional marketing organizations, where networked-negotiated marketing will be most appropriate, and the shift from marketer control to customer control may occur without any intermediate steps. And it is about these consumers that marketers have the least information, knowledge, insights and experience since most academic and commercial research in the past has been conducted in Western markets.

A Marketing Communication Research Agenda

With this background in mind, we present a new marcom research agenda. We have identified areas that we feel have been under-researched or recently emerged. The agenda is organized around the framework in Figure 15.2. All illustrate how the new marketplace is developing and why this networked and negotiated approach is appropriate. Here are the basic content areas where academic research can contribute the most.

Understand Network Models

Marcom approaches are mostly based on outbound, linear, stimulus-response models. Today's systems are now one giant network connecting customers with each other as well as the firm. This means marketers must learn how networks are created, how they are dynamically expanded, contracted and reformed on all levels. New types of research techniques will need to be employed such as object-oriented modeling, principal-agent analysis, game theory, evolutionary learning and network models for the diffusion of innovation (Valente, 1996). Another difference in this networked-negotiated marketplace is that the traditional marketer cannot continue to send out messages, offers and so forth exclusively through outbound systems; they must learn to respond appropriately to the user-generated content (UGC) that is developed outside the traditional marketing system. These can be considered in-bound *trigger events* (Malthouse, 2007). Often, these are contacts the firm did not initiate and with which it may not externally agree (arrow D). In other words, the marketer moves from "external talking" to "external listening," an area that is not well developed in most selling-oriented organizations.

Firms must understand when and how to respond to customers who post content to social media, discussion forums, review sites and so forth. We suspect that a firm can ignore at least some, and perhaps much, of the UGC, but what criteria determine which content can be ignored and which demands a response? For the UGC requiring a response, what communication strategies should a firm follow in crafting a response? What metrics can the firm use to monitor social media and gauge the effectiveness of its interactions with customers?

Negotiation and Relationships

Most academics are not accustomed to researching in negotiated marketplaces, where haggling in bazaar-like situations is a way of life. This will require the development of new forms of understanding consumer behaviors and generating customer insights. Marketers must move away from the view that they create and maintain product or service value to one where relationships are reciprocal.

The concept of cocreation, where consumers participate in the creation of value, has been discussed for decades, but it is not fully understood along with the technology used to create these new opportunities for its use. How can the firm use marcom to stimulate consumers to cocreate brand meaning, benefits and value? For decades the firm has decided what the brand should be and then created advertising to convey its meaning to passive consumers. Now, consumers create alternative brand messages and post them on social media and the Internet. How effective is UGC brand messaging compared to traditional advertising, and how can it be monetized? How does the firm respond when the consumer's views of the brand differ from what the marketer intended? What are the best ways to prompt consumers to create such content? How does creating, sharing and viewing UGC affect purchase behaviors (not just "engagement" metrics such as the number of Tweets)?

Decreasing Brand Loyalty

Another challenge created by the networked-negotiated marketplace is that consumers have more relevant, high-quality products and services available from which to choose (Schultz, Block, & Viswanathan, 2013). For example, at one point a consumer who was looking for a product would have gone to the local retailer and bought whatever that retailer stocked. Alternatively, the consumer may have sought out some catalogs and mail-ordered the item. The Internet, search and the widespread availability of efficient delivery systems have now changed this. Consumers can find a manufacturer or distributer on another continent. At the same time, there is more parity in the quality and functionality of products so that consumers become less attached to particular brands. An important issue is how to develop, nurture and maintain brand loyalty in this competitive marketplace. One possible solution is for firms to develop customer *engagement* with products and services. Marketers agree that customer engagement is important but do not agree on what it is (Brodie, Hollebeek, Juric & Ilic, 2011) or how to develop or maintain it.

Synergy, Integration of Contacts and the Growth in Channels and Devices

Over the past several years, the focus of marketing has been to identify the one or two primary marcom tools, optimize them and observe marketplace success. The traditional Western marketer approach of "starting with TV and adding a few other media forms to fill out the holes" will decline. Going forward, the emphasis must be on identifying what combination of marcom forms is optimal. This task is being made more difficult by the growth in the number of advertising channels, devices and titles within a channel. In addition to print, TV and out-of-home advertising, there are many more delivery channels including computers on the Internet, mobile devices, text messaging, paid search and so forth. The number of, for example, TV channels and programs is also growing, creating increased fragmentation. This increases the complexity of allocating media budgets. We need better methods of understanding the effectiveness of each vehicle, as well as how vehicles and channels interact with one another—media and message synergy. Measuring and demonstrating the return on investment of individual media and combinations of media will continue to grow in importance.

The traditional marketing belief has been that if we know all the pieces and parts, we can reassemble them to our benefit. Increasingly, however, we see that that all the moving parts interact. Customers are holistic. They take in, assemble and activate the knowledge they need, when they need it, in the form they need it. Marketers must become holistic in their views as well. Integration will be a key skill for marketers going forward, of what their customers, influencers, recommenders, detractors and all the others in the marketing network do.

RESEARCH METHODS

Data has always been the most challenging aspect of academic research. Thus, acquiring or capturing relevant marketplace data has driven the academic research agenda for decades. Today, there is a plethora of data, generated by both marketers and customers, floating about in various marketing systems. Capturing and harnessing that data will be one of the key skills of researchers in the new marketplace. That means new research tools will have to be developed, tested, proven and then implemented to take advantage of the new data explosion typified by "the cloud." Survey research, the traditional workhorse of both academic and professional researchers, will likely become less important as it becomes easier and easier to capture actual marketer and customer behaviors. Some sets of research tools that seem especially important for marketers in the future include the following.

First, marketers should become more skilled at using all the variables available on social media and the rest of the Internet. Marketers need to become better at working with unstructured data—doing network analysis, string processing and text mining—while recognizing the limitations of such data sets, such as them being convenience samples and the inherent selection biases with consumers who self-select into sharing content, etc. These methodologies have existed in computer science for many years, but most marketers are usually not trained to use them, and they are not covered in any marketing research textbooks. The extant classification of word of mouth (WOM) is simplistic and is typically positive, negative or perhaps neutral. Surely, however, not all negative WOM is the same, nor deserving of the same responses. As part of text mining, we need more granular descriptions of WOM. Graph theory and network analysis are also not covered in marketing research and other marketing courses.

Second, marketers must learn more about computer science algorithms and artificial intelligence. Many of the new-media advertising decisions—for example, those that center around paid search terms, bidding for banner and display ad space, selecting hosting sites for ads, picking a set of products to recommend to a customer visitor to a webpage and so on—must be made millions or even billions of times each day. Automated computer algorithms are required. Therefore, these decisions must be made in a fraction of a second, and so issues such as whether a model or algorithm can produce a recommendation in such a short time must be considered. Another modeling issue is that the marketplace is constantly changing and the firm is constantly acquiring more data, requiring "real-time" updating. Marketers have traditionally used models where the model parameters are estimated once, then embedded in a "batch" model. They are then held constant until the model is re-estimated, again in a batch model. It will become important to develop models where the parameter estimates change dynamically as more data become available and the marketplace changes. Such issues have traditionally not been concerns of marketing scientists or researchers, but they are today.

Third, marketers will have to figure out how to take advantage of the data explosion that is created by digital devices and other technology. The amount of data collected about customers has expanded by several orders of magnitude over the past few decades because of the Internet, social media, mobile devices and so forth. Such data can be overwhelming but creates new opportunities for more relevant and effective marketing contact points. We can think of these new data sets as expanding the set of variables that a marketer can "condition on" when delivering contact points. For example, at one point media buying decisions were made primarily on the basis of assumed or estimated demographics—an advertiser might be looking for women between the ages of 25 and 40, and such a demographic block was assumed to be homogeneous. Marketers can now decide on contact points for an *individual customer* based on previous purchase history, what the individual has said in social media, where the customer is (including GPS information from mobile devices), the "role" of the consumer in a network of consumers and more. How can marketing contact points be made more effective by using all this data, e.g., better targeting of messages or personalizing the content of messages? How can such data be used to generate new ideas for products and services? Data quality issues must be addressed, since there may be, for example, changes to collection procedures that are unknown to the analyst, and there are selection biases over who participates in social media, etc. The use of such data will also create new questions around privacy.

How does an organization determine whether a "reciprocal relationship outcome" is being achieved? This is developed from the view of the customer, not the marketer, which is an area not well developed today. Organizations already have a good idea of how to measure outcomes that benefit itself, such as customer lifetime value, customer equity and brand equity. More work is needed to understand whether the consumer is realizing value or perceives that the relationship is worthwhile in terms of time, effort and monetary cost. Measuring customer satisfaction has become standard practice across many different industries, but satisfaction is not necessarily the same thing as value. We must understand the relationship between value and satisfaction. If satisfaction is a consequence of value, then it may be a convenient proxy, but it will not be diagnostic in that it helps identify specifically where there is a problem or, more importantly, an opportunity. This discussion on customer experiences and engagement may be a way to characterize and understand value, yet this is an undeveloped area for most marketers (see Mersey, Malthouse & Calder, 2012; Hollebeek, et al., 2014).

A related question is whether there is a synergy between the value of the interaction between the organization and customer—in other words, is the value of one party enhanced when the other party receives high levels of value or is it decreased when problems occur? (See Larivière et al., 2013 for a discussion of value fusion.) This would suggest that organizations and consumers share a symbiotic relationship in a customer-organization ecosystem. This represents a strikingly different way of thinking about customers than the first two phases, where the firm targets segments of customers and contacts them with various marketing messages so that they buy, to the benefit of the organization. Thus, can longer-term, reciprocal measures be developed that will help explain the value to both?

Integrating the Organization

One of the most difficult challenges to marketing in the future is that many customer touch points are not managed by the "marketing" group.

Information technology (IT) departments often "own" many of the operational databases that record, in great detail, a wide variety of customer interactions including transaction history, website browsing and page view histories, click logs, mobile location-specific records, call-center logs and so forth. IT also often oversees customer relationship management systems, which are responsible for many contact points with customers such as e-mail and other forms of direct marketing. In addition to providing information about customers, these databases and systems also target contact points at individual customers so that organizations can allocate different amounts of marketing resources in different customers. The messages from IT departments may not be coordinated with what marketing is saying about the brand. Computer science and IT may excel at managing large data sets in real time, developing efficient and scalable algorithms for recommending cross-sell opportunities and testing endless variations of messages, but such optimizations could do more harm than good if they undermine the brand-building messages created by marketing departments and ad agencies. IT professionals must know more about marketing and branding. It would seem appropriate that these activities should be coordinated with the brand-building messages in "advertising or other forms of marketing communication." What seems to be missing is the testing of these propositions and the effect of synergy across such touch points. Again, these are activities that either do not exist or have been under-researched in the past.

While traditional marketing sometimes excels at developing brand and market strategies, it has been less specific about issues central to direct and database marketing such as lifetime value, managing customer databases and measuring the outcomes of marketing actions at the customer level. Marketers need better training in how other departments think and carry out their marketing-related activities, including analytics, finance and IT.

There will always be a need for people who can do something exceptionally well, but those with specialized knowledge and skills should understand that their area is one piece in a larger puzzle, that it is becoming more important for the pieces to be connected and that they have a role to play in putting the pieces together. Simply creating a new view of organizational structure is a task in which the entire organization must engage as it is well beyond the venue of marketing alone. Managers at all levels will need even better peripheral vision along with systems and processes that will enable action to be taken.

CONCLUSION

We have presented our view of how marketing and marketing communication have developed and evolved over the last half century. Inherent in this view is the fact that most of the changes have come as the result of technologies that have benefited both the marketer and the customer. These technologies will continue to emerge and evolve. Thus, we view marketing and marketing communication as a dynamic system, where traditionally only snapshots in time were possible. These snapshots, after some period of time, can now be assembled into a moving picture, which is what we have tried to do in this chapter. That moving picture can provide insights into why and how things developed as they did, but it is limited in its ability to predict the future. Thus, we have built two historical models to explain what has happened. The second model, which we call the CN^2 (the N^2 refers to negotiated and networked) marketplace, is an attempt to place in perspective a current "snapshot" of the marketplace. We believe it suggests some new methodologies and approaches that must be developed if marketers and academics are to improve and understand the dynamic and ever-changing marketing system in which all of us find ourselves. All the areas of future research that we have suggested are rich areas for new thinking and new development. Going forward, we believe much of the new thinking must come from the developing markets and economies of Asia-Pacific, Africa and South America. It is here that technologies are seeing their most rapid development and markets are evolving most quickly. In our view, it will likely be the Asia-Pacific area where much of the new thinking will originate. Thus, the domination of Western thinking in marcom must be tempered with the emerging market experiences being developed, which represent another form of integration and likely are the most important of all.

REFERENCES

Achrol, R. (1991). Evolution of marketing organization: New forms for turbulent environments. *Journal of Marketing, 55,* 77–93.

Aggarwal, P. (2004). The effects of brand relationship norms on consumer attitudes and behavior. *Journal of Consumer Research, 31*(1), 87–101.

Blattberg, R., Glazer, R., & Little, J. (1994). *The Marketing information revolution.* Harvard Business School Press, Cambridge, MA.

Brodie, R.A., Hollebeek, L.D., Juric, B., & Ilic, A. (2011). Customer engagement: Conceptual domain, fundamental propositions and implications for research. *Journal of Service Research, 14*(3), 252–271.

Day, G.S. (1994). The capabilities of market-driven organizations. *Journal of Marketing, 58*(4), 37–52.

Deighton, J., & Kornfeld, L. (2009). Interactivity's unanticipated consequences for marketers and marketing. *Journal of Interactive Marketing, 23*(1), 4–10.

Hennig-Thurau, T., Malthouse, E., Friege, C., Gensler, S., Lobschat, L., Rangaswamy, A., & Skiera, B. (2010). The impact of new media on customer relationships. *Journal of Service Research, 13*(3), 311–330.

Ho, J. (1997). Evaluating the World Wide Web: A global study of commercial sites. *Journal of Computer-Mediated Communication, 3*(1).

Hollebeek, L.D., Glynn, M.S. and Brodie, R.J. (2014). Consumer Brand Engagement in Social Media: Conceptualization, Scale Development & Validation. *Journal of Interactive Marketing*, Forthcoming.

Humby, C., Hunt, T., & Phillips, T. (2004). *Scoring points: How Tesco is winning customer loyalty.* London: Kogan Page Publishing.

Humphreys, A. (2010). Co-producing experiences. In A. Peck & E. Malthouse (Eds.), *Medill on media engagement.* Cresskill, New Jersey: Hampton Press.

Kitchen, P.J., & Schultz, D.E. (2009). IMC: New horizon/false dawn for a marketplace in turmoil? *Journal of Marketing Communications, 15*(2–3), 197–204.

Kotler, P. (2002). *Marketing management.* Upper Saddle River, New Jersey: Prentice Hall.

Krause, S., & Magedanz, T. (1996). Mobile service agents enabling intelligence on demand in telecommunications. *Proceedings of the 1996 IEEE Global telecommunications conference,* GLOBECOM '96, 1, 78–84.

Larivière, B., Joosten, H., Malthouse, E.C., Van Birgelen, M., Aksoy, P., Kunz, W., & Huang, M.H. (2013). Value fusion: The blending of consumer and firm value in the distinct context of mobile technologies and social media. *Journal of Service Management, 24*(3), 268–293.

Lavidge, R.J., & Steiner, G.A. (1961). A model for predictive measurements of advertising effectiveness. *Journal of Marketing, 25,* 59–62.

Malthouse, E.C. (2003). Scoring models. In D. Iacobucci & B. Calder (Eds.), *Kellogg on integrated marketing* (pp. 227–249). New York: Wiley.

Malthouse, E.C. (2007). Mining for trigger events with survival analysis. *Data Mining and Knowledge Discovery, 15* (3), 383–402.

Malthouse, E.C. (2013). *Segmentation and lifetime value models using SAS.* Cary, NC: SAS.

Malthouse, E.C., Haenlein, M., Skiera, B., Wege, E., Zhang, M. (2013). Managing Customer Relationships in the Social Media Era: Introducing the Social CRM House. *Journal of Interactive Marketing, 27* (4), 270–280.

Mathews, J. (2009). China, India, Brazil: Tiger technologies and the building of national systems of economic learning. *Asian Business and Management, 8*(1), 5–32.

Mehta, R., & Sivadas, E. (1995). Direct marketing on the Internet: An empirical assessment of consumer attitudes. *Journal of Direct Marketing, 9*(3), 21–32.

Mersey, R.D., Malthouse, E., & Calder, B. (2012). Focusing on the reader: Engagement trumps satisfaction. *Journalism & Mass Communication Quarterly, 89*(4), 695–709.

Nel, D., van Niekerk, R., Berthon, J.P., & Davies, T. (1999). Going with the flow: Web sites and customer involvement. *Internet Research, 9*(2), 109–116.

Schultz, D. (2012). The marketing and communications implications of social media: A new digital Silk Road? *Proceedings of the Beijing Forum,* Peking University, Beijing, China, November, 2012.

Schultz, D., Block, M., & Viswanathan, V. (2013, June). Brand preference being challenged. *Proceedings of the European Advertising Academy Conference (ICORIA),* Zagreb.

Schultz, D., Barnes, B.E., Schultz, H.F., & Azzaro, M. (2009). *Building customer brand relationships.* Armonk, New York: M.E. Sharpe Publishing.

Schultz, D., Kerr, G.F., Kim, I., & Patti, C. (2007). In search of a theory of integrated marketing communication. *Journal of Advertising Education, 11*(2), 1–27.

Scott, D. (2007). *The new rules of marketing and PR.* New York: Wiley.

Thorson, E., & Moore, J. (Eds.). (1996). *Integrated communication: Synergy of persuasive voices.* Mahwah, New Jersey: Lawrence Erlbaum Associates.

Tuli, K.R., Kohli, A.K., & Bharadwaj, S.G. (2007). Rethinking customer solutions: From product bundles to relational processes. *Journal of Marketing, 71,* 1–17.

Vargo, S.L., & Lusch, R.F. (2004). Evolving to a new dominant logic for marketing. *Journal of Marketing, 68,* 1–17.

Valente, T.W. (1996). Network models of the diffusion of innovations. *Computational & Mathematical Organization Theory, 2*(2), 163–164.

16 Marketing Self-Branding Strategies for Social Presence in Digital Media

Robert Pennington

Digital media are emerging as a new of location for community development. Through increasing capacity for user-generated content and interactivity, virtual communities become more richly detailed in their appearances. These new living spaces attract users by satisfying the same values that attract users to actual communities. The result is virtual communities analogous to actual communities.

Virtual communities have evolved from telephonic verbal communication to highly interactive digital electronic media that provide the rich audiovisual sensory detail that gives consumers presence, the sense of being in an environment both physically and socially. Because communities are essentially social, digital media users especially need tools for social interactivity.

In actual communities, brands have evolved from signifiers of property rights through signifiers of product attributes to signifiers of consumer attributes. As components of cultural discourse, brands have become an important mode of consumer communication. Self-branding identifies and distinguishes consumers as social objects within consumer market culture. In analogous virtual communities, self-branding will be a critical factor in generating presence.

Marketing effective self-branding strategies will maintain authoritative control of brand meaning while providing consumers with tools to establish social presence. By communicating cultural roles and relationships in virtual environments, self-branding will transfer to and reinforce marketing in actual environments.

Communities

Traditional societies are self-sustaining communities of people within specific geographical boundaries. Behavior determines social value. Objects signify prior behavior. The transition from behavior to objects as signs of community value is a practical development. For the purpose of individual identity, which is individual value in the community, acquiring signs gains increasing importance relative to other productive behaviors. Sign acquisition becomes a productive behavior as individuals produce themselves and establish their identities in terms of community values. Because communities establish sign meanings, individual identity can extend no farther than the area in which other individuals recognize and respond similarly to common signs. It cannot extend beyond the boundaries of community culture. Individuals find their fulfillment within the bounds and boundaries of culture (Benedict, 1934).

Virtual Communities

Technology breaks the boundaries of culture because it permits the extension of a representational system beyond interpersonal contact. The development of technology for sustaining community through culture propagation inevitably led to the blurring and even the loss of boundaries. Technology intended to sustain culture by breaking the boundaries of time also broke the boundaries of space with consequent diffusion, dilution, or contamination. The term "technology" tends to evoke relatively recent development of electronic tools. But the forerunners of electronic tools were the strictly manual means of producing signs as representations: clay tablets, papyrus, paper, and pigments.

The origins of virtual communities lie in that primitive technology through which individuals could represent a community entirely through the creation of signs. A reed pressed into wet clay did not put an actual community into the clay, but only a representation. Yet the purpose was to convey an organic sense of the community. Those who were educated in the use of representational systems did not interpret the signs as mere signs. Rather, they interpreted the signs as the community. Although it did not have the features of twenty-first-century electronic, digital technology, this was the virtual community—a community that is not actual, but that users interpret as actual.

Culture substitutes a technological representation for actual reality. Culture itself is a virtual reality. What contemporary discourse calls virtual reality is just the current technologically sophisticated version of an integral component of human development. Current technology affords the possibility for broader use of icons, a type of sign that shares a physical resemblance with its representation. Humans have created such signs for tens of thousands of years but not to the extent that contemporary technology permits. The earliest technology, and even some recent technology, entailed a high possibility of attracting attention to itself. Pigments on stone could easily appear to the viewer as just what they actually were: pigments on stone. Although contemporary technology can just as easily call attention to itself, it affords such richness in sensory detail that viewers fail to acknowledge that the environment is only virtual and not actual. Regardless, it still relies on the original principle of cultural substitution either for a coincident actual environment, for an entirely imaginary environment, or for a range of blends.

Coincident Worlds

People live simultaneously in two worlds, an actual world and a culturally constituted world. The actual world occurs unmediated by any technology. The culturally constituted world may have a base in the actual world, but it can be completely independent. Nudler (1990) uses the terms "environment" and "world" to distinguish them. However, the two are so melded that either without the other would be incomplete in human perception. Individuals interpret and complete a purely actual world by mentally applying the cultural forms that constitute experience (Hall, 1973). Individuals mentally interpret and complete the purely representational worlds of signs by mentally supplying the physical sensations that culture has associated with the technologically produced signs. Although the sensations produced may be imaginary, the individual can perceive them as actual. Although the social world may include actual physical sensations, its dominant components are signs that reveal culturally defined relationships. These signs can be identical in both the actual world and the technologically produced world of digital media. Therefore, individuals can perceive themselves to be socially in an environment regardless of whether it is actual or technologically produced.

Humans continually endeavor to satisfy needs. They must secure their physical survival (Maslow, 1943; Bay, 1990), but this is not a human need because it applies to all living organisms. However, without physical survival, the question of other distinctly human needs is moot. It is the platform for all other needs, whether basic or derived. Digital environments impose a need for secure physical survival as well. Hardware, software, electricity, and online constitute the physical platform of the digital environment. Without them, the question of human needs in digital environments is moot. Because the physical platform need applies to all, it cannot satisfy a distinctly human need. Among a range of writers who often disagree with each other concerning basic human needs, one most fundamental need stands out: identity (Rubenstein, 1990). Humans enter digital environments along with their distinctly human needs. Because the need for a physical platform is common to all, it cannot identify because it cannot distinguish. Digital environments, however, afford greater capacity than actual environments to satisfy identity needs because they are worlds of signs only, and humans construct their identities through signs. Although digital environments appear on the physical platform that makes them possible, users easily disregard the platform just as they disregard their physical platforms in actual environments. The ability to satisfy this basic human need in digital environments entails the capacity to enter such environments as an actual human. When individuals construct and recognize their known cultural identities and relationships in any world of signs, they perceive themselves to be present in that world.

Presence

The essence of presence is a reduction of the amount of mental construction required for the user to create and modify the environment. Presence occurs only in the mind of the individual. Some have applied the concept to distinguish direct experience in actual environments (Coyle & Thorson, 2001; Klein, 2003; Steuer, 1992). Others studies use presence as a shortened form of telepresence (Li, Daugherty & Biocca, 2002; Lombard & Ditton, 1997; Lombard & Snyder-Duch, 2001), the sense of being in a distant environment mediated by technology. Because culture is the use of technology, this study finds the distinction superfluous. A range of technologies can evoke presence, but digital media draw particular attention because of continual advances in the capacity to produce the critical factors of presence: vividness and interactivity. The range and richness of the sensory inputs that technology provides are the components of vividness. To date, the range of sensory inputs in digital media does not extend beyond sight and sound. Interactivity is the ability to effect changes to the inputs available for sensation in real time. We can also apply the concept of richness to interactivity as the range of possible changes and the facility with which the user can affect the changes.

The effect of presence is not simply hypnotic. In utilizing vividness and interactivity, technology must create an environment the user perceives as one the user could actually be in. Merely providing a range of richly detailed sensory inputs with which the user can interact in real time does not elicit presence. The user must be able to make sense of the environment. The user may detect patterns in a broad range of detailed technologically generated inputs and be able to act upon them in real time and in a range of ways. However, no matter how much they may arrest the user's attention and occupy the user's consciousness without cultural definition, patterns and interactions cannot constitute environments.

The user must be able to organize sensory inputs into recognized, identifiable patterns that sufficiently conform to expectations of what actual environments could be. Culture provides those expectations along with a range of possible deviations. Fantasy has definite latitudes of acceptability. The same organizing function that culture plays in actual environments also applies to digital media environments. The templates for actual and virtual experience are cultural products. For presence to occur, technological vividness and interactivity must create an environment that is culturally plausible, one that fits cultural forms without too many distracting anomalies. However, even anomalies must eventually find explanation through the existing system of cultural components and interrelationships. The user must perceive the virtual environment as a representation of an actual or possible world in which the user can be present.

Virtual Cultures

For digital media to elicit cultural presence, sign choice and organization are critical. No matter how richly vivid and interactive a digital environment may be, details must lie within users' cultural norms. Otherwise, users will feel presence, but in a foreign culture. In this situation, users may lose awareness of the mediating technology but not lose awareness of the signs or organization. Technological vividness and interactivity facilitate psychological processing to foster presence in digital environments. But poorly selected and organized signs will hinder presence in cultural environments. Whether the virtual culture may diverge from actual culture and to what degree depends on users. That latitude derives from the norms of users' actual-world cultural environment. Users may want to feel present in a digitally mediated foreign environment. What constitutes even a foreign environment depends upon the signs and organization principles of users' base culture. Presence in any kind of virtual culture emerges from prior experience, which is culturally constituted.

Through cultural agreement, individuals project meaning onto the material world. The exchange of objects is the exchange of meaning. All exchange constitutes meaning transfer. Object possession attaches meaning to the possessor by cultural agreement (Douglas & Isherwood, 1979). Individuals endeavor to acquire objects based on cultural meaning. Signs are repositories of meaning. The specific and exclusive purpose is to convey and assign meaning that still only resides in the human psyche. Brands have always been signs even though their meanings have evolved. Even as an expression of property, that meaning does not reside in the brand itself. However, because individuals transfer meaning so completely to signs, brands do not just signify property or any other attribute. Brands become attributes. From a disinterested view outside of brand culture, acquiring a brand is a process of acquiring a sign of an attribute. From within brand culture, the brand is the attribute. Therefore, consumers do not acquire brands as signs of extent attributes. Rather, they acquire the actual attributes. An individual can have no meaning without a sign of that meaning, and brands are the signs.

In digital environments, individuals associate themselves with meaningful signs that can occur in those environments, just as they do in actual environments (McWilliam, 2000). Consumer brands are especially useful because they can occur in digital environments exactly as they occur in actual environments. The material world signifies. In the actual world, objects signify something about the environment or context within which they occur. Objects that humans create represent the cultural values of those who create and recognize them. Culture also designates naturally occurring objects as meaningful. Digital environments do not contain either human-created or naturally occurring objects. The entire environment is a context of signs only, unintelligible except through conventions imported from actual environments.

Technology can provide vividness and interactivity to create an illusion that users perceive as actual. But an actual car, for example, cannot occur in any digital environment. Only a representation of an automobile can occur. Even the most sophisticated computer-aided design does not produce an actual automobile. Manufacture is restricted to the actual world. The brand Ford, however, can occur in digital environments exactly as in actual environments because it is only a sign. Although human created, signs are still component elements of the material world. Further, as components of the actual material world, their inclusion in digital environments provides a material connection to actual environments, facilitating meaning transfer and consumer identity from actual to digital.

Authoritative Control of Signs

Language development and sharing begin informally. But cultures develop formal systems of dissemination that seem to restrict freedom in language use, breaking the dynamic of development. Formal systems establish authoritative sources as arbiters of language use proper to respective linguistic communities. Authoritative sources facilitate community growth through consistent application of rules that originally emerged informally. As the linguistic referees, authoritative sources specify the designations of the symbolic representations that constitute language. Because symbolic representations convey meaning within the community, authoritative sources control what community members can mean in the formal use of a language. Because language represents a system of concepts and interrelationships, authoritative control formally specifies the concepts that communities can recognize and formally relates those concepts.

In everyday use, language eludes authoritative control. Users tend to conform to prescribed patterns for various practical and psychological reasons. The linguistic community establishes minimal informal standards less rigorous than authoritative formal standards. Consequences of violating standards tend to isolate individuals from the community to some degree through differentiation and distinction. Such isolation can have positive or negative value for individual or community. Although the purpose of authoritative control is to direct everyday use, everyday use ratifies authoritative control. The common and the informal ultimately guide the authoritative and formal. Authoritative forms must serve community symbolic requirements if they are to be anything but arcane esoterica. Further, language is but one dimension of a community's symbolic representational systems. All designations that a community shares are system components. Language, however, tends to draw the greatest attempts at authoritarian control because by its nature it elicits a great amount of attention.

Consumer brands are another type of designation often fundamentally associated with authoritarian control. Brands tend to be a most public mode of communication. Whereas language most often occurs at the interpersonal level, brands are a fundamentally mediated form. Written language forms are based on the oral forms (Saussure, 1986). Brand forms fundamentally are written. Oral expression of brands is based on the written form. Because brands lack the basic interpersonal contextual cues to meaning, people can respond to brands however they please. They can attach to brands whatever meaning they want. When exposed to a meaningless sign, people will attach meaning arbitrarily and eventually develop agreement (Baudrillard, 1988). But brands have developed to achieve specific communication purposes that would fail if brand meaning were consigned to public whim. To achieve brand purpose, authoritarian control of meaning is imperative.

Meaning Transfer and Brand Significance

Brand identity, what a brand can mean, derives from the signifying context. For consumers, brands constitute a portion of their signifying contexts. Brand meaning transfers to consumers, creating consumer identities. The process can be conscious or unconscious, deliberate or haphazard. One some level, however, consumers construct identities by selecting culturally meaningful signs. Their emotional attachment to and involvement with signs and their combinations determines individual identity. Brand selection is critical to consumer culture because brand meaning defines identity through meaning transfer.

In advertising, brands signify the symbolic environment in which they occur. Brands acquire meaning from collocation with other components of the symbolic representational system that is culture. Products do not appear in advertising. Nor do consumers and their environments. Culturally recognized signs constitute advertising. The image or icon of a product is not the product itself (Mick, 1986) but rather a cultural convention for representation. An isolated representation communicates only the cultural recognition of the represented object or concept. Further cultural meaning depends on actual observation and interaction with the represented object. Advertising includes representations of seemingly ancillary objects and concepts to support product meaning. Ancillary representations are critical to the meaning of the focal representation. Supporting representations define and refine the cultural meaning of the focal representation. Surrounding representations are more than mere combinations. The composition of cultural representations evokes cultural meanings that transfer to the focal representation, which is the brand.

Context of occurrence defines meaning. Although a sign may occur in many contexts, the more common and consistent contexts determine dominant meaning. With brands, when the more common and consistent contexts are interactions with producers, sellers, marketers, or products, then consumers more strongly associate those interactions with brands. Examples of such brands abound. However, they tend to be brands with less exposure to consumers through advertising and other marketing communication. They are less likely to be the top-of-mind brands that constitute the everyday inventory of cultural signs available for identity construction. The brands available for identity construction in consumer culture commonly and consistently occur in the context of advertising that abstractly represents consumers' actual everyday contexts. Advertising asserts that specific brands belong in specific contexts. The context means the brand, and the brand means the context. Interaction with a product may be a context element, but with competing branded products, interaction results are identical. Therefore, brand meaning derives from other elements of context that represent consumers' social context. Within a cultural framework, abstract brand contexts closely resemble consumers' actual or anticipated contexts.

A brand is not a unique occurrence. It cannot indicate any specific consumer alone. As a sign, a brand signifies all possible occurrences of a context. Brands signify all possible occurrences of a value that cannot inhere in the brand and so must be external to the brand. When attached to an object, including a social object, brands signify value potentially applicable to other objects. Consumers define object values and the significance of brands and their physical platforms. Through brands, consumers define values of objects, including themselves and each other as social objects. Brands represent culturally valued qualities not unique to any individual consumer. No individual consumer may actually have the exact quality the brand exactly signifies because values are often ideals—attractive end states or goals that none may ever achieve. The significance of consumer brands, then, is an ideal consumer type rather than any specific consumer as token.

Branding Consumption

Consumption is communication that establishes a system of relationships through analogy. The utility of all cultural signs and of culture itself resides in the capacity to represent an abstract world that culture asserts is analogous to the actual world. In consumer culture, consumption continually establishes, renews, reiterates, revises, modifies, and reinforces relationships through symbolic analogy. Consumers embed meaning within the range of consumption acts and through those acts retrieve meaning for social and cultural application. Consumption acts occur in the actual world but constitute a discourse that constructs an independent world dependent on social agreement. Within the consumer world, the range of concepts and relationships is limited to the range of signs that constitute the world. However, because the number of distinct signs is unlimited, the number of possible concepts and relationships is unlimited.

Consumers identify with brands on a personal level because their presence in consumer culture depends upon brands. Consumer culture, as any culture, is a social creation. Being within any cultural environment—not just the sense of being but being itself—can only occur through the system of signs. When consumers think of themselves and of other consumers, they do not think of individuals external to and independent of the cultural system. Each consumer has a physical body that is external and independent. Physical appearance alone signifies in any culture but only in the context of other signs. The absence of signs signifies. Descartes may have convinced himself that his own thinking was sufficient evidence of his being. But his thinking was in terms of cultural signs that constituted his language; his thinking and his being were within culture. Within consumer culture, brands are far more than differentiating and distinguishing signs. Brands are who consumers are. To say, "I consume, therefore I am," may seem to be hilarious crass commercialism. However, to remove all of any consumer's brands, leaving nothing but unbranded products, would be to deprive that individual of personhood and being.

Self-Branding

What the market supplies is more than the means to sustain the material conditions of existence. The market supplies the means to exist within a culture. On some level, consumers fail to acknowledge the mediating role of material goods in generating their cultural environment. Those material goods as platforms for brands evoke cultural presence through vividness and interactivity in meaning. The vividness that brands create is the range of cultural concepts and the richness of cultural detail available to consumers for representation. The interactivity that brands permit is the ability to compose and modify meanings appropriate to any social context. For those who achieve cultural presence, consumers literally are the brands that they consume. They are not external to or independent of the brand symbolic system. Self-branding is a redundant term because without branding, one has no self within consumer culture. The market supplies individuals with their very being. Even to rebel against or to reject all brands as individual identifiers is a means of distinction through the brand signification system. One cannot be an anticonsumer without first accepting the concept of consumer (Gabriel & Lang, 2006).

Self-branding in digital environments makes sense because of meanings transferred from actual environments. Consumers can feel presence in any environment that provides vividness and interactivity. But it is only fantasy without *cultural* vividness and interactivity. Without recognizable and expected cultural signifying interaction, the digital environment is only a fantastic animation. Over time, users would ascribe qualities to the digital environment similar to those they ascribe to the actual environment, transferring digital signs into actual environments. But presence in either environment would not transfer to the other. As a major component of the actual-world sign system, branding allows consumers to enter digital environments with their culture intact, integrating the two environments as culturally identical. The digital and actual environments can appear culturally seamless when brands provide the vividness that makes consumers oblivious to technology. Consumers do not have to process new information to make sense of digital environments when familiar cultural elements constitute those environments. The known system facilitates consumers' entry into those environments.

Brand Linguistics

Recent research into consumers' use of brands validates prior linguistic research. Kervyn, Fiske, and Malone (2012) have found that consumer relationships with brands fit the warmth and competence of the Stereotype Content Model (SCM). The warmth concept is not temperature but the metaphor of a good feeling that an object or sign evokes. The competence concept is the sense of ability and capacity that an object or sign evokes. These two concepts are congruent with the factors of evaluation and potency that emerged from extensive cross-cultural studies Osgood, May, and Miron (1975) conducted 40 years ago. Those studies were the foundation for Semantic Space Theory (SST). Kervyn and colleagues (2012) also found support for an agency dimension that appears to be highly congruent with the activity dimension of SST. The later studies do not refer to SST, and the researchers do not indicate any awareness of SST or its possible contributions to brand research. Therefore, the congruence and validation are particularly noteworthy because the later studies implicitly show the linguistic quality of brands to locate concepts within semantic space. Esch and colleagues (2012), however, did specifically note results easily interpreted as the three dimensions of SST.

Fournier (1998) has found substantial similarities between consumer-brand relationships and social relationships. The findings are important because they support what we would expect based on discussions of advertising by Leymore (1975) and Williamson (1978). Fournier and Álvarez (2012) augment and reinforce that work by noting that brand relationships, like human relationships, require two parties. As one of those parties, the consumer assigns human-like qualities to brands in the process of meaning production. These findings reinforce assertions that consumers are active meaning producers (Cleveland, 1986; Fiske, 2010; Hirschman & Thompson, 1997). Fournier's contributions are invaluable in recognizing consumers' role in brand meaning creation. But those contributions are somewhat like Columbus discovering America: many had already arrived by different routes before Columbus, or Fournier, reached the same destination. Even so, their conclusions leave little room for doubt concerning earlier assertions, conjectures, or anecdotes.

Strategies

All cultures provide an inventory of identities defined by specific designating representations. All cultures are grammatical systems in the sense that identities interrelate to form a proper and legitimate structure. The system specifies who may or must carry a certain identity and rules for the proper acquisition and display of identifying signs. The system only occurs through actual practice. Some cultures are more dynamic than others in the flexibility of the representational system to develop through innovative designations. But even the extent of cultural extrapolation must not exceed the cultural ability to comprehend innovation within the fundamental paradigm. Any seemingly new identity is mostly, if not entirely, a composite or rearrangement of prior identities. Although any individual could establish a completely new and unique identity, that identity would be extracultural and, therefore, not an identity at all except as an outsider such as a foreigner or rebel.

Within consumer cultures, individuals have enormous flexibility for identity construction through gradations of quality signifiers. Brands are the ingredients in the cultural recipe for identity, especially in digital environments. Although current technology can convey signs quite accurately, the spatial range of inputs available for interaction is less than that of the actual environment. Consumers do not need the 11 billion bits per second (bps) of information that the actual environment presents to our senses. They only need the more salient of the 50 bits per second that we can process. Yet spatial and temporal placement contributes to comprehension. The 50 bps surround us in the actual world whereas the digital environment confines them to the location of video and audio displays. Those displays can be expansive but expensive in monetary costs and their own spatial requirements. Practical digital environments utilize very limited dimensions. For a sense of presence, the technology must draw attention to displays so that the physical limits become perceptually obscure. The 50 bps of processing must fall within the boundaries of digital displays.

As Plassmann, Ramsøy, and Milosavlljevic (2012) have noted, hearing or seeing one's own name tends to draw attention to a context of interrelated elements. As consumers utilize brands in identity construction, the display of an identity brand achieves an effect similar to perceiving one's name because the brand and the name serve the same function, which is to identify and distinguish. The availability of brands in digital environments draws attention to the environments, permitting not only a sense of being in the environment but of being the environment. Through brands, consumers convert themselves from analog to digital, integrating themselves with the environment.

Individual consumers are both compositors and components of digital environments. Their communication goals are to define their relationships with other compositor components. As in actual environments, individuals do not so much seek to understand the environment as to organize the environment according to what they already understand. The widespread availability of brand advertising in actual environments establishes a familiar and convenient means for organizing digital environments. Relationships that consumers project onto brands in actual environments transfer readily to digital environments. The challenge for consumers is to assemble brands into the syntagmatic chains (Leymore, 1975) that most effectively elicit the desired sense of relationship from other compositor components. Judgments concerning effectiveness take the form of signifying feedback, just as in actual environments. But in digital environments, the feedback takes the forms available within those environments. Brand signifiers are important elements of those forms.

Digital Brand Acquisition

The challenge for marketers in the digital environment is to satisfy consumers' self-branding wants and needs through convenience, appropriate cost, and effective communication. The astute reader will notice the parallel between this challenge and that of actual environments. We can expect this parallel because consumers bring their actual cultures to digital environments to integrate themselves and their environments. Brands must be available for personal attachment to consumers through various digital locations until consumers decide to suspend display. Then, brands must continue to be available for retrieval so consumers can resume display as they choose. The attachment, display, suspension, and resumption require that marketers serve consumers' identity needs. Mere brand display unattached to any consumer in a digital environment may suggest that a consumer belongs in that environment, but it does not contribute to consumer identity. Without unattached brand display, the digital environment may seem foreign because of widespread unattached display in actual environments. But even in actual environments, brands do not contribute to consumer identity until consumers acquire and attach them.

Consumer attachment is not just a preference, liking, or recommendation on a social networking site. Attachment is a consistent signifying brand display available for others to observe in the digital environment. It can take the form of an appearance on a personal page so that the brand is a decorative signifying element of digital home decor similar to actual home decor. In this way, the brand assumes the function of defining a consumer's personal digital space. The consumer expresses identity within personal boundaries that digital society recognizes. Attachment also means that the brand is a constituting element of the consumer in digital space and time. The brand is an integral component of the consumer avatar, a relatively fixed physical appearance in relation to surrounding digital signs. Through the fixed appearance, consumers make themselves known, establishing themselves as components of the digital environment. Through such insertion, given sufficient branding and interaction opportunities, consumers feel presence not merely as observers but also as participants.

As cultural participants, consumers are the ultimate arbiters of brand meaning. But to meet consumer needs, brands must be recognized and understood by surrounding social elements—that is, other consumers. Display in association with other cultural signs transfers meaning to brands. Consumers themselves are cultural signs. So consumers derive their identities from brands that derive their meanings from consumers. This might be a chicken-and-egg conundrum except for the role of marketers. The initial right of brand use belongs to the marketer, who controls the media and vehicles for brand distribution and who proposes an associated meaning through strategic communication. Once acquired, however, the brand belongs to the consumer (Schultz & Barnes, 1995), who relies on the marketer for consistent identity. Original brand loyalty is from brand to consumer. The brand that provides a consistent, valued identity component will find reciprocal consistent, patterned use in the consumer's behavior.

Imperative to digital strategy is that brands appear in the contexts that serve consumer wants and needs. Brand display as a consumer awareness or reminder device will generate poor attitude toward the brand, as results from Jeong, Bohil, and Biocca (2011) show. Consumers attribute human qualities to brands. The quality of calling attention to oneself just for awareness or reminder finds little value among consumers. People who exhibit that quality are at best childish and immature, at worst annoying and rude. Therefore, when Jeong and colleagues (2011) found lower attitude toward the brand from gratuitous display, they could have expected that finding because brand appearance was self-serving. Had they displayed an image of users' mothers instead of a brand, the result would likely have been a lower attitude toward the mother. In the same digital context, if the study had offered an acceptable brand as a user manifestation, the likelihood of improved brand attitude would have increased. Some marketers might not like to think of themselves as servants, but that is exactly what they are in both actual and digital environments. Serving consumer wants and needs is paramount.

In actual environments, brands are usually affixed to some vehicle, a product for interacting with the environment that yields tangible results. Yet that product and its interactive results also supply cultural identity and distinction. The brand affixed to the product supplies further identity and distinction among those who engage in similar tangible interaction with the environment. Ultimately, the brand is affixed to the consumer rather than the product. Digital environments may seem to differ because consumers do not need digital brand vehicles, which are digital products, for interacting with the digital environment, that yield digitally tangible results. But developing sophistication in creating such environments entails increasing the availability and even necessity of such products. This rapidly emerging congruence between actual and digital fosters greater presence in the environment itself. Utilizing brands as fixtures on digital products for transfer to consumers fosters digital cultural presence virtually identical to and indistinguishable from actual culture. Self-branding in the digital environment, then, is a necessary component of consumers' integrated communication system in market culture. The integrated market will supply the effective branding opportunities in both environments that will enable consumers to construct integrated identities.

CONCLUSION

Individuals find fulfillment through culture, but technology has broken the traditional boundaries. For millennia, people have superimposed culturally constituted worlds onto actual environments. Digitally generated virtual worlds add another layer of experience. Because digital environments are cultural products, they reflect the cultural habits, inclinations, inhibitions, and characteristics of those who construct them. Widespread migration to the digital frontier will submerge the habits of pioneers. The emerging cultures will greatly resemble the cultures that immigrants carry with them as they develop virtual communities.

As observed in actual worlds, culture is a representational system of signs. Because of their nature, digital environments are strictly symbolic constructions and therefore better suited for meeting strictly human needs. A fundamental human need is for identity with a group and within a group. Group identity is manifest in a shared symbolic system. Individual identity within a group is manifest in the unique combination of signs selected from the symbolic system. People can and do move between groups and systems. The systems, however, are often independent: group and individual identity in one system does not affect identity in another. System integration forges common identity.

But behavior effects in one system may not influence effects in another. The validity of any cultures depends upon its utility when superimposed onto actual environments. All cultures are virtual in that they consist of representations, of which accuracy is irrelevant. However, the capacity of digital virtual environments to influence effects in actual environments depends on the accuracy between digital and nondigital cultures. Behaviors constitute the fundamental meaning system of all cultures. Individuals cannot physically enter digital environments to behave just as they do in actual environments. But in actual environments, the individual self is culturally constructed from meaningful acts and other signs. Digital symbolic representations can mimic actual behaviors, which users accept as equivalent to actual behaviors when surrounded by other appropriate signs.

In contemporary consumer culture, brands are essential components in identity construction. Brands are nothing but signs with meanings acquired through association and collocation with other culturally meaningful signs. Consumers themselves are among those signs that give meaning to brands. Consumer products serve as vehicles for brand dissemination, but even products depend upon consumers as vehicles for dissemination. Marketers expose consumers to brands through advertising and other forms of marketing communication that utilize the cultural system of representations. But ultimately, consumer acceptance solidifies, ratifies, and reinforces brand meaning in identity construction.

Self-branding in actual environments entails product acquisition because products are the immediate brand vehicles. The ultimate vehicle is the tangible consumer who collocates with the tangible product to which the brand is affixed. Consumers thereby utilize the identity-constructing capacity of brands. The resulting market activity satisfies both consumers, who continuously construct identity, and marketers, who receive reimbursement for serving consumers and gain the means to construct their own identities.

The tangible and intangible, concrete and abstract, symbolic and substantial continually reinforce each other in material needs and cultural meaning.

Digital environments enable consumers to enter a world seemingly unencumbered by physical constraints. But that world is perceptible only through sight and hearing. Consumers may believe that taste, touch, and smell are available for perception in the digital world though they lack the sensory devices necessary to perceive them. Consumers' brains supply the missing senses based on similarity of context with the actual world. In the same way, consumers perceive social presence in digital worlds by supplying social components that would probably occur in similar actual-world contexts. Brands are important clues to the identities of social components because they establish relationships that parallel relationships in the actual world.

The challenge for marketers is to recognize consumers' digital identity needs and provide the necessary means for identity construction through self-branding. Marketers must include digital environments in their integrated communication plans. They must also recognize that consumers will use brands in their own integrated communication plans. The loyal brand will guarantee consumers the ability to maintain personal integrity by erasing social and cultural boundaries between actual and digital environments. Marketers can expect consumers to reciprocate by acquiring products in actual environments that are vehicles for the identifying brands that construct their actual and digital social environments.

REFERENCES

Baudrillard, J. (1988). *Selected writings*. (M. Poster, Trans.). Stanford, CA: Stanford University Press.

Bay, C. (1990). Taking the universality of human needs seriously. In J. Burton (Ed.), *Conflict: Human needs theory* (pp. 235–256). New York: St. Martin's Press.

Benedict, R. (1934). *Patterns of culture*. Boston: Houghton Mifflin Company.

Cleveland, C. E. (1986). Semiotics: Determining what the advertising message means to the audience. Vol. 3. In J. Olson & K. Sentis (Eds.), *Advertising and consumer psychology* (pp. 227–241). New York: Praeger Publishers.

Coyle, J. R., & Thorson, E. (2001). The effects of progressive levels of interactivity and vividness in web marketing sites. *Journal of Advertising, 30*(3), 65–77.

Douglas, M., & Isherwood, B. (1979). *The world of goods*. New York: Basic Books.

Esch, F., Möll, T., Schmitt, B., Elger, C. E., Neuhaus, C., & Weber, B. (2012). Brands on the brain: Do consumers use declarative information or experienced emotions to evaluate brands? *Journal of Consumer Psychology, 22*, 75–85.

Fiske, J. (2010). *Understanding popular culture*. 2nd ed. London: Routledge.

Fournier, S. (1998, March). Consumers and their brands: Developing relationship theory in consumer research. *Journal of Consumer Research, 24*, 343–373.

Fournier, S., & Álvarez, C. (2012). Brands as relationship partners: Warmth, competence and in-between. *Journal of Consumer Psychology, 22*, 177–185.

Gabriel, Y., & Lang, T. (2006). *The unmanageable consumer*. 2nd ed. London: Sage Publications.

Hall, E. T. (1973). *The silent language*. Garden City, NY: Anchor Press/Doubleday.

Hirschman, E. C., & Thompson, C. J. (1997). Why media matter: Toward a richer understanding of consumers' relationships with advertising and mass media. *Journal of Advertising, 26*(1), 43–60.

Jeong, E. J., Bohil, C. J., & Biocca, F. A. (2011). Brand logo placements in violent games: Effects of violence cues on memory and attitude through arousal and presence. *Journal of Advertising, 40*(3), 59–72.

Kervyn, N., Fiske, S. T., & Malone, C. (2012). Brands as intentional agents framework: How perceived intentions and ability can map brand perception. *Journal of Consumer Psychology, 22*, 166–176.

Klein, L. R. (2003). Creating virtual product experiences: The role of telepresence. *Journal of Interactive Marketing, 17*(1), 41–55.

Leymore, V. (1975). *Hidden myth: Structure and symbolism in advertising*. London: Heinemann.

Li, H., Daugherty, T., & Biocca, F. (2002). Impact of 3-D advertising on product knowledge, brand attitude, and purchase intention: The mediating role of presence. *Journal of Advertising, 31*(3), 43–57.

Lombard, M., & Ditton, T. (1997). At the heart of it all: The concept of presence. *Journal of Computer-Mediated Communication, 3*(2). Retrieved from www.ascusc.org/jcmc/vol3/issue2/lombard.html

Lombard, M., & Snyder-Duch, J. (2001). Interactive advertising and presence: A framework. *Journal of Interactive Advertising, 1*(2). Retrieved from http://jiad.org/vol1/no2/lombard

Maslow, A. H. (1943). A theory of human motivation. *Psychological Review, 50*, 370–396.

McWilliam, G. (2000). Building strong brands through online communities. *Sloan Management Review, 41*(3), 43–54.

Mick, D. G. (1986, September). Consumer research and semiotics: Exploring the morphology of signs, symbols and significance. *Journal of Consumer Research, 13*, 196–213.

Nudler, O. (1990). On conflict and metaphors: Toward an extended rationality. In J. Burton (Ed.), *Conflict: Human needs theory* (pp. 177–201). New York: St. Martin's Press.

Osgood, C. E., May, W. H., & Miron, M. S. (1975) *Cross-cultural universals of affective meaning*. Urbana: University of Illinois Press.

Plassmann, H., Ramsøy, T. Z., & Milosavlljevic, M. (2012). Branding the brain: A critical review and outlook. *Journal of Consumer Psychology, 22*, 18–36.

Rubenstein, R. E. (1990). Basic human needs theory: Beyond natural law. In J. Burton (Ed.), *Conflict: Human needs theory* (pp. 336–355). New York: St. Martin's Press.

Saussure, F. (1986). *Course in general linguistics*. Peru, IL: Open Court Publishing.

Schultz, D. E., & Barnes, B. E. (1995). *Strategic advertising campaigns*. 4th ed. Lincolnwood, IL: NTC Business Books.

Steuer, J. (1992). Defining virtual reality: Dimensions determining telepresence. *Journal of Communication, 42*(4), 73–93.

Williamson, J. (1978). *Decoding advertisements: Ideology and meaning in advertising*. London: Marion Boyars.

Part IV
Marketing Strategies
Country Case Studies

17 Technology and Competition in U.S. Television
Online versus Offline

Ryland Sherman and
David Waterman

Over the past decade, as both broadband adoption by consumers and Internet bandwidth capacity have rapidly grown, the online distribution of television and other video programming has emerged as a viable industry. As one sign of its importance, Netflix alone accounted for over a quarter of total peak North American fixed Internet traffic in the second half of 2012 (Sandvine Intelligent Broadband Networks, 2012, p. 7). In other terms, though, the floodgates are yet to open. By various estimates we report, online distribution probably accounted for less than 5% of total television industry revenues in 2012. And in contrast to most other U.S. media, the standard television industry has been remarkably resilient, in terms of both viewing and revenues, as broadband technology has developed and diffused.

It is evident, however, that online video distribution has the potential to be very disruptive to the established offline television industry. In this chapter, we explore, from an economic perspective, the development of the online television industry, its threats to standard television, and its future. Our main focus is on professionally produced television programming that is also exhibited on standard TV by U.S. broadcast or cable networks. Most of the firms involved in online and offline television distribution are thus the same or have direct ownership ties. Many of them also supply theatrical movies and other types of video programming; thus our analysis often overlaps with that of the broader online video industry. Among the central questions we address: What explains the persistence of offline television in the broadband era? How have business models and competition in the online television industry developed? What are the economic advantages and disadvantages of online compared to standard delivery of television programming, and what factors will determine the future of online TV? As we will see, digital technology has played a key role in the recent development of the offline as well as the online TV industry.

There has been understandably little economic research in such a new industry, but a number of scholarly works on the economics of online media provide a foundation for this chapter. Among earlier works, Owen (2000) addressed the potential of the Internet for television delivery, and Shapiro and Varian (1999) and Eisenmann and Brown (2000) explored ways that online content providers could use the Internet for competitive advantage and create value for consumers. Several authors in Kahin and Varian (2000) discussed economic and legal aspects of Internet media delivery. Among more recent works, several edited books, notably Noam, Groebel, and Gerbarg (2004), Gerbarg (2008), and Noam (2008), have addressed the emerging technology, economics, and content of Internet television and video. A series of Federal Communications Commission reports (1994–2012) on the television and video industries have provided valuable data and insights. Fontaine, Le Borgne-Bachschmidt, and Leiba (2010) provide another European perspective on television's transition. Simon and Bogdanowicz (2012) report on a series of European Commission studies about the digital transition of media industries in European Union member countries. We cite other works as we proceed. (See also Waterman, Sherman, and Ji (2013) for further literature on this topic.)

We begin in the next section with the standard TV industry and its persistence. In the following section, we turn to online TV: its historical timeline, its main revenues models and programming, and the phenomenon of content aggregation. We then discuss the competitive advantages of utilizing the Internet for video distribution, and conclude in the final section with a discussion of economic factors that will affect the future of online television.

Television in Historical Context

The economic performance of the television industries is illustrated in Figure 17.1 for the period from 1980–2010 as a percentage of all economic activity, as measured by GDP. The "Internet" category includes national TV distribution, such as via Hulu.com and CBS Interactive, and local TV station websites.

Television grew steadily as a proportion of GDP over this period—including a relative increase of about 20% from 1999–2010 (0.93% of GDP to 1.12%), even as U.S. household broadband adoption grew from less than 3% to 67% (Pew Research Center, 2011). During the 1999–2010 time frame, in fact, the media industries as a whole, led by newspapers, music, and radio, declined by about 20% as a fraction of GDP (Waterman & Ji, 2012).

Extraordinary technological change—especially digital conversion—has combined with an expanding appetite for TV viewing to fuel this economic growth.

One aspect of TV's economic growth has been a massive conversion from "free" (ad supported) to "pay" TV (i.e., multichannel subscriptions). When television began in the 1940s, direct payment was awkward and inefficient, but by the 1970s, direct payment systems—first terrestrial cable, then digital broadcast satellite (DBS), and most recently, the telecommunications companies—have excavated a consumer willingness to pay for TV that in the aggregate has now exceeded advertiser revenues. In 1980, less than 1

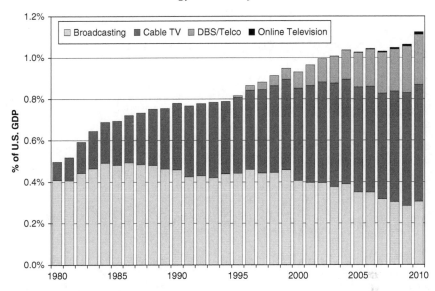

Figure 17.1 Television industry revenue by category, as % GDP, 1980–2010.
Sources: U.S. Bureau of the Census, trade associations, industry analysts, 10-K reports, author estimates. Adapted from Waterman & Ji, 2012.

in 5 TV households subscribed to services of these and other multichannel video programming distributors (MVPDs); by 2010, 86% subscribed. Partly reflecting the secular decline of broadcast television, direct payments as a percent of total television industry revenue increased from about 15% to 56% over this same period (Waterman & Ji, 2012).

Another aspect to television's growth is its increasing value to consumers due to dramatic expansions in channel capacity, accompanied by much higher financial investments in television programming and, especially since the mid-1990s, the advent of HDTV (high-definition TV). Partly responsible were the launch of geostationary satellites for commercial television beginning in the mid-1970s and steady increases in cable system transmission capacity via fiber optics. The dominating cause, however, was conversion from analog to digital distribution technologies. In early years, analog was cheaper and more efficient than digital. Over time, though, the balance shifted dramatically in favor of digital, which allows for higher quality and quantities of TV at lower cost. Modern DBS, launched in 1994, was entirely digital from the beginning. At about the same time, cable systems began converting to digital tiers, which dramatically expanded their channel capacity, in turn stimulating entry by hundreds of new television networks, especially those catering to niche audiences as MVPD viewers migrated away from broadcast channels. A larger and higher quality set of programming options has probably also contributed to a one-third increase in TV usage from about 43 hours per week per TV household in the early 1970s to nearly 58 hours in the early 2010s (TV Dimensions, 2012, p. 76).

These developments have continued to drive increasing revenues of standard television into the Internet broadband era. From 2000 to 2011, the number of channels available to the average U.S. TV household was reported to rise by over 60%, from 72 to 137 (TV Dimensions, 2012, p. 26), and the number of networks transmitting in HD increased from a handful to hundreds. Consistent with these trends, basic cable network programming investments reportedly rose by 334% just over the 2000–2011 period (SNL Kagan Research, 2012a). TV viewers have continued to come along for the ride, displaying the formidable competitive advantages of standard TV that online confronts. According to Nielsen, average U.S. individual TV viewing rose from 29 to 34 hours per week from 2000 to 2012 (Nielsen, 2011a, p. 16; Nielsen, 2013, p. 9).

Online Commercial Television

Industry Development

Although the online video industry dates to the mid-1990s, few of its pioneers survived the "dot-com" bust of 2000–2001. By the mid-2000s, however, broadband household adoption and speeds had become sufficient to usher in a period of vibrant entry and competition that has formed today's online television industry.

In 2005, iTunes began offering some recent TV series episodes for direct payment. Also in that year, YouTube was created to enable Internet users to upload and distribute videos from their digital video recorders. Full episodes of major network series programs, however, were soon being illegally posted by YouTube users. After an initial period of tolerance, the networks and program suppliers issued "takedown" orders under the Digital Millennium Copyright Act, and lawsuits followed. It was not until 2008 and 2009 that NBC and Fox (later joined by ABC) launched Hulu and CBS started tv.com (later CBS Interactive),[1] primarily as online outlets for some of their regular series programming. Since 2010, several others have entered the online television market, notably the launch by MVPDs of "TV Everywhere" services (an umbrella term for the online programming services of a number of cable, DBS, and telecommunications providers).

As Figure 17.1 illustrates, the online component of the television industries remains small, accounting for under 2% of revenue from all sources in 2010, although both online advertising and direct payments have clearly grown much faster than have those of standard television since 2010.[2] These financial contrasts are generally reflected in viewing estimates. Nielsen reported that the average individual watched 34 hours of television per week in the fourth quarter of 2011 compared to 68 minutes of Internet video, about a 30 to 1 ratio (Nielsen, 2013, p. 9). Available viewing information shows less extreme contrasts for the more narrowly defined category of broadcast and cable network programming. One analyst estimated that about 5% of all prime-time broadcast network program viewing in 2010 was online (Convergence Consulting Group, 2012), and another that 8% of all U.S. TV viewing was online in that year (Screen Digest, 2011a, p. 210). These ratios are surely rising as well, but the orders of magnitude continue to reflect the economic dominance of offline television as of this writing.

Revenue Models and Programming

Table 17.1 summarizes characteristics of several significant providers of online commercial television programming as of Spring 2013. While some providers, including Amazon and Hulu, have adopted more than one revenue model, five main business models that define principal economic

Table 17.1 Some major online commercial television suppliers

Service	Primary Content	Primary Business Model(s)
iTunes	Broadcast and cable programs; movies	Pay to download/rent
Amazon	Broadcast and cable programs; movies	Subscription; pay to download/rent
Netflix	Broadcast and cable programs; movies	Subscriptions
Hulu	NBC, ABC, and Fox TV series; some cable network content/ web-only video	Advertising and subscriptions
CBS Interactive	CBS broadcast programs	Advertising
Viacom Digital	Viacom cable networks (MTV, Comedy Central, BET, Nickelodeon, etc.)	Advertising
Crackle	Sony-owned movie and TV content	Advertising
YouTube	User-generated content; funded professionally created 'channels', other professional content	Advertising; subscription
Comcast Xfinity	Broadcast and cable programs; movies; Netflix-like 'Streampix' premium content service offered beyond MVPD geographic areas	Free to offline cable subscribers by package level; Subscription (Streampix)
Verizon FiOS	Broadcast and cable programs; movies	Free to offline cable subscribers by package level
HBO-Go	HBO exclusive series and licensed movies	Free to offline subscribers
TBS	TBS television programs	Free to offline subscribers, with advertising

segments of the online TV industry have emerged: a la carte rentals and purchases, subscriptions, ad-supported professional content, ad-supported user-generated content, and verification-dependent content bundled by MVPDs (TV Everywhere).

In all but the latter category, a leading firm has emerged, but programming content, levels of content aggregation, and support of media player devices vary widely within the online industry.

With 63% of the total online movie and TV downloads in the first half of 2011 (Screen Digest, 2011b, p. 294), iTunes is the evident leader in the a la carte rentals (via streaming) and purchases (via download) category. Building on its successful digital music sales market, Apple's popular line of media devices provide seamless interchange among their devices and their own online video and music markets. Other online rental/purchases firms, such as Amazon, generally lack Apple's competitive advantage of design integration into an entire hardware product line, as well as widespread device adoption. Amazon's line of Kindle tablets and Microsoft's recent product developments (such as Windows 8, iPad-like tablet options, and Xbox Live), have sought to capture some of the convenience premium that has helped iTunes to be so successful in both music and video.

In the subscription category, Netflix dominates with its mix of mostly TV programs and movies. The bandwidth demands of its 25 million subscribers as of July of 2012 were 18 times greater than those of Amazon, it main direct competitor, which reportedly had about 10 million subscribers (Sandvine Intelligent Broadband Networks, 2012, pp. 20–21; Sharma & Bensinger, 2013). Netflix' streaming service is available on computer web browsers, the major three video game consoles, and a long list of other devices. As of 2011, Nielsen found that roughly 50% of users watched Netflix through their game consoles (Nielsen, 2011b). Although much of their programming is similar, both Netflix and Amazon have recently announced exclusive programming deals in a heated battle to differentiate themselves for competitive advantage, including some relatively expensive original programming, such as Netflix' $100 million investment in the *House of Cards* series.

In the ad-supported professional content category, Hulu.com is currently the leading firm, earning the fourth-highest comScore ranking for "total ad minutes viewed" and the highest number of average ad minutes per viewer at the end of 2012 (comScore, 2013). Since its origins as a joint venture between owners of three of the four major broadcast networks, Hulu has steadily added more content partners, including the CW Network, AMC Network, Viacom's cable channels, BBC America, Univision, and Sony's Crackle. Several of these groups, including Viacom channels and Crackle, also distribute their content through their own ad-supported portals. Comedy Central's *The Daily Show* is an example of an individual program that is distributed through its network's own portal as well as Hulu.

While competing online VOD suppliers, such as iTunes and Amazon, sell roughly the same menus of more popular TV series and movies (analogous to the offline sale of DVDs in multiple big-box stores), the distribution of the same content through competing online ad-based portals does not seem to have a significant offline counterpart. Different ad-supported providers also support different consumer devices. Comedy Central programming, for example, is not directly distributed through any smartphone, tablet, game console, or set-top box systems, while Hulu Plus, that firm's premium subscription service, supports all these devices, enabling *The Daily Show*, for example, to be distributed to a larger total viewer base.

YouTube remains the dominant ad-based amateur content distributor, and in terms of unique viewers, the number of videos displayed, and minutes per viewer is the top online video content distributor overall by a large margin. As of the end of 2011, its global share of number of videos watched was 43.8%, 20 times greater than its next biggest competitor, China's Youku, with 2.3% (comScore, 2013). To continue expanding, YouTube has shifted toward offering professional content, financing 100 "channels" of niche programming in late 2011 (Bond & Szalai, 2011). YouTube's limited foray into professionally produced content is an apparent milestone in top-down creation of "long-tail" (Anderson, 2006) programs that are ostensibly narrow in appeal (e.g., professional skateboarder channels, *Vice* and *InStyle* magazines)—and also very inexpensively produced. YouTube's total stated budget for the 100 channels was $100–150 million, and YouTube recently announced that it would invest another $200 million while adding 60 more channels (Efrati, 2012).

Finally, in the still-nascent authentication-dependent TV Everywhere (TVE) segment, competition is at the local geographic market level, so the mix of MVPD competitors (except for DBS-based services) varies market by market. So far, TVE services are available for free, but only with "authentication" that the user is a paid monthly subscriber of an MVPD's offline services. TVE is thus always bundled with offline MVPD services, obfuscating its contribution to the revenues of their parent companies. Generally these portals provide online access to a portion of the content that subscribers already have access to with their MVPD subscription. For example, Comcast's TVE service, Xfinity, offers programming from TNT and other Turner Broadcasting System ad-supported channels to all Comcast subscribers whose subscriptions include those channels. In some cases, users access TVE programming through the specific channels' web pages. For example, HBO-Go.com, a website that offers the same movies and TV programming that the familiar HBO monthly subscription channel provides, is available only to users who also subscribe to HBO via participating offline MVPD services.

Most of the larger MVPDs offer TVE services. Availability becomes less likely among relatively small MVPDs. New intermediaries like Synacor, however, have appeared to provide business-to-business services assisting smaller MVPDs to manage TVE portals. In terms of content diversity, TVE systems of larger MVPDs tend to offer the most programming. So far, however, even the largest MVPDs offer only a small subset of the programming available with the subscribers' MVPD packages. A likely reason for these contrasts is that MVPDs have reportedly encountered a snare of contracting problems that limit online program distribution rights.

Of course, the providers in all five of these industry segments compete with each other, but they have some other differentiating features in terms of programming content, including a growing number of Internet-original programs. The great majority of these original programs, along with obscure foreign movies and TV shows, are surely part of the long tail of programs too narrow in appeal or too low in quality to be profitably supported offline. Apart from several relatively expensive original programs (e.g., *House of Cards*), however, economically viable television content offered by online video services is overwhelmingly "windowed" programs that have already appeared, or that appear at about the same time, on offline media (Owen & Wildman, 1992; Wildman, 2008).

In the TV program case, the windowing model is in flux, but most programs on ad-supported Internet services such as Hulu, CBS, and Viacom Digital generally appear with a delay of one day to a few weeks, with more complex windowing strategies occasionally used. For online VOD (and the advertiser- and subscription-supported Hulu Plus), delays are often shorter, and live streaming of major network programming to mobile devices (though with a different set of commercials) is now emerging. For most subscription services such as Netflix and Amazon, however, windows are generally several months later for both TV programs and movies, comparable to the movie release windows of monthly subscription cable networks like HBO and Showtime.[3]

Content Aggregation and Disaggregation

At least for the leading online providers, aggregation of commercial television and other programming from multiple creators or copyright owners appears to be a dominant business model. As noted earlier, Hulu aggregates mainly programs from the three major broadcast networks that co-own the site, but also from many other "content partners." Netflix's subscription service offers a large menu of TV programs and movies that come from many different owners. iTunes offers a menu of TV programs from numerous broadcast and cable networks as well as distributors of theatrical movies. At the other end of the spectrum, a number of online video businesses are essentially stand-alone networks, such as HBO-Go, ESPN3, and several individual basic cable TV networks. Viacom Digital, CBS, and Disney are intermediate cases in that they offer numerous broadcast or cable programs, although mainly those produced or distributed by the website's corporate owner.

The efficiencies of online content or product aggregation have been studied by several authors, notably Bakos and Brynjolfsson (1999, 2000). They showed that the extremely low marginal carriage or capacity costs of Internet distribution allow content aggregators to average consumers' demands over a great many different products at once, enabling more accurate pricing to extract consumer surplus.[4] Bakos and Brynjolfsson's model, however, appears to presume a collection of products sold at one price, such as AOL and other Internet service providers (ISPs) offered in early days of the Internet. While that model potentially applies to modern subscription services such Netflix and Hulu Plus, a more apparent source of economic efficiencies of online aggregation is analogous to well-established reasons that brick-and-mortar department stores exist. Consumers have a one-stop shop and can compare prices of many different brands directly.

A number of other authors, notably Shapiro and Varian (1999) and Eisenmann and Brown (2000), have also recognized that Internet architecture offers unusual efficiencies of aggregation; links to a virtually unlimited amount of programming content can be offered by a single seller at extremely low marginal costs. On the other hand, the Internet also makes *disaggregation* of content more efficient. Cable television and other MVPDs evidently realize strong economies of scale with respect to the amount of programming they deliver and the number of subscribers they serve due to high infrastructure costs. Individual networks, however, can potentially bypass—and thus potentially "unbundle"—MVPDs simply by making themselves available online as stand-alone services. The Internet infrastructure also has large fixed costs, of course, but like a national postal service, those costs are shared among great numbers of content providers and other businesses. Thus, the Internet makes both aggregation and disaggregation of programming content more efficient.

Whether content aggregation or disaggregation by online video providers eventually dominates is simply an empirical question. An evident advantage of online aggregators is a strong brand identity among a vast number of competing websites, clearly one objective of aggregators such as iTunes and Hulu (Yao, Queiro, & Rozovsky, 2008). A look at online video suppliers at the other end of the range, such as HBO-Go and ESPN3, suggests that suppliers that already have well-established names are prominent among successful content disaggregators.

On balance, online content aggregation appears to be a compelling model. Other Internet developments also seem to display its economic advantages in the television case. Google TV, for example, partially serves as an aggregator of program suppliers who are willing to be sold as part of an online package that can be watched on a TV set. The Microsoft Xbox 360, Sony PlayStation 3, a variety of set-top boxes, tablets, and similar hardware devices essentially function as content aggregators as well.

This leads us to the role that TV Everywhere, at least potentially, may play in the aggregation of online video content. As we noted earlier, TVE systems currently accomplish only limited levels of aggregation, but they can be viewed as nascent attempts to achieve large-scale, MVPD-like levels of online content aggregation. MVPDs are aggregators not only of a great variety of programming but also of business models, including adver-tiser and fee support, monthly subscription, and VOD. In that respect, TVE can be seen as a potentially comparable large-scale aggregation of the still-developing online TV components of subscription (e.g., Netflix), advertiser-support (e.g., Hulu), and VOD (e.g., iTunes) services.

Whether MVPD-level aggregation will prove in the long-term to be a suf-ficiently differentiated or valuable option for consumers is uncertain, but the history of the television industry indicates that to be a plausible outcome. Waterman, Sherman, and Ji (2013) develop economic models that interpret MVPD bundling of offline and TVE services as a price discrimination device by which "low value" consumers are offered online video for free in order to decrease the likelihood of that they will "cut the cord." It is likely that TVE has other strategic advantages to MVPDs in their attempts to enter the online video market.

Comparative Efficiencies of Online Television

The massively parallel nature of the Internet is potentially a great boon to both consumers and distributors of television and other video program-ming. "Appointment television" contrasts fundamentally with the asyn-chronous on-demand Internet architecture that enables consumers to watch the programming whenever they please. The volume of programming that can be profitably offered is greatly expanded by the long tail made possi-ble by the Internet's extremely low capacity costs. The small but increasing quantities of original programming offered by Hulu, Netflix, YouTube, and other online suppliers parallels the early development of cable television in the late 1970s and early 1980s. Online video's potential is greater, however, as foreshadowed by the range of niche-appeal channels created by YouTube and other suppliers. The recent proliferation of tablets and other portable media players is increasingly fulfilling the "anywhere" as well as the "any-time" promise of online video distribution.

Internet technology offers theoretical improvements in both advertis-ing and direct-payment business models. On the advertising side, online video portals incentivize the tracking of individuals' consumption patterns in order to target advertisements to individuals directly.[5] Many portals, such as Hulu, allow consumers to choose between different ads and often allow feedback about whether ads were relevant or satisfying. The data collected can be used to analyze individuals' overall consumption patterns, and sophisticated suggestion engines can lower consumers' search costs by linking them more directly to products they are likely to view or buy. Online direct-payment systems can also be more efficient, such as by use of micro-payments and mobile phone applications and by facilitating price discrimi-nation with dynamic pricing and instantaneous price changes.

Enabling all of these advantages of online television is the remarkably efficient two-way interactivity made possible by personal computers and their communications. Without easy search for content within and among online video websites, neither the vast aggregations nor the disaggregations of online programming would be possible in practice. Similarly for the efficient direct pricing and management of online VOD. Targeted advertising and suggestion engines also depend on interactivity and improved interface options.

Of course, MVPDs have themselves advanced well beyond the rigorous model of appointment television with their own end-user computers in the form of set-top boxes and the DVR. "Pay-per-view" systems that relied upon staggered start times of the same popular movie on several dedicated channels have been replaced by VOD systems having hundreds or thousands of different movies or TV programs. The versatility and efficiency of computer communication within the open architecture of the Internet, however, is more advanced and shows greater promise.

CONCLUSION: THE FUTURE OF ONLINE TELEVISION

The technological marvels and vibrant entry into online television may seem in sharp contrast to the reality of its small audiences and revenues and the economic persistence of standard television.

One possible explanation for these contrasts is that at this moment, offline MVPD television is simply more convenient and familiar to the great majority of households. It offers a large selection of content with relatively low search costs, with on-screen program information grouped by familiar channels on a single device specifically designed to be plugged into any TV or home entertainment system. In contrast, online video often requires additional devices to be displayed on a home entertainment system, like a Roku or a game console. Most people have not adopted these devices, and many adopters may be unwilling to switch between different programs across different devices on any regular basis. For most people, changing the cable channel is simply easier than switching from Hulu through a game console to an iTunes library on a personal computer. The very range of different online services available on different devices can lead to a confusing and time-consuming search process that may discourage all but the most price sensitive or tech savvy from regular use.

As the speed and quality of online video transmission continues to rise, as broadband diffusion grows, as more efficient and portable media players continue to proliferate, and as the interaction between consumers and video content providers becomes more seamless, the economic viability of the online video entertainment industry seems bound to improve. Perhaps TV Everywhere packages, the online content bundle most similar to offline MVPD video services, will also become unbundled as MVPDs seek to regain a portion of users who will have cancelled their services in favor of online video.

Foreshadowing changes to come are rapid shifts in online video use among a small but growing base. Nielsen reported that the amount of time the average person spends per week watching all online videos nearly doubled between the fourth quarters of 2011 and 2012 (from 38 to 68 minutes per person; see Nielsen, 2013, p. 9). The most intensive online video user group in the later Nielsen study, 18- to 24-year-olds, watched 129 minutes of Internet video on average. Perhaps most telling, Nielsen decided in 2013 to include "Zero-TV" households into its samples (Nielsen, 2013, p. 4). Comprised of roughly 2 million U.S. homes in 2007, this traditional TV–avoiding group had grown to 5 million households by the start of 2013 (p. 5).[6]

It would be a mistake, however, to view the transition of television purely in terms of any presumed rate of viewer migration from offline to online. Even as technological constraints of online video fall away, and as inevitable demographic shifts occur, the online video entertainment industry faces significant uncertainties and constraints in the reasonably near future. We conclude with mention of four of these.

First, the economic future of online video depends critically on the development of successful online business models, notably advertising, to support greater program quality and variety, especially Internet-original content. To the advantage of television content suppliers, the within-program video ad model transfers directly to online. However, although cost-per-thousand (CPM) advertising rates for Hulu are reportedly comparable to or above those of prime-time broadcast TV, the number of commercials sold is much lower, resulting in relatively low advertising income per program online. Convergence Consulting Group (2012) estimated that compared to the earlier-cited viewing proportion of about 5% in 2010, the broadcast networks earned only 2.7% of their advertising revenues from online exhibition. The viability of video advertising is apparently increasing, but the rate of improvement will have an important effect given the 44% of total television industry revenues coming from advertising in 2010.

A second uncertainty is comparative technological improvements in competing offline media. Cable TV technology in particular is a very efficient means for simultaneous downstream delivery as well as pricing of television services to consumers. Though improving rapidly, the Internet is less well designed for simultaneous real-time delivery of television programming such as sports. The usability of MVPDs' VOD systems, as well as their recent innovations in targeted advertising, are also variables.

A third issue is how video delivery costs, content provider prices, and ISP pricing structures will evolve as consumer bandwidth demands for online video continue to grow. We noted at the outset that online video already is a major part of broadband traffic. As online video demand increases, will ISPs be able to scale up their infrastructure accordingly? For example, more widespread adoption by ISPs of bandwidth usage–sensitive pricing could result in heavy video entertainment users paying effectively higher prices per movie or TV program, reducing demand for online video.

Finally, a major economic constraint on the online television industry could be limits on the availability of programming from content providers. We also noted that the online exhibitions of most windowed television programs are at this writing usually delayed, at least slightly, from their offline television exhibition. Although windows are still settling, these delays presumably reflect lower returns per viewer from online exhibition. Undoubtedly, these delays have slowed television audience migration to online at least to some extent. How soon, and whether, television premieres will be simultaneous with, or perhaps before, offline exhibition, could be a crucial factor in viewer migration and economic growth of online television.

ACKNOWLEDGEMENTS

Some of the material in this paper was presented by David Waterman at the Digital Media and New Media Platforms: Policy and Marketing Strategies conference, National Chengchi University, Taipei, Taiwan, March 29, 2012. We are grateful to Yu-li Liu, Robert Picard, and other attendees at that conference for their contributions. We are also grateful to audiences at the 40th Annual TPRC Conference on Communication, Information and Internet Policy in Arlington Virginia, September 21–23, 2012, and at the Dynamics of the Media and Content Industries conference, sponsored by the European Commission (IPTS), October 25–26, 2012. An anonymous reviewer of this chapter provided valuable comments. All shortcomings remain our responsibility. Some sections of this chapter draw upon Waterman, Sherman, and Ji (2013).

NOTES

1. CBS Interactive is the umbrella company for CBS.com, which distributes long-form TV programming, and tv.com, which now distributes short-form content.
2. eMarketer (2012) reported a growth in the ratio of all online video advertising to total offline TV and online video advertising from 2.35% in 2010 to 4.3% in 2012. SNL Kagan Research (2012b) reported 59% growth in total TV industry revenues from online consumer direct payments (subscription plus video-on-demand, or VOD, revenues) of $1.8 billion to $3.1 billion between 2010 and 2011.
3. Netflix and Amazon have recently accelerated the acquisition of exclusive rights to a few major films and TV programs that have substantially shorter windows.
4. Conceptually, their model is similar to the empirically based explanations by Crawford and Cullen (2007) and Crawford and Yurukoglu (2012) for why cable TV systems bundle programming into various packages for different prices.
5. In addition to earlier works already cited, Evans (2009) and Anderson (2012) offer surveys of a growing economic literature on Internet advertising.
6. While three-fourths of "Zero-TV" households own televisions, two-thirds view their content on other devices, and roughly half subscribe to an online video service (p. 5–6). They tend to be younger, with fewer children, and are more likely to live alone (p. 7). A third of them identify cost as the reason they do without MVPD video services, and only 18% of them consider subscribing (p. 8).

REFERENCES

Anderson, C. (2006). *The long tail: Why the future of business is selling less of more.* New York: Hyperion.

Anderson, S. (2012.) Advertising on the Internet. In M. Peitz & J. Waldfoge (Eds.), *The Oxford handbook of the digital economy. Vol. 1* (pp. 355–396). New York: Oxford University Press.

Bakos, Y., & Brynjolfsson, E. (1999). Bundling information goods: Pricing, profits and efficiency. *Management Science, 45*(12), 1613–1630.

Bakos, Y., & Brynjolfsson, E. (2000). Bundling and competition on the Internet. *Marketing Science, 19*(1), 63–82.

Bond, P., & Szalai, G. (2011, October 28). YouTube announces TV initiative with 100 niche channels. *Hollywood Reporter.* Retrieved from www.hollywoodreporter.com/news/youtube-tv-channels-kutcher-poehler-254370

comScore. (2013, January 14). *comScore releases December 2012 U.S. online video rankings.* comScore Press Release.

Convergence Consulting Group. (2012). *The battle for the American couch potato: Online & traditional TV and movie distribution.* Company White Paper.

Crawford, G. S., & Cullen, J. (2007). Bundling product choice, and efficiency: Should cable television networks be offered a la carte? *Information Economics and Policy, 19*(3–4): 379–404.

Crawford, G. S., & Yurukoglu, A. (2012). The welfare effects of bundling in multichannel television markets. *American Economic Review, 102*(2), 423–438.

Efrati, A. (2012, July 30). YouTube to double down on its "channel" experiment. *Wall Street Journal.* Retrieved from http://online.wsj.com/article/SB1000087239 6390444840104577549632241258356.html,

Eisenmann, T. R., & Brown, A. (2000). *Online content providers.* Harvard Business School. Background Note. No. 9–801–261. Boston, MA: Harvard Business School Publishing.

eMarketer. (2012). *A sample of eMarketer's topic coverage.* Retrieved from www. emarketer.com/Coverage/Video.aspx

Evans, D. S. (2009). The online advertising industry: Economics, evolution, and privacy. *Journal of Economic Perspectives, 23*(3), 37–60.

Federal Communications Commission. (1994–2012). *Annual assessment of the status of competition in the market for the delivery of video programming.* Various annual reports, including the 2012 (ed.), released July 2012, FCC 12–81, MB Docket No. 07–269.

Fontaine, G., Le Borgne-Bachschmidt, F., & Leiba, M. (2010). Scenarios for the Internet migration of the television industry. *Communications & Strategies, 77,* 1–14.

Gerbarg, D. (Ed.). (2008). *Television goes digital.* New York: Springer-Verlag.

Kahin, B., & Varian, H. R. (Eds.). (2000). *Internet publishing and beyond: The economics of digital information and intellectual property.* Cambridge, MA: MIT Press.

Nielsen. (2013). *The cross-platform report.* Retrieved from www.nielsen.com/us/en/insights/reports-downloads/2012/the-cross-platform-report-q4-2012.html

Nielsen. (2011a). *The cross-platform report.* Retrieved from www.nielsen.com/us/en/insights/reports-downloads/2012/the-cross-platform-report-q4-2011.html

Nielsen. (2011b). What Netflix and Hulu users are watching ... and how. *Nielsen Newswire.* Retrieved from www.nielsen.com/us/en/newswire/2011/what-netflix-and-hulu-users-are-watching-and-how.html

Noam, E. M., Groebel, J., & Gerbarg, D. (Eds.). (2004). *Internet television.* New York: Routledge.

Noam, E. M. (Ed.). (2008). *Peer-to-peer video: The economics, policy, and culture of today's new mass medium.* New York: Springer.

Owen, B.M., and Wildman, S. (1992). *Video economics*. Cambridge, MA: Harvard University Press.

Owen, B.M. (2000). *The Internet challenge to television*. Cambridge, MA: Harvard University Press.

Pew Research Center. (2011). *Broadband and dial-up adoption, 2000–2011*. Pew Internet & American Life Project. Retrieved from www.pewinternet.org/Trend-Data/Home-Broadband-Adoption.aspx

Sharma, A., & Besinger, G. (2013, June 5). Dora, SpongeBob jump sides in fickle web-video world. *Wall Street Journal*.

Sandvine Intelligent Broadband Networks. (2012). *Global Internet Phenomena Report*. Retrieved from www.sandvine.com/resources/resource-library.html

Screen Digest. (2011a). Timeshifted TV viewing increases (p. 210). *Screen Digest*.

Screen Digest. (2011b). US online movie market up 25% (p. 294). *Screen Digest*.

Screen Digest, Inc. Shapiro, C., & Varian, H.R. (1999). *Information rules: A strategic guide to the network economy*. Cambridge, MA: Harvard Business Press.

Simon, J., & Bogdanowicz, M. (2012). *The digital shift in the media and content industries*. Policy Brief. Joint Research Centre, Institute for Prospective Technological Studies, European Commission. Retrieved from http://is.jrc.ec.europa.eu/pages/ISG/MCI.html

SNL Kagan Research. (2012a, September 26). *Motion picture investor*.

SNL Kagan Research. (2012b, November 30.) *Motion picture investor*.

TV Dimensions. (2012). Media dynamics incorporated. Retrieved from www.medi adynamicsinc.com/products/tvDimensions.cfm

Waterman, D., & Ji, S.W. (2012). Online vs. offline in the U.S.: Are the media shrinking? *The Information Society, 28*, 5.

Waterman, D., Sherman, R., & Ji, S.W. (2013). The economics of online television: Industry development, aggregation, and "TV Everywhere." *Telecommunications Policy*. Vol. 37, 725–736

Wildman, S.S. (2008). Interactive channels and the challenges of content budgeting. *International Journal on Media Management, 10*(3), 91–101.

Yao, D., Queiro, F., & Rozovsky, J. (2008). CBS and online video. *Harvard Business School Cases*. No 9–709–447. (Revised 2010) Boston, MA: Harvard Business School Publishing.

18 Multiscreen Services

User-Centric Marketing Strategies

Donghee Shin

Television viewing habits are rapidly traversing platforms in the digital realm and influencing the evolution of multiscreen services. A multiscreen (often referred to as an N-screen) service allows users to view the same smartphone content on multiple devices, such as a desktop computer or a home TV, anytime and anywhere. Multiscreen service has become popular as the number of people who own multiple smart gadgets (e.g., smartphones, tablet PCs, and smart TVs) has rapidly increased. The increase in consumers has motivated telecommunication companies to introduce multiscreen services that enable data sharing on different platforms. Multiscreen has steadily gained popularity since its introduction in 2011 as smart technologies have advanced. Multiscreen technology will likely become a more important service in the future as technologies become seamlessly interconnected across different platforms. It is predicted that the number of multiscreen users will exceed 100 million by 2014 and 288 million by 2016 (FitzGerald, 2012). This is because consumers want to view the same content on multiple devices by connecting smartphones, computers, and TVs through the same network. For example, when users who are watching a movie leave their living room, or even their home, they can continue to watch the movie on the subway or bus through their smartphone or tablet PC. Such attributes make multiscreen a major rival to the most valuable services in the telecommunications industry and threaten to change major facets of the global communications industry (Shin, 2013).

Despite advances in technology and optimistic predictions, several obstacles hinder the widespread use of multiscreen (Kim, 2010a). The most significant hindrance is the lack of interoperability across various platforms to different devices. Porting content across digital devices requires considerable processor power; current mobile phones cannot handle large applications that transform regular data into specific data and then send it to a data channel (Ha, Kang, & Lee, 2010). Thus, interoperability is a key factor in multiscreen development, as the service aims to provide content across a variety of platforms such as TV, PC, and mobile devices that can be shared and consumed seamlessly by users.

There is also conflict in the regulation and distribution of multiscreen. The emergence of multiscreen has prompted network neutrality issues

(Korea Information Society Development Institute [KISDI], 2011), which have recently become a heated topic in the field of telecommunications. Regulatory bodies are facing bottlenecks over the issue because of the new 3G and WiMax technologies (De Reuver, Bouwman, De Koning, & Lemstra, 2009). Consequently, regulators have become concerned with how networks should be accessed and available to users. Currently there are no established control mechanisms or regulations to enforce network neutrality (Shin & Choo, 2011). There are also obstacles from within the industry (Sibley, 2011). Some mobile operators have prohibited the use of multiscreen within their mobile networks, and some have imposed a surcharge to avoid cannibalization of their service revenue streams (Ha et al., 2010).

However, consumer indifference may be the most significant barrier to multiscreen development. Consumers have seen many technological changes and have been given numerous optimistic promises over the last decade, although many mobile services have yet to become widespread (e.g., Shin, 2010) for mobile virtual network operators (Noh & Kim, 2010; Yu, Ha, Choi, & Rho, 2005; Funk, 2007). While there is current widespread enthusiasm for multiscreen, skeptics consider it to be a gimmick or, at best, an immature service. Nevertheless, most of the services recently introduced into the market have not created great value for consumers and have been quickly withdrawn from the market, often before they had a chance to create any demand.

Despite the increasing importance of user acceptance and market diffusion, only a few researchers have addressed the issues of multiscreen adoption and marketability. Multiscreen services are investigated from a consumer adoption perspective in this study in order to determine implications for policy and managerial practices. Mazzoni, Castaldi, and Addeo (2007) stated that policies formulated by governments should be based on the customer's perspective (i.e., how consumers feel about multiscreen services, current users' experience with services in various contexts, and how future consumers will engage with such services). Similarly, Cecere and Corrocher (2011) contend that telecom firm strategies should be grounded in consumers' behavior in relation to new services.

Indeed, a new and multifaceted ecosystem can create campaign planning challenges for brand marketers and agencies, and there is a lot to learn about how consumers use multiple screen interfaces. For example, what are the experiences of multiscreen TV viewers? How are multiscreen viewers consuming content, and how engaged are they with each media? How can brands stay ahead of the curve by effectively building multitouch cross-media campaigns? In light of these questions, the following research questions were prepared to guide this study:

RQ1: What are the factors that influence the acceptance of multiscreen?
RQ2: What are the determining antecedents of consumer intentions?
RQ3: What policy and managerial implications can be drawn from user acceptance?

A consumer acceptance model can be examined by collecting data from multiscreen users. This model can reveal critical factors for multiscreen acceptance that can help develop managerial and policy directives. Theoretically, we suggest a model that can identify both the antecedents of multiscreen usability and the development of user multiscreen adoption. The new model is an improvement on previous technology acceptance research because it integrates quality and perceptual values as primary factors. Previous studies focused on telecom acceptance have often been criticized for their lack of context-specific understanding (Mallat, Rossi, Tuunainen, & Oorni, 2008; Venkatesh & Agarwal, 2006), which leads to acceptance models with low explanatory power. Thus, by incorporating technology-specific factors into an adoption model, the model can better explain how the technology is accepted at an individual level and how it eventually diffuses into the market and society.

From a practical standpoint, the findings of this study can be used to guide regulators to create effective policy, which will facilitate diffusion and help the industry shape effective strategies to attract multiscreen consumers. Globally, regulators have attempted to devise an effective policy model that addresses the introduction of network neutrality (Shin & Choo, 2011). Likewise, the industry is facing the challenge of how to develop multiscreen services that are useful, seamless, interoperable, and, most importantly, user centered. A better understanding of how user factors will affect adoption and diffusion will provide insight for marketers and will allow them to plan appropriate multiscreen strategies. The results of this study represent a set of guidelines to help the multiscreen industry understand users' perceptions of multiscreen development and how users contribute to ongoing adoption and usage.

LITERATURE REVIEW

Definition of Multiscreen

Multiscreen services allow users to easily access content and information across a range of multiple screens and has been envisioned and anticipated by both the industry and consumers (Shin, 2013). Multiscreen service has become more feasible with the rapid development of cloud-computing technologies. Multiscreen is based primarily on cloud-computing technology and is aimed at providing content across a variety of platforms such as televisions, PCs, and mobile devices so that users can seamlessly share and consume content (Oldroyd, 2010). Cloud storage separates content and applications from a device and then delivers them from data centers on the network. Mobile cloud technology will significantly increase the rate of this migration as users rapidly appreciate the value of the cloud and the ease of accessing it through any device.

The key component of multiscreen service is a platform that mediates the use of content or services on multiple devices. An interface with content providers and replay and synchronization technology are required for each device. Open application programming interface (API) and Open Marketplace can be used actively for the multiscreen platform. Open API allows the number of usable devices to be increased while Open Marketplace is suitable for expanding transactions between content providers and consumers. Cloud technology is essential to the multiscreen platform for service synchronization on multiple devices.

Multiscreen can be described as a multiscreen strategy because it uses similar operation strategies. Service providers are currently developing multiscreen strategies to offer competitive content services that help retain customers and increase their subscriber base. The move toward multiscreen content delivery is an industry-wide trend and represents the next phase in the evolution of broadcast delivery models.

Current Multiscreen Development

The diffusion of multiscreen has been rapidly developing and shows the next generation of the media evolution, which was preceded by the transitions from terrestrial, cable, and satellite systems to Internet Protocol TV (IPTV), and now to hybrid IPTV/ Over-the-Top (OTT) systems, eventually leading to pure open Internet-based broadband TV models.

Broadcasters, content providers, and manufacturers are attempting to capitalize on new viewing trends by extending live, time-shifted, and interactive content to new platforms. Korean manufacturers have started to release products that feature multiscreen technology, touting its ability to allow consumers to watch content on smartphones, PCs, and TVs with little difficulty. Within the changing telecom sector in Korea, KT is competing with its biggest rival, SK Telecom, to enjoy more first-mover merits by promoting the multiscreen strategy in the saturated local market (Kim, 2010b). In early 2011, LG Uplus introduced a wireless multiscreen service that enables data sharing on multiple platforms such as mobile phones, tablet PCs, televisions, and personal computers (Uplus Shoot and Play). LG Uplus allows the application to be downloaded on their devices without uploading content or making other interdevice connections.

Samsung's multiscreen product, named the Hoppin smartphone, is similar to the current smartphone technology but contains a number of upgrades including multiscreen technology. In conjunction with the launch of SK Telecom's Hoppin service, the Galaxy S Hoppin also acts as a set-top box. When the Galaxy S Hoppin is connected to a TV, users are able to play smartphone-stored content on the TV and can also search and buy content. The Samsung Galaxy S Hoppin also supports wireless content sharing through the Digital Living Network Alliance (Kim, 2010b).

Multiscreen Technology Worldwide

Multiscreen has been developed under different names and in different forms depending on the location and market around the globe. This technology has been developed under various titles including multiscreen strategy, quadruple play service, or 3-screen service (Oldroyd, 2010). In the U.S., Verizon FiOS includes bundled Internet access, telephone, and television services that operate over a fiber-optic communications network. Verizon FiOS services are delivered over a fiber-to-the-premises network via passive optical network technology, and voice, video, and data travel over three infrared spectrum wavelengths.

In 2010, AT&T started to offer 3-Screen service, which included a TV, a PC, and a wireless device. Backed by a quartet of voice, video, broadband, and wireless services, AT&T is making applications and content available on all three screens. With this new 3-Screen service, a user who watches a football game on TV can continue viewing the game on his or her laptop and then leave the house and watch the game on his or her cell phone (FitzGerald, 2012). In the UK, the BBC iPlayer service reaches millions of users and provides a wide variety of connected devices with live, constantly-updated, interactive content. KPN, a Dutch multiscreen technology, extends its IPTV service to multiple screens, offering catch-up, interactive, and live pausing features (Research & Markets, 2011).

The popularity of multiscreen technology has increased rapidly worldwide. Specifically, the surge in smart devices is expected to trigger an expansion of the multiscreen market. Mueller (2012) estimated that the number of multiscreen users will rise from 10 billion in 2014 to 150 billion by 2016. In light of these positive predictions for the mobile phone market, more telecom companies are making adjustments to their overall business strategies to adopt and adapt emerging multiscreen options to mobile subscribers.

Korean Media Landscape: Digital and New Media Platform

South Korea is an Asian powerhouse in the global digital revolution due in part to leading technology brands such as Samsung and LG. The South Korean online community uses a multitude of digital tools and channels for online activities. Prominent activities include the use of social networking sites (SNS) and online trade. Recent figures reveal that there are more than 3 million Twitter users in Korea. The Korea Chamber of Commerce and Industry determined that 60% of people in their 20s have used social commerce. Some short-listed examples of popular channels that are used by digitally connected South Koreans are listed in the following.

South Korea is home to one of the largest blogging communities in the world, second only to China. There are 10.93 million active social networkers; of these, only 33% are content sharers. This is still relatively low compared to other countries such as the U.S. or the Philippines, which report

51% and 60% of content sharers, respectively. South Koreans use an array of instant messaging tools such as NateOn, KakaoTalk, Buddybuddy, Sayclub Tachy, and MSN Messenger. Outside of work, many teenagers prefer to use SMS and instant messaging to communicate. The top five search engines in Korea are Naver, Google, Daum, Yahoo, and Nate. Other digital media platforms include location-based services (LBS), social commerce, and Quick Response (QR) Code technology.

Research Model

In this study, an adapted technology acceptance model (TAM; see Davis, 1989), which consists of quality factors along with traditional components of other theories, is proposed. While TAM is one of the most influential research models in the study of the determinants of technology acceptance (Venkatesh & Agarwal, 2006), several researchers have identified significant limitations of the model (Yu et al., 2005). Given the wide applicability of the TAM to emerging technologies, it is expected that the path causalities found in its theories are also applicable to multiscreen technology (Kuo, Wu, & Deng, 2009). Therefore, the following hypotheses are proposed:

H1: Attitude toward multiscreen positively influences the intention to use multiscreen.

H2: Perceived usefulness (PU) has a positive effect on the intention to use multiscreen.

H3: Perceived ease of use (PEoU) has a positive effect on the intention to use multiscreen.

H4: Customers' perceptions about multiscreen reliability positively influence the PU of multiscreen.

H5: Perceived access positively influences the PU of multiscreen.

H6: Perceived portability has a positive effect on the PEoU of multiscreen.

H7: Perceived availability positively influences the PEoU of multiscreen.

H8: Social norm (SN) positively influences users' intentions to use multiscreen.

Study Design

Consumer Modeling

There were four phases in the survey method of this study. First, individual in-depth interviews were conducted with current and prospective multiscreen users. Ten respondents were asked to explain their attitudes about and experiences with multiscreen. These preliminary interviews provided an overview of multiscreen use as it is currently in the early stages of diffusion. Second, five focus groups consisting of current and prospective users were organized, with the help of five multiscreen providers based in Korea. Interviews were conducted with groups of four to six individuals who discussed how they currently use the services and what factors would influence their use in the future. The goal of the individual interviews and focus group sessions was to test and validate the research model, to identify items that were missing from the model, and to gain a preliminary understanding of the factors that have an impact on usage behaviors.

Third, a final survey questionnaire was developed based on focus group session feedback and by eliciting comments from an expert panel composed of professors and researchers in the field of telecommunications, as well as experts in the mobile technology industry. Representatives from actual multiscreen providers were also consulted for questionnaire development. Prior to use, a pilot survey among possible users was administered to test the questionnaire; this provided a comprehensive review of individual responses to the survey. In the pilot survey, 30 respondents participated. The items were worded based on the pilot test findings, and then the survey was reviewed and modified by experts in quantitative research.

The finalized survey was administered by a marketing firm that specializes in survey development, data collection, analysis, and reporting. The company has already collected robust panel data related to various cloud services. The marketing firm was used to ensure data quality due to the low penetration of multiscreen technology. A total of 370 responses were surveyed by the company over a 7-month period. To refine and increase the validity of the survey data, 41 responses that contained answers with systematic errors or inconsistent information were excluded. The quality of the collected data was cross-verified and validated by a third agency. The results of the cross-validation indicate that the data are reliable and representative and that the final sample reflected the general population of cloud-computing users. AMOS, a maximum likelihood-based structural equation modeling software program, was used for statistical analysis.

Results

Structural Model

The overall fit of the model is satisfactory, and all of the relevant goodness of fit indices were greater than 0.90. Chi-square statistics show nonsignificance in the structural model, indicating that the model adequately fits the data. The Goodness of Fit Index (GFI) is 0.95, the Adjusted Goodness of Fit Index (AGFI) is 0.91, and the Tucker-Lewis Index (TLI) is 0.91. Similarly, there is no evidence of misfit, with the Root Mean Square Error Approximation (RMSEA) showing an acceptable level of 0.067. An RMSEA value in this range can be favorably compared to the findings of Joreskog and Sorbom (1996), who suggested that RMSEA values of 0.06 or greater indicate a close fit. The standardized Root Mean Residual (RMR) was also very good at 0.027, which is well below the threshold for a good overall fit. Another positive test statistic was the normed chi-square value of 1.98. Such a value is well below the benchmark of 3, indicating good overall

Table 18.1 Adjusted *t*-statistics and standardized path coefficients

Hypothesis	Path coefficient (β)	*t*-value	Significance (two-tailed)	Support
H1: Attitude → Intention	0.42**	5.010	$p < 0.01$	Yes
H2: PU → Attitude	0.55***	7.941	$p < 0.001$	Yes
H3: PEoU → Attitude	0.42**	5.210	$p < 0.01$	Yes
H4: Reliability → PU	0.44**	5.011	$p < 0.01$	Yes
H5: Connectivity → PU	0.53*	3.329	$p < 0.05$	Yes
H6: Portability → PEoU	0.58**	4.561	$p < 0.01$	Yes
H7: Availability → PEoU	0.44**	4.651	$p < 0.01$	Yes
H8: SN → Intention	0.28	1.3529	$p < 0.05$	No

*$p < 0.05$; **$p < 0.01$, ***$p < 0.001$

model performance. Because the model exhibited satisfactory fit indices, the structural model path coefficients could be assessed.

Structural Paths and Hypothesis Tests

To test the structural relationships, the hypothesized causal paths were estimated; seven hypotheses were supported while one was marginally rejected (see Table 18.1). The results support the proposed model, confirming the key roles that are influenced by quality and utilities. The findings highlight the significant role of quality in determining users' perceived PU and PEoU, which, in turn, directly affect intention. A user's intention is influenced by attitude, which supports H1 (β = 0.42, *t* = 3.120, *p* < 0.01). Additionally, it can be stated that a user's intention is indirectly influenced by quality and values. Given the strong paths, four factors (quality,value,attitude, andintention) can be established as a series of key relationships specific to multiscreen. Call quality is found to be the most significant factor (β = 0.55, *t* = 5.981, *p* < 0.001) in this relational path. Approximately 52% of the variance in the intention to use multiscreen can be explained by the variables in the model (R^2 = 0.520). The R^2 of PU is explained to approximately 32% by the two exogenous constructs in the model. About 29% of the variance of PEoU is explained by mobility and coverage. Both R^2 values were relatively higher than those in previous studies on PU and PEoU.

Consumers' Intention: Logit Regression Analysis

Because the structural equation model (SEM) findings were significant, logistic regression was performed to examine the statistical significance of each of the coefficients in the equation (Bewley & Fiebig, 1988). Logistic regression was selected to determine which of the factors identified in multiscreen adoption were the most significant with regard to predicting the probability of subsidence. The path coefficients from the SEM did not help identify the relative significance among the factors. Using the raw survey response data, the logistic regression method gives estimates of model coefficients that can be used to quantify the probability of subsidence. Logistic regression is well suited to the present study of multiscreen adoption as it allows for an estimation of the probability that multiscreen will emerge based on a set of specified factors.

Independent variables were drawn from the variables of the model. The dependent variable used in the analysis was whether or not multiscreen is adopted. Logit regression was jointly performed for all the factors. A Logit model is helpful for understanding the extent to which certain factors influence a customer's choice of technology. The model evaluates the influence of independent variables on an event that is either happening or is not happening and whether multiscreen is accepted or not. In the independent variable analysis, each of the categories was assessed for its impact on the dependent variable. A series of people were questioned as to whether or not they would accept multiscreen (accept: 1 = yes, 0 = no).

The logistic regression procedure was jointly run for all of the factors, with the exception of the SN since it was rejected in the hypothesis testing. One model is presented in Table 18.2, and the dependent variable is whether or not consumers would adopt multiscreen depending on the independent variables. Seven Logit models were estimated (Table 18.3), each with a binary dependent variable. The basic model consisted of seven independent variables. The percentage-correctly-estimated (PCE) index shows the

Table 18.2   First logistic regression results

Explanatory variable	Coefficient	Chi-square	p-value
Reliability	6.1146	31.13	0.0113**
Connectivity	8.2102	8.13	0.0043***
Portability	7.2677	43.65	0.001***
Availability	5.0223	0.21	0.0229**
Usefulness	2.3358	4.61	0.0317**
Ease of use	3.1245	2.43	0.001***
Attitude	4.3276	28.16	0.0498**
Log Likelihood			11.63
PCE			59
Chi-square			0.373 for alpha = 0.05

Adjusted pseudo R^2 = 0.35
*p<0.1, **p<0.05, ***p<0.01

maximum estimated level of accuracy of a model. the PCE is 60%, which is not much better than a random 50/50 chance. In addition, the overall explanatory power of the model is quite low, though it is significant at the 0.05 level (adjusted pseudo R^2 = 0.24, $p < 0.05$). Therefore, each of the selected variables was analyzed by one-to-one alternative models.

The results indicate that consumers believe reliability is an important factor. Users are more likely to adopt multiscreen with stable reliability because the reliability of the multiscreen system is critical in delivering content and services seamlessly. The coefficient of the reliability variable has a Wald statistic (Pawitan, 2001) equal to 1.314, which is significant at the 0.01 level (99% confidence level) with a critical value of 6.32 [df = 1]. The overall model is significant at the 0.01 level according to the model chi-square statistic. The model correctly predicts 61% of the responses. McFadden's R^2 is 0.25, which indicates that around a quarter of the variation in the dependent variable is explained by the logistic regression model. Model 2 includes the compatibility variable. According to the block chi-square statistic, Model 2, which incorporates connectivity, is superior to Model 1 in terms of overall model fit. The block chi-square statistic is significant at the 0.01 level (critical value = 9.11 [df = 2]), and in this model the percentage of correct predictions increases by 6%, and the McFadden's R^2 value is almost 100% greater. Model 3 adds portability, which has consistently been identified as an important variable of mobile technologies in previous studies. The results from Model 3 show that consumers are concerned with the portability of multiscreen services. The higher the portability of multiscreen, the more likely consumers are to choose it. The coefficient of the observability variable has a Wald

Table 18.3 Logistic regression model analysis

	Model 1	Model 2	Model 3	Model 4	Model 5	Model 6	Model 7
Reliability	1.314*	1.231	0.932	1.232	0.326	0.234	1.031
Connectivity		1.720**	1.383	1.111	1.391	1.099	0.001
Portability			2.148**	2.074	2.001	0.991	1.331
Availability				3.895**	2.031	0.099	1.431
Usefulness					4.001***	2.010	3.001
Ease of use						2.931**	0.914
Attitude							1.301*
Model x^2	24.1	9.11	35.7	34.6	29.2	19.4	24.6
McFadden's R^2	.25	.46	.53	.55	.59	.63	.64

*$p<0.1$, **$p<0.05$, ***$p<0.01$

statistic equal to 17.32, which is significant at the 0.01 level (99% confidence level) with a critical value of 4.235 [df = 3]. The statistics demonstrate that Model 3 is slightly superior to Model 2. In the same manner, Models 4, 5, 6, and 7 add availability, usefulness, ease of use, and attitude, respectively. The subsequent models show that the added variables play significant roles in the willingness to adopt multiscreen (Table 18.3). With the addition of each variable, the new model becomes slightly superior to the previous model.

When all of the variables are considered, the logistic regression results show that quality characteristics are significant predictors of the diffusion of multiscreen technology (Table 18.4). Connectivity and availability are the two most significant factors that affect customers' intentions. Other variables such as reliability and portability are also associated with relatively high coefficients. Interestingly, while quality characteristics were found to be significant, traditional TAM factors such as PU and PEoU were negligible. One interpretation is that consumers may want defined and concrete features rather than vague perceptions of usefulness or ease of use. The overall findings of this study agree with the SEM findings. The adjusted pseudo R^2 for the model is 0.54 ($p < 0.01$), suggesting that the factors provide substantial and statistically significant explanatory power that accounts for variance in users' decisions about multiscreen. Finally, statistical significance testing for the modified model was conducted to examine whether neighborhood significantly affects the model. The following equation was employed to assess the chi-square test of the likelihood ratio:

$$\lambda = \frac{L_0}{L_1} < 1$$

where L_0 denotes the likelihood of the basic model and L_1 denotes the likelihood of the study model.

$Log\ l = L_0 - L_1$

$-1198.283 = -1366.197 - -167.914$

$-2Logl = 2396.566$

In the prior expression, L_0 is derived from the initial logistic regression, while L_1 is taken from Model 4. The statistical testing suggests that the factors significantly improved the model's performance.

DISCUSSION

The results of this study augment understanding of future multiscreen diffusion in a rapidly evolving convergence environment. Consistent with previous studies on technology adoption, the findings show that both PU

Table 18.4 Selected independent variable Logit analysis

Independent variables	Multiscreen intention		
	Standardized β	S.E.	p-value
Reliability	0.504***	0.568	0.002
Connectivity	0.678**	1.731	0.007
Portability	0.543**	0.444	0.0183
Availability	0.750**	3.215	0.031
Usefulness	0.219*	1.122	0.849
Ease of use	0.180*	0.0164	0.364
Attitude	0.224*	0.012	0.049
Constant		0.000**	
Log likelihood		164.788	
PCE		88	
Chi-square		3.95 (for alpha = 0.05)	

Adjusted pseudo $R^2 = 0.54$
$*p < 0.1$, $**p < 0.05$, $***p < 0.01$

and PEoU have considerable impacts on attitude and, eventually, the intent to use multiscreen. Specifically, it was demonstrated that these TAM factors are greatly influenced by quality and that various quality factors play antecedent roles in both PU and PEoU. Additionally, the effects of quality have a much stronger impact on intention than previous studies have indicated (DeLone & McLean, 1992; Koivisto, 2009). While extensive research has been conducted in the area of consumer adoption, the contextual antecedents of PU and PEoU have yet to be clearly examined in a specific context. In this study, the antecedents of the two variables in the TAM were identified in the context of multiscreen. The results represent a modest theoretical advancement, grounding new variables in the TAM. This work was applied to an emerging technology within a particular context in Korea with a series of specific factors. Researchers who have studied the TAM and diffusion (e.g., Kim & Zhang, 2009; Venkatesh & Agarwal, 2006) argue that there is increased interest in modeling context-specific (as opposed to generic) behaviors with specific technological artifacts. In addition, context dependence has been alluded to in the domain of user behavior. Researchers have acknowledged that evaluation criteria differ with respect to technology products, users, and situations. Future telecom technologies in a ubiquitous environment will be considerably different from other technologies in terms of their capability, coverage, and level of service quality (Teng & Yu, 2009). In a future convergence era, seamless and pervasive networks that are able to provide multiple broadband applications, Quality of Service (QoS), and high bandwidth content will be developed with service-related functions that are independent of the underlying transport networks (Fabrizi & Wertien, 2007). It is important to note both this cloud context and the ubiquitous specific factors. This study determined that the new variables of perceived reliability and perceived availability, which reflect the network capability and the service dimension, respectively, were valid and significant. Such a result warrants a consistent model for multiscreen drivers and stable theory development. Hence, the model proposed in this study is a meaningful contribution to the emerging body of literature on future telecom environments.

IMPLICATIONS FOR POLICY AND MANAGERIAL PRACTICE

The emergence of multiscreen technology has revealed unchartered avenues for regulators and businesses that will develop the future of telecommunications (Ha et al., 2010. This study provides entities with guidelines to prepare for future technology changes based on the implications for policies and management. The results imply that the regulator fulfills a role that should guarantee the competitiveness of the telecommunications market and ensure that the consumer's demands are met. While third-party players such as content providers may enter the market and use network data access to target early multiscreen service adopters, network owners or mobile operators are able to suppress such moves. The findings also clarify the practical implications of developing effective multiscreen services.

Policy Implications

Policy issues such as network neutrality and interconnections are highly debated topics that are beyond the scope of this study. However, our findings confirm the importance of such issues, and regulators should be well prepared to address them, as well as consider the following questions:

1. Are there any regulatory barriers to multiscreen introduction that will need to be removed?
2. Are there any anticompetitive barriers restricting the move to multiscreen?
3. Do regulators have an active role in promoting multiscreen interconnection, or should the transition to multiscreen interconnection be managed by the general telecom market?
4. How can cooperation and coordination among different industry players be ensured?

Managerial Implications

The findings provide insight into different ways that users interact with their devices, implying that marketers should consider unique attributes of devices as they develop messaging and content plans. For example, content grazing is the most common way users interact with multiscreen services.

A number of users view two or more screens simultaneously to access unrelated content—for example, watching a show on TV while checking e-mail or texting.

Engaging users within an increasingly complex and competitive market is a challenge for any telecom provider. Telecoms must deliver the right content with the right device at the right time. They must also create user experiences that not only engage and retain existing subscribers, but also appeal to new audiences who increasingly want more flexible, interactive, reliable, portable, and seamlessly accessible services.

For multiscreen technology, network quality and network neutrality may be the two most significant factors for development (Kim, 2010b). While these factors reflect a changing environment in the telecom industry, the factors are also well suited to findings from the consumer model by the SEM. In the model, reliability, connectivity, and quality are highly significant factors. The importance of employing reliability and connectivity in a TAM may be unique to 4G technologies, which provide increasingly ubiquitous and pervasive accessibility. Numerous studies have already determined that the user's desire to easily access content anywhere, anytime, on any device continues to increase, and smart devices continue to be developed to satisfy such needs. This trend will persist worldwide as the convergence continues to forge ubiquitous environments. With this in mind, multiscreen service providers should work to increase user awareness that multiscreen is available at any time on a ubiquitous basis. Additionally, based on the analysis, it can be inferred that the multiscreen industry will face the following challenges:

1. A lack of multiscreen awareness
2. A limited number of broadband connections available in specific areas
3. The high monetary cost of multiscreen services and the lack of established standard rates that service providers adhere to
4. A lack of a standard architecture in multiscreen services
5. Limited interoperability across different platforms and networks, which will decrease the connectivity and mobility

To address the challenges stated here, the industry must do the following:

1. Continue to develop a differentiated offer in a fiercely competitive market
2. Develop an effective partnership ecosystem to deliver new content/ services quickly and efficiently
3. Ensure multiscreen service can deliver enhanced functionality to support a more sophisticated and reliable multiscreen strategy

Strategic Implications

A principle of transparency that induces contributions from many different players and active cooperation with other industries will be vital factors in multiscreen market success. With the principle of transparency, the multiscreen service market is expected to develop in two main directions that will help expand the user base and create a larger and more profitable market.

First, the popular "one person multi device" trend is currently demanding technologies that make it easier for users to shift content between devices. Content shifting allows users to freely access the same content regardless of the device and network. Multiscreen will become more popular as multiscreen providers' efforts are directed to enhance service compatibility and convenience by establishing standardized technology.

Second, an entirely new value will be created through services that were previously nonexistent. Not only will the number and type of devices for multiscreen increase, but there will also be a wide variety of services that are available for the same content that will reflect device characteristics. Moreover, these differentiated and valuable services supplied by multiscreen service providers will lead to the emergence of many third-party firms and new business models, thereby enriching the multiscreen ecosystem and market. Multiscreen market stakeholders that work with a wide range of industries should focus on openness and cooperation. They should also focus their efforts to enhance consumer convenience and benefits, which will allow their multiscreen business to thrive. Increased value for consumers will ultimately foster value and expand market creativity.

Currently, there are players in the new media market that endorse a defensive strategy instead of seeking an appropriate level of agreement to create a profitable market for multiscreen services. For example, firms experience challenges in copyright and publication, which includes the time period and number of screens that certain content can be used for when content is sourced. With the widespread diffusion of smart devices and telecom networks advances, content consumption will become centered on multiscreen services. In consideration of future changes, market players should proactively collaborate with one another and assume leadership to generate a market environment that focuses on producing new value for customers in the new multiscreen era. A principle of transparency that incorporates numerous player participation and active cooperation with other sectors will become key factors in the future success of the multiscreen market.

CONCLUSION

Consumers are driving cloud evolution by demanding converged cross-screen services and a superior quality experience. The findings of this study imply that consumers want a flexible experience that allows quality content to be mobile and want the ability to shift from one device to another. However, most users have a fragmented experience with current multiscreen technology that lacks true cross-screen capabilities. In addition, current services offer limited reliability, partial availability, restricted mobility, and narrow connectivity.

This study provides explanations for the relationship between multiscreen factors and a consumer's intent. The factors that relate to quality significantly affect the adoption behavior of consumers. The perception that multiscreen is easier to use, is more useful, is of higher quality, or provides more value will entice users to adopt this technology. Therefore, managers should launch promotions that improve value perceptions of multiscreen.

High quality, convenience, and usefulness are key factors from the consumer's perspective that can be prerequisites for multiscreen success. Compared to competitors, multiscreen faces significant barriers to mass consumer adoption. Such barriers include inadequate quality, insufficient cost savings, and an unconvincing user experience. Thus, multiscreen vendors should devote additional efforts to systematic management of quality and features. The findings on PU and PEoU indicate that user intent affects consumption behavior, and this study recommends that vendors determine and establish customer multiscreen perceptions. This can be achieved by ensuring that the carrier's services are conducted in accordance with users' expectations—namely, that their content is high quality, that services are reliable, and that promises and commitments are upheld.

Future studies may further examine multiscreen strategies and focus on device makers, telecom carriers, and Internet service provider strategies. Finally, a stakeholder approach may provide a good framework to investigate interaction dynamics between investors.

REFERENCES

Bewley, R., & Fiebig, D. (1988). A flexible logistic growth model with applications in telecommunications. *International Journal of Forecasting, 4*(2), 177–192.

Cecere, G., & Corrocher, N. (2011). The intensity of VoIP usage in Great Britain. *Telecommunications Policy, 35*(6), 522–531.

Davis, F.D. (1989). Perceived usefulness, perceived ease of use, and user acceptance of information technology. *MIS Quarterly, 13*(3), 319–340.

De Reuver, M., Bouwman, H., De Koning, T., & Lemstra, W. (2009). How new billing processes reshape the mobile industry. *Info, 11*(1), 78–93.

DeLone, W., & McLean, E. (1992). Information systems success. *Information Systems Research, 3*(1), 60–95.Fabrizi, S., & Wertien, B. (2007). Roaming in the mobile internet. *Telecommunications Policy, 32*(1), 50–61.

FitzGerald, J. (2012). *How multi-screen consumers are changing media dynamics.* comScore Research Report. Retrieved from www.comscore.com/Insights/Presentations_and_Whitepapers/2012/How_Multi-Screen_Consumers_Are_Changing_Media_Dynamics

Funk, J. (2007). The future of mobile shopping. *Technological Forecasting and Social Change, 74*(3), 341–356.

Mueller, J. (2012). *Network market trends and strategies.* Gartner Research Report. Available online, www.gartner.com/technology/research/

Ha, K., Kang, K., & Lee, J. (2010). N-screen service using I/O virtualization technology. *2010 Proceedings on Information and Communication Technology Convergence* (pp. 525–526).

Joreskog, K.G., & Sorbom, D. (1996). *LISREL 8.* Chicago: Scientific Software International.

Sibley, K. (2011). *Multi-screen strategy case studies*. New York: Jupiter Publishing.

Kim, Y. (2010a). Analysis on N-screen strategy and trends. *Information Communication Strategies, KISDI, 22*(20), 1–23.

Kim, S. (2010b). Building a sustainable UX ecosystem under N-Screen and cloud computing paradigm. *Journal of the Ergonomics Society of Korea, 29*(4), 553–561.

Kim, Y., & Zhang, P. (2010, December). *Continued use of technology: Combining controlled and automatic processes*. Proceedings of the International Conference on Information Systems (ICIS), St. Louis, MO.

Koivisto, M. (2009). Acceptance of mobile communication technologies in student communities. *International Journal of Web Based Communities, 5*(2), 164–178.

Korea Information Society Development Institute (KISDI). (2011). *2011 Media and Communication Outlook of Korea*. Seoul: Korea Information Society Development Institute.

Kuo, Y., Wu, C., & Deng, W. (2009). The relationships among service quality, perceived value, customer satisfaction, and post-purchase intention in mobile value-added services. *Computers in Human Behavior, 25*, 887–896.

Mallat, N., Rossi, M., Tuunainen, V., & Oorni, A. (2008). The impact of use context on mobile services acceptance. *Information & Management, 46*(3), 190–195.

Mazzoni, C., Castaldi, L., & Addeo, F. (2007). Consumer behavior in the Italian mobile telecomm market. *Telecommunications Policy, 31*, 632–647.

Oldroyd, J. (2010). *Multi-screen strategy case studies*. (2010, February). Ovum Research Report.

Noh, M., & Kim, J. (2010). Factors influencing the user acceptance of digital home services. *Telecommunications Policy, 34*(11), 672–682.

Pawitan, Y. (2001). *In all likelihood: Statistical modeling and inference using likelihood*. New York: Oxford University Press.

Research and Markets. (2011). *N-screen & multi-device business trends in Asian market*. Research and Markets Research Report.

Shin, D. (2010). MVNO services: Policy implications for promoting MVNO diffusion. *Telecommunications Policy, 34*(10), 616–632.

Shin, D. (2013). N-screen: How multi-screen will impact diffusion and policy. *Information, Communication and Society, 16*(6), 918–944.

Shin, D., & Choo, H. (2011). Demystifying Internet neutrality of Korea with stakeholder analysis. *Review of Policy Research, 28*(6), 557–583.Teng, W., & Yu, H. (2009). Exploring the mass adoption of 3G mobile phones in Taiwan. *Telecommunications Policy, 33*(10), 628–641.

Venkatesh, V., & Agarwal, R. (2006). Turning visitors into customers. *Management Science, 52*, 367–382.

Yu, J., Ha, I., Choi, M., & Rho, J. (2005). Extending the TAM for a t-commerce. *Information & Management, 42*(7), 965–976.

Contributors

EDITORS AND CONTRIBUTORS

Yu-li Liu, Ph.D. (Indiana University), is professor in the Department of Radio and Television at National Chengchi University in Taiwan. She served as one of the first-term commissioners of the National Communications Commission from 2006 to 2008. She is president of the Chinese Communication Association (CCA) (September, 2013–August, 2015). She has received grants from the U.S. Fulbright Foundation and Taiwan's National Science Council for research projects in the areas of convergence, broadband networks, digital TV, and new media policy. She was also granted Excellent Research Award by the National Science Council in 2013.

Robert G. Picard is one of the world's leading academic experts on media economics and management and government communications policies. He is director of research at the Reuters Institute, Department of Politics and International Relations, University of Oxford. He has written hundreds of articles on media issues for scholarly journals and industry publications. He has also been a consultant for government agencies and ministries in North America and Europe, international agencies, investment firms, and numerous media companies and media labor organizations.

CONTRIBUTORS

Peng Hwa Ang is a professor at the Wee Kim Wee School of Communication and Information and director of the Singapore Internet Research Centre at Nanyang Technological University in Singapore. His research is in the areas of Internet governance and media law and policy. In 2004, he was appointed by the UN secretary general to the Working Group on

Internet Governance and later cofounded the Global Internet Governance Academic Network (GigaNet), where he was elected the inaugural chair.

Jef Ausloos is a doctoral researcher at the University of Leuven (iMinds— ICRI). He holds an LL.M degree in information technology and intellectual property law from the University of Hong Kong and has working experience in U.S.-based civil society organizations (Electronic Frontier Foundation, Center for Democracy & Technology) and academia (Berkman Center for Internet & Society). At ICRI, he mainly focuses on the intersection of privacy, freedom of expression, and intermediary liability rules on the Internet.

Rob Frieden holds the Pioneers Chair and serves as professor of telecommunications and law at Penn State University. He has written over 70 journal articles and several books, most recently *Winning the Silicon Sweepstakes: Can the United States Compete in Global Telecommunications*, published by Yale University Press. Professor Frieden holds a B.A., with distinction, from the University of Pennsylvania and a J.D. from the University of Virginia.

Richard A. Gershon, Ph.D. (Ohio University), is professor and codirector of the Telecommunications & Information Management program at Western Michigan University, where he teaches courses in media management and telecommunications. He is the author of *Media, Telecommunications & Business Strategy* (2013). Dr. Gershon is a Fulbright scholar who has held visiting appointments at the University of Navarra, Spain, and Nihon University, Japan.

Petros Iosifidis completed his M.A. in communication policy studies and Ph.D. in media policy at City University and University of Westminster respectively. He is currently professor in media and communication policy at City University London. He is author of five books and has published extensively in refereed journals. He serves as an ESRC Peer Review College reviewer and as a national expert for European Commission projects. He is editor of the *International Journal of Digital Television* and coeditor of the Palgrave Global Media Policy and Business Book Series.

Hyangsun Lee is a senior research fellow of the Korea Communications Standards Commission. She earned her Ph.D. in mass communications, with a minor in law, at Indiana University. Her research interests are in content regulation in broadcasting and on the Internet. Her current work mainly focuses on developing workable coregulatory methods in the convergent and smart media environment. Dr. Lee worked as an associate editor for the *Federal Communications Law Journal* and a senior researcher of the Korea University Research Institute for Information and Culture.

Peter Looms holds degrees from the University of Cambridge. He has worked for more than 30 years in Denmark on broadcasting policy and strategy. He took part in DTV4ALL, which assisted the European Commission in promoting digital television accessibility across Europe. Peter is currently chairman of an ITU-T Focus Group working on digital media accessibility. He teaches at universities in Denmark and Hong Kong, writes on media accessibility, and is involved in accessible TV projects in Argentina, China, and India.

Edward C. Malthouse is the Theodore R. and Annie Laurie Sills Professor of Integrated Marketing Communications and Industrial Engineering at Northwestern University and research director for the Spiegel Institute on digital and database marketing. He was the coeditor of the *Journal of Interactive Marketing* from 2005–2011. His research interests center on media marketing, database marketing, advertising, new media, and integrated marketing communications. He is the author of *Segmentation and Lifetime Value Models Using SAS* and the coeditor of *Medill on Media Engagement*.

Linda Mory studied Media Communication at Chemnitz University of Technology (Germany) and European Public Relations at the Dublin Institute of Technology (Ireland) and Leeds Metropolitan University (Great Britain). From 2008 to 2012, she was a doctoral student and research assistant to the Chair for Information and Communication Management, German University Speyer. Linda holds a doctoral degree from the German University of Administrative Sciences and now works as an internal strategic consultant at the SAP AG. Her publications focus on electronic business/government, media management, and corporate social responsibility.

Yoko Nishioka is the professor of the faculty of Global Media Studies at Komazawa University. Her primary area of research is institutional changes in global communication industries. Her recent book, *Form and Change of Global Telecommunication Institutions*, won three incentive awards. She received her Ph.D. in media and governance from Keio University in Tokyo, Japan, and an M.A. in communications from Annenberg School for Communication, the University of Pennsylvania, in Philadelphia.

Philipp T. Nitzsche studied industrial engineering at the University of Karlsruhe (Germany). Since 2009 he has been a doctoral student and research assistant to the Chair for Information and Communication Management, German University Speyer. His publications focus on electronic business/government, business model management, and innovations.

Robert Pennington, Ph.D. (University of Wisconsin, 1991), has held faculty positions at several universities in the U.S. and Taiwan in departments of communication, management, and foreign languages and cultures. He specializes in the cultural development implications of communication technology. His general interest concerns consumption and marketing communication as cultural processes for satisfying basic human needs. He has written previously about marketing communication development, advertising and brands within consumer culture, the meanings of consumer brands, and psycholinguistic methodology.

Amit Schejter, Ph.D. (Rutgers), is associate professor of communications at Ben-Gurion University of the Negev and at Penn State University, where he serves as codirector of the Institute for Information Policy. He is the author or editor of 4 books and more than 40 journal articles, law reviews, and book chapters in four languages. Dr. Schejter teaches courses on regulation, law, and policy; media and information industries; comparative media systems; and media activism. He is founding coeditor of the *Journal of Information Policy*.

Don Schultz, professor (emeritus-in-service) of integrated marketing communications at the Medill School, Northwestern University, Evanston, IL, holds a B.B.A. from University of Oklahoma and an M.A. and Ph.D. from Michigan State University. He is president of Agora, Inc., a global marketing, communication, and branding consulting firm. He is also author/coauthor of 26 books and 150 trade, academic, and professional articles. He is a featured columnist in *Marketing News* and *Marketing Management.*

Ryland Sherman is a Ph.D. student in telecommunications at Indiana University–Bloomington with a law degree from the IU Maurer School of Law, an A.B. with honors in economics and psychology from the University of Chicago, and additional M.B.A. coursework at the Kelley and Booth Schools of Business. He is primarily interested in how media technology innovations interact with intellectual property law and competition strategies.

Donghee Shin is a professor and chair of the Department of Interaction Science, Sungkyunkwan University, Seoul, South Korea. Dr. Shin has been appointed as a World Class University Project Scholar by the Ministry of Education, Science, and Technology in Korea. In 2011, Dr. Shin was awarded SKKU Fellow, the highest honor in Sungkyunkwan University. He has been researching on telecommunications management and policy, and he had various consultancy experiences in the field of telecommunications and information industry. Dr. Shin is the author of 60 international journals and 5 books.

Minoru Sugaya is a professor and vice director of media policy and economics at Keio University, Tokyo, Japan. He is a former president of the Japan Association of Information and Communication Research. He was visiting researcher at the Kennedy School at Harvard University in 1991 and at Michigan State University in 1992. He has published and edited a number of books in the field of telecommunication, broadcasting, and film industries. He has also served as a member or chairperson of several government committees, including those on universal service, cable television, and media convergence.

Miklos Sukosd is associate professor at the Journalism and Media Studies Centre at the University of Hong Kong. Previously he served as academic director of the Center for Media and Communication Studies at Central European University, where he also taught as associate professor of political science. His research focuses on media in China and postcommunist Central and Eastern Europe; media, sustainability, and the environment; and media and Buddhism. He has published over 20 books and many book chapters and journal articles about media and politics.

Mabel Tan is a postgraduate student at the Wee Kim Wee School of Communication and Information at Nanyang Technological University in Singapore. Formerly an assistant vice-president at Singapore's info-communications company StarHub, her research interests center on price wars for exclusive sports on pay TV, where she had published two opinion articles in the national newspaper, the *Straits Times*, in October 2009 and May 2013, with analyses on the problems and policy actions taken.

Yasu Taniwaki, councilor, cabinet secretariat (deputy director-general, National Information Security Center), joined the Ministry of Internal Affairs and Communications (MIC) in 1984. After serving in several positions, including economic councilor and telecommunications attaché at Embassy of Japan in U.S. (2002–2005), director of Competition Policy Division (2005–2007), director of Telecommunications Policy Division (2007–2008), director of Information Policy Division (2008–2011), and deputy director-general, Information and Communications Bureau (2012–2013), he has served in his capacity since June 2013.

Noam Tirosh is a Ph.D. candidate in the Department of Communication Studies at Ben-Gurion University of the Negev. In 2012 he completed his M.A. in the Politics and Government Department at Ben-Gurion University. Now, his research focuses on the relationship between collective memory, information and communication technologies, and democracy as seen in a broad perspective. His work has been published in such journals as the *Information Society* and has been presented in several national and international academic conferences.

Peggy Valcke is research professor at the University of Leuven (iMinds—ICRI). She is visiting professor at the University of Tilburg and teaches media and communications law at the University of Brussels and in the Florence School of Regulation at the European University Institute. She has served as an expert for organizations like the European Commission, the Council of Europe, and the German Media Concentration Commission, as well as administrations and authorities in Belgium. She is one of the five members of the General Chamber of the Flemish media regulator and assessor in the Belgian Competition Council.

David Waterman is professor in the Department of Telecommunications at Indiana University, Bloomington. In addition to many journal articles and book chapters on the media industries, he is author of *Hollywood's Road to Riches* (2005, Harvard University Press) and coauthor of *Vertical Integration in Cable Television* (1997, MIT Press, with Andrew Weiss). Professor Waterman has presented his research in testimony before the U.S. Congress and served as a consultant to the Federal Communications Commission, the U.S. Department of Justice, and other government agencies.

Bernd W. Wirtz (wirtz@uni-speyer.de) studied business administration in Cologne, London, and Dortmund. In 1994, he was awarded a doctorate in the field of new media and competition strategies. Since 2004, he has been a full professor (chair for information and communications management) at the German University of Speyer. He is an editorial board member of the journal *Long Range Planning*, the *International Journal on Media Management*, the *Journal of Media Business Studies*, and the *International Journal of Business Environment*. He has several years of experience in consulting on strategy projects for leading media and telecommunication enterprises and the European Commission.

Euisun Yoo is a professor of the Division of Media Studies at Ewha Womans University. He earned his Ph.D. in telecommunications at Indiana University. Dr. Yoo currently serves as a member of the Korea Press Arbitration Commission. He also served as a member of the Media Diversity Commission. Dr. Yoo is president of the Korean Association for Broadcasting & Telecommunications Studies for the 2013–2014 term. He also served as president of the Cyber-Communication Academic Society and editor of the *Korean Journal of Journalism and Communications Studies*.

Index